HANDBOOK OF
COMMUNICATION MODELS, PERSPECTIVES, STRATEGIES

Uma Narula

ATLANTIC
PUBLISHERS & DISTRIBUTORS (P) LTD

ATLANTIC
PUBLISHERS & DISTRIBUTORS (P) LTD

7/22, Ansari Road, Darya Ganj, New Delhi
Tel.: +91-11-4077 5252, 2327 3880
E-mail: orders@atlanticbooks.com
Web: www.atlanticbooks.com

Published by Atlantic Publishers & Distributors (P) Ltd.

Reprinted in 2014, 2022, 2023, 2025

Printed & bound in India by Atlantic Print Services

For My Family

To

Holistic and Integrated Scenario of Communication Decades

Preface

New Ideas, new Models of communications and newer perspectives through which communication has been studied, applied, or practiced have evolved and changed overtime. Accordingly many of its theories have undergone change. But they all exist in juxtaposition so as to present a holistic and integrated scenario in 2000 decade of communications *per se*.

This book is an effort to present this holistic scenario. The book is unique in presenting communication in holistic and integrated perspectives to the readers: students, teachers and trainers, researchers, practitioners, professionals, and educators who deal in diverse areas of Communications and focus on the critical issues pertaining to them.

There is no book published currently in the last ten years in communication discipline to present Communication Models, Perspectives, and Strategies in a handbook in an integrated and holistic communication perspective *per se*. Though there have been books written, including my four books that have focused on a single subject-matter exclusively in a particular book.

The compilation of Basic Communication Models is based on the evolution of communication models as developed by communication exemplars over a period of time developed in consequence to our changing understanding of the concepts, elements of communication process and communication rules. Other Models vis-à-vis Development Communication Models, International Communication and Globalization Models, Intercultural Models, Technology Models, Communication Management Models, Communication Research Models and Models for Communication Strategies are the product of my four decades of Communication Research in Theory and Practice and publishing widely in the areas of development, culture and information technology.

My communication researches in diverse communication areas, from diverse perspectives and in different geo areas have provided depth in presenting Communications from seven diverse perspectives, and the Communication planning viz strategies in a cohesive and understandable pattern.

There are two reasons to warrant the publication of this book. First, it deals with sensitizing concepts and strategies from diverse Communication perspectives. Further, a rigorous research based approach to these topics is taken in the book. Therefore, this book provides integrated and holistic perspectives of Communications since the last six decades.

The book is organized in three parts, Introduction and Conclusions chapters. Introduction focuses on Communication Framework, Concept of Communication and why we need to take a Communication Perspective.

Part 1 presents Communication Models in eight sections. The Models focused are:

Section 1: Basic Communication Models

Section 2: Development Communication Models

Section 3: International Communication and Globalization Models

Section 4: Intercultural Models

Section 5: Technology Models

Section 6: Communication Management Models

Section 7: Communication Research Models

Section 8: Models for Communication Planning and Strategies.

Part 2 presents seven perspectives from which human communications is practiced, interpreted and analyzed. These are:

1. Basic Communications Perspective
2. Development Communications Perspective

3. Information Communication Technology (ICT) Perspective
4. International Communication and Globalization Perspective
5. Intercultural Communication Perspective
6. Communication Management Perspective
7. Communication Research Perspective.

These perspectives do overlap and all these perspectives are intertwined as *a Communication Perspective.*

Part 3 discusses the significance of Communication Planning and Communication Strategies in the context. The role of positive and negative communication strategies is discussed in the context of seven perspectives.

In Afterword — the concluding chapter, a few communication scenarios are highlighted to address the contextual significance of the seven perspectives. We foresee that the above-mentioned seven perspectives from which we have analyzed communications *per se* may undergo several changes. The changes may occur when particular perspective's scope is widened.

The demand for an integrated and holistic approach to communication scenario in 2000 decade by the communication scholars, teachers and practitioners stimulated me to write this book.

UMA NARULA

Contents

PART 3

COMMUNICATION STRATEGIES

List of Figures

Pages

International Communication Models

Information Communication Technology Models

Intercultural Communication Models

Introduction

Vision 2000 decades—perspectives on how love, or peace, family, race, art, literature, community, spirituality, politics, science and technology will change for future generations.

Communication Framework

Over the last six decades there has been increasing interest in the study, applications, practice and research in Communication discipline. Research in Communication has conceptualized communication *per se* in 40s and 50s, and to develop Model and Theories. In short, to learn what communication is, how it works, and to develop means of communicating more effectively in diverse areas affecting human conditions in societal and economic contexts.

Earlier, Communication discipline had borrowed concepts and models from other disciplines of psychology, sociology, and anthropology etc. Over a period of time, it developed its own concepts, models, theories and assumptions through Communication Research. Such research has supported, refuted or improved upon various assumptions, constructs and other factors that have impact on changing perspectives on communication models, theories and practice. Various factors such as the historical analysis of communication theories, assessment of ongoing socio-economic and political realities, new insights and experiences gained through empirical research has created diverse communication perspectives. Moreover, human communication itself undergoing change due to various factors has impacted these perspectives.

Looking at communication as an essentially organizing feature of human society, over a period of time, different scholars with different assumptions and methods developed different paradigms to assess and evaluate the human communication *per se*.

Over a period of time different Mass Communication Models developed in consequence to our changing understanding of the concepts, elements of communication process, and communication rules.

Researches also advocated, supported and developed different perspectives from which communication has been studied and applied overtime.

Change is an ongoing process in the human communication environment, in societal set-up and in information and communication technologies (ICT), and also in the development efforts by the societies. Such changes in these areas create new prospects for communication *per se*, for communication environment, and changes in conceptualizations both in theory and practice to meet the ever-changing demands.

The major constraint of these ever-changing demands is that communication is getting complex overtime. There are complexities in communication opportunities both technologically as well through social access. To coordinate communication complexities and the demands of the masses, newer rules and regulations, censorship and controls are created to restrain the opportunities. Another constraint is that, on one hand, the efforts to practice and create a globalization perspective on communication have made communication complex. On the other hand, it has created demands for culture specific models and communication perspectives since there is realization that every society has its own cultural identity, communication environment, role, rules and strategies.

But these two constraints have rather stimulated more theory and research and diverse perspectives in Communication discipline.

Concept of Communication

Communication is interaction with ourselves, with others and with our external and internal environments. The focus of our communication is sometimes defined, sometimes undefined and vague. Similarly not all times we are conscious of our purpose of communication or the effects that our messages will have on the targeted receivers. Our communication may not be comprehensible all time and for everyone. But communicate we must and we must express ourselves. It is necessary and important human activity to survive and grow.

The animals, the birds, the insects, the tree and the plants all communicate. To us it may not be comprehensible just as our communication may not be comprehensible to them.

Human communication and non-human communication through technology is the context of our discussions.

The human effort is to discover nature, essence, and dynamics of communication to learn what communication is and how it works and to develop means of communicating more effectively. Over the last few decades, there has been increasing interest in the study and practice of 'communication'. As a result, knowledge and definition of 'communication' has varied widely in terms of purpose, nature, level of abstraction and scope.

In human (public) communication, three major elements play a significant role. These are Ethos, Logos, and Pathos. Ethos refers to the character of the speaker, Logos is power of reason and evidenced in text and speech and Pathos is emotions elicited in an audience.

Communication is a social process, and countless ways in which human beings keep in touch with one another. The messages in a shared environment could not only be oral, written, non-verbal, visual or olfactory but these could also be laws, customs, practices, ways of dressing, gestures, buildings, flags, gardens, exhibits, etc. Language and body synthesizers that are culture specific are essential components of messages. People in communication define the various types of society, sub-society and groups. The characteristics of these depend on the modes of communication they possess, media exposure, rituals and personal relationships.

The conventional concept of communication is that we use communication to express our inner purposes, attitudes, and feelings; to describe events and objects of the external world and to produce sharing between the speaker and the audience addressed. The patterns of social communication constitute the world, as we know it.

Pearce (1989) presents the premise that we live in communication rather than outside of communication and use communication for our own purposes. In the era of communication revolution, communication is far more important and central to human condition than ever before realized. There is recognition that multiple forms of communication exist in human society. These forms are not neutral. They are alternative forms of being human. Each qualitatively different form of communication affords a particular array of opportunities and problems.

Communication is the locus of forces through which persons create and manage social realities. Social reality includes concept of Self, Community, Institutions, and Cultures. Through communication we create concept of SELF–who we are, we create relationships within the community and build institutions. We communicate and act together to create and recreate community relationships that are managed within a culture.

Communication has been subjected to numerous and diverse conceptualizations. However, most definitions agree that:

> Human communication is a process of transmission of ideas through feelings and behavior from one person to another.
>
> Communication is persuasive and seeks to obtain desirable response to what is being transmitted.
>
> Communication is not linear but is a two-way and multi-way process.

Modes of Communication have evolved overtime, from oral traditions to electronics and wireless. They have expanded from local to regional, national and global, thus crossing all the physical barriers. There are three main divisions of communication modes: Non-verbal communication is thorough silence, gestures, tactile, olfactory and space-time cues. Verbal communication comprising of spoken word is through both interpersonal and electronic channels. Written communication is through Print media, electronic media and wireless and online channels.

Three types of channels are used for the above three modes of communication: Interpersonal, Non-verbal, and Mass Media both electronic and wireless.

In interpersonal, there can be one on one, and small group communication like in group meetings, seminars and teaching classes. Both verbal and non-verbal channels are used. Sometimes in group meetings supportive written communication may be used such as flip charts, posters and brochures etc. In impersonal interpersonal mode the mass audience is the communication focus such as audience in political rallies. Body language, space and time cues are important when non-verbal cues are used in interpersonal communication. Thus the oral traditions of interpersonal through various modes and the oral traditions that we label now as traditional media or popular media are the folklores and performing arts; are the earliest form of human communications through ages.

The earliest communication scenario thought of communication as linear activity. This was a simplistic presentation of human communication. Sender sends the message through a channel to the receiver. But an interaction and processural perspective of communication evolved through research in theory and practice.

It evolved that communication activity is a process. The essential elements are: there is interaction so there is sender/s and receiver/s within a context. There is a message to be conveyed through a channel. The objective of the interaction is to have intended or unintended effects on receivers (targeted audience), to assess the effectiveness, their should be loops of feedback between the sender and receiver.

In the process of transmission, certain distortions get added which are not part of the message sent by the source. This they called NOISE. There is *Channel noise* that suggests interference with the transmission of the message. Channel noise has various connotations. In media channels, it could be identified with the state of technology, operation of technology, physical (through purchasing power), and social access to these channels; and people's actual exposure to these messages. In interpersonal communication, channel noise may be any distraction or distortion of message between the source and the receiver.

Semantic Noise occurs when message is misunderstood because of lack of understanding of communicator's frame of reference. The receiver does not ascribe the same meaning to the message as intended by the communicator. Or the receiver does not understand the message because the communicator may use difficult words and unknown terminology.

In case the sender is not satisfied with the passive reception of the message irrespective of such passivity from mass media or interpersonal channels. He/she wants more control on communication — i.e. whether the message has the intended effect or not. The concept of linear feedback is added. Further, control can be achieved if the sender knows receivers' reactions to the messages. Thus it is necessary for the receiver to give feedback to the sender and certain cues about the message. This helps the sender to maintain control over the intended effects and adjust future messages.

The need for communication channels, messages and audience for the focused issues varied and these developed accordingly over the time periods. The communication policies related to these issues are formed to organize the communication scenario effectively.

Taking a Communication Perspective

The propensity to differentiate Communication from NOT Communication follows one of Aristotle's laws of identity. In contemporary thought, Aristotelian heritage is expressed in the assumption that one communicates not only by speaking, reading and writing but also by sleeping, eating, running, etc. There is little difficulty in identifying a particular instance of social action as *Communication.* The problem arises in specifying what human actions are *not communications.* It is impossible to identify a set of "critical attributes" to differentiate between what is communication and what is not communication. Any form of social action can be shown to be communication.

Narula & Pearce (1986) argue that communication is better understood as a perspective or context from which any act may be examined or understood. The assumption is that any action has a message value. One cannot, *NOT COMMUNICATE.* Whatever one does or does not do can be looked at from a communication perspective.

From a communication perspective, the human actions are seen as the process by which people collectively maintain social realities. Human beings simultaneously live in a symbolic universe (social reality) and are engaged in sequences of interactions with their environments and with other people. They actively strive to create coherent stories drawing from the "resources" of their social reality and from the practices in which they are engaged with others.

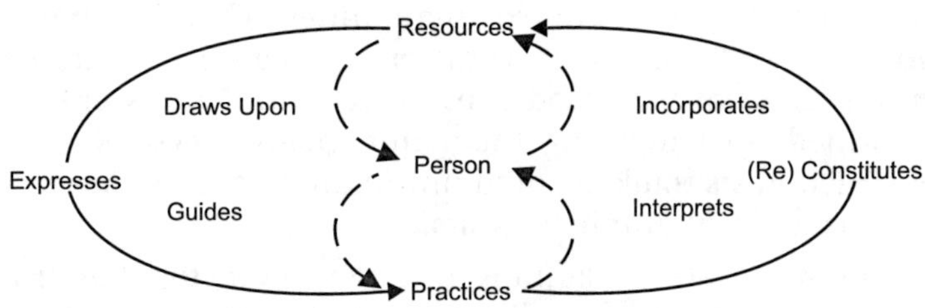

Fig. 1. Communication Perspective

Implications are that the 'communication perspective' facilitates interpretative and critical analysis. The result of this analysis is that meanings of actions, both of one's own and that of others, are made transparent and increase the possibility of communication. Thus from the point of theory, research and practice, communication - whether inter-personal or mass media always has a context in which it is presented, received, reacted to and acted upon. The contexts could be cultural, development, international, and technological. Thus utilization or effectiveness of communication is placed in contexts and is therefore context specific.

In these specific contexts we present seven perspectives (in following sections) from which human communications is practiced, interpreted and analyzed. These are Basic Communications, Development Communications, Information

Communication Technology (ICT), International Communication and Globalization, Intercultural Communication, Communication Management, and Communication Research. These perspectives do overlap and all these perspectives are intertwined as *a Communication Perspective.*

From these perspectives, many social actions that otherwise would not be defined as instances of communication, are shown to be powerful means of creating and managing social reality. For example, consider public works and legislation; from a communication perspective, both powerfully construct the social realities of the masses and the government itself.

Social constructionist perspective on communication treats actions as real, pivotal events rather than simply as transitory states of or between pre-existing entities. That is, the events and objects of the social world exist because of patterns of actions that have accrued previously, and actions are being performed now to bring them into being. Secondly, social constructionists think of communication in terms of interactive patterns and not atomistic units.

Communication planning through interactive patterns is an integral part of a holistic communication perspective. Communication planning is necessary to make (varied perspectives) action oriented. Communication planning involves, communication strategies, media planning (channel planning) and resource management culminating in communication policies.

PART 1

COMMUNICATION MODELS

A MODEL is presentation of the real phenomenon in abstract terms that can be applied in different forms at different times. Communication is an extremely complex process that becomes more complex with ever-changing communication phenomenon. Complexity and constant change in communication process makes it imperative that it is presented in simple and generalized way to explain and understand the structure and functions of communications. Communication Models present this simplification.

1

Basic Communication Models

Classification of Communication Models

The format of communication models depends on how we define and understand the process of communications and how these are applicable to different forms of communications. Communication Models are classified in three categories: stages, types, and forms of models. There have been four stages in the development of Communication Models: *Action, Interaction, Transaction and Convergence.* There are two types of communication models: *Linear and Non-Linear.* These can be presented in various forms such as *Symbolic Model, Physical Models, Mental Models, Verbal Models, Iconic Models, Analog Models and Mathematical Models.*

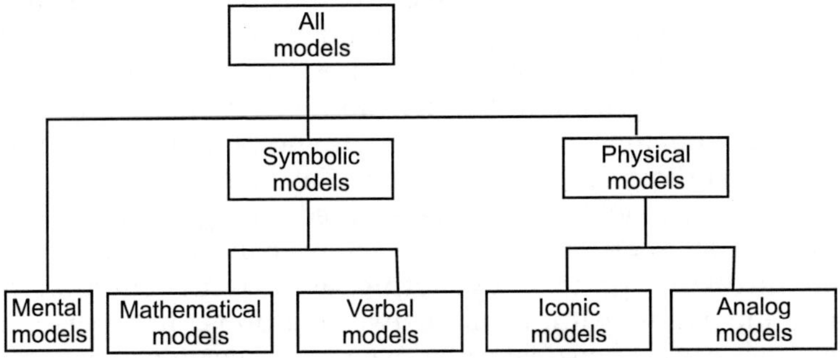

Fig. 1.1. Types of Communication Models

This presents taxonomy of models. In communication we are concerned with Symbolic models that comprise of Verbal models and Mathematical models. Physical models comprises of Iconic and Analog models. Verbal model is simply the theory stated in words. Verbal models are useful in terms of stating hypothesis or presenting results of a study. Verbal models could be SMCR models of communication process, SMCRE model of David Berlo and Gerbner's general model of communication.

Graphic models present schematically what verbal models present with words. Graphic models of communications are : Gerbner's general Model of communications, Westley and Mclean's ABC mass communication Model, Defleurs expansion of Shannon and Weavers Model and Vora's Model for diffusing concepts. These models are discussed in later section.

Iconic models are photographs, sculptures, and paintings of person, objects and scenes. Analog models bear a defined structural relationship to the subject they represent but do not look like them. The computer may be described as an analog of the human brain.

Mathematical models are not frequently encountered in communication field except for graph theory in the analysis of communication networks and the statistical concepts of information processing. Communication theories generally have not been expressed in mathematical symbols.

Communication system comprises of two general models: Media systems and Oral systems. In media systems, the information flow is activated through professional communicators for transmission through media channels such as print, radio, television, film, video, telecommunications etc. The messages are descriptive and impersonal. In the oral systems, the messages are point to point emanated from sources authorized to speak by social hierarchy. Messages are prescriptive and they are transmitted through oral channels to highly differentiated audience. Each primary group completes the diffusion pattern by acting as a relay channel of communication within and between groups. Interpersonal channels can be personal when the communication is between or among the individuals. The direction of change is from oral to media systems in all societies. But at the same time they coexist and are supportive of each other.

Linear and Non-linear Models of Communications. This is second classification of models. The media system and oral system models are classified into Linear and Non-linear Communication Models.

Linear Model is unidirectional model that portrays the message flow from speaker to audience with or without effect. These models could be both vertical and horizontal. In Non-linear models the message flow is bi-directional or multidirectional. These models are circular and convergence models.

Most of the earlier models of communication in 40s and 50s were linear models. They are foundation models and suggested new, useful and significant concepts, which were later, developed into non-linear, interaction, transaction and convergence models.

The linear communication models were useful for, and designed for experiments that assumed one-way causality for the study of propaganda and mass persuasion. These models described a simple communication act and not the process. Although Berlo in 60s defined communication in terms of communication process but in his subsequent research he did not pursue this idea. In fact Berlo (1977) acknowledged that S-M-C-R was not intended as a communication model but it was developed as an audio-visual aid to develop recall of the components of the communication relationships.

There are limitations of the linear models. Kincaid (1979) pointed seven biases of linear models for human communications:

- The linear models give a one-way-act usually vertical, and not cyclical-two-way process overtime.
- A source biased based dependency rather than on the relationship of those who communicate and interdependency.
- A tendency to focus on the objects of communication as if they existed in vacuum, and isolated from their context.
- A tendency to focus on the messages *per se* at the expense of silence, punctuation, and timings of the messages.

- A tendency to consider the primary function of communication to be persuasion rather than mutual understanding, agreement and collective action.
- A tendency to concentrate on psychological effects of communication on separate individuals rather than the social effects and relationships among the individuals.
- A belief in one-way mechanistic causation rather than mutual causation, which characterize human information systems that are fundamentally cybernetic.

Freire (1973) suggested that these seven biases are interrelated and cumulative, each tend to support the other and tend to create a coherent image of the communication process in spite of the limitations and problems it produces.

The ***Non-linear Models*** follow the cybernetic principle. The four most important elements of cybernetic explanation are the concept of information, feedback, networks and purpose. The analytical concepts of interaction, self-generation, mutual exchange and sharing explain the human communication in non-linear models of communication.

Deutch Karl (1968, p. 390) advocated that human systems are not connected and coordinated by mechanical means or force of matter and energy but rather by exchange of information. The most important for information sharing is the communication network circuits, by which individuals within the system are interconnected. A circuit is a circular loop with two-way exchange of information that is a prerequisite for feedback. Feedback produces action in response to input of information and through its reactions modify its subsequent behavior.

Capra (1975, pp. 286, 296) suggests a '***Bootstrap Model***'. It suggests that process of communication is self-generating by mutual sharing and exchange of information. According to this model, the universe is a dynamic web of interrelated events. Mutual interrelation determines the structure of the web. None of the property of any part of the web is fundamental. They all follow from overall consistency.

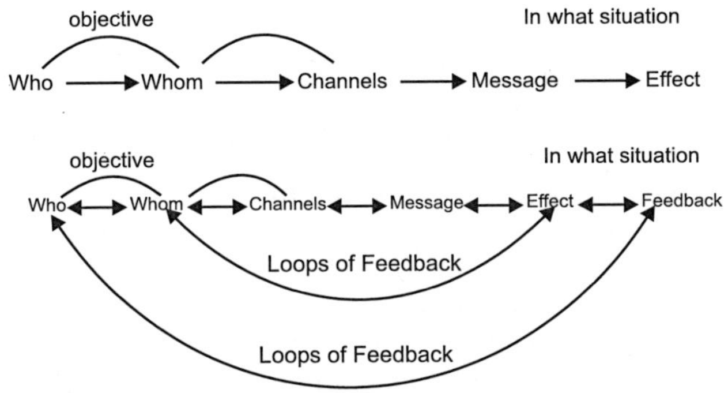

Fig. 1.2. Linear and Non-linear Models of Communication

The third classification of communications model is: Action Model, Interaction Model, Transaction Model and Convergence Model. Action, interaction, transaction and convergence concepts developed these types of communication Models. They were rather the developmental stages of communication models.

The Action Models are sender-oriented. They emphasize how a sender must construct a message to secure a desired result. How must the sender act, or speak in order to transmit his message and persuade his listeners.

Action models may work with media channels but they do not work well with interpersonal channels. From the action model point, the miscommunication may come from two perspectives. One, the source did not structure the message correctly for transmission. Two, the listeners did not correctly listen to the message or the listeners applied their own meaning to the message.

The action model is implicit model for both listening as well speaking. Listening is the act of receiving the message, and it is acting upon the message. People who operate from action model presume that listening just happens and it does not require the active participation of the people. Listening skills need not be developed and people are natural effective listeners. To them, listening is unrelated to the source. These misassumptions make the mass mediated messages ineffective at times. The early models (1.3 to 1.10) were action models.

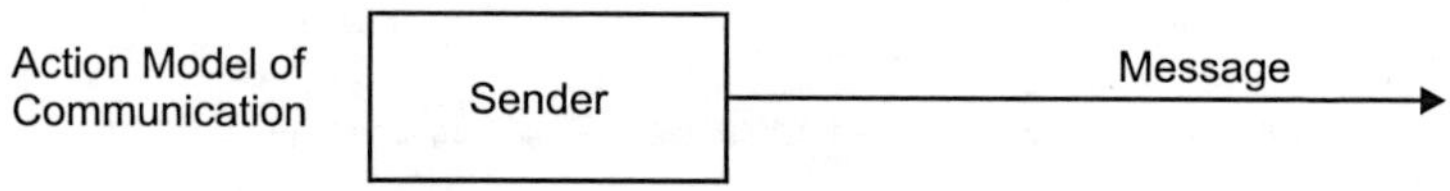

Fig. 1.3. Action Model of Communication

Interaction Models focused on interaction and relatedness between the sender and receiver. The concern was the effect of the message on both senders and receivers. The communication theorists and researchers were not satisfied with the passive reception of the message. They wanted more control on communication i.e. whether the message has the intended effect or not. They added the concept of linear feedback. Further, control can be achieved if the sender knows receivers' reactions to the messages. Thus it is necessary for the receiver to give feedback to the sender and certain cues about the message. This helps the sender to maintain control over the intended effects and adjust future messages accordingly.

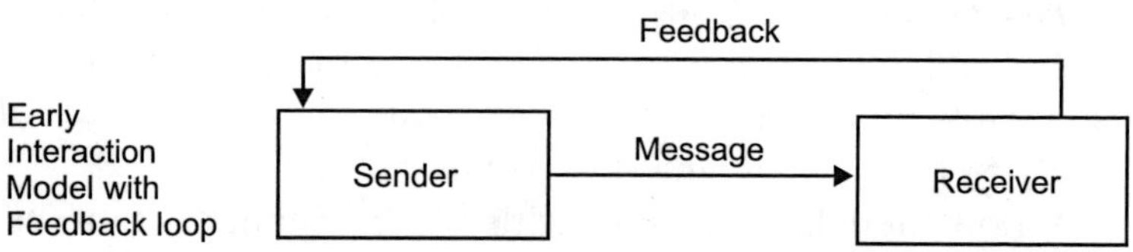

Fig. 1.4. Interaction Model of Communication

When the dimension of 'time' was added in the model, the linear qualities of the model became more apparent. It is apparent from Fig. 1.4. that the exchange of message is taking place overtime. The sender is alternatively sending a message and receiving feedback from the receiver. There is continuity of responses between the sender and the receiver. Sender has control over the intended effect of the message and adjusts future messages as desired by the sender to be effective message.

In an interaction model, *listening* becomes a process of listening, receiving, decoding, interpreting and acting upon messages. When the receiver acts upon the message; that behavior is seen as *feedback* and is seen as *response* to the sender's message.

Mother tells the child, 'Tara, please clean your book bag'. She comes after a few minutes and finds Tara cleaning the study desk including the book bag. Since the message did not have the desired behavior on child's part, mother gave another message, 'hey I only wanted you to clean your book bag'.

There was interaction listening between mother and Tara. People who listen interactionally are not essentially good listeners. They are so preoccupied with how they are going to respond to the message that they do not receive the message as intended or distort the message received. As an alternative, if Tara had given the feedback that she would like to clean the study table along with the book bag, then mother could have adjusted her second message accordingly.

The concept of information is a significant contribution in interaction approach to communication. What is *new* is informational, what is not *new* is redundancy. In communication, the relationship between information and redundancy is meaningful. Wherever there is redundancy, there is repetition of elements forming a pattern. These patterns and differences in patterns are meaningful within interaction. They are *patterns of interaction*. In communication, patterns of interaction and variations are more meaningful than the information itself.

Although information is an important concept in communication theory, but we tend to base our behavior more on variations in pattern of interactions than on the amount of information in our communications. Communications may be personal or mass mediated.

There are two limitations of Interaction Models. One, the true interaction is lacking between the sender and the receiver. Separate behaviors (action and responses) are exchanged in interaction models that alternate in sending and receiving messages. Second, interaction models lose their clarity when they are applied to the multiple message systems operating simultaneously.

Transactional Models of Communication view communication as simultaneous responses whereas linear feedback is central in the interaction models. In transaction models, while 'A' is speaking, 'B' is generating messages or feedback in many ways ... through body postures, facial expressions, eye movements, hand gestures, spatial distance from 'A' and verbal language use.

If we attempt to diagram the flow of these messages and potential messages generated by both A&B through their specific message systems; the overlapping lines begin to merge into simultaneous interactions. That is the characteristic of transactional model.

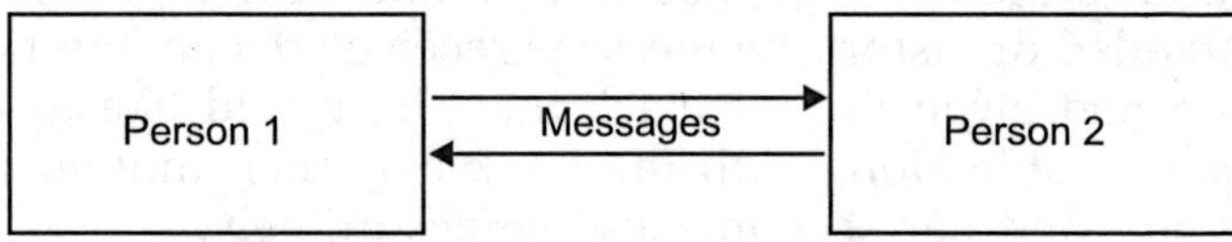

Fig. 1.5. Transactional Model of Communication

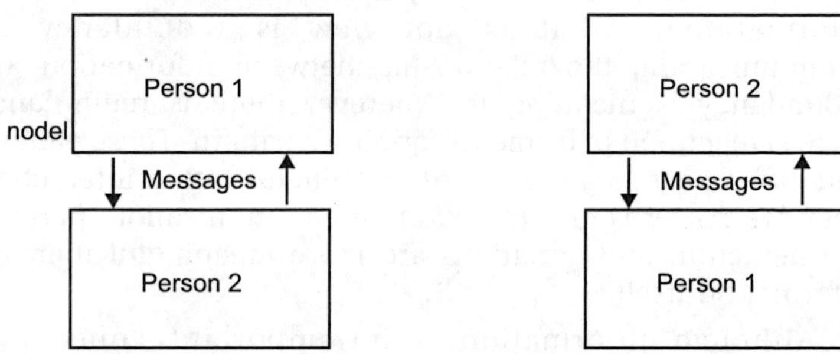

Fig. 1.6. Transactional Model of Communication

In Interaction model 'A' may be interacting with 'B' and there may be linear feedback. But in Transaction Model both A&B are participating simultaneously in the communication situation. They mutually perceive each other. Both, sender and the receiver are making adjustments to the messages exchanged within transactions. Thus both the parties are engaged in the process of creating meaning in a relationship.

In the Transaction Model, we observe the entire communication situation rather than isolating a sender or a receiver. Because we view the entire transaction, we view the progress of communication by re-examining the transaction at a later time.

In transactional models, the concern is with the *patterns of communication behavior* within the relationship formed between the senders and the receivers; and not with *patterns of information and redundancy.* Communication can be effective by making use of these identified patterns of communication behavior. It is not necessary to know what causes such behavior patterns, what motivates them or even how they are created. As long as a pattern of behavior can be defined and observed, it can be used advantageously. Advertisers spend millions to discover patterns of product users' behavior.

Convergence Model of Communication is based on the principle of cybernetics. The four most important elements of cybernetic explanation are the concept of information, feedback, networks and purpose. The analytical concepts of interaction, self-generation, mutual exchange and information sharing and mutual understanding explain the human communication in convergence models. They are non-linear models of communication.

Kincaid (1979) developed a convergence model. According to this model, effective feedback creates convergence and ineffective feedback creates divergence. The participants converge and diverge on their relative positions overtime to reach mutual understanding of the issue. In this model *communication is reaching mutual understanding.*

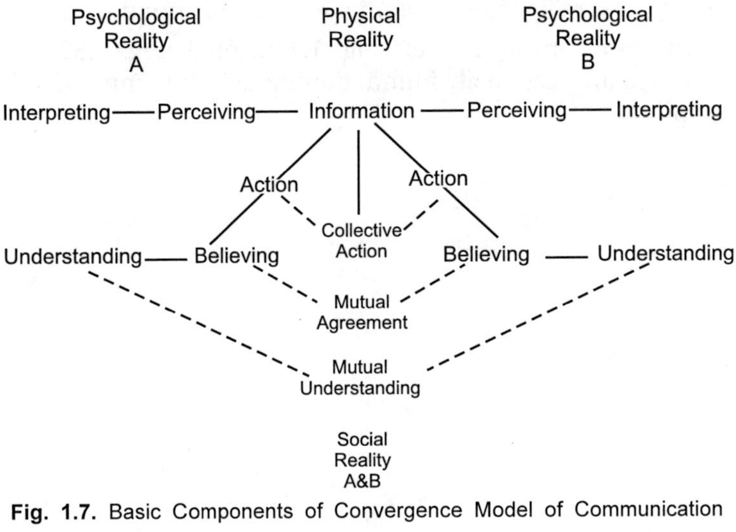

Fig. 1.7. Basic Components of Convergence Model of Communication

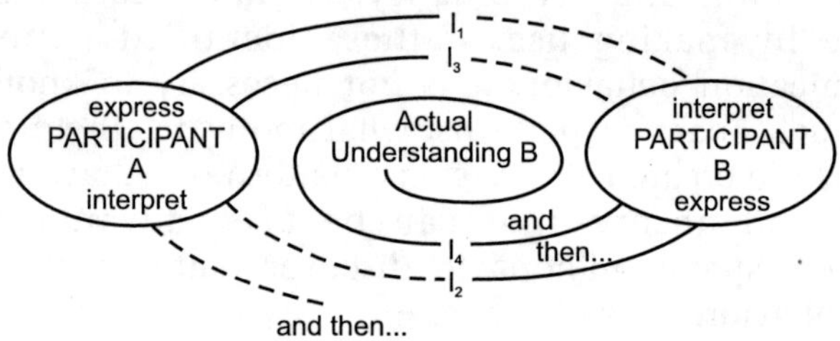

Fig. 1.8. Convergence Model of Communication

In the last six decades there has been a great model hunt for Communication Models. Empirical and Communication research influenced the evolution of these models.

The basic linear models of 40s and 50s are foundation models and suggested new, useful and significant concepts which were later developed and integrated into non-linear interaction, transaction and convergence models of 80s. These models developed the new concepts of multiple feedback loops for mutual understanding among the participants, and contextual approach in communication act and situation. Further, the emphasis has been in developing specific models rather than a Meta Communication Model. Specific models may be culture specific, system specific and situation specific.

Therefore, basic models Fig. 1.7 through Fig. 1.32 given in our text are essentially foundation models in communication discipline.

Fig. 1.9. Models Communication: Summary

Lasswell (1948)	Gerbner (1956)	Berlo (1960)
WHO Communicating organizations, their nature and function.	1. SOMEONE (Source, communicator 2. perceives an event 3. and reacts 4. in a situation to make available	SOURCE Press, publishing research organizations, governments, churches and other social organizations, television, radio and publishing
says WHAT The nature of the content: informative entertaining, educative.	6. MATERIALS 7. in some form 8. and context 9. conveying content through some	MESSAGE Words, mathematical symbols, pictorial images
in which CHANNEL Print media, audiovisual media automatic data processing.	5. MEANS channels; media; physical engineering administrative and institutional facilities for distribution and control.	CHANNEL Print, electronic media
to WHOM The nature and receptivity of the audience.	1. SOMEONE (destination, audience) 2. perceives an event 3. and reacts 4. in a situation	RECEIVER General audiences, specialized audiences
and with what	of some	
EFFECT The nature and effect or response of the audience; the way in which it *affects* the communicator.	10. CONSEQUENCE Someone perceives an event and reacts in a situation through some means to make available materials in some form and context conveying content of some on sequence to.	

Fig. 1.10. Models of Communication: Summary

	Sources	Type of Model	Main Components of the Model	Definitions of Communication
1.	Claude Shannon and and Warren Weaver (1949)	Linear	source encoder message decoder destination noise feedback	All the procedures by which one mind may affect another.
2.	Charles Osgood and others (1957)	Linear	message decoder interpreter encoder message decoder	One system a source, influences another, the destination by manipulation of alternative signals which can be transmitted over the channel connecting them.
3.	Bruce Westley and Malcolm MacLean (1957), based on Newcomb (1953)	Linear	messages sources (advocacy roles) gatekeepers (channel roles receivers (behavioural system roles) feedback	Person A transmit message about an object X to person B through gatekeeper C.
4.	David Berlo (1960)	Linear	source message channel receiver feedback	A process by which a source intentionally changes the behaviour of a receiver.
5.	Wilbur Schramm (1973)	Relational	informational signs relationship among participants active receivers	A set of communication acts focussed on a set of informational signs within a particular relationship.
6.	D. Lawrence Kincaid (1979)	Conver-gence	informtion uncertainty convergence mutual understanding mutual agreement collective action networks of relationships	A process of convergence in which information is shared by participants in order to reach a mutual understanding.

Functions of Communication Models

Communication Models are visualization of the communication process. They are basics about the elements of communication, how they operate and interact.

Models may serve any or all of the four general functions. First, models organize the various elements and the process of the communication act in a meaningful and interesting way. Second, they help in discovery of new facts about communication. It generates research questions. It serves heuristic function. Third, these enable us to make predictions concerning communications i.e. what will happen under certain conditions. Fourth, models may provide the means of measuring the elements and processes involved in communication.

Frank E.X. Dance (1983) suggested that we adopt a family of communication models. Each of these models highlights some aspect of the process of communication and distorts others. Most communication theorists agreed. After 1970, few more models of communication were developed and those models of communication were not unidirectional. For detailed discussion on evolution of Models of Communication, refer to Narula (1994, pp. 45-69).

The various Communication Models that developed in the last six decades reflect on the process of communication. The revised concept of communication is based on empirical communication research and deliberations of scholars in the discipline. Key points of these revised models are:

- Communication is processural and reflexive
- Sequence of events is important
- Meaning of events is derived from their locations within an ongoing sequence
- We learn to focus on "patterns" rather than on individual messages, and on interactions rather than on movements of messages from one place to another
- Participants in the communication process contribute to the meaning of any given aspect of communication and function as 'sources' and 'receivers' as they participate.

- There is interaction between the sender and receiver through several communication networks and feedback loops.
- Contextual approach to meaning in a communication act and situation is important and mutual understanding among the participants is necessary for effective communication.

The essential elements of the process are presented in the following five versions of the Basic Communication Model:

1. Sender—message——channel——receiver
2. Sender—message——channel
3. Sender—message——channel——receiver——effects
4. Sender—message——channel——receiver——effects——feedback
5. Sender—message——channel——receiver——effects——feedback loops

Fig. 1.11. Basic Communication Model-1

In version 1 of the Basic Model, the objective of the sender is to send message through a channel to the targeted receiver. The sender's immediate concern is not receivers' reactions, comprehensibility, and intended effects e.g. communication through public meetings or presentation on TV. Here the receivers are not differentiated mass and there could be both short and long-term effect that the sender is not assessing. In version 2 of the Model, the targeted audience exists but it is their choice to attend the public meeting or switch on the TV.

In version 3 of the Model, the targeted receivers are differentiated; sender is concerned about the intended effects of his/her message. He/she is vaguely aware of the effects; but he/she has no way to assess the effects. In version 4 of the Model, the targeted receivers are differentiated, sender is concerned about the intended and unintended effects of his/her message and he/she assesses the effects through audience feedback.

In version 5 of the Model, the targeted receivers are differentiated, sender is concerned about the intended and unintended effects of his/her message and he/she wants his/her audience to comprehend his/her message. In order to assess the effects on the audience and to facilitate comprehensibility of the message, feedback loops are necessary. Feedback loops from sender to receiver and from receiver to sender are necessary in these contexts. The receiver can choose a channel of his/her choice for feedback, which is equally accessible to him and the primary sender.

These basic Models for communications evolved overtime.

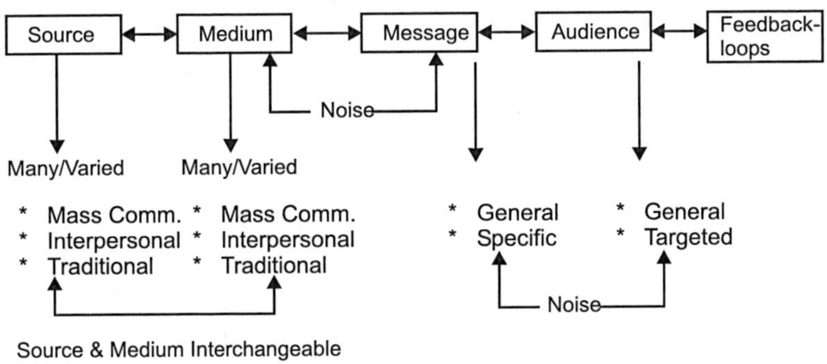

Fig. 1.12. Basic Communication Model-2

Aristotle's Model of Communication

Aristotle proposed the earliest communication model some 2300 years back. This is simple and linear. This model included five essential elements of communication: the speaker, the speech or message, the audience, the occasion and the effect. Aristotle advises the speaker on constructing a speech for different audience on different occasions and for different effects. This model is actually more applicable to public speaking than interpersonal communication.

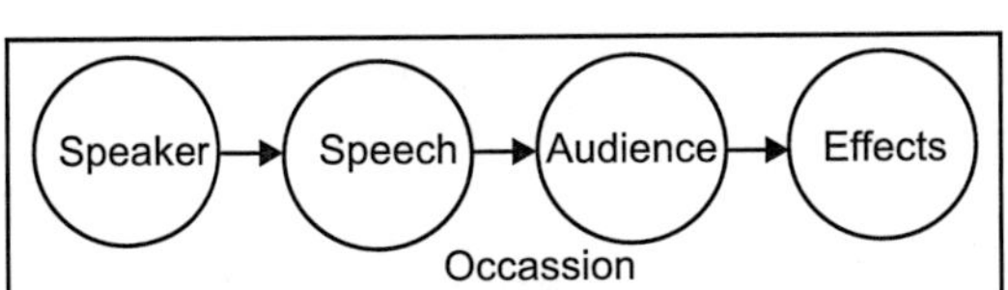

Fig. 1.13. Aristotle's Model of Communication

Lasswell Model of Communication

Lasswell proposed a communication model in 1948 that was not different from Aristotle. This model suggests the message flow in a pluralistic society with multiple audiences. The message flow is through numerous channels.

Communication Component	Research Area
Who	Control Analysis
Says What	Content Analysis
In What Channel	Media Analysis
To Whom	Audience Analysis
With What Effect	Effect Analysis

Fig 1.14. Lasswell Model of Communication

Shannon and Weaver Model of Communication

In 1949, Claude Shannon and Warner Weaver proposed a Communication Model. The speaker selects a desired message from all the possible messages. The message is send through a communication channel and changed into signals (messages). The receiver receives the signals. In the process of transmission, certain distortions get added which are not part of the message sent by the source. This they called NOISE.

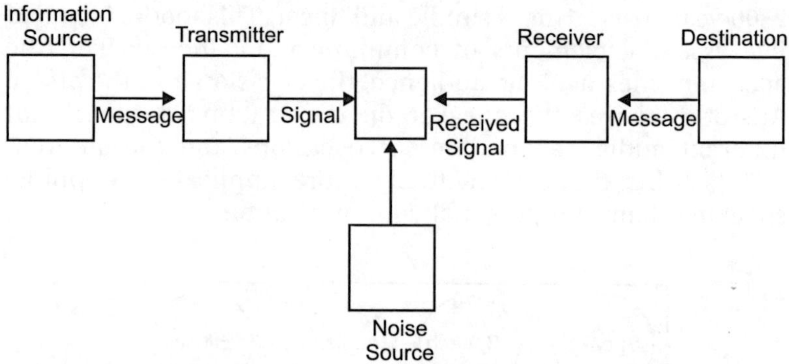

Fig. 1.15. Shannon and Weaver Model of Communication

This model led to the technical improvements in the message transmissions and it stimulated scholars from several disciplines to study communication scientifically. Their effort was towards developing a *Unified Model of Communication.* The focus of this Model was three components viz. Channel Noise, Semantic Noise, and Feedback. These three components were considered for the first time in the communication process. *Channel noise* suggested any interference with the transmission of the message. *Semantic Noise* occurs when message is misunderstood. *Feedback* is the third component to assess the 'effects' and comprehend the intended message adequately.

Narula (1994) discussing about 'Noise' i.e. distortions in communication transmission suggests that channel noise has various connotations. In media channels, it could be identified with the state of technology, operation of technology, physical (through purchasing power), and social access to these channels; and people's actual exposure to these messages. In interpersonal communication, channel noise may be any distraction or distortion of message between the source and the receiver.

Further, *Semantic Noise* occurs when message is misunderstood because of lack of understanding of communicator's frame of reference. The receiver does not ascribe the same meaning to the message as intended by the communicator. Or the receiver does not understand the message because the communicator may use difficult words and unknown terminology.

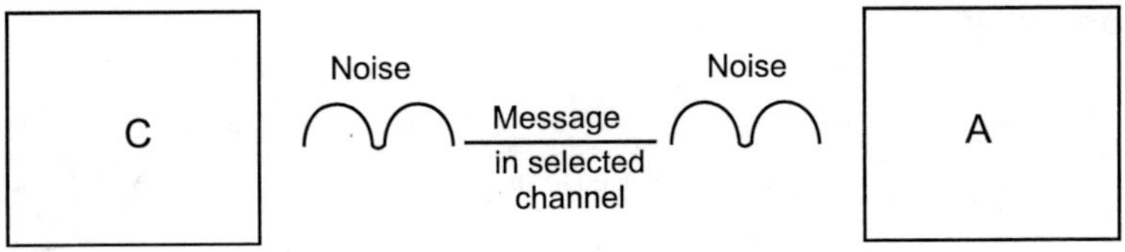

Fig. 1.16. Channel Noise

Communicator places his message in a selected channel to reach audience (A), but it is subject to noise interference.

Communicator and audience member (A) has same frame of reference so they understand the message, A1 is partially receptive, A2 is unable to understand.

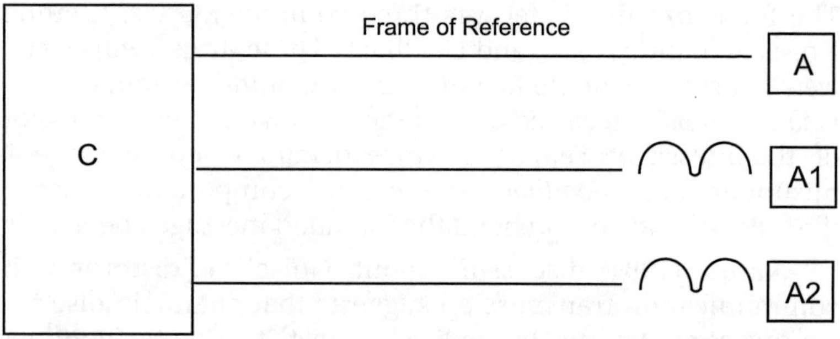

Fig. 1.17. Semantic Noise

Communicator in a channel controlled by 'E' reports source message. For instance, pro family planning messages of the government (source) is reported by professional communicators through opinion leaders to the villagers. Opinion leaders are second in line communicators to the people. The original source can pass messages through two-step communicators. Some can receive message directly if they have direct exposure to media channel, others indirectly through opinion leaders. Messages may not register at all with others who are inattentive to them.

Thus the feedback interactions occur along the communication route. But these feedback interactions are only one-way.

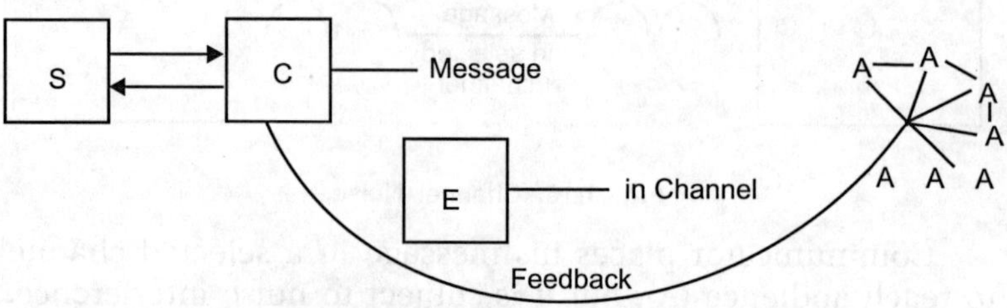

Fig. 1.18. Channel and Semantic Noise

Shannon and Weaver did discuss the semantic or pragmatic problem in communication and the channel noise in the transmission of messages. But their model failed since other human communication researchers who used this model did not consider enough about the semantic or pragmatic levels of communications. They did not pay enough attention to the channel noise. It did not register with them that feedback component is a significant component in communication process.

Principle of redundancy i.e. the repetition of the main idea of the message is used to reduce channel noise both in mass media and interpersonal communication channels. The semantic noise can be reduced if communicator adjusts his vocabulary to audience needs, interests and understanding. But the interpretation of intended meaning depends on feedback loops between the source and the receiver.

Wendell Johnsons Model of Communication

Wendell Johnsons proposed one of the most insightful models in 1951. It is a simple model explaining the complex process of communication.

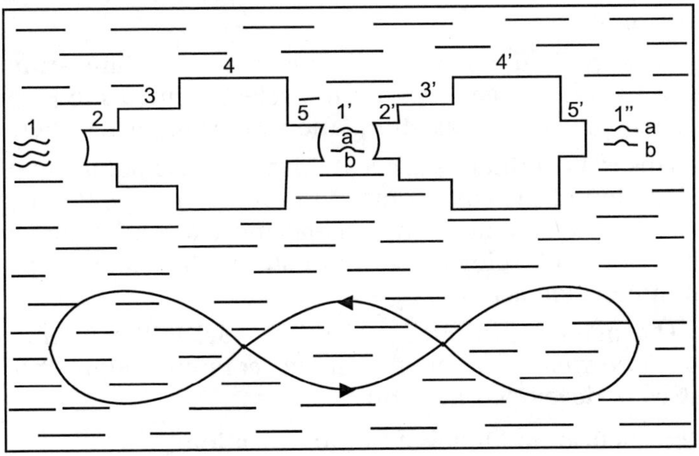

Fig. 1.19. Wendell Johnsons Model of Communication

In the figure, the surrounding rectangle indicates that communication takes place in a *context*. This context is external to both the sender and the receiver and even to the communication process as well. The curved loop indicates that the various stages of communications are actually interrelated and interdependent.

Stage 1 in the figure denotes communication event and the actual communication process begins at this point. This event is the external stimulus to communication. Although all communication may not have reference to this event. Johnsons argues that communication make sense when it relates to the external world. Stage 1' is the external event of spoken or written words that served stimulation for the speaker.

At stage 2, the receiver is stimulated through one or more sensory channels. The opening at 2 is shown relatively small to emphasize that out of a large number of sensory stimulations, only a small part stimulates the receiver. At stage 2' the receiver is stimulated

At stage 3, the organic evaluations occur. Certain bodily changes are affected such as muscular tensions. At stage 3' there are organism evaluations.

At stage 4, the feelings that are aroused at stage 3 are translated into words in accordance with individual's unique language habits. Stage 4' feelings of receiver are translated into words.

At stage 5, the selected linguistic symbols are arranged into a pattern. Stage 5' shows the selected linguistic pattern. These symbols serve as stimulation for another receiver.

This is a continuous process. This model is not a complete explanation of the communication process *per se*. It is rather an attempt to picture some of the most essential elements, processes and relevant relationships that make up the communication act.

The major contribution of this Model is the *Interaction* and *Contextual* components in the communication models that were developed later on.

Wilbur Schramm Model of Communication

Wilbur Schramm was influential in facilitating use of linear models in 1950's and later on moved to develop relational models in 1973. Empirical and communication research influenced his models.

1. The Sender → Receiver model of early 40s based on bullet theory.
2. The Sender → Message → Receiver (as Schramm realized the importance of message)
3. Sender → message → channel → receiver. (On further research the importance of channel was evidenced).

   Sender → message → channel → receiver → effects.

Fig. 1.20. Wilbur Schramm Model of Communication

In his relational models of 70s Schramm was concerned with the effects of communication on the receivers. He used the *effects* and *effects analysis* components from Berlo's Model of 1960. He implicitly suggested *Interaction* component when he talked about active, selective and manipulative audience in his relational model. He argued that the most dramatic change in general communication theory in the last 40 years has been the abandonment of the idea of passive audience. Audience is a full partner in the process of communication.

David Berlo's Model of Communication (1960) explains the various components in the communication process. The four basic components are source, message, channel and receiver. There are five channels for each of these four components. It was for the first time that the '*Effect*' component was initiated in the communication process. Berlo suggested that message must have some effect positive or negative on the audience and that effect must be assessed through effect analysis.

Source →	Message →	Channel →	Receiver → Effects
Communication Skills	Elements	Seeing	Communication Skills
Attitudes	Structure	Hearing	Attitudes
Knowledge	Content	Touching	Knowledge
Social System	Treatment	Smelling	Social System
Culture	Code	Tasting	Culture

Fig. 1.21. Berlo's Model of Communication

Gerbner's Model of Communication

Gerbner's Model of Communication (1956) considers these elements in the communication process. There is source that reacts to an event in a situation through some channel. The content and the consequences of the communication act are conveyed in some form and context. This model emphasized the importance of *effects* and *context* in the communication process and act.

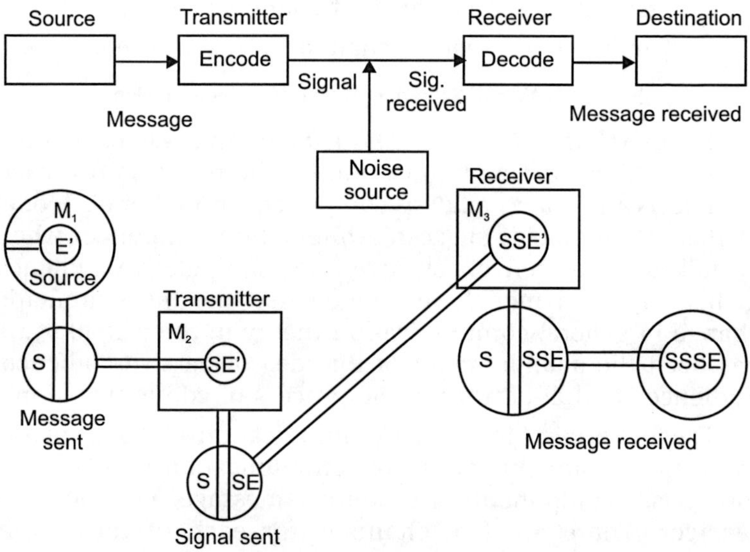

Fig. 1.22. Gerbner's Model of Communication 1

Communication Component	Research Area
Someone	Communicator/Audience Research
Perceives an Event	Perception Research and Theory
And Reacts	Effectiveness Measurement
In a Situation	Physical/Social Setting Research
Through Some Means	Media Investigation
To Make Available Materials	Administration; Distribution
In Some Form	Structure; Organization; Style
And Context	Communicative Setting
Conveying Content	Content Analysis; Study of Meaning
Of Some Consequence	Overall Changes Study

Fig.1.23. Gerbner's Model of Communication 2

Westley and MacLean Model of Communication

Westley and MacLean's Model (1957) expanded on the Newcombs ABX model (A communicates to B on topic X) with the inclusion of C as gatekeeper as developed by Lewin. The A_s representing advocacy roles select and transmit messages purposely to modify B_s perception of X. The B_s (perceivers and audience members representing behavioral system roles) respond in terms of their needs and requirement for messages as means of orienting themselves to the environment. The C_s (representing channel roles or gatekeepers) are agents of the B_s who non-purposely select and transmit information for them.

Linear feedback is an important component of this model and introduced first time in the communication model.

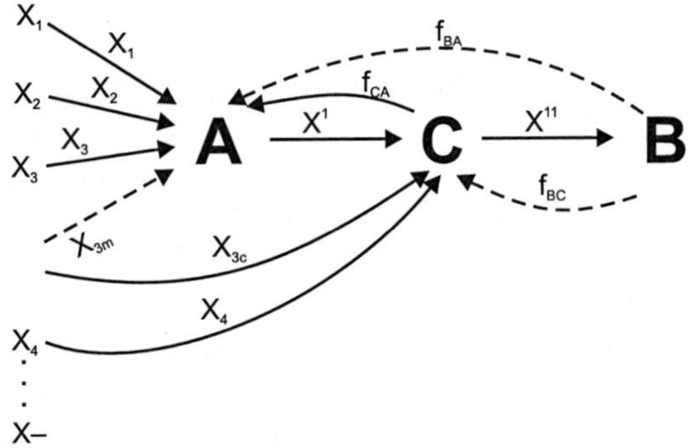

Fig. 1.24. Westley and MacLean Model of Communication

DeFleur Model of Mass Communication System

The DeFleur Model (1966) expanded on the Shannon and Beaver Model and interjected a mass medium device. Based on Westley and MacLean Model suggested feedback device to demonstrate that communication process is circular and thus implicitly suggested two-way feedback. The 'noise' in the model may interfere at any stage in the mass communication process. DeFleur pictures the source, transmitter, receiver and destination as separate phases of mass communication. The components of *two-way feedback and targeted audience* (as separate from receiver) were introduced first time in the Communication Model.

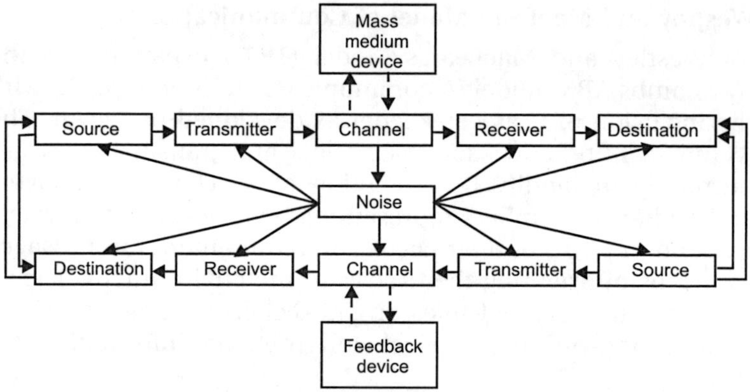

Fig. 1.25. DeFleur Model of Mass Communication System

Hiebert, Urgurait and Bohn (HUB) Model of Mass Communication

In this model, communication is perceived as a set of concentric circles much like the waves formed when a pebble is thrown in a pool. The pebble that is analogous to the communication content causes ripples that become ever widening circles until they hit the shore (audience) and bounce back (feedback).

The idea is that initial content goes through a series of actions and reactions labelled as pool of human affairs. The focus on content development was given attention for the first time.

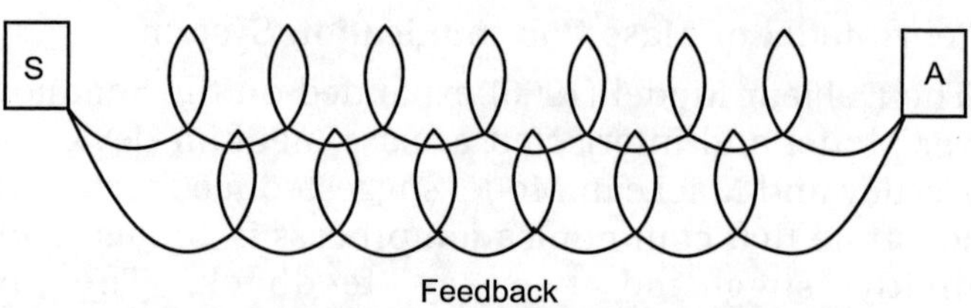

Fig. 1.26. HUB Model of Mass Communication

Vora's Model for Diffusion of Concepts

Vora's model is a complex model. It presents the concept of diffusion, knowledge, attitude change, and behavior change in a dynamic and progressive spiral that utilizes mass media and interpersonal channels. This model emphasized the *external and internal environment and effects components* in addition to source, message, channel and receiver components in the mass communication process for diffusion of concepts.

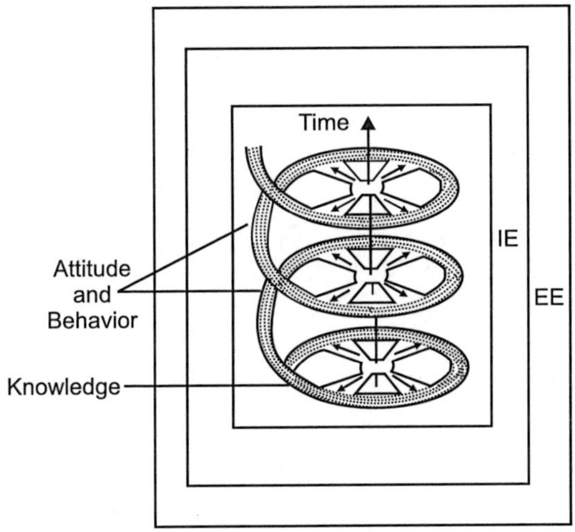

Fig. 1.27. Vora's Model for Diffusing Concepts

Effective Interpersonal Communication Model

Generally any good communication is labelled as effective if it reaches its targeted audience. Both mass media and interpersonal communication need to be effective to achieve its objectives.

Interpersonal communication describes the relationship between the 'Self and Others' and the coordination between the two. Effective interpersonal communication is characterized by five qualities of openness, empathy, being supportive and positive. Openness is willingness to reveal information about oneself that is relevant in the interpersonal encounter. Empathy is feeling as the other person feels and one identifies with the other. This helps in understanding the attitude and behavior of the other persons. Supportive environment facilitates the open and empathetic communication and it becomes effective. Person must have positive regard for oneself. Equally important is having positive feelings about the other persons. This encourages active and meaningful participation and interaction. Positive feelings of general communication situations are important for effective interaction.

Interpersonal Communication Models

Bois' Model of semantic reaction (1973) referred as 'Semantic Reactor's is most useful and insightful for interpersonal communication.

Fig. 1.28. Bois' Model of Semantic Reactor

The Self responds to stimuli as a whole, a reaction is determined by actual situation, spoken word, the thought occurs and that what it means to the individual.

Self-moving activities include movements of bodily organs, feelings, activities of needs, drives, wants, fear, hopes, thinking activities include all those functions that involve symbolic process of abstracting, conceptualising, speaking, writing, listening, asking questions, decision making, strategy formulation, etc. The electrochemical activities refer to bodily movements which begin with operation of DNA and RNA in the genes and includes neuronal activity. All these activities are interrelated and mutually dependent. Thus Self must be viewed as a unit which acts and reacts as a whole.

The environment as indicated in the model suggests that Self always moves in the context of environment. At times environment is close to the Self and limits the range of possible behavior, at other times it stretches for and does not exert great influence on the Self. The environment influences the Self and vice-versa.

The 'context environment' has four different dimensions which are basic and important: the physical dimension refers to the place we are, the social dimension to the type of functions we are attending — whether we are in a party, professional meeting, wedding, etc. The social dimension shows whether the environment is friendly, hostile, indifferent, etc. The cultural dimension suggests the prevailing value systems, the unwritten codes of acceptable or unacceptable behavior.

The Self functions in relation to 'time'. The Self operates in the present but with some reference to past experience and future envisions.

Thus Bois Model defines a human being as a thinking, feeling, self moving electrochemical organism in continuous interaction with a space-time environment.

Constraints of the Model: The model talks about only reacting to the environment but we react as well as act. Moreover Self and environment are not in clear cut contrast but they are in fluid interaction. The model is static whereas Self is constantly moving, changing and reorganising.

Thus we look at communication as exchange of semantic reactions.

There should be tacit recognition that both the parties are valuable and worthwhile to each other and have something important to contribute. Both parties should be allowed to convey and listen to messages and thus given opportunity to interact.

Homophily and hetrophily are significant for effective interpersonal communication. Homophily refers to degree of similarity between the parties engaged in interpersonal communication. Hetrophily refers to differences between the parties. Research evidence is that interpersonal communication is more effective when the parties are similar in age, gender, religion, socio-eco status, educational level and even professional and political leanings. But in certain communication situations, heterogeneity of the other parties becomes a necessary condition. Consider these two instances: when experts impart training, and diffusion process of innovations. In these two instances, change is often brought when the parties involved are 'optimally hetrophilious'.

Source credibility is important point for effective communication both for interpersonal and mass media. Source is seen as possessing or lacking credibility for its messages and interactions.

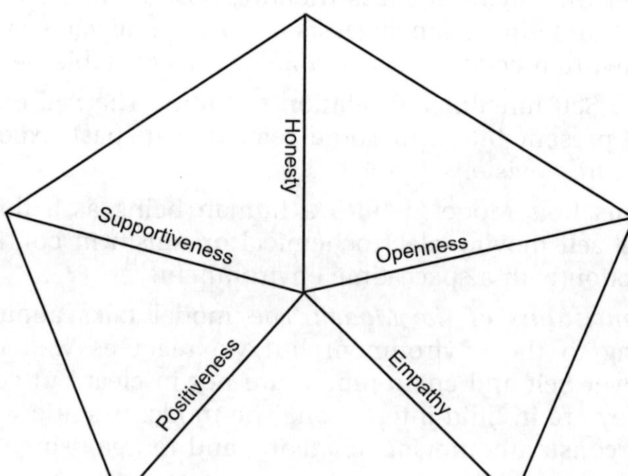

Fig. 1.29. Effective Interpersonal Communication Model

Society, Media and Audience Reciprocal Relationships

Mass media addresses the audience dependency on media information that is ubiquitous condition in modern society. It is a key variable in understanding why and when media messages will alter beliefs, attitude and behavior and help maintain a sense of connectivity with social reality. Media operates in 'contextual environment', which varies in different societies.

The effectiveness of the communication through media channels depends on the reciprocal relationships between media, society and audience. The socio-economic, political, cultural and technological environments affect the media systems. The mass mediated messages aims at and creates awareness, knowledge and change in attitudes and behavior among the audience.

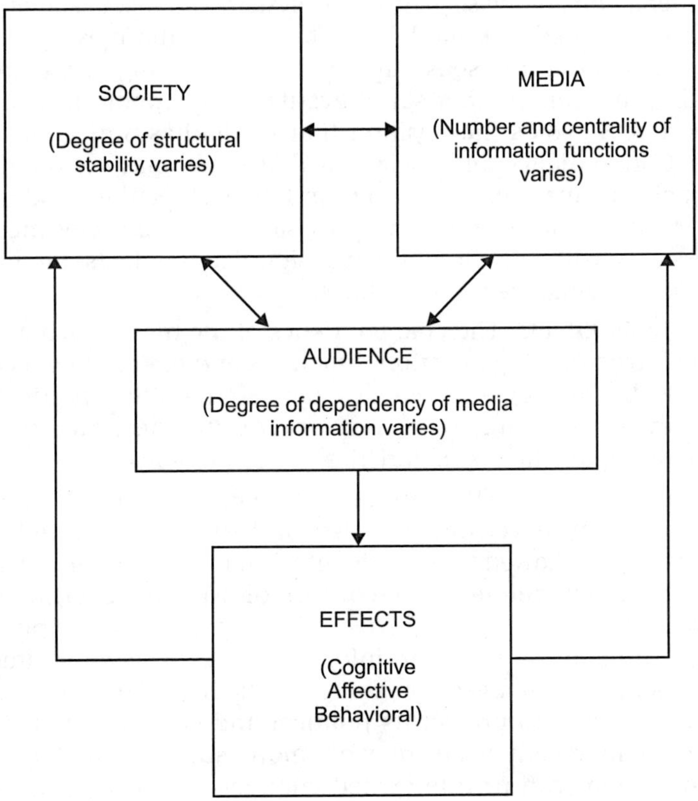

Fig. 1.30. Society, Media and Audience Reciprocal Relationships

DeFleur and Rokeach (1982) discuss the dependency theory of media effects. The proposition is that the potential for mass media messages to achieve a broad range of cognitive, affective, and behavioral effects will increase when media systems provide many unique and central information delivery services. The potential will further increase when there is structural instability due to conflict and change in society. The audience's changing cognitive, affective and behavioral conditions can feedback to alter both society and media. Thus there is tripartite relationship between media, audience and society.

The model given below allows for a continuous process of interaction among society, media system and media audience. It is also a feedback model of effects of media messages on the audience in the sense that effects of ongoing events may set into motion another set of events. Most important is that this model avoids the position that media has no significant effect on audience and society or that media has unbounded capacity to manipulate people and society. Rather it allows us to specify in a limited way to say when and why media messages will or will not have significant effects on how audience thinks, feel and behave.

Media Effects. The characteristics of the media such as its goals, structure, organization, functions and operating policies affect the messages. Messages delivered in this particular framework can have desired or counter-desired effects depending on the characteristics of the audience.

For instance, TV in India is partially owned but wholly controlled by government. A few Indian private owned TV channels are allowed to operate but within the program content and other guidelines and control of Indian government. Government has the objective of being pro-social and its major function is to create information, knowledge, attitude and behavior changes for some of its major development programs; and to project its political and economic policies. Though in recent years to woo more audience and be in competition with private owned channels, it has changed its policies to deliver healthy entertainment programs also.

The media messages thus delivered by government or

non-government channels construct the social realities of its people and people manage their social realities accordingly in a social set up where culture and society are not open. But in this age of globalization when people and particularly younger generation is exposed to global cultures and ways of life through TV messages and visuals there is conflict among people. They try to change or adopt to newer ways. The government is more concerned about foreign influence on the people's cultural ways and values and it takes action to control or censor.

Cognitive media effects occurs in three ways. First it is in terms of change in belief systems and attitudes and values. Second is media role in agenda setting. Agenda setting is an interactional process. The topics are selected by the media and presented to the public. Information about such topics is selectively assembled and selectively disseminated. The public sorts out the issues and information selectively. The list of issues that emerge is the agenda of media audience. Third is the expansion of people's system of beliefs. People's knowledge and belief system expands since they learn about other people, places and things from mass media.

Media has impact on values. Media information may not change the basic values but they play significant role in creating conditions for 'clarifying the values'. One way of clarifying such values is presenting information that precipitate value conflict within the audience. Once the mass mediated messages identify and clarify the value conflicts, the audience articulate their own value positions. In this process genuine values get clarified.

The affective effect of media messages is on audience feelings and emotions. For example, prolonged exposure to violence on media desensitizes people or creates fear and anxiety.

Forms of Communication

Interpersonal and Media are two basic forms of mass communication. There are different interpersonal and media channels through which people communicate. There are four forms of interpersonal communication: intrapersonal, dyadic communication, small group communication and public

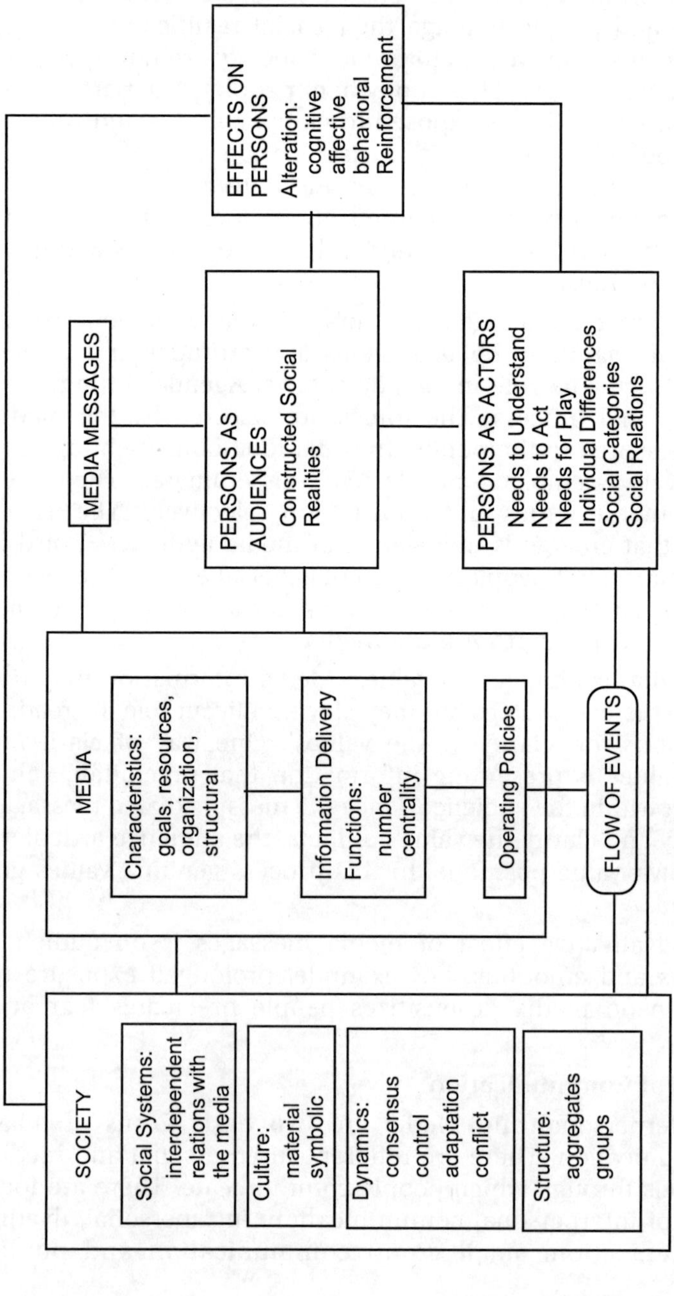

Fig. 1.31. Integrated Model of Media Effects

speaking. The conventional mass communication channels are print, radio, TV, film, photography and exhibitions etc. With the advent of modern information communication technologies, other ethnotronic communication devices of video

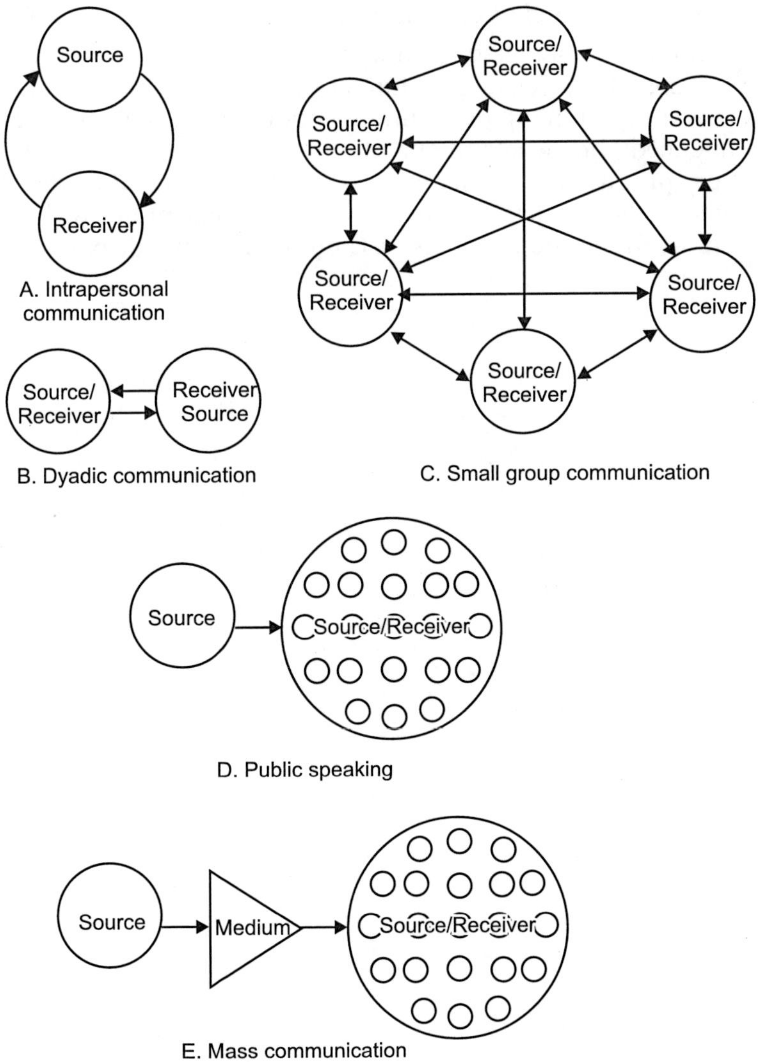

Fig. 1.32. Forms of Communication

player and camcoder (video camera), audio players, audio and videocassettes and CDs have become ubiquitous and play supportive role for the conventional media channels. Telecommunication, Internet through world wide web and channelled through computer has become an important and significant channel of communication.

The basic models of communication evolved since 40s to 70s. These four decades of model development were crucial to the development of communication discipline. Research influenced the development of these models from a bullet theory premise to interactions, comprehensions and feedback loops in the models. It would be more appropriate to label them as foundation models in Communications discipline.

2

DEVELOPMENT COMMUNICATION (DEVCOM) MODELS

The dynamics and dysfunction of development have impeded or facilitated the devcom models operating in a particular society at a particular point of time. When the dynamics of development change, the devcom models undergo changes to fit the social, economic and political realities of the society and the global contexts in which they operate.

The various models given in this chapter are associated with Development Communication Perspective discussed in Chapter 2 in Part 2. A detailed discussion supports these models.

The focus of development has always been growth. In 50s and 60s, it was envisaged that economic growth could be through industrialization and modernization. Modernization presented the problems of social structural constraints. Lerner (1958) was the exemplar of modernization model. He pointed that urbanization, literacy and exposure to mass media are the indices of modernization.

Urbanization → Literacy → Economic and Political Participation

↘ ↙

Mass Media Exposure

Fig. 2.1. Lerner Model of Development

The trickle down theory assumed that the benefits of industrialization and modernization would trickle down from rich to poor and from developed countries to developing countries.

Capital gain, and gain in awareness and knowledge would

trickle down to poor from rich, and from developed countries to developing countries. But the theory did not work as assumed and rather created gap. The emphasis on mass media exposure created communication gap between the have and havenots because of limitations of media opportunities and media access. Urbanization created peripheral slum areas around urban metros and towns as rural population migrated to urban areas in search of employment opportunities and better quality of life. The efforts towards literacy were a slow process.

For detail discussion on this approach, refer to Modernization approach in Development Communication Perspective section in Part 2.

The dynamics of development are the patterns of interaction and social realities of various agents of development. Political leadership, development administration, rural and urban masses are the agents of development. The major dynamic factor for development is 'development efforts' by all the agents. Development efforts comprise of development awareness, motivation for development and participation in development.

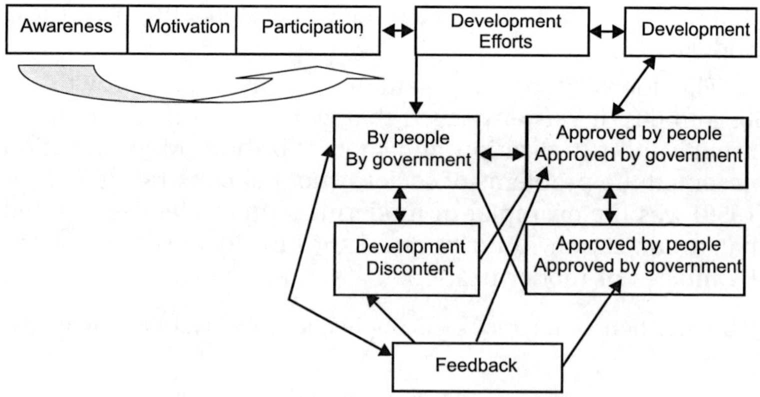

Fig. 2.2. Dynamics of Development Communication

There is relationship between development awareness, discontent, motivation and feedback linkages with participation, approval and adoption of development projects.

The analysis of six development decades suggests that development discontents in the developing countries were created by the interaction patterns of the above mentioned development agents.

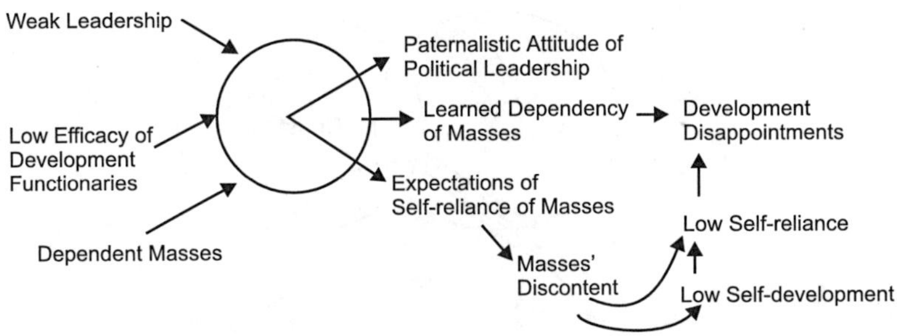

Fig. 2.3. Dysfunctional Factors in Development

The above figure shows that coordination was not achieved among people's participation, local leadership and effective development administration. The 'affordances' of the social system resulted in weak local leadership, ineffective functionaries in the development bureaucracy and masses that remained dependent. Though they shifted their dependence from the local community to the central government. The government's goal to improve the material wellbeing of the masses within a context of democratic socialism is difficult and contains some unresolved contradictory tensions.

Discontent and personal inefficacy are serious concerns for development because they make all the participants in development describe themselves as helpless in achieving the development objective, make people blame each other and withdraw from commitment to democratic participation in development.

Pervasive discontent with development program is a problem if it leads to withdrawal from participation but otherwise discontent *per se* need not be a problem. It would rather motivate to achieve the development objectives.

The assumption is that future development programs are built as a result of interactions between people and social-economic-technological opportunities. Once we gain a deeper understanding of the directions of change, we may define with greater measure of confidence our region of feasible action as shown in Fig. 2.4.

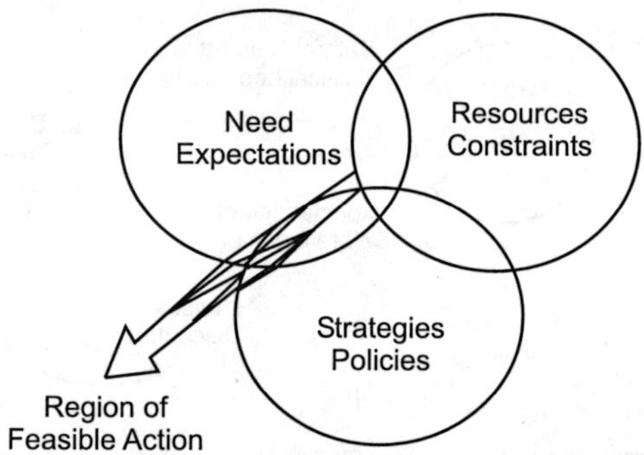

Fig. 2.4. Region of Feasible Action

Development communication needs and expectations are subjective categories. There are three sets of problems related to it: (i) there are behavior orientations related to all media, (ii) affective orientation with regard to major national development communication expectations, needs and constraints of resources, (iii) cognitive orientations with respect to major national development communication strategies and policies.

Development threshold concept suggests being receptive to development to a certain point. For example, there is a marked difference between the development threshold of rural and urban society, between elite and masses, and even men and women within rural and urban society. These differences in threshold are termed as 'development gap'. The development gap hypothesis is that patterns of communication may lead the have-nots away from the mainstream of development and thus create development gap.

This also suggests that people at different development thresholds need different communication strategies for effective development. Human and localized approach suggests communication efforts tailored to the needs and psychological dispositions of people.

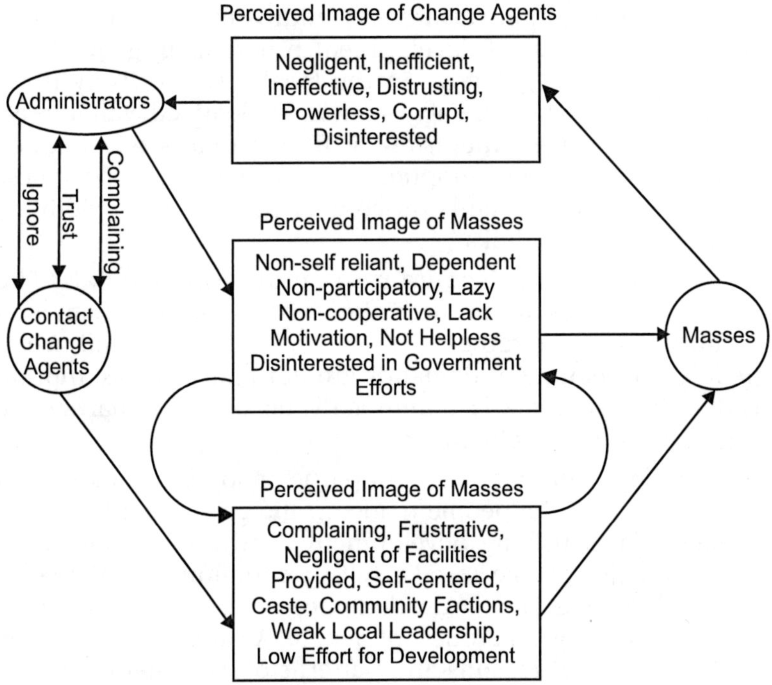

Fig. 2.5. Communication Gap for Development Participation

Development Effort is identified with what activates people to participate in development. The development effort is further defined as development awareness, development discontent, and motivation for participation in development programs.

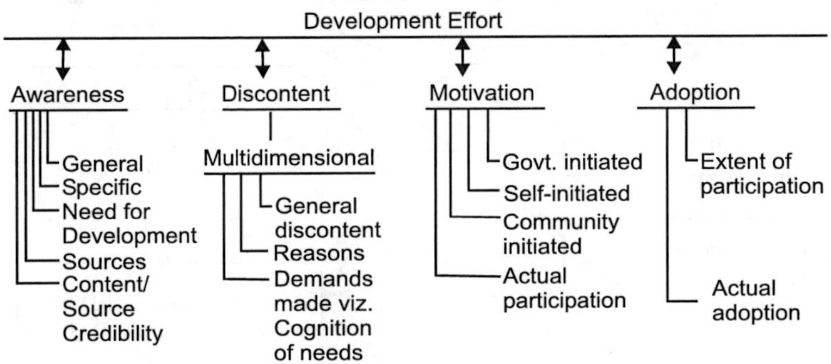

Fig. 2.6. Development Efforts
Source: Narula: Dynamics of Development

The development awareness addresses the question of people's awareness of development programs in general and specific activities going on in the local areas or likely to be taken in future. The general awareness is identified with interest and arousal stage, whereas specific awareness is identified with participation and adoption stage. The extent of awareness as high and low depends on source, content and credibility of communication links.

Development discontent is multidimensional. The discontent could occur with the existing development and communication strategies. People get discontented when people's development demands are not met. The assumption is that development discontent activates people to participate aggressively in development.

Development motivation for participation is identified with the demands of the people made on the government or other agencies for satisfying development needs. Such motivation also stimulate people to take self or community initiative to do development. The motivational force for development may be the psychological arousal of people. Awareness, knowledge of the issues and reasons and patterns of discontentment are necessary and sufficient for motivation.

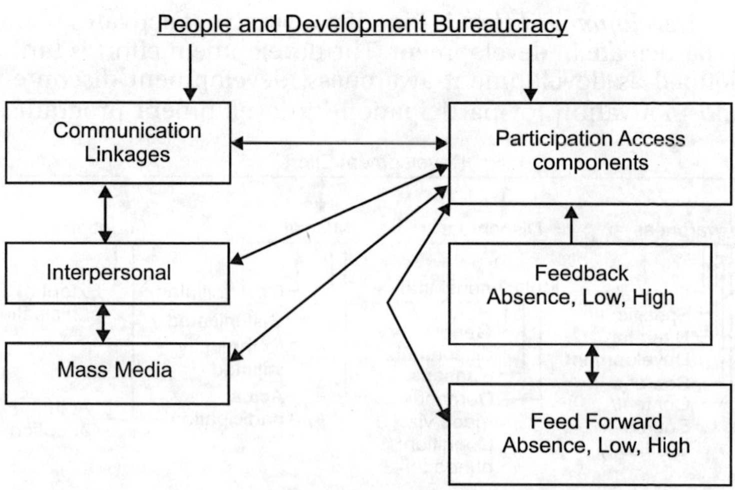

Fig. 2.7. Participatory Communication Patterns for Development

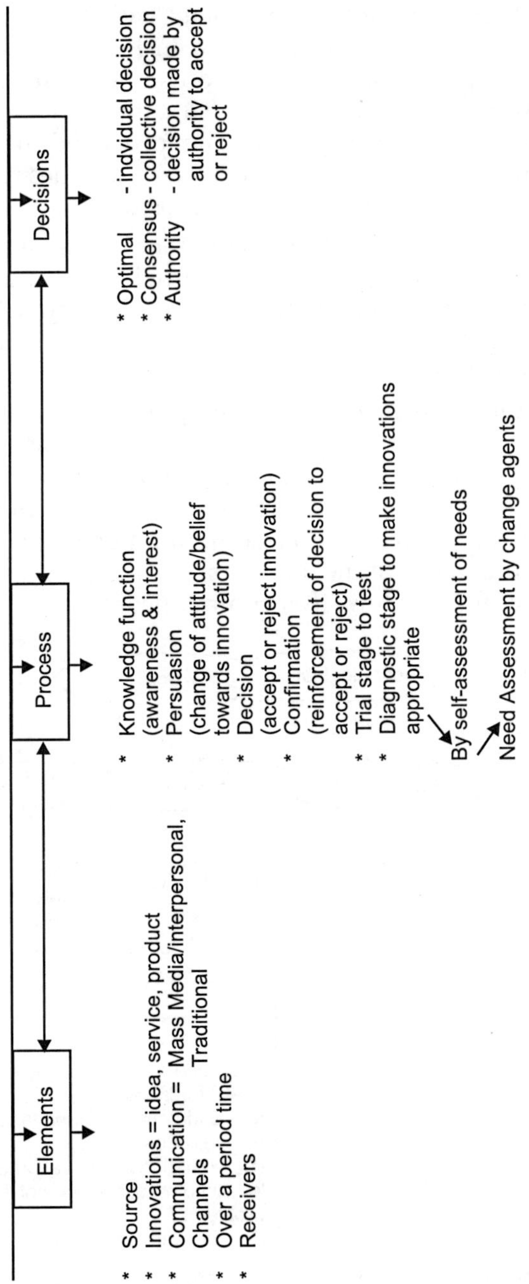

Fig. 2.8. Roger's Basic Diffusion Model

Development participation happens with the individual and community initiated participation in local development activities in the past, present and to do so in the future. The degree of involvement is identified with the frequency with which people discuss development. The forms and the modes of participation differ considerably in different societies reflecting local, economic, political and social variables.

What, who and how of participation is augmented by consideration of how the context of participation may affect its extent and substance. Analysis of the development task and the salient features of development environment may make the context explicit.

Diffusion of Innovations is the adoption of technological and social innovations through diffusion of new ideas, services and products. Diffusion of both material and social innovations is necessary for development. The individual and community decisions for acceptance and rejection of innovations depend primarily on the needs of the adopters, what is communicated about innovation, and how it is communicated.

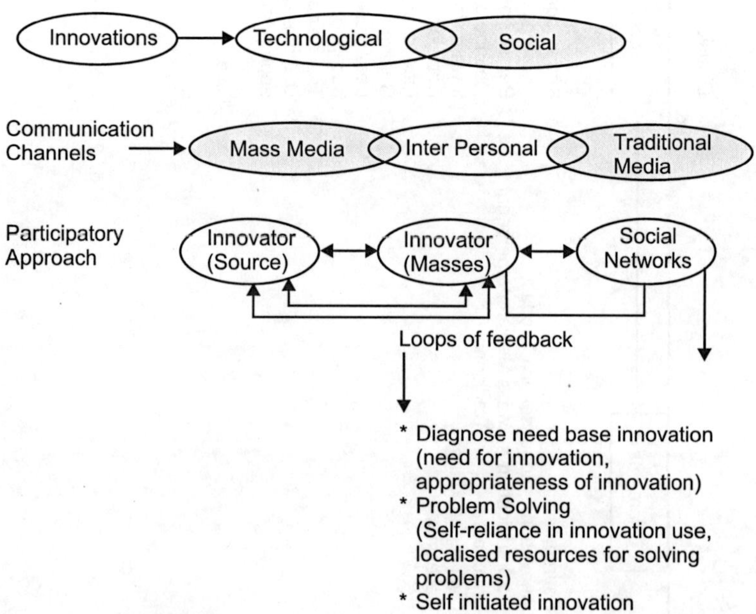

Fig. 2.9. Diffusion — A Communication Strategy for Development

The three important stages in such communication are: create awareness by *reorienting* the products, services by introducing the changed innovative elements. Creating knowledge and interest by *refocusing* the attention on the innovations. Further, innovative ideas have to be *reinforced* by both intensive and extensive media and interpersonal campaigns. The reinforcement helps in making decisions and adoptions.

The notion of how development works in developing countries. The development planners have a definite notion of how the various groups should interact to bring about development. They envision all agents as actively participating in a fully circular process. In this process, their own role is that of providing expertise that guides the action of others.

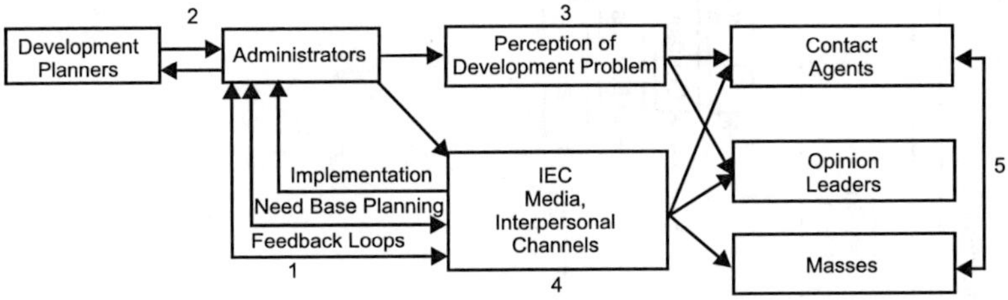

Fig. 2.10. Planners' Concept of How Development Works

The administrative change agents blame the masses for the failure of development projects, citing their passive participation. The pattern of actions and attributions made by the administrative change agents is shown in Fig. 2.10.

There is a complex and now familiar pattern of interaction between the administrators and the masses. The administrators are frustrated because they do not have adequate resources to provide all the services the masses need. The combination of assumed responsibility, inadequate provision of services and expressed frustration elicits a complex response by the masses, including a high degree of development awareness, discontent and dependency. There is rapid, reiterated cycle of exchanges in which each blames the other.

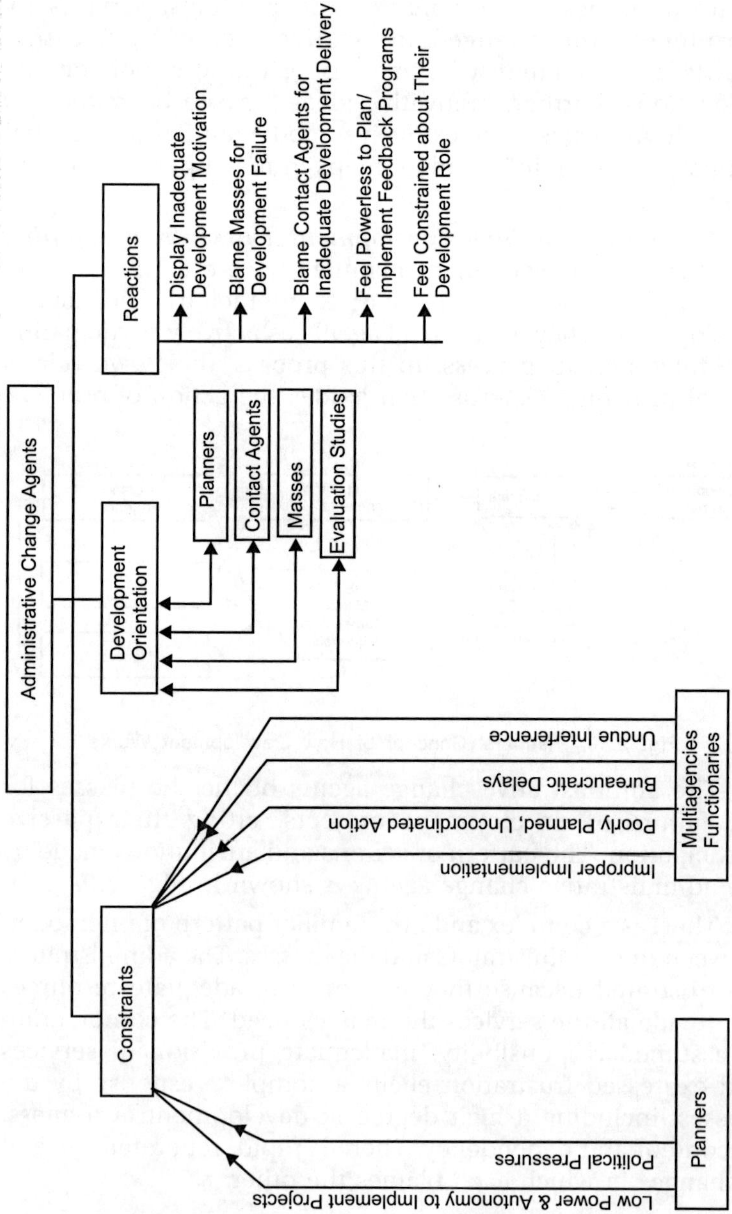

Fig. 2.11. Administrative Change Agents' Interaction with Planners

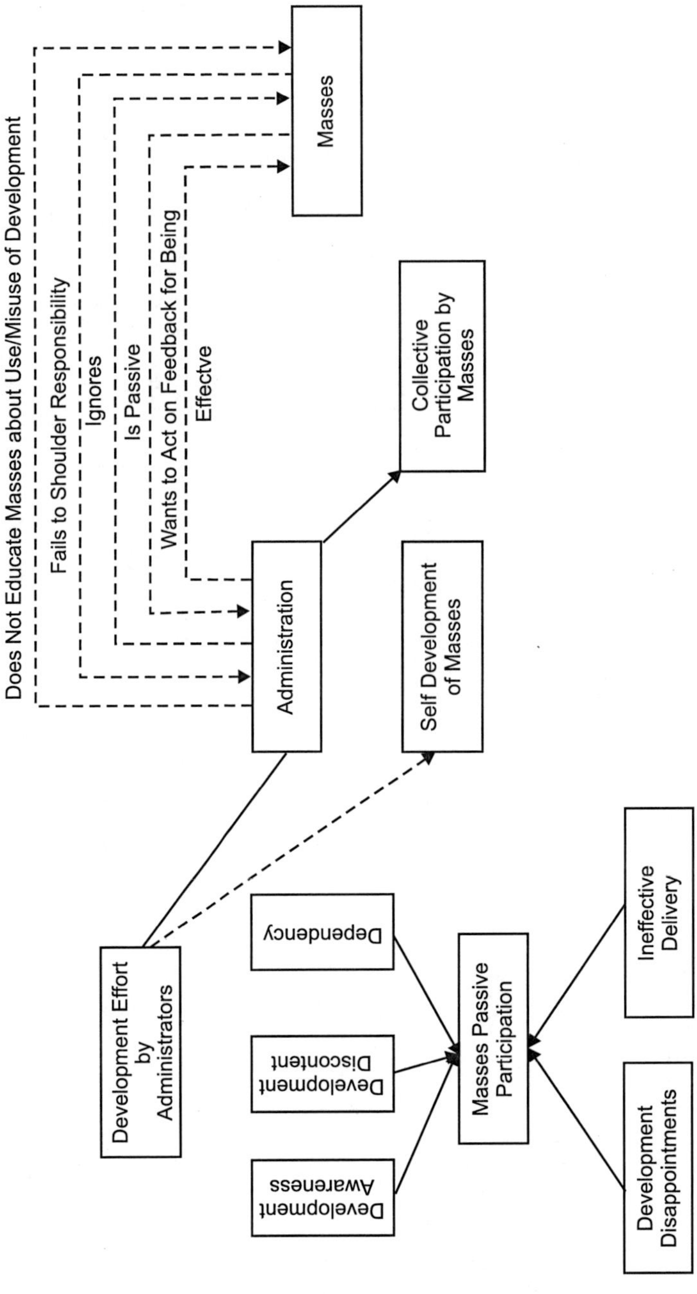

Fig. 2.12. Administrative Change Agents' Interaction with Masses

Fatalism	Characteristics Perceived as Problems	Government Intentions	Development Efforts	Actual Effects
Contentment	Yes	Improved quality	Motivate (e.g., create discontenment with things as they are)	Discontenment
Dependency	No	—	—	Dependency (on the government rather than on fate, landlords or social hierarchy)
Unaware of innovations	Yes	Inform	Educate	Aware of innovations
Exploited	Yes	Emancipate	Legislate protective policies: inform people of rights	Well informed of personal rights; an attitude of having been victimized and now entitled to unearned benefits. The government offered itself as paternalistic; to the extent that development communication is successful, people take the role of cilents.
Participation limited to the local social hierarchy	Yes	Develop the individual or prossessing identity and rights	Intrude into existing hierarchies with radio, TV and personnel linking individuals to the government	Learned dependency; participation consists of accepting things offered as owed, and of "complaining" (that is, "informing the government that it its not doing its job.")

Fig. 2.13. Effects of Development Communication Programs

Development dialogue focuses on application of policy skills, development of administrative infrastructure, communication infrastructure and dialogue strategies. Participatory development and good governance are necessary conditions for dialogue for development. The emphasis is on micro level action contexts, local resistance to change, community participation, and empowerment of people through participation. Simple, moral, accountable, responsible and transparent (SMART) government is advocated for development. With the two components of participation and good governance; strategies can be built around the development issues to reach a consensus to do development. In this context, the government knows people's needs and the people know limitations of the government; and they agree to do development within this framework of partnership.

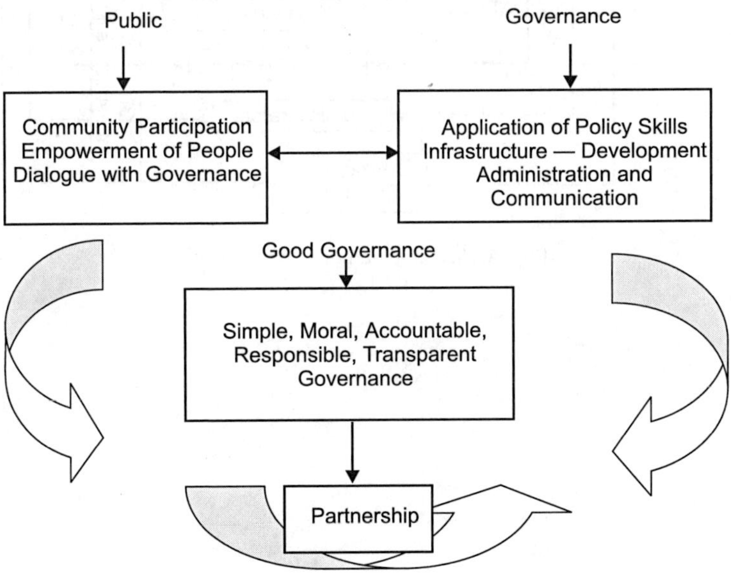

Fig. 2.14. Development Dialogue Strategies

The basic model of development suggests the various components of development and its dynamics that are discussed above in specific contexts.

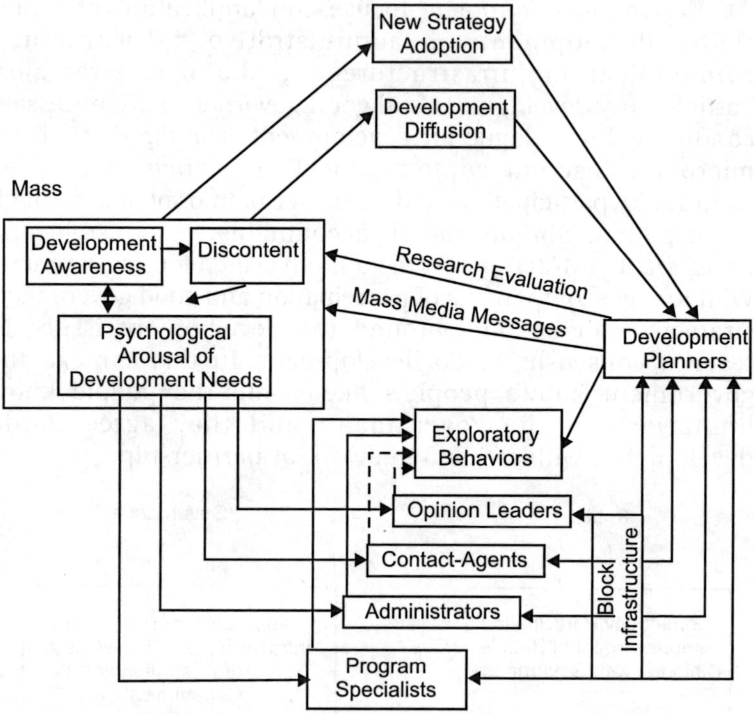

Fig. 2.15. Development: Basic Model

3

International Communication Models

International Communication is sending messages to international community. It may cross the physical boundaries of countries or without that. People are talking to other people in different countries on phones, on Internet and through video-conferences etc. without leaving their homes or work places. They communicate about themselves through content messages on TV, radio, or cinema. People communicate face-to-face with the people when they visit those countries and places. Letters, books, newspapers from one country may cross over to other countries and they communicate about people's concerns, their cultures and life styles.

Messages could be oral, written, visual or action. One or many may receive the message through one or multi-channels. The form may be products, services, infrastructures and ideas. Senders could be individuals (one on one), group organizations, governments, and international organizations from different countries. Channels could be multimedia and interpersonal. Message may be issue-specific or interest evoking issues.

The important components of the model are: interaction with different countries and nations. It is important that the messages are of interest to both senders and receivers. Both media technologies and interpersonal channels are used to facilitate communication. Noise element is incomprehension of what sender wants to convey till it is brought to the level where receiver is able to comprehend for further feedback and action. Circular communication is essential since main objective in many instances is to reach mutual understanding. Therefore, feedback, reaction is sought on the messages conveyed which could be both positive and negative depending on the circumstances. In the model given below the first and the fourth components i.e. interaction and comprehension of the message are the most important.

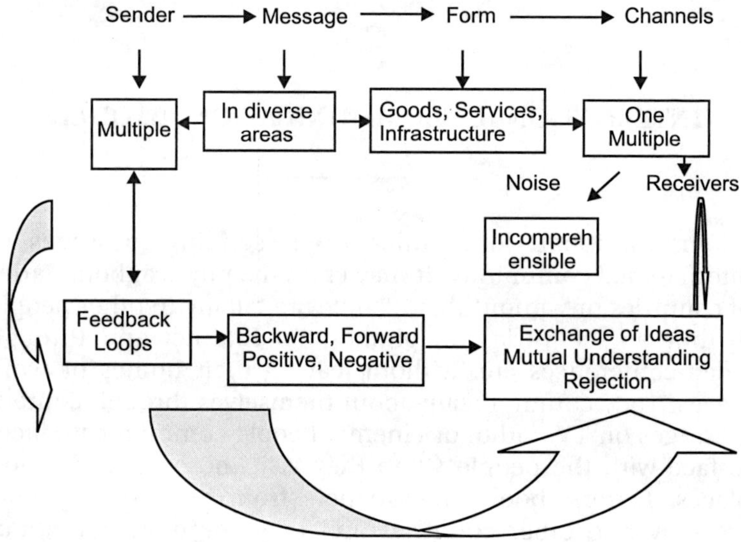

Fig. 3.1. Nature of International Communication

Television shows us life styles of people from different lands, their varied socio-cultural, political concerns. There is instant feeling that their behavior, values are totally different

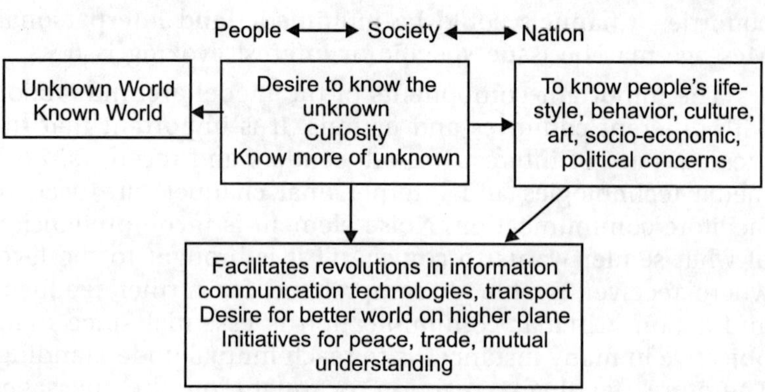

Fig. 3.2. Key Factors in International Communication

or somewhat different. The print media also reflect these dimensions. The curiosity to know these dimensions better and to integrate those cultural practices stimulate us to communicate and interact with people in other countries through personal or impersonal, interpersonal and media channels.

The deliberations of 'Right to information' debates of 70s-80s of MaCBride commission led to the 'New World Information and Communication Order' (NWICO). Where it was advocated that developing countries should have the right to present information about their countries in the global context. They should have control over their communication channels. The international flow of information would be restructured to allow a balance of communication power between western countries and developing nations.

Absence of a consensus on the shape of a 'New world information and communication order' demonstrates that we are in an age of paradigm shifts. Our political and economic institutions are clearly lagging behind the accelerating pace of scientific, technological and cultural change. For international relations, the significant change is through expansion of global communication.

NWICO can be best constructed by developing communication competence for the voiceless. Pluralism in voices however requires pluralism in structures of media access. No single system of media control (governmental, commercial, public, or community) can alone guarantee the plurality of voices. A balance among them might use the expanding channels of communication for an expanding plurality of voices more reflective of the international community.

It calls for free and balanced flow of information among the billions inhabitants of this world, who are caught up between the imperatives of pre-modern, modern, and postmodern worlds to which they belong. NWICO may be conceived of as a network of networks of NGOs, to mobilize the global civil society, to empower the urban and the rural communities, to enhance their communication competence and media capabilities, to negotiate with the State and Non-State actors to redress their conditions.

Global Communication is imperative these days to connect to people globally not only on just one on one basis but across many countries because of growing needs and demands on many fronts viz. political, economic, socio-cultural, technology etc. A network of communication across countries, inter-country and cross-country leads to globalization. Several countries communicate at bilateral or multilateral levels on specific issues.

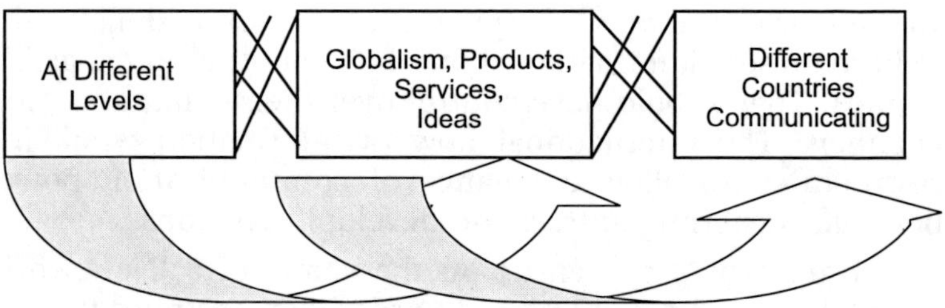

Fig. 3.3. Global Communication Model

Globalization Contexts. The frequent inter-country and cross-country interactions depend on their (each country's) needs and demand to interact. These could be economic

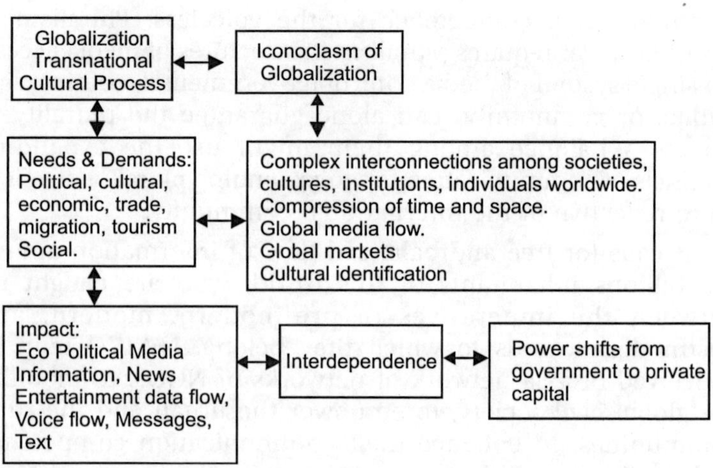

Fig. 3.4. Globalization Contexts

including trade, political, technology, cultural, migration, social and tourism. The forces of interdependence of nations do create a close knit global economy and other systems. The force of globalization shifts power away from governments to private capital. ICTs have been the main driving force and facilitator in all these contexts.

Interdependency Model addresses the issue of international interdependency for international development and resolving crucial issues of political conflicts and war. Communication is an important component.

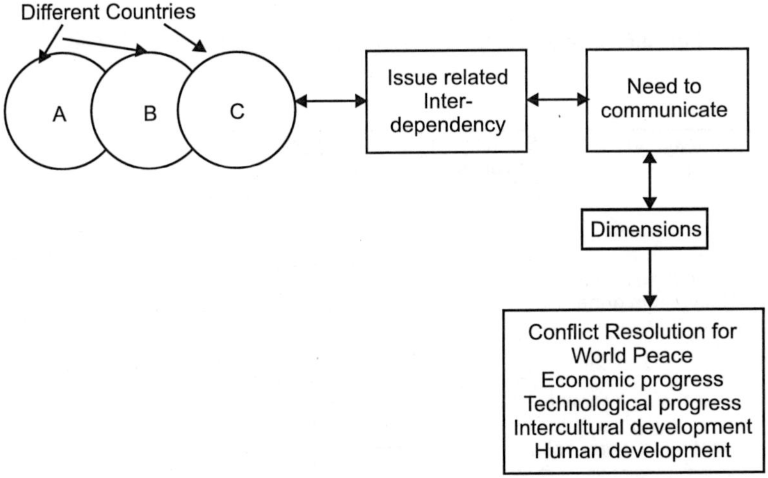

Fig. 3.5. Global Interdependency Model

Technological breakthroughs, innovations, re-inventions are researched and developed by many countries' scientists and technologists. Ultimately the end product may be achieved and patented by one country but the ultimate objective is to let all benefit by it whether it is telephone, electricity, television, radio, computer etc. The ICTs of present decade suggest global networking. Whether it is e-mail through computer, varied uses of telecommunications or broadcasting, and use of satellites. These ICTs work when there are global interconnected efforts for both hardware and software. These do not exist or survive by the efforts of a single country.

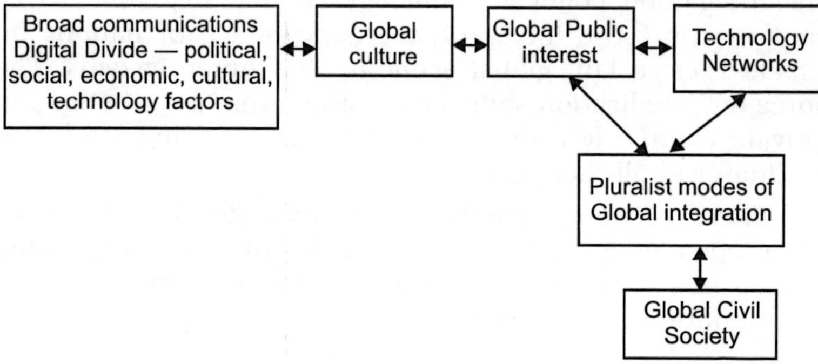

Fig. 3.6. Global Technology Networking Communication Model-1

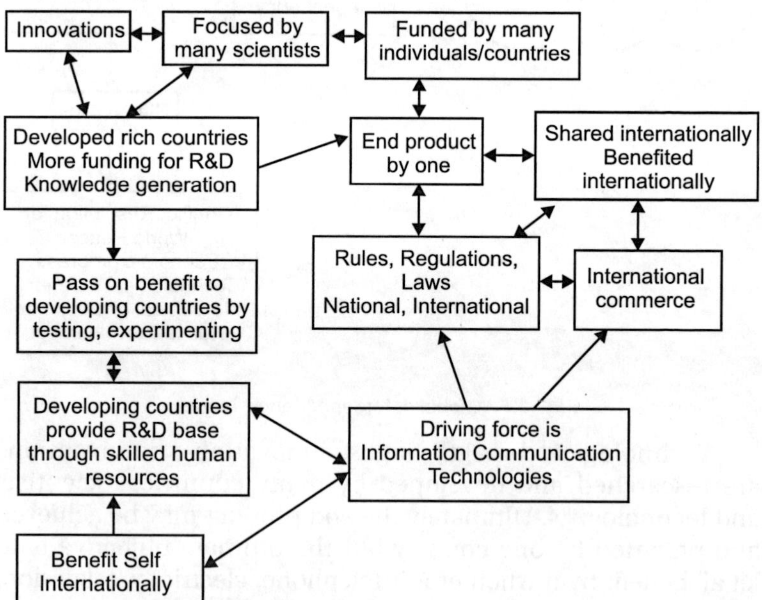

Fig. 3.7. Global Technology Networking Communication Model-2

4

INFORMATION COMMUNICATION TECHNOLOGY (ICT) MODELS

Information resources, national policies, needs and demands for information technology interact to create specific information environment, culture and models. These are universal concerns for ICTs. But there are models within the framework of these universal concerns, which are very specific to each country when applied. This is evidenced by case study research.

In the last six decades the communication revolutions in ICTs have impacted the social and working lives of people around the world.

Every change in ICTs throughout human history has produced anxious voices. There have been dilemmas of innovations.

Social technologies are imperative for the diffusion of communication technologies. The concept of social technology is acceptance of a particular medium as well as the message meaning relayed through the individual and the social system. The performance demands of technology must fit into existing patterns of human interactions to be meaningful in the particular social system and must meet the standards of their social traditions that act as guideline for acceptance, rejection and censorship both by government and the people. The adoption of technology is a social decision so it has social implications.

The salient examples are computer and video technologies in India from 90s to date. In India, the adoption of computer was resisted in 90s. It had gone through the stages of anxiety, fear and apprehensions of losing jobs. In 2000 decades it is now well accepted and ubiquitous. In 90s the video was accepted as an inexpensive means of entertainment through video parlors. Indian government has to censor the video entertainment for its misuse.

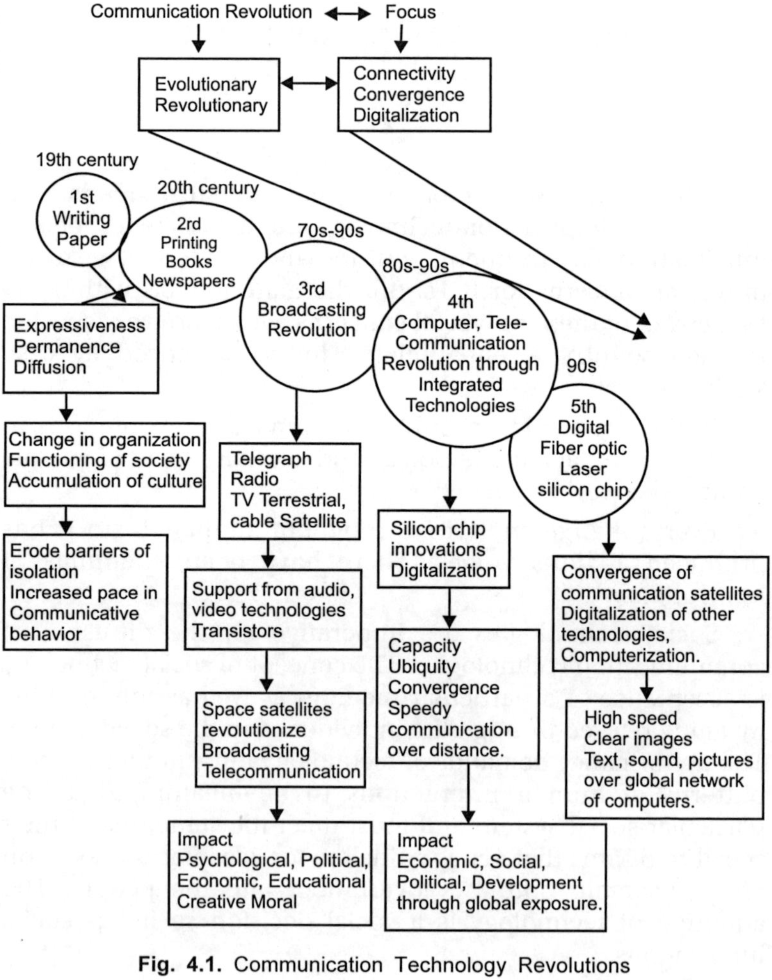

Fig. 4.1. Communication Technology Revolutions

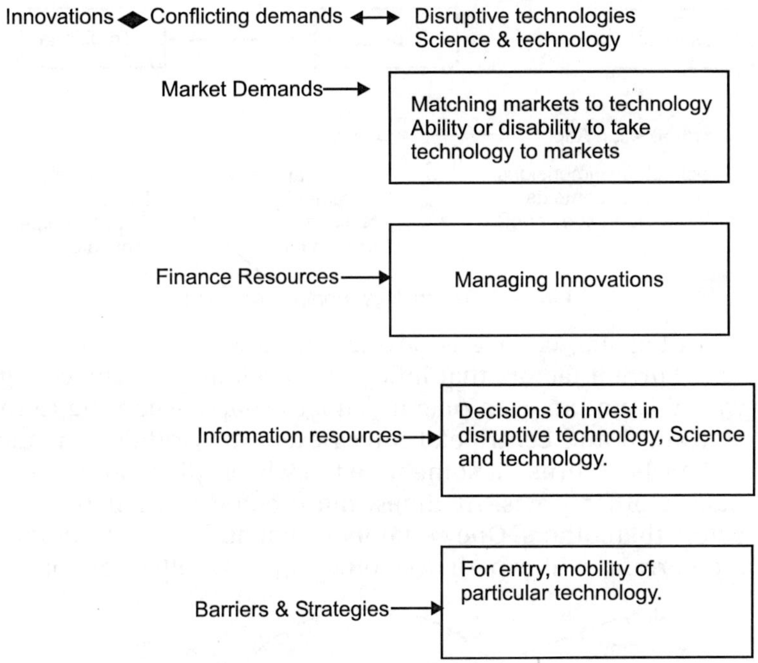

Fig. 4.2. Dilemmas of Innovations

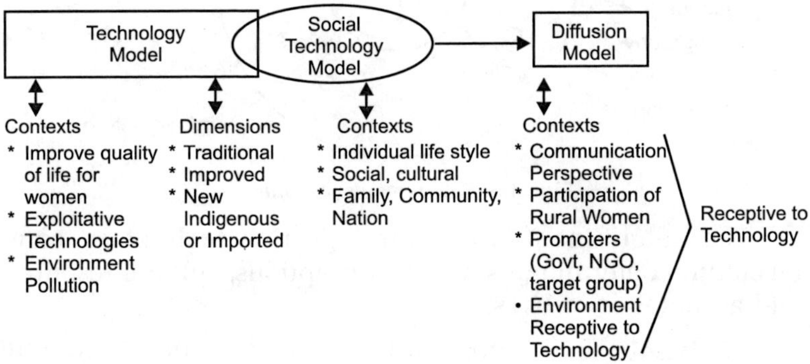

Fig 4.3. Technology Promotion Model

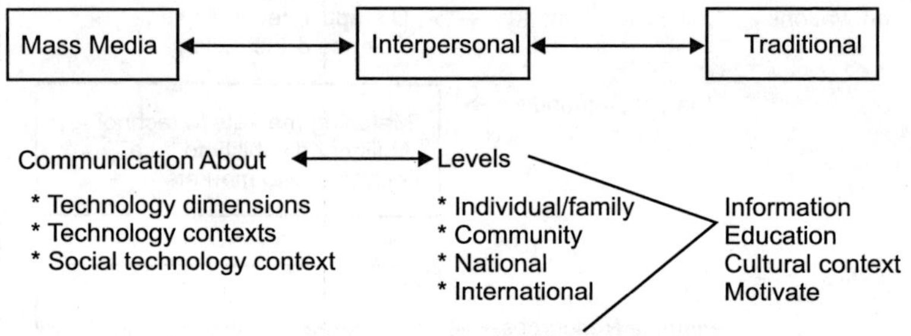

Fig. 4.4. Technology Perspective Model

In Fig. 4.5, change is positioned between traditional and other current factors that influence development. The change 'wheel' is not an even one; it changes shape according to the centrifugal and centripetal forces exerted by other dynamics as the wheel turns. At some time the wheel spins more rapidly than at other times. At times, more change is felt by some factors than others. One certainty is that all factors (traditional and current) will experience some aspect or effect of change.

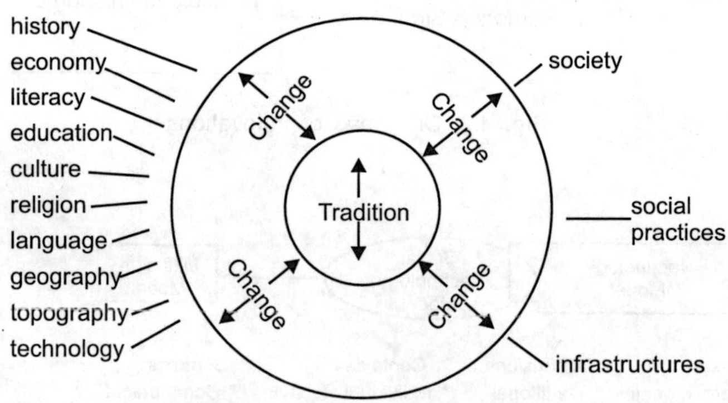

Fig. 4.5. Components of Change

The determinants for communication technology could be cultural determinants, value assumptions, cultural resources and acceptance of ICTs.

There are two important dimensions of technology diffusion. On one hand, there is interaction of scientific and technical factors; and on the other hand, there is interaction of economic, social, and political factors. The overall 'interaction points' of these two dimensions determine technological development, its applications, and communication.

Communication Perspective	Cultural Challenges
1. Perspective of Government * Accelerate development pace by IEC * Efficient Communication Network * Optimum information accessible to Majority	Pro-social Role for Culturally Diverse Multitude
2. Perspective of Masses * Technologies should be available, accessible, cost effective, meaningful performance * Diffusion of science and technology at grassroot levels * Quality of life	Assimiliate Pro-social Messages in the Social System

Fig. 4.6. Communication Technology Determinants

Culture Specific → Communication Forms → Communication Acts

	Cultural Challenges
1. Cultural Determinants * Cultural values of elites and masses * Super imposed societal values * Cultural Policies of Government * Media structures, controls and practices * Work ethics, organizational practices	Creation of social technology
2. Five Value Assumptions * Regard for human nature * Relationship of man to nature * Time orientation * Orientation towards activity * Types of relation among people	Developing social competence
3. Cultural Resources * Language, Religion, Ideology * Values, Ways of doing and Making things * Myths, Stories, Artifacts * Typifications, Interpretative procedures	Putting cultural resources at risk
4. Accept Technology - Challenges related to 1,2,3 are accepted	Cultural–LAG

Fig. 4.7. Communication Technology Determinants–Integrated

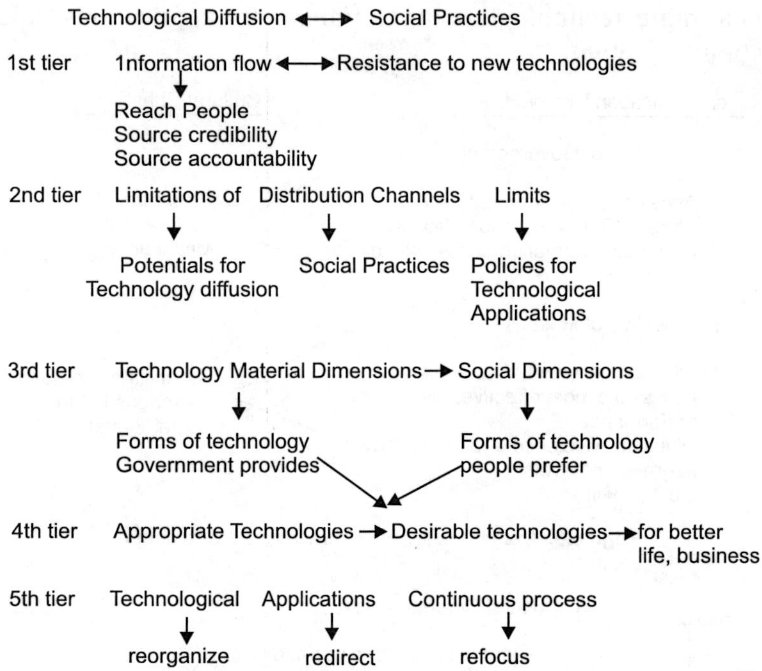

Fig. 4.8. Diffusion of Technology Tiers

When society is using Advance Information Technology in its varied applications; it focuses on varied dimensions to make information technology effective.

Rapid technological change, unpredictability of consumer demands, and diversity of innovative applications have created much uncertainty about the speed of development and diffusion; and economic, social, and cultural impact.

Social research can refine understanding of the complex roles that social, organizational and cultural processes play in the development of ICTs in various sectors of society. Yet the complexities and interdependencies of technological, organizational, and social change make prescriptions for policies and practice highly problematic and contingent on the special and historical context.

The social process of ICTs and its effect on the society represents a new perspective on social and behavioral processes. They seek guidance through research to improve social interventions using technology in domains such as education, mental health, work productivity etc. Scientists and technologists highlight the human side of electronic communications and they think about the social processes and effects of ICTs designs, applications and policies.

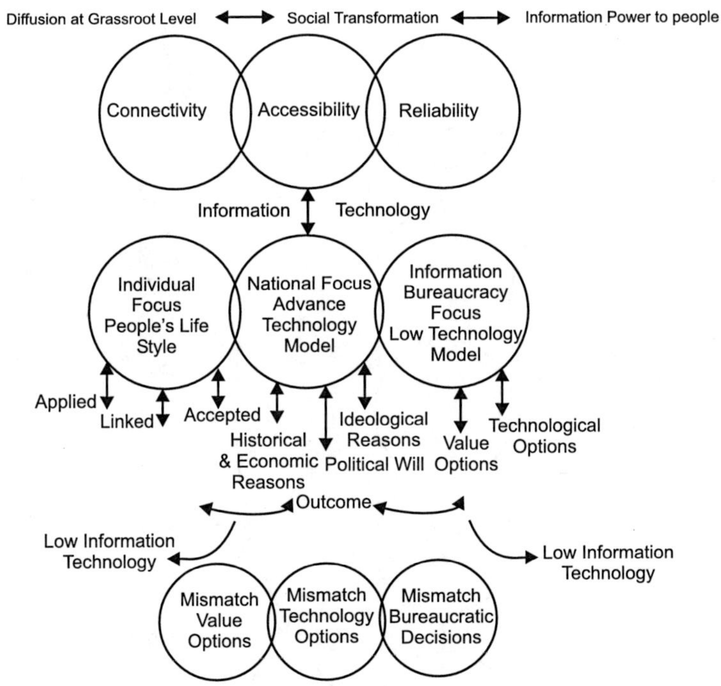

Fig. 4.9. Information Technology Model

Every society differs in the race for information technology and building of information society. The general model provides background to information technology efforts.

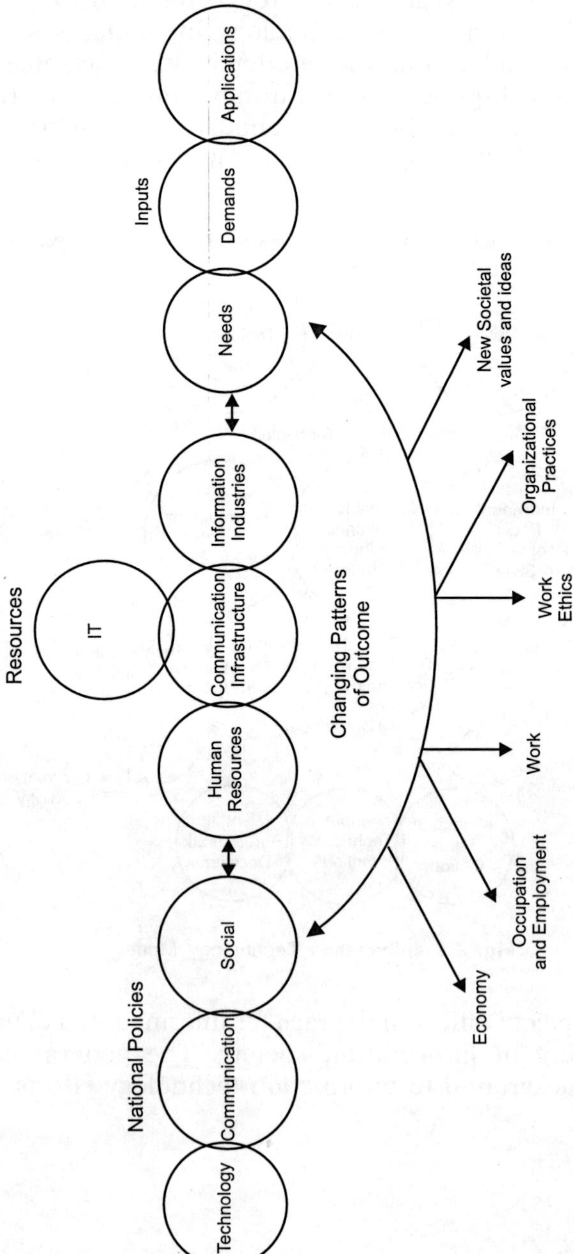

Fig. 4.10. Advance Information Technology Model

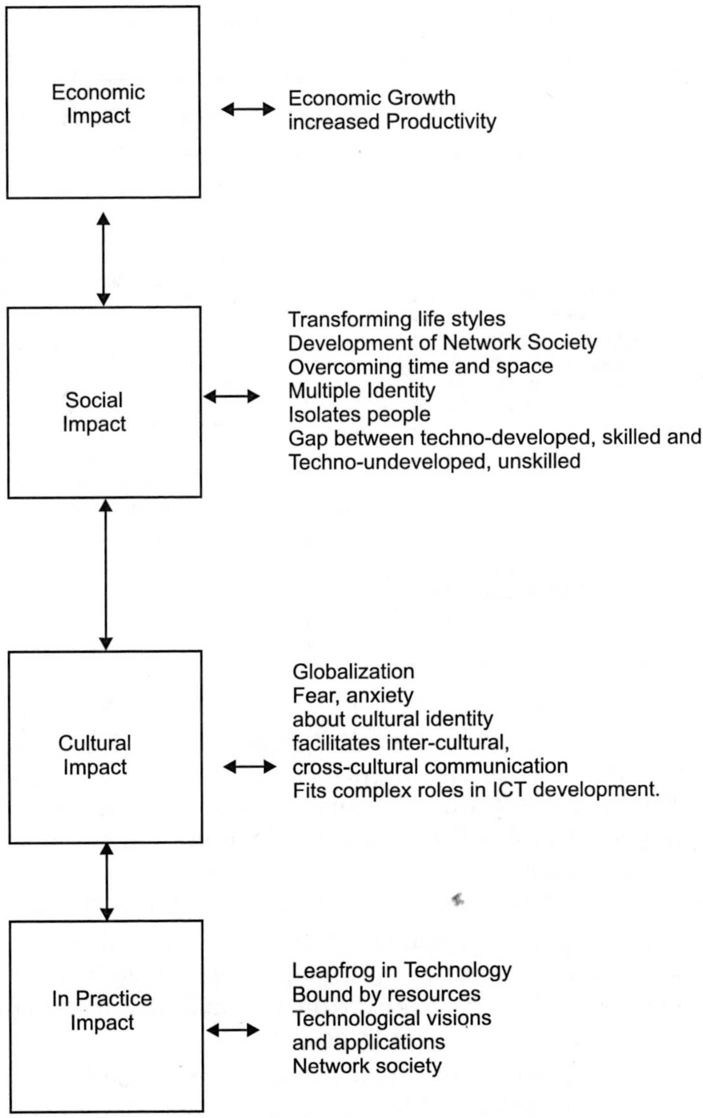

Fig. 4.11. Information Technology Impact

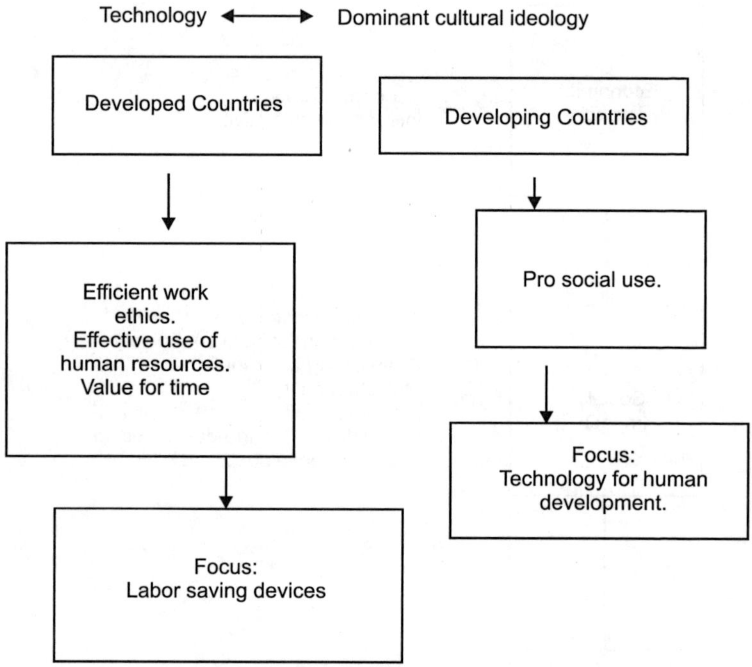

Fig. 4.12. Communication Technology Context

Fig **4.13** suggests that the development of information society depends on the interplay of resources, national policies and inputs. When these factors interact, the outcome is the changing patterns of economy, occupations and employment, work and work ethics, and organizational practices. Thc changing patterns result in new societal values and ideas.

The information society develops to the advance stage through development of information technology culture and its diffusion. This has impact on national and international levels and facilitates gaining power.

Management of information causes increasing problems for the organizations: (i) how to make a whole of the scattered information, (ii) how to screen out relevant information, (iii) how to extract from the information environment those messages likely to have significance for the organization. Two important communication skills are needed in this context: Knowledge Management and Impression Management.

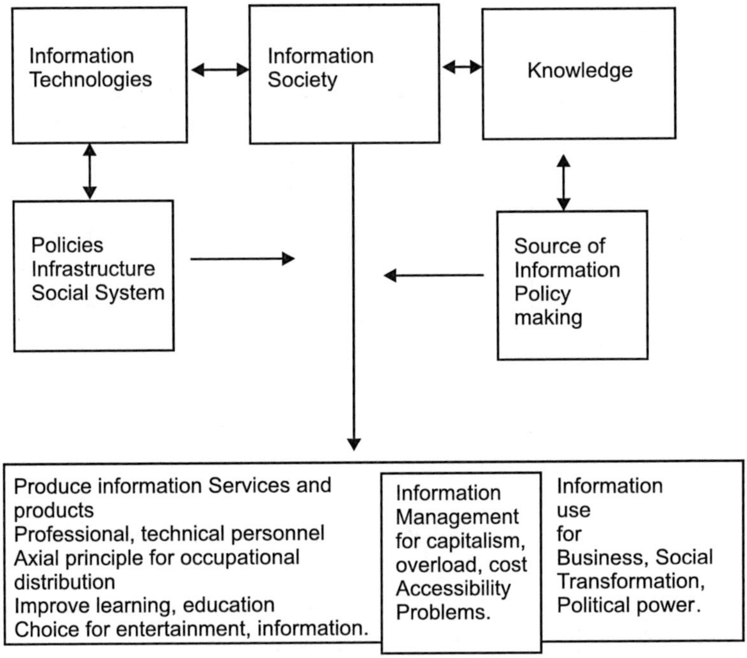

Fig. 4.13. Information Society: General Model

Knowledge management of scientific information helps in innovations. Management of other kinds of information helps in decision-making and leadership roles. Impression management is needed for visual professional competence. It is the direct visual impression that creates the illusion of credibility and not visual information itself. Advertising and marketing industries work hard to find more and more effective visual means of impression management.

Digitalization is another technological possibility that offers a universal system that is distributed through satellite or through fiber optics. Digitalization of information makes the same channel of communications more useful by doubling up on the amounts of information carried through conventional conduits.

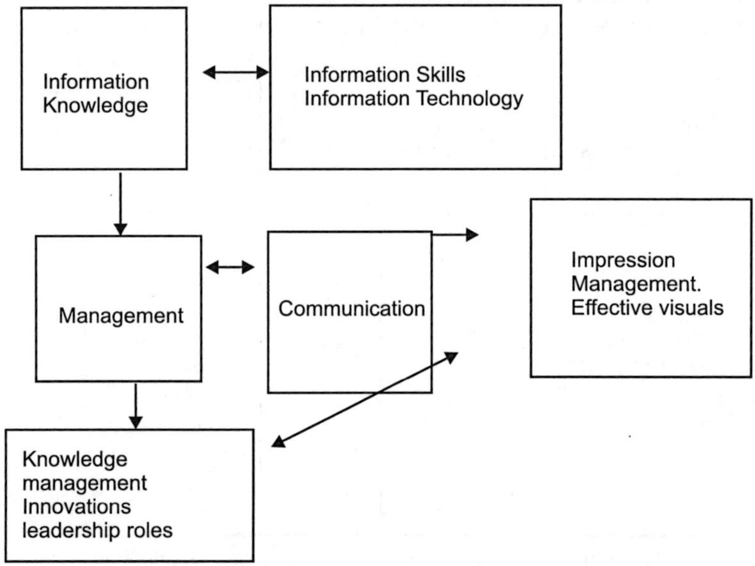

Fig. 4.14. Global Information Economy Management

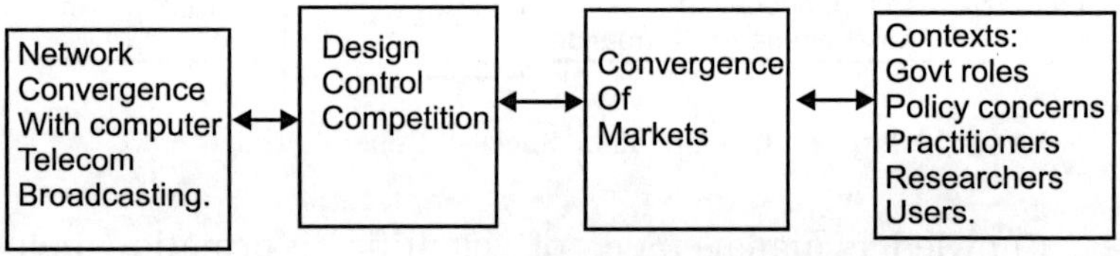

Fig. 4.15. Digital Convergence

The potential impact of digital convergence is on the pre-digital media system of print, film, radio, television, computer and telecommunications. Production technology has become more computer-based and is creating new media forms. Technological and economic drivers of such convergence will have social, cultural and economic impacts. The policy concern, players and stakes will be different in each context.

Internet is fast expanding and is ubiquitous in all walks of life. It is having tremendous impact on people's life and how the businesses are being conducted and has facilitated globalization. Information gathering, sharing is the major focus and much is achieved through it. Internet is a *New World* for social behavior.

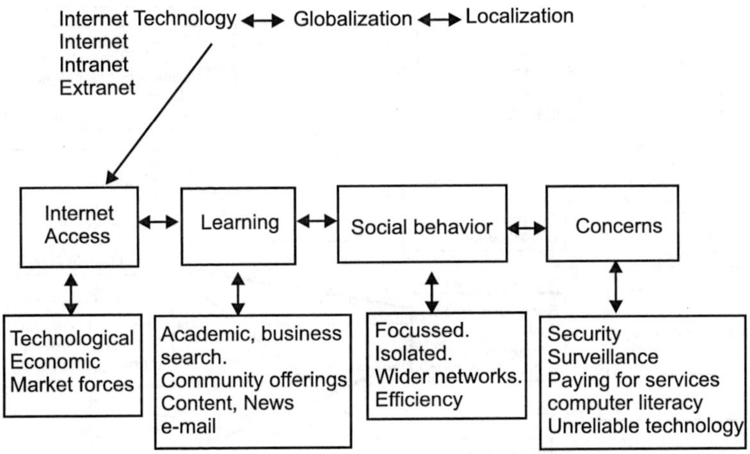

Fig. 4.16. Internet

Presently, there is multimedia approach to ICTs. The convergence of mainstream ICTs and supporting ICT, and an integrated approach to information technologies is having social, cultural and economic impact on the lifestyle and societies globally.

Information technology is important for globalization process. It has impact on globalization and vice versa. Importance of information and ICTs addresses three concerns: the liberalization of markets, encouragement of competition between different systems, and the globalization process in the context of third world.

The powerful flow of information, news, and various broadcasting programs not only saturate the world markets but are also having tremendous impact on people's life.

Complex process of global interconnectedness, time-space compression and action at distance re-envisaged the world. This creates iconoclasm of globalization. Transculturation, hybridization, and indigenization are important in understanding the cultural influences. These rethink of cultural

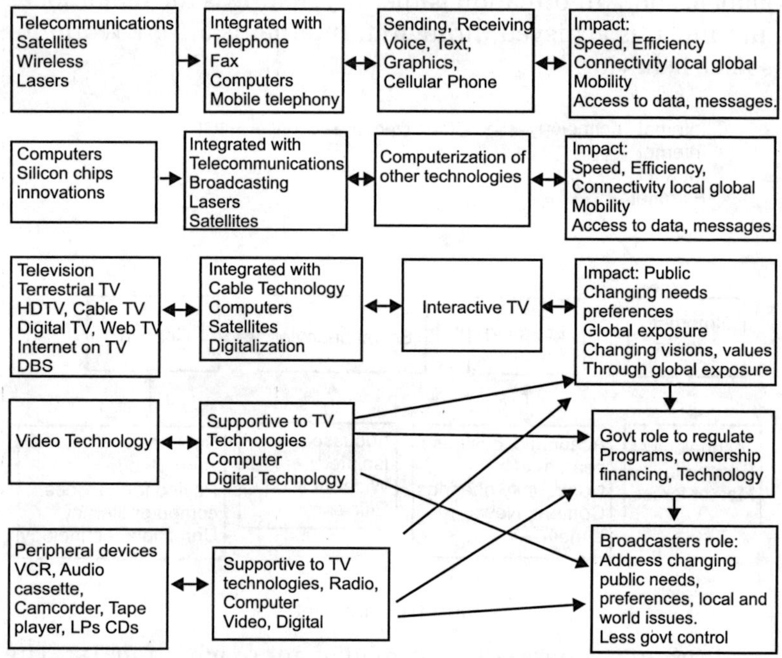

Fig. 4.17. Information Technologies: Integrated Approach

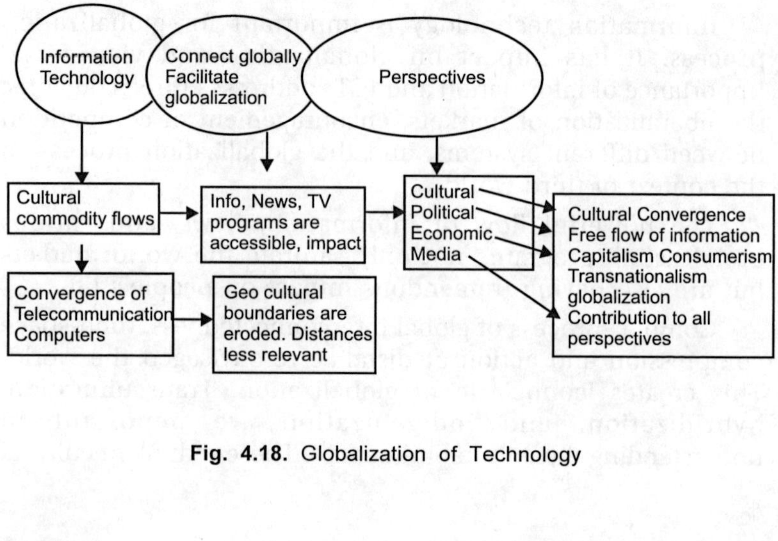

Fig. 4.18. Globalization of Technology

power not as cultural imperialism but as a process of cultural integration. The communication in global contexts presents cultural challenges.

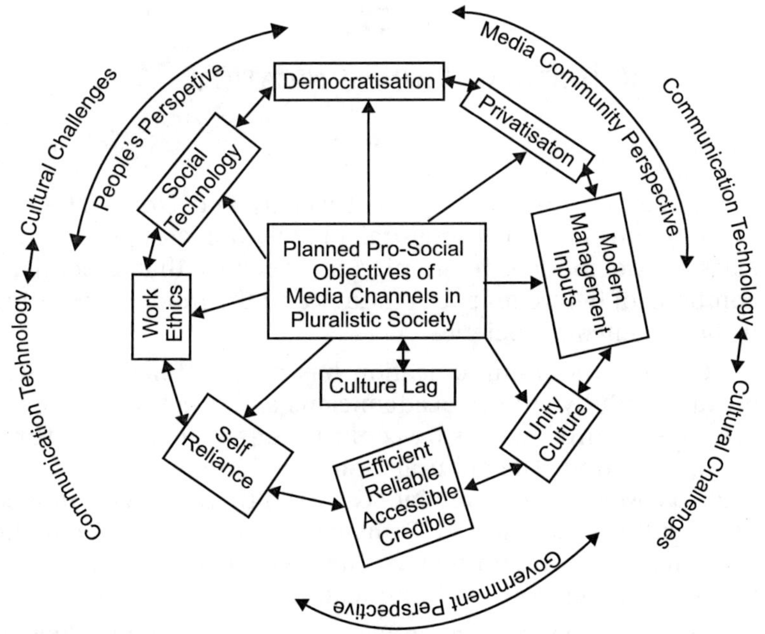

Fig. 4.19. Communication Technology and Cultural Challenges

Technology is a component of culture and is understood in its cultural context and the choice of technology is within this system. Communication technology presents cultural challenges. It poses cultural challenges for preserving or destroying the cultural identity and values of a particular society. It can pose challenges for cultural vitality, diversity and intercultural understanding. These challenges are also culture-specific.

5

Intercultural Communication Models

All cultural models suggest *Diversity* and *Unity.* There is unity in diversity. The cultural models are grouped in two classes: the models in immigrant societies that essentially comprise of heterogeneous cultures and the models operating in homogeneous societies.

Culture and communication has been defined in variety of ways both by culture academicians and practitioners. Both are basic and necessary components of intercultural communication. The cultural models in immigration societies such as Melting Pot model, Cross-cultural Images model, Multi-culture model, and Trans-culture model highlight the diversity, cultural influences, and contexts. These create intercultural tensions and multiculturalism.

Figure 1 'Communication Perspective' given in introduction chapter in context of cultural communication suggests that the particular forms of communication shape the social institutions and social traditions. People interpret their environments and experiences. People derive their power of communication from their resources of cultural habits and practices. They reconstitute and reinterpret them when faced with alien culture and interact with coordination and coherence.

The contact situation is viewed in terms of ecological contexts and the demographic characteristics of people. The patterns of conjunctive relations are envisaged in terms of intercultural role networks. The cultural (acculturation) process includes several sub-processes such as intercultural transmission (diffusion), cultural creativity, cultural disintegration, and reactive adaptations. Cultural fusion, assimilation, and a stabilizing pluralism are the lasting outcome of acculturation.

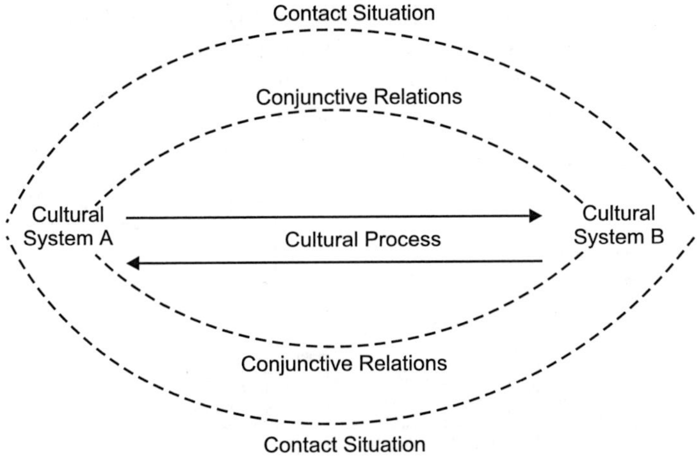

Fig. 5.1. Approach to Cultural Communication

The model subsumes the effects of pre-migration factors, and situational determinants in the receiving society. These are concerned with socio-psychological aspects. Length of residence in the receiving society is taken as an independent variable that interacts with both pre-migration and situational determinants to modify the objectives and subjective modes of adaptation.

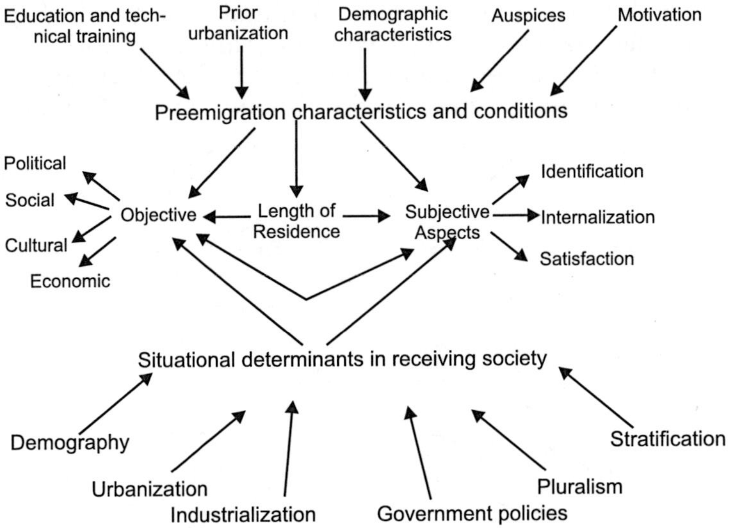

Fig. 5.2. Multivariate Model for Immigration Adaptation Process

The model given below reflects how socio-demographic characteristics and various communication variables involved in the process of acculturation of ethnic groups function and interact with one another to facilitate or impede acculturation.

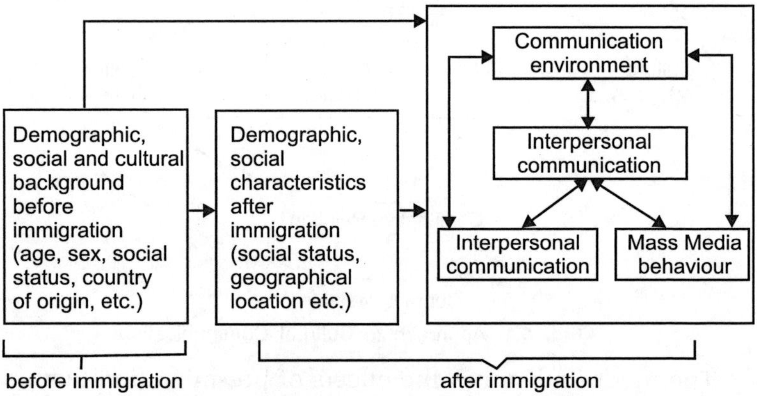

Fig. 5.3. Communication Model for Acculturation

Technology and media connectivity not only exposes people to cultural ways and cultural diversity but it also diffuses the same to a global audience and shape unique cultural ways. The interaction of culture specific images of self and others, stereotypes, prejudices, multicultural settings and media exposure create Intercultural Images which are further facilitated by social communication networks, and intercultural communication competence for wider political, social, economic, business, and technological ramifications.

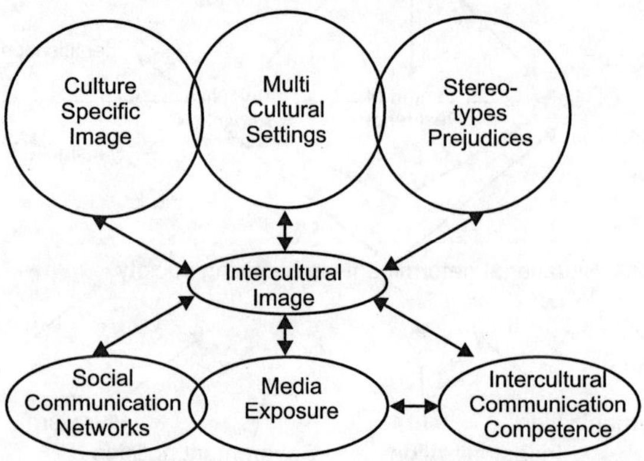

Fig. 5.4. Cultural Diffusion: Intercultural Image

Communication technologies are apparatuses through which cultural invasion and cultural domination may take place. This may in turn create cultural dilemmas, crisis of cultural identities, and related tensions. The dynamics are how the cultural diversity is managed.

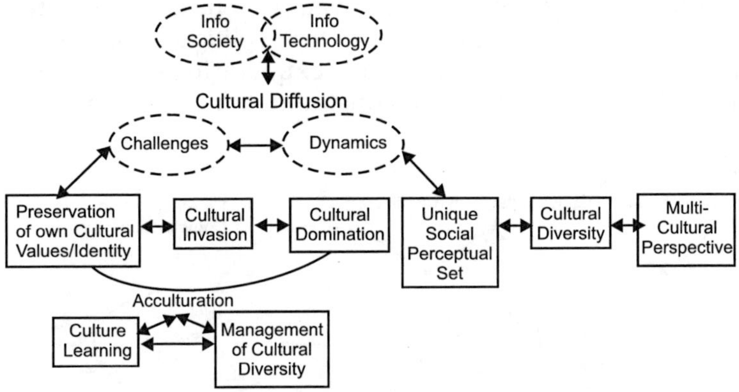

Fig. 5.5. Cultural Diffusion: Challenges and Dynamics

This figure below presents a holistic viewpoint of cultural diffusion from the point of various milieu and communication variables.

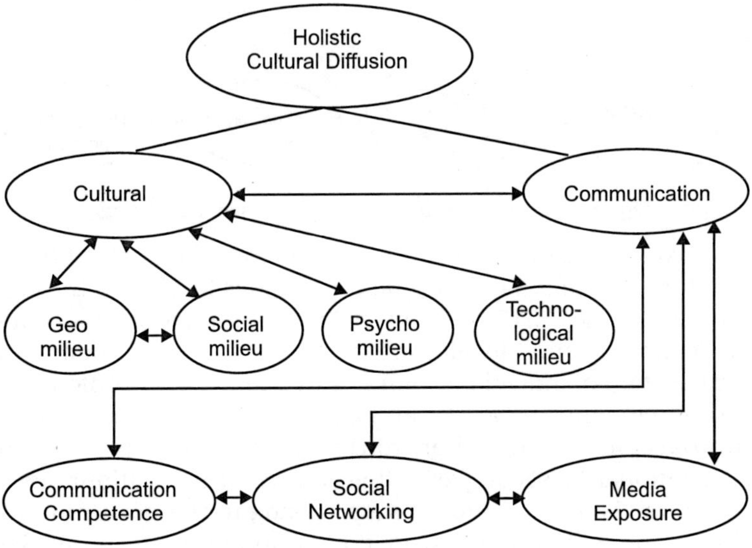

Fig. 5.6. Cultural Diffusion: Integrated Perspective

The major prospect of cultural diffusion is in its being the agent of intercultural change, intercultural understanding and political peace. Intercultural change depends on human communication environments, intercultural contexts, technologies and the immigration policies. The right type of information, knowledge about various cultures can create intercultural understanding and in turn political peace. Political and economic demands and expectations created by intercultural contexts create constraints for cultural diffusion.

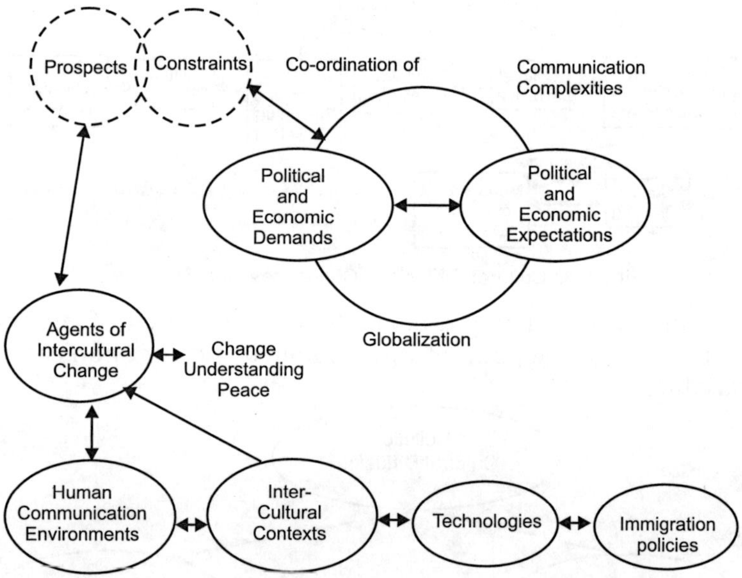

Fig. 5.7. Cultural Diffusion: Prospects and Constraints

Take the instance of the phenomenon of globalization as an effort for women development at various levels and through various focuses. This has implications for global visibility, transparency and development strategies for women. The participation of individual countries in international conferences and agreements means that nations expose themselves for comparisons with other nations. Transparency at the international levels suggests that abuses at the national level are more visible and more embarrassing to the governments. That many governments over the world appear to be willing to commit to women's rights and gender equality.

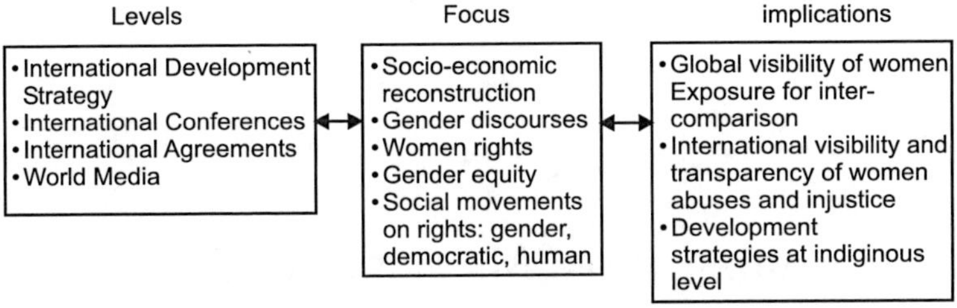

Fig. 5.8. International Strategies for Women Development

We observe that every culture-society differs in the race for information technology and building of information society. Beside technology, the cultural resources and practices play significant role in these efforts. We do face the communication challenges in cultural contexts. A cultural perspective in globalization addresses how cultural diffusion can facilitate globalization. Conflicts are generated through complexities in cultures.

6

Communication Management Models

Communication is an important component in every human activity. It is effective when it is managed well. Therefore it is important how communication is managed in various streams

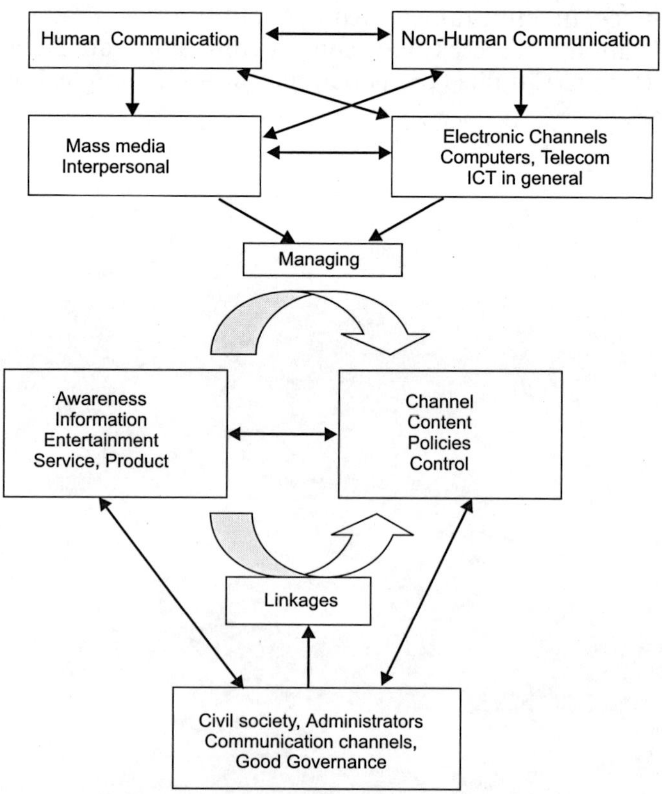

Fig. 6.1. Communication Management Competence

for effective delivery of ideas, products, and services. The management could be of both human and non-human (computer, telecommunication etc) communications. In fact, management of knowledge is the significant component in communication management. A few salient areas are discussed in the communication management perspective in Part 2 of the book. Models associated with those areas are presented in this section.

Management approach calls for holistic approach to communication in any particular area, be it business, entertainment, information technology or development. The necessary conditions for such a holistic approach are IECM strategies, linkages between civil society, administrators and communication channels, and good governance. Management competency is important.

Business Communication Models

The focus of business communication is on diverse dimensions of businesses. The various Business Communication Models take four approaches. First is general approach to business communications. Second is special approach that handles business communications from various perspectives in specific aspects of different business sectors. Some of these may include negotiations in business dealings, management of products and services, product-cycle, advertisement and public relations, globalization, information technology, training (including intercultural training) etc. and overall effective communications.

The third approach focuses on communications for human relations in businesses. These include employee relation management (ERM), customer relation management (CRM), product relation management (PRM) etc. Fourth approach focuses on business and economic intelligence and analysis, economics of business communications.

Business intelligence and its social components, changing dimensions and areas of businesses, and the new and wider applications of ICTs create a specific business culture for a particular business. Communications through conventional and new media technologies, and interpersonal channels play significant role in managing these three business communication components. Internet and various modes of mobile communications have facilitated global business and globalization in business. Through newer technologies of Internet we are stepping into e-commerce.

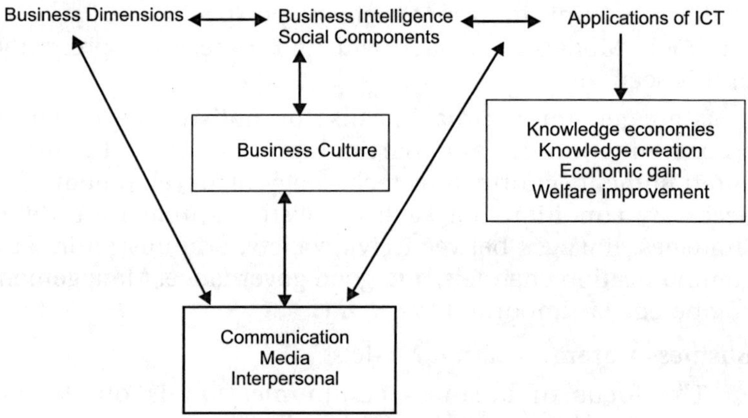

Fig. 6.2. Business Communication Management

Managing knowledge economy for economic gain through business and economic growth culminating in improvement of welfare is important. It is the efficient use of knowledge in this context.

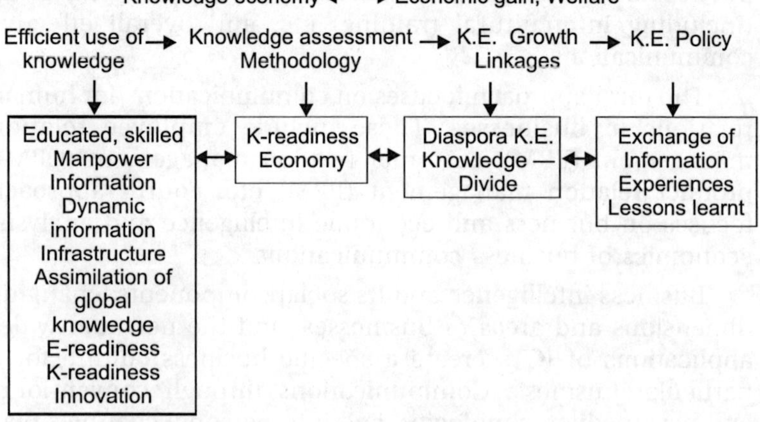

Fig. 6.3. Managing Knowledge Economies

Knowledge as an important component of communications needs management for its effective use in varied sectors of activity. This model addresses the issues of knowledge management competencies and dynamics, various components, applications, techniques, and its impact on number of variables.

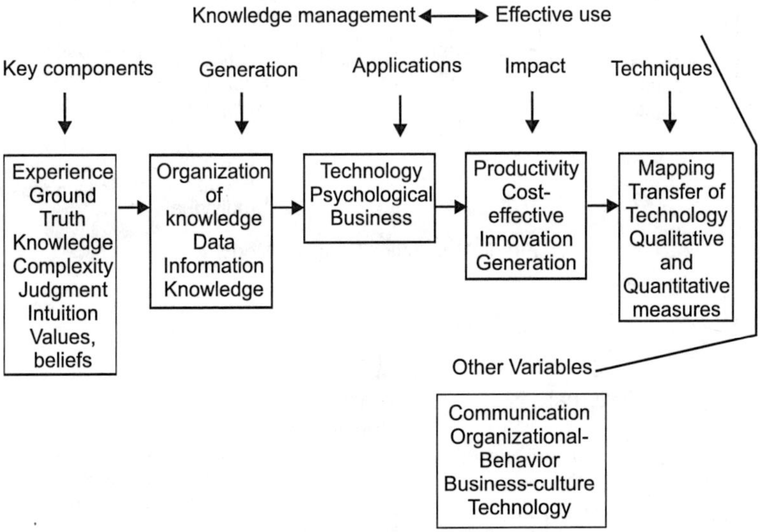

Fig. 6.4. Knowledge Management Model

Conflict Management Models

The figures given below deal with conflict process, variables of conflict, and the conflict resolution efforts through conflict management. Efforts of various stakeholders manage conflicting information to achieve balance and justice.

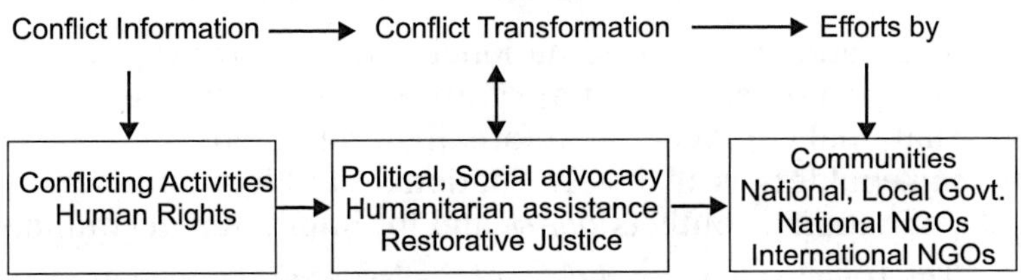

Fig. 6.5. Conflict Management Model

Conflict is a process and it erupts when there is a saturation point pertaining to certain variables. The two models given below map the variables in conflict when there is disturbed peace crisis. Peace dimensions design helps in conflict resolution.

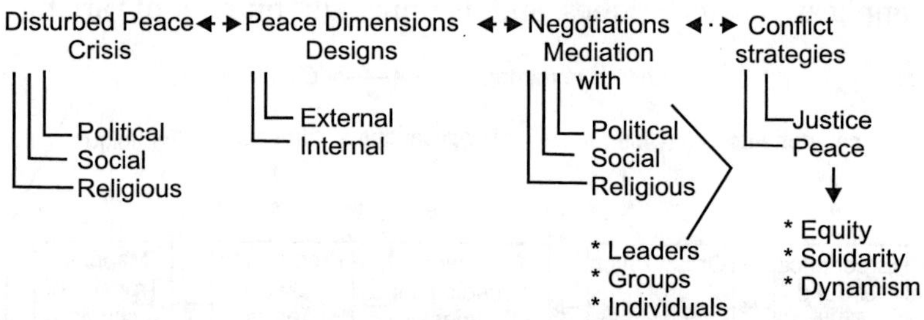

Fig 6.6. Conflict Process Model

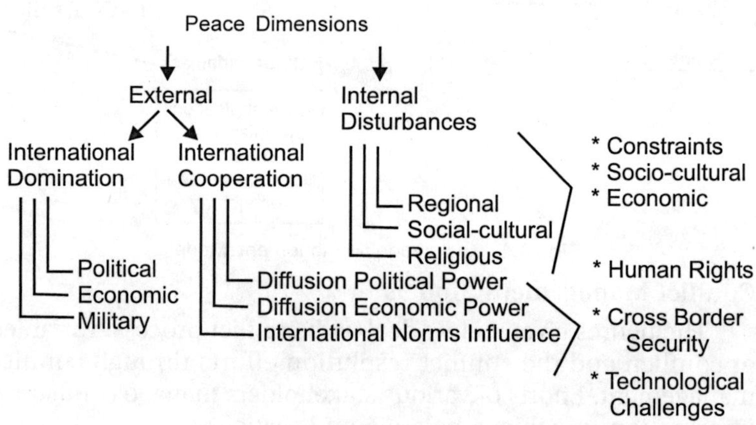

Fig. 6.7. Peace Dimensions for Conflict Resolution

The national and international conflicts are triggered by many variables. National conflicts can culminate in international conflicts. Therefore, the preliminary steps taken by stakeholders is to resolve national conflicts both for the sake of national conflicts *per se* and for international conflicts.

The triggering of conflicts with its issues and consequences, its escalation and de-escalation is modelled. Further, when the social conflicts are protracted, certain dynamics are significant.

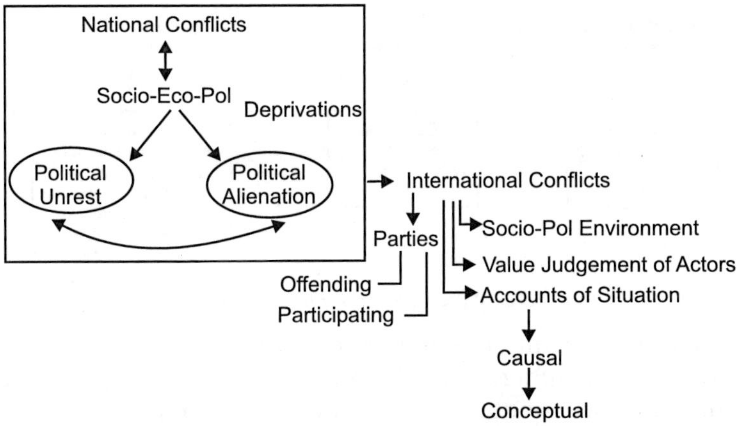

Fig. 6.8. Conflict Variables Model

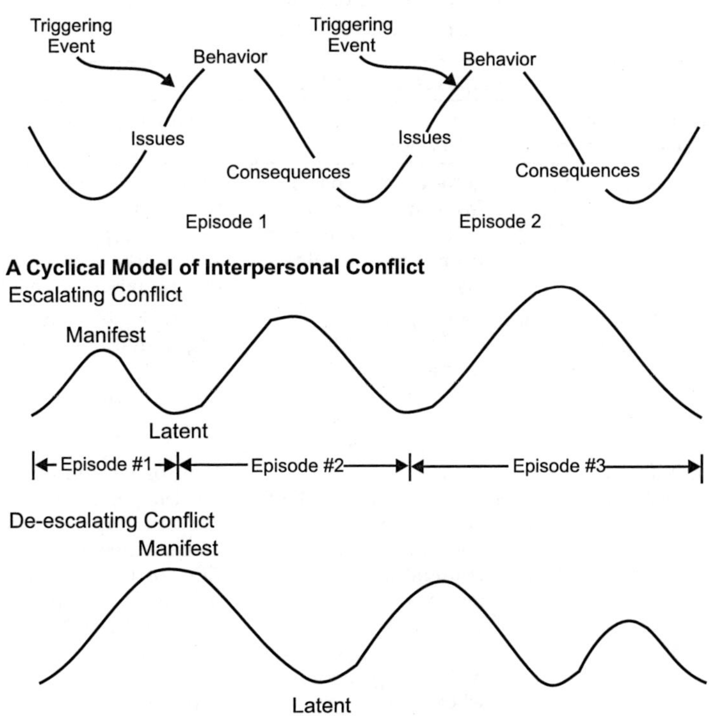

Fig. 6.9. Diagnostic Model of Interpersonal Conflict

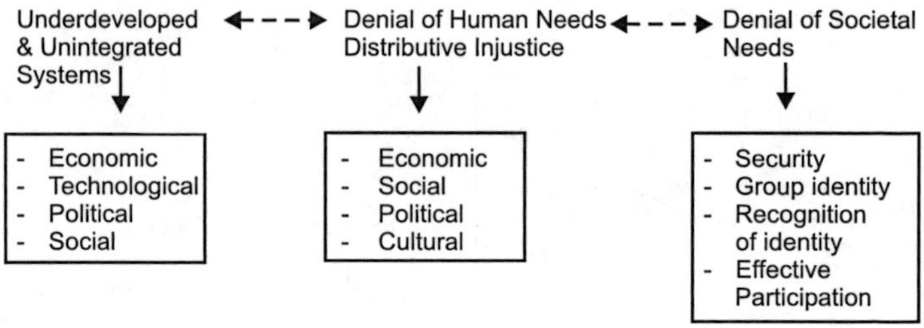

Fig. 6.10. Dynamics of Protracted Social Conflicts

Third party intervention and communication can help resolve the conflicts. The four components — aggression, conflict, negotiations, order and peaceful change manipulate the parties for conflict resolution.

Understanding conflict dynamics helps in conflict management. The conflict dynamics are issues, triggering events, resolution initiatives and consequences.

Purposes of Conflict Dialogue		
Elements of Conflict Cycle or Episode	Diagnostic Objectives	Action Objectives
1. Issues in conflict	Differentiate basic from symptomatic issues and resolvable from unresolvable issues	Resolve by compromise or integration of substantive differences and working through of emotional differences
2. Events or conditions that trigger manifest conflict	Identity barriers to conflict or conflict management behaviours and events that precipitate such behaviour	Control by avoiding triggering new episode unless constructive purpose will be served
3. Manifest tactics or resolution initiatives	Understand how characteristic conflict behaviours can generate additional issues	Control by limiting destructive tactics, encouraging constructive initiatives
4. Consequences, including feelings produced by conflict	Understand the feelings generated by conflict episodes how they are coped with, and therefore whether they are fueling the next episode	Control by assisting principals to cope better with feelings and other consequences of conflict

Fig. 6.11. Conflict Dynamics and Conflict Management

Figure given below presents an integrated model to manage conflicts. Conflict resolution requires integrated efforts of parties in conflict focusing on flexibility of attitudes, dialogue among the parties, negotiations and action taken accordingly. Even for negotiated actions it is necessary to make integrated efforts by both the parties.

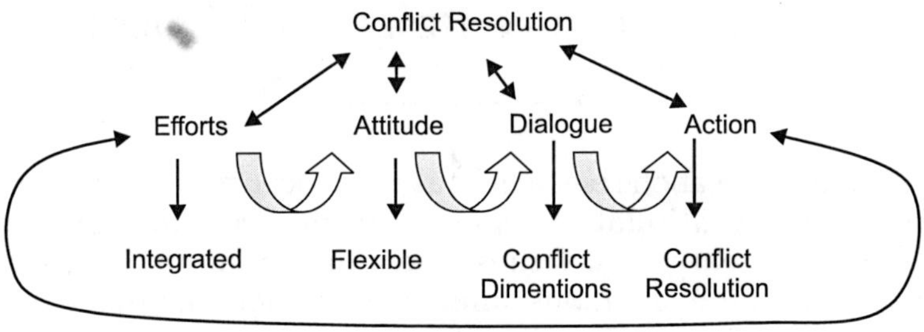

Fig. 6.12. Conflict Resolution Integrated Model

7

Communication Research Models

Communication research focuses on local, regional, national and international issues from communication point. The early researches and confrontation with new communication situations stimulated further communication research in specific areas of source, audience, message, channels and effects (both mass media and interpersonal), communication rules, content and contextual research. Besides this, urban, urban periphery and rural areas are also researched for the specific related issues.

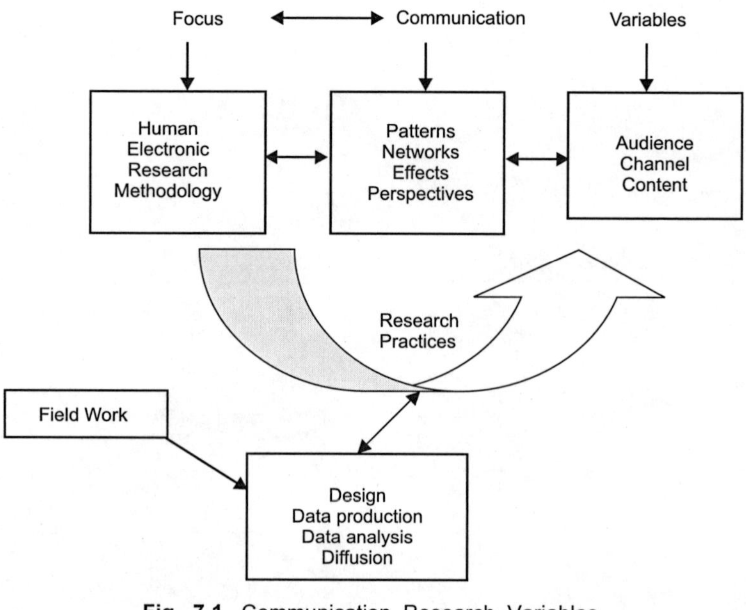

Fig. 7.1. Communication Research Variables

Thus the research models differ according to the above focuses, and categorizations and they are issue related. Even the research models are impacted by the upcoming and newer applications of media technologies. Research in different communication variables changes the communication scenario over a time period. Such changing communication scenario can represent specific research models. Thus there could be numerous research models. To present them from every single perspective would be beyond the scope of this book. We present only salient communication research models.

Research is conducted with greater sensitivity to cultural and political concerns and with methods reflecting those concerns. New Research methodologies, new research techniques are experimented and adopted to gain better insights in human communications.

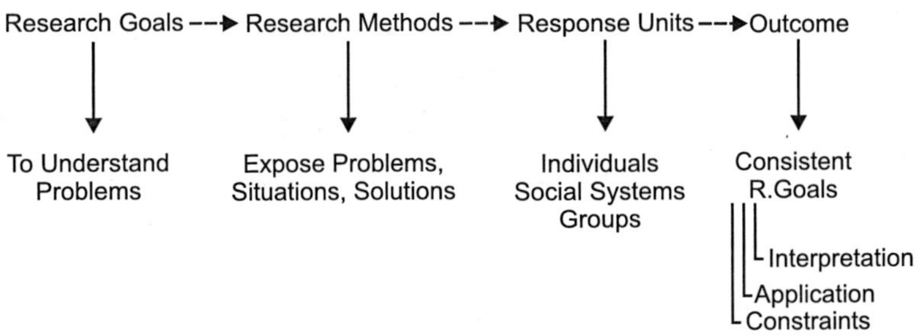

Fig. 7.2. Social Research Investigative Paradigm-1

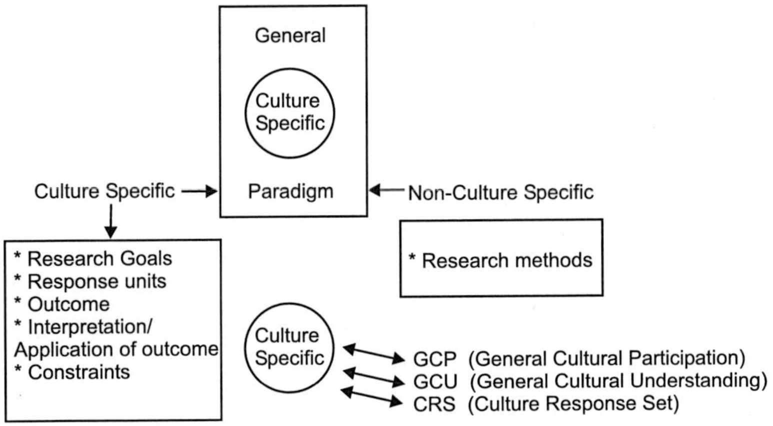

Fig. 7.3. Social Research Investigative Paradigm-2

The research practices are constrained by practical problems and some of those problems are politics and culture specific.

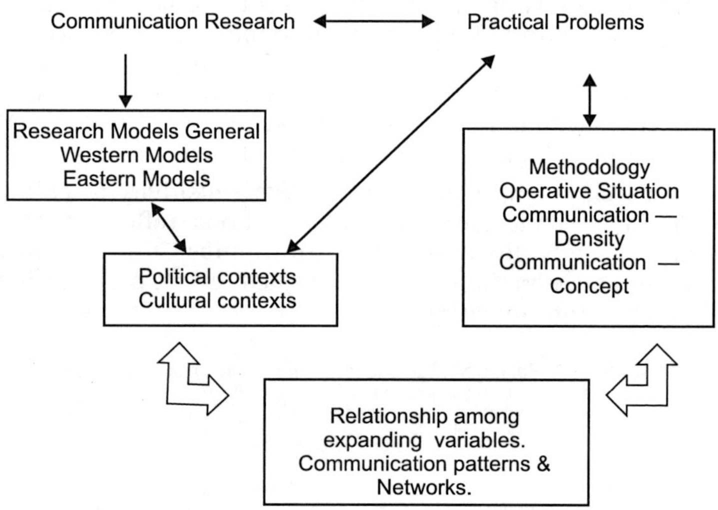

Fig. 7.4. Practical Constraints in Communication Research

Over a period of time different Mass Communication Models developed in consequence to our changing understanding of the concepts, elements of communication process, and communication rules. Communication research facilitated these.

8
Communication Planning

Communication strategies are based on field experiences and theoretical analysis of focused activity areas. Varied communication strategies are used (planned) both by government and people to communicate effectively to their targeted audience. Communication planning involves — communication strategies, media planning (channel planning) and resource management culminating in communication policies.

The dimensions focused in the strategies must be managed well in order to make the programs delivered to the targeted audience effectively.

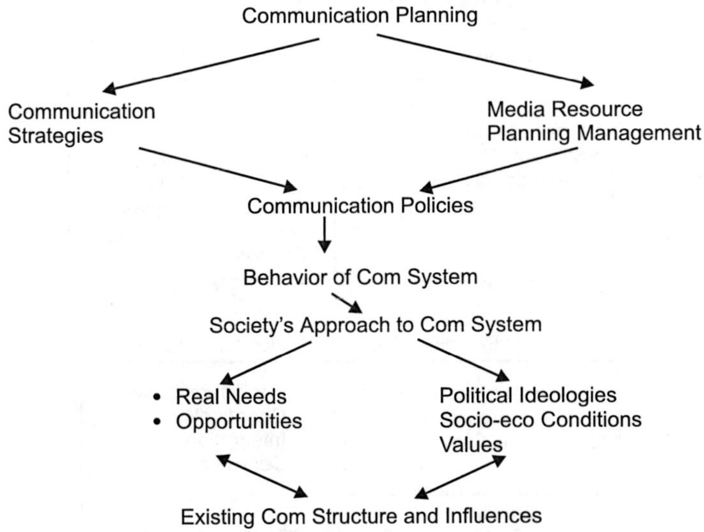

Fig. 8.1. Communication Planning and Policies

The interaction of State, market and public is significant for communication planning.

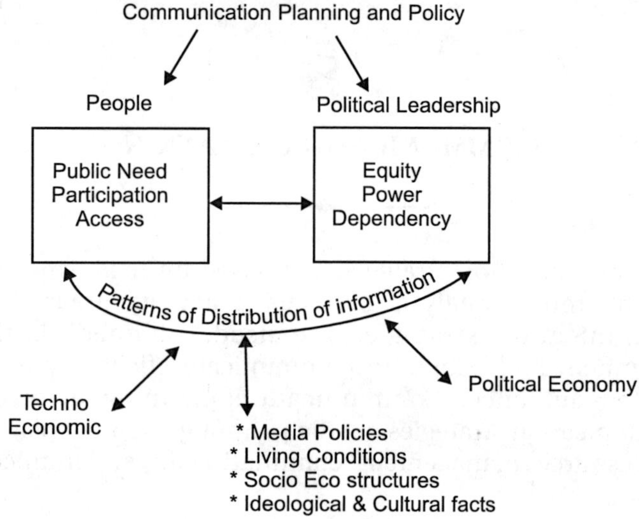

Fig. 8.2. Political Economy of Communication Planning

Different components of vertical, horizontal and cyclical communication planning structure the policies.

Fig. 8.3. Components of Communication Planning

The planning constraints could be human, technical and other resources.

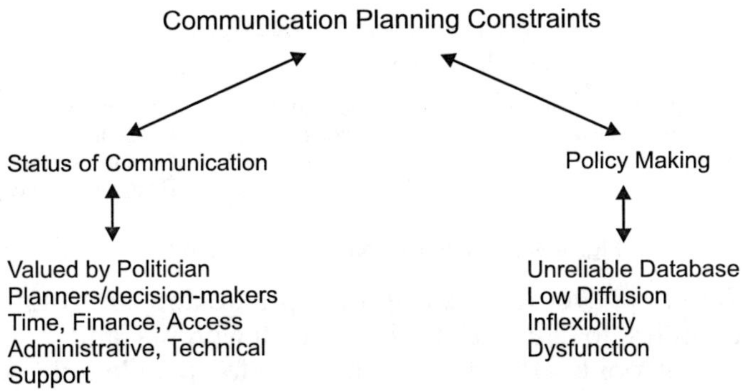

Fig. 8.4. Communication Planning Constraints

These strategies could be both positive and negative. They are both media and interpersonal focused. Nature, forms and types of communication strategies suggest mostly who would use these strategies, with what objectives and with what effects.

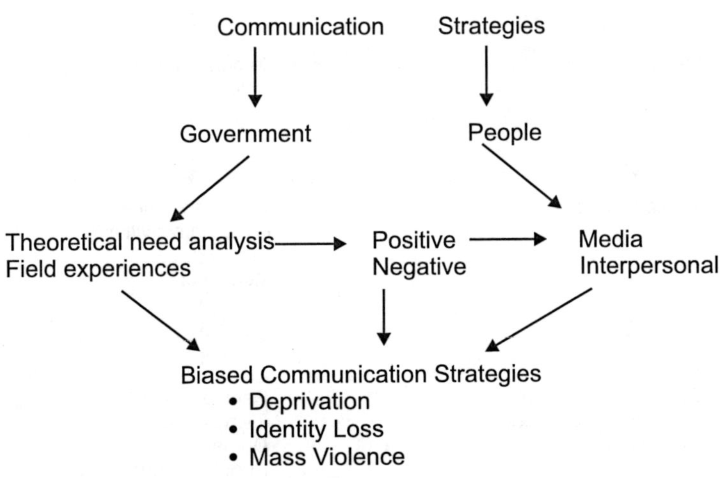

Fig. 8.5. Communication Strategies Model 1

The assumption is that biased communication strategies create deprivation, loss of identities and mass violence.

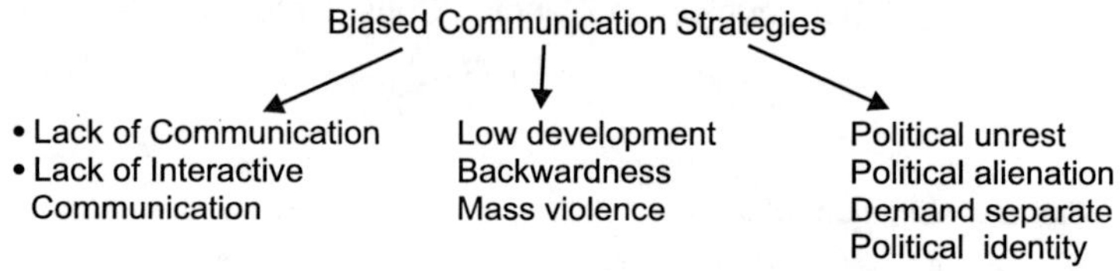

Fig. 8.6. Communication Strategies Model 2

National governments use, manipulate and control media technologies to channel their own viewpoints and policies and to set political and social agenda for people's thinking. People use power of media to express their demands, viewpoints and set their own agenda. This public agenda sets the government for interaction with the public's viewpoints and opens way for public discourses on many issues.

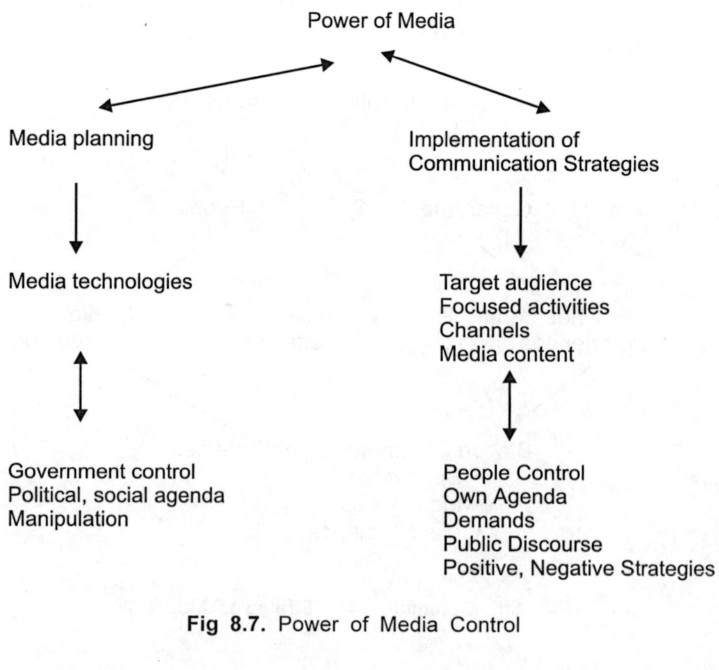

Fig 8.7. Power of Media Control

The International governments, organizations and communities control and influence the media to set political agenda with the national governments and social agenda for people. Media in combination with information, education, communication and motivation (IECM) strategies control and influence the communities.

Media control is a vertical strategy. Mass media can be the ideological army in support of globalization, but can also become the grassroots weapons to fight its impact. Ethics in Media is challenging.

PART 2

COMMUNICATION PERSPECTIVES

There are seven perspectives from which human communications is practiced, interpreted and analyzed. These are: Basic Communications, Development Communications, Information Communication Technology (ICT), International Communication and Globalization, Intercultural Communication, Communication Management and Communication Research. These perspectives do overlap and all these perspectives are intertwined as *a Communication Perspective*.

9

Basic Communication Perspective

The journey of a Dream does not end with the Dreamer but with the Communicator.

A Framework

The focus of this perspective is on the basics of communications *per se* in any field of activity:

- Communication Concepts,
- Communication rules, contexts, patterns, networks and effects,
- Priorities and functions of communications,
- Audience demographics, organization and structural changes,
- Communication channels and consumption,
- Communication content,
- Evolution of Communication Models

These seven factors set up the basic communication perspective framework. The other specific perspectives operate within this framework. Discussion of these factors in Chapter 15 of Part 2, 'Communication Research Perspective' addresses how research has changed the above six factors overtime. Other perspectives presented in later sections highlight the research and development in those specific areas as supported by the basic framework.

Concept of communication: The conventional concept of communication is that we use communication to express our inner purposes, attitudes, and feelings; to describe events and objects of the external world and to produce sharing between the speaker and the audience addressed.

Over the last few decades, there has been increasing interest in the study and practice of 'communication'. As a result, knowledge and definition of 'communication' has varied widely in terms of purpose, nature, level of abstraction and scope. The modes of communication are changing and so are the channels of communications. These are add-ons. The basic concept of the communication remains the same but communications are getting more and more complex.

The complexity in interaction results from human and non-human communications. The add-ons are changing the interactions in human-to-human communications. This has changed the process, forms and focus of communications. As we stated earlier, to handle complexity, it is argued that communication is better understood as a perspective or context from which any act may be examined or understood. The assumption is that every action has a message value. One cannot, *Not Communicate*. Whatever one does or does not do can be looked at from a communication perspective.

The second factor that adds complexity to communication interactions is migration of human being around the world. In the developed world, over the last three decades the communication concept has changed due to immigration and hybridizing. One cannot expect indigenous society. In developing world, there is no significant immigration impact because immigration is low. More regional cultural impact is noticeable within the country. Emigration brings the bounce back effect in this context.

Thus migration with its assimilated cultural resources and non-human technologies has been changing the concept of communication. The changed concept further contributes to change in its modes, demands, messages, audience and effects.

There is research evidence that the principles of coherence, coordination and mystery in human condition are achieved by everyone but in different forms and these differences are different forms of communication. Variety of factors can affect these differences in forms. These factors could be different forms and characteristics of communication channels, exposure and access to these channels, and effects of both media system and interpersonal systems on people in a particular society and in global contexts.

Context: Communication always occurs in a *context* and not in a vacuum. Communication environment is the context. Sender sends the message in *his* context, the receiver receives the message in *his own* context. The message is understood and is effective when the contexts of both of them match. In 80s, the communications contexts widened its scope three-way: society specific context, specific–society context within global context, and global context of communications. The global context has assumed importance as a context in itself and also for consideration of development of communications in a particular society.

Even the early Communication Models of 50s, Gerbner (1956) and Westley and McLeans (1957) have suggested the significance of 'contextual environment' in communication. In later years, communication research established the importance of 'context' by developing contextual and related theories, identifying contextual research and its effects in high context cultures and low context cultures. In 70s culture specific contexts became significant for communications. Importance of global contexts for communication was put forth in 80s. The advance communication technologies have been promoting globalization in its various facets.

Communication rules: Whatever may be the forms of communication; it must be organized, and governed by certain rules. Communication Rules research of 70s and 80s has given new perspectives to communications. Rule theories can explain, predict, and control communicative behavior. Rules research is concerned with explicating symbolic regularities in communicative behavior. Communication can be organized by communication rules, by communication patterns, by achieving communication competence, and through developing communication networks.

Communication patterns: In communication there is repetition of elements forming a pattern. These patterns and differences in patterns are meaningful within interaction. They are patterns of interaction. In communication, patterns of interaction and variations are more meaningful than the information itself. These patterns predict the likely attitudes and behavior of audience in a particular communication situation and among specific networks. The concern is with the *patterns of communication behavior* within the relationship formed between the senders and the receivers; and not with *patterns of information and redundancy.* Communication can be effective by making use of these identified patterns of communication behavior. Four social categories affect the patterns:

- Individual differences that focus on personality differences and traits, physical, psychological and material environments and exposure to opportunities and communication accessibility mold the communication patterns.
- Social categories perspective focuses on communication patterns in rural, urban and urban slum areas as well as between and among various social stratifications.
- Social relations categorized by age, gender, income, education, occupation and social status determine the patterns.
- Group relationship that focuses on patterns in interpersonal communication in dyad, large, small groups and in opinion leadership.

It is important to understand the communication contexts and patterns in a society in order to understand it, issues that it faces, and its communication density. Researches have established the importance of context and communication patterns as affected by various social categories.

Communication effects: It is assumed that very communication message or act must produce effect as desired by the sender. Sometimes that effect may be latent, manifest and not comprehended by the receiver.

Effects can be assessed in terms of creating awareness, knowledge, attitude and behavior change through relationship between communication channels, targeted audience and society

Communication priorities and functions: The major function of communication is connectivity. This could happen through any communication channel. The connectivity is further categorized into getting mutual understanding, creating conflicts, being pro-social and global etc. Within the broad range of connectivity, communication functions differ and get prioritized according to the priorities set by different countries.

Communication function could be directive or persuasive for bringing three types of changes: (1) creating awareness and disseminating information, (2) bringing attitudinal and behavioral changes for mutual understanding, (3) by educating and motivating people, and 4) providing entertainment. There is interplay of source, message, communication channels and audience in different permutations for communication but the dynamic interplay of these is necessary for effective and successful communication.

Communication research did set up three significant points by 80s. One, media and oral systems comprise of general models of communications. Two, the direction of change is from oral to conventional media systems and thence on to electronic media systems as the technology progresses. They both coexist and are co-significant. Third, that human nature is ever changing in societal contexts due to variety of factors. The degree of change in human communication behavior correlate significantly with the behavioral changes in other social systems.

Priorities and functions of communication theory, applications and practice also keep changing due to changes in technology and human communication behavior. The changing communication scenario globally creates demands and priorities for communication conceptualizations and its diverse perspectives. These priorities will differ in developing and developed countries and even within specific countries among developing and developed countries.

The five fold priorities for communication in developing countries focus on control, pro-social messages, access to ICT, and political communication. First, there is control, censorship and privatization exercised by nationalization or semi-government control of media channels. These countries have major concern about threat of foreign communication invasion through cultural domination, consumerism, and political propaganda. The second priority is pro-social communication, wider reach of media technology, and social innovations to the masses. The third priority is to have access to update ICT through indigenous efforts, transfer of technology and external support. Further, to facilitate optimum social access to these technologies to the masses. The fourth priority is development of planned Interpersonal oral channels infrastructure for delivery of pro-social messages. Fifth priority is political communication to support the process of democratization and development etc. These five priorities may differ in order in different countries and all of these may run concurrently also.

The developed countries have six priorities. First concern is the control, privatization and independence of media channels. Second is the use of advance technology for media channels. Third is the research and development of new communication technologies and information society. Fourth, media technologies are used for political communication. Fifth is providing entertainment and news in the domestic and global contexts thus creating an international communication order. Sixth is the political and consumerism communication internationally, particularly to the developing countries. These priorities may differ in order in different countries and all of these may run concurrently. These priorities may relate one or together to communication scenario internationally or in developing countries.

Communication functions differ and get prioritized according to the priorities set by the countries. These functions could be pro-social, promote consumerism, disseminate information, awareness and knowledge and provide entertainment etc. The ongoing process of communication research also sets forth agenda for these functions.

Over a period of time, certain research questions have been posed, why do we want to communicate, interact personally, send messages through communication channels? We found we communicate to inform as well seek information, to educate and get educated, motivate and get motivated and mobilize people for these functions. Thus when communication is directive it aims at creating awareness, attitudinal change, behavioral changes and action implementation. When it is persuasive, it aims at bringing over the desired change in its targeted audience.

Audience: People in communication define the various types of audiences and sub-audiences. Their characteristics depend on the modes of communication they possess, media exposure, geo areas, rituals and personal relationships on one hand; and on the other hand, the social, economic, gender and political issues posed define the targeted audience.

Audience is an important component in the communication process. Receptive and effective communication depends on the characteristics of the targeted audience, which should be compatible with the issues and geo areas targeted, type of messages and the communication channels selected. The perception differentials of the different audiences and the effects of the media or interpersonal channels on them depend on the selected variables.

Communication models of 70s and 80s i.e. the Convergence Model and feedback loops component in the models suggested that audience are not passive but active and participatory. By participation, interaction through feedback loops and making demands, they influence the content of communication. Thus audience shapes the communication content and the communication contents constitute an audience. Further, development communication models have supported the participatory role of the audience.

Communication channels and consumption: In the last six decades, many new communication channels are initiated in the world over. These decades have also seen development of basic and conventional media technologies like print, radio, television, telephone and computer on one hand; and on the other hand developing corollary technologies such as video, audio-cassette and record player, DVD player, cassettes and DVD, cordless and cell phones, laptops, floppies and CDs and Internet etc. Thence on 90s onwards were the decades for developing more of functional and structural improvement in both basic and corollary technologies as well their applications. There is no equal distribution, physical and social access of these communication channels in developed and developing countries.

Even there are many structural and functional changes in both formal and informal interpersonal communication channels in developing countries both as impact of changing media technologies as well planned to suit the needs and practices of the people.

Source credibility is important point for effective communication both for interpersonal and mass media. Source is seen as possessing or lacking credibility for its messages and interactions. There are three types of credibility: *Initial* or *extrinsic* credibility that the source commands because of its title or position or brand channel in the mass media. *Derived credibility* is what the listener perceives. It depends how a speaker communicates i.e. the degree of conviction, intelligence, and competence of the speaker. The content of the discourse and how it is presented and what takes place on the whole during the interpersonal encounter or media presentation affects the credibility. The perceived credibility can be changed and rebuilt if it is not favorable. *Terminal credibility* is what the source is seen to possess after interpersonal interaction is over.

In case of mediated messages, the brand image built over a period gives the initial credibility. But its derived credibility depends on the importance and reliability receivers give to its messages. For instance, to start with, government news broadcasting channel may have credibility. But it may lose credibility, if over a course of time people find that they get censored, delayed or distorted news through the government controlled channel. Derived credibility matters most in mass mediated communication and initial credibility is secondary.

In interpersonal communication both initial and derived credibility is important. People trust political and social leaders who they know are competent and intelligent and are able to convince them about their ideas, policies and programs. Terminal credibility varies in both types of sources.

Media consumption is the interplay of utilization of mass media, actual exposure to mass media, and opportunities for exposure to mass media channels and messages. These are socially constructed and maintained practices.

The kind of media used, and extent of media consumption changes overtime. The change depends on variety of factors such as media technology availability, resources, purchasing power, physical and social accessibility to media channels and the type of media content provided.

In developing countries, the media consumption may be low for TV and video in villages for two reasons: One, due to physical inaccessibility to these channels because of low purchasing powers or the technological difficulties. Secondly, non-accessibility to community TV provided by government due to social constraints such as higher castes and higher income group not allowing the lower castes and low income groups to watch TV with them; or not allowing women to watch when males are watching. In such situations, even many of the pro-social messages or entertainment value is lost.

There may be other constraints also. For example, the government in India wanted to use the video in villages for entertainment and pro-social messages; since film medium has low reach. This experiment did not work in desert villages of Rajasthan in India because of dusty environment; the video heads would often get clogged and the technician help would be miles away.

Print has low consumption in villages because of low rate of literacy and limited circulation of Newspapers, magazines, books and other printed literature and affordability by low-income group. Film has low reach because of nonexistence of cinema houses in these areas. There is more consumption of traditional media of folklores and other oral traditions. Computer has low reach because of low purchasing power as well as low electricity power. Earlier, rural telephones were non-existent in many developing countries but the revolution of mobile telephones and inexpensive rural exchanges have increased telephone density in rural areas. This is true of Indian villages also and this is creating social change.

It is worst in urban slum low-income areas; either the community TV sets are not accessible due to social constraints of lack of organized cohesiveness in a slum. Even if some people may have their own TV sets, they can't connect them for such reasons: there may be lack of electricity connections in slum areas, they may not be able to afford to pay for cable TV connections and electricity consumed. There is research evidence that in many slum areas in India, people would buy and subscribe for cable TV more for escapist fun and entertainment. They may even sacrifice some of the daily essentials for it. They have access to print, film and telephones. There consumption of film and mobile phones is higher as compared to print medium. They can't afford to buy newspapers, magazines and books but they do have access to community newspapers, and mobile libraries for magazines and books in their native language.

Comparatively media consumption for basic conventional technologies and its developing corollary technologies is more in urban areas because of higher purchasing power, more physical and social accessibility of various media channels and higher rate of literacy. Film and Print, Computer and its corollary technologies have wider reach in urban areas.

Thus people in villages, urban slums and low-income groups in developing countries have low media consumption due to above-mentioned reasons. They are the people who need higher exposure because many of the pro-social messages by different groups are targeted to them and they also need this for entertainment also as they cannot afford other channels of personal entertainment.

Many developing countries including India support media with structured interpersonal communication both formal and informal for pro-social messages. They also encourage them to create and develop folk traditions in entertainment.

ICTs access and consumption in these areas is also getting attention of many government and NGOs to facilitate social and economic development for this segment of society. The effort is to fill the media consumption and digital divide.

Comparatively there is higher rate of media consumption in developed countries because of availability and accessibility of high technology end media products and services; and higher rate of literacy. Even in these countries the low-income group may consume substantially electronic channels but print medium consumption is low because of low literacy.

Consumption of interpersonal communication: Informal interpersonal communication is used all times spontaneously. Our focus is here about formal interpersonal communication used in various domains. There is horizontal interpersonal communication among people to people when they want to discuss among themselves the various issues. There is top to bottom formal interpersonal communication when there are public discourses by leaders and by those in authority. There is bottom to top interpersonal communication when people want to give feedback to leaders or authorities or convey their demands or discontents. In dialogue strategies also this mode is used. In many developing countries this is a significant channel for conveying pro-social messages for persuasion and for information, education, communication and motivation (IECM) campaigns. Even in some countries such as in India government has planned interpersonal infrastructure in rural areas to facilitate these communication activities. On the whole this channel plays supportive role for media channels and coexist with media channels.

In developed countries, there are also pockets of poverty and low literacy among the population still there is low reliance on formal interpersonal communication for pro-social messages since there is high level of physical and social accessibility of media channels. Formal interpersonal communication is often used for political communication campaigns and both top-bottom and bottom-top as well horizontal modes are used in this context.

Communication content (message) is important component in the communication framework. The messages in a shared environment could not only be oral, written, non-verbal, visual or olfactory but these could also be laws, customs, practices, ways of dressing, gestures, buildings, flags, gardens, exhibits, etc. Language and body synthesizers that are culture specific are essential components of messages.

The important dimensions of content — message is listening, interpretation and understanding, feedback, choosing the content, and distortions.

In an interaction model, *listening* becomes a process of listening, receiving, decoding, interpreting and acting upon messages. When the receiver acts upon the message, that behavior is seen as *feedback* and is seen as *response* to the sender's message.

People will choose a TV or radio channel depending on the messages they are looking for. Are they looking for political or social news, entertainment or adventure? This may be true while selecting films to watch—is it escapist fun or the reality that they want to experience through cinema. Other media or ethnotronic channels are used according to what messages we want to receive or give. The different kind of messages chosen can be serious news about politics, economy, health and technology; pro-social entertainment, crime, war and political upheavals etc. Our choice of these messages can also express our involvement or indifference to the issues focused through the contents.

People look for reliability, credibility, utility, emotional and rational appeal when choosing content whether it is through media or interpersonal communication channels.

The miscommunication may come from two perspectives. One, the source did not structure the message correctly for transmission. Two, the listeners did not correctly listen to the message or the listeners applied their own meaning to the message. Thus distortions do occur due to intentional or unintentional interpretation of the content. This does happen in case of spreading of rumors. Content may get distorted because of incomprehension of the subject-matter or meaning. In print media language difficulty or lack if literacy may constrain knowing the content and distorting it. The recipient to suit its own preconceived notions may distort even content from an alien culture.

Evolution of communication models. These were developed by Communication exemplars over a period of time. These are further developed in consequence to our changing understanding of the concepts, elements of communication process, and communication rules etc. through ongoing process supported by research and development. Actually these are the foundation models in communication discipline. The evolutionary process of these models is discussed in Part 1.

Practitioners, researchers and academicians developed pertinent communication models through communication research and development in different aspects and domains of communication *per se*. Some of these evolved based on the earlier foundation models and suggested new, useful and significant concepts, which were later developed; and others present new dimensions.

These models provide significant insights into communication nature, process and forms, modes and utilization of channels to develop perspectives related to different domains.

In this chapter we have introduced the various dimensions of communication framework. There is brief and salient discussion of each in this chapter. In context of subsequent perspectives in the following chapters; these dimensions are discussed in detail as relevant and salient to a particular perspective.

Summary

The main tenets of basic communication perspective are concepts, source, channels and audience, message (issue related content), communication rules, contexts, patterns, networks and effects and communication models.

The dynamic interplay of source, message, communication channels and audience is necessary for effective and successful communication. Such communication has concerns for its priorities and functions. Priorities differ from developed to developing countries. Communication functions differ and get prioritized according to the priorities set by the countries and consumption of communication channels that are socially constructed and maintained practices.

The changing communication scenario globally, creates demands and priorities for communication conceptualizations and its diverse perspectives.

The functions, applications and practice of communications also keep changing. The changing communication scenario presents diverse communication models. Some of these developed on the earlier foundation models and suggested new, useful and significant concepts, which were later developed; and others present new dimensions.

10

Development Communication Perspective

Government is problem not the solution for development in developing countries. —*Anonymous*

The communication flow in developing societies is systemic. It is a system, interacting and exchanging influences with the environment. Input is, influences received by the environment and output is products, services delivered by the system to transform its environment. A development communication program is a goal establishing system, formulated with a set of objectives which programmer can change as the program proceeds. This system can be *state-determined system* where one set of goals can determine the next set of objectives. It can be *Markov system* where a chain of events influences the system. It includes many types of causal relationships including reciprocal causation. There could be equifinality where many causes will have the same effect and multifinality in which one cause may have many effects.

Integrating the dynamics of development and the dynamics of communication is the challenge of our time. It calls for greater understanding of communicators of what they can communicate towards development and an understanding of development agencies of what they could get out of communication system.

Keys to Development: Access to development modes, empowerment of the people, and good governance are three keys to development:

- *Access to* development is through physical, social, and economic modes. People are in physical contact with the development channel; they are allowed socially to access it; and over and above have the purchasing power to buy it. For example, if people have to benefit through development messages on TV. People should have exposure to TV either at community centers and other public places or at homes. If at public places; then there should be no caste, class, gender, time and space restrictions to watch the programs. There should be electric power as well government ready to buy community sets or people could afford to buy them. This could be true of any interpersonal channel. People can benefit from the development messages if they have access to these three modes.

- *Empowerment* of people of all classes, caste and creed to demand, participate and act for development for themselves as well as to enjoy its fruits.
- *Governance*: good governance is precondition for development to empower people, to give them access to development. Good governance presupposes intelligent, knowledgeable, hardworking, conscientious, honest people forming the government (though a government may not be having all these characteristics; but a balance of these could create good governance). Such a government is able to create right ambiance for development by generating awareness and knowledge about newer development modes, sharing such knowledge with its people, and letting people grow in the right direction.

Approaches to Development

Each sub-community of development theorists and practitioners worldwide has acted out of overlapping but still somewhat different paradigms. The mission statement of each community might be similar, even identical and all would endorse a common goal if stated at a sufficient level of generality and abstraction. However, within the common perspective, they operate with very different assumptions, practices, and values, and often take their differences as very important.

A historical analysis of development models since 50s provides insight into the changing development models. These changed with the changing dynamics of development, and the technological breakthrough in the mass media channels. There have been *four approaches* to understand development in national and international contexts. The four approaches are exemplar for development and present the historical perspective. The restructured development approach presents the current scenario. These changing models addressed three questions:

How to do development?

How did the problem of underdevelopment start?

Why do development efforts not work in some of the developing countries?

One, Modernization approach viz. Dominant Paradigm and New Paradigm of Development. Dominant Paradigm was operative in 50s. This paradigm was based on the observations that the differences in per capita income between developed and developing nations could not be explained in terms of differences in natural resources or other factors outside human control. Add to this is a value structure that identified an absence of certain modern conveniences and material culture demanding redress, and the conditions of most of the nations was interpreted as a plight caused by their own failure to use their human and natural resources as full potential. The problem might be due to lack of technology, an inability to put natural resources to their best use, an inability to harness optimum potentiality of their human resources, the lack of adequate economic institutions, or the inefficiency of government or market machinery.

In this context, the developed nations were taken as the ideal. Development focus was on increasing productivity, economic growth and industrialization through capital-intensive investments.

The second emphasis derived from an analysis of cultures of developing nations was that the attitudes and folkways of traditional people were ill suited for the demands of modernization. Therefore, a planned change of values, attitudes and behavior was necessary. Communication and uncritical faith in its power was seen as an indispensable tool for making people modern (Lerner, Inkles and others noted).

In 70s New Paradigm emerged. It is a 'Metamodel' of development. It assumed that there are many efficacious pathways to development; and development can and should take a variety of forms. Which pathway is appropriate depends on a particular country's social, political and economic structure, development needs, and the availability of resources and technology.

The New Paradigm presents dimensions of dialogue and multilogue. Communication in which masses can participate actively. It advocates that the planning and implementation of development program should be carried *out* with people rather than *for* them. But actual occurrence of these patterns posed threat to existing political institutions that are otherwise perpetuated by the docile acquiescence of the masses. Development objective was improving the quality of life of people. The shift of emphasis was on an explicit recognition of their importance of maintaining continuity with traditional lifestyles rather than importing western model of society and forcing indigenous people to adapt to it. The ideal development was envisioned as locally unique blending of modern and traditional values and institutions.

The modernization perspective in both the Dominant and New Paradigm attempted to foster development while working within the international structures. Modernity was seen as a set of personal attitudes, technological innovations and social institutions that originated in the west and for several reasons could and should be shared with less fortunate nations.

These paradigms were committed to 'international equity'. They blatantly opposed the social structure within many nations and between developed and developing countries. In fact, they explicitly blamed the international economic order for creating and perpetuating underdevelopment.

Second approach is Interdependency Model. Nordenstrang and Schiller (1979) argued that the issue of economic development could not be understood on a nation-by-nation basis. Rather, the network of interrelations among nations must be analyzed. The Interdependency Model is a critique of the dominant paradigm's identification of domestic factors as the causes of underdevelopment. It claims that *the international social and political system decisively determines the course of development within each nation.*

The development of individual countries depends largely on economic and political factors outside their national boundaries. For developing nations, the implication is, that domestic development projects — no matter how well conceived — may be ineffective, overpowered by the effects of actions taken by other nations. For developed nations, implication is equally striking; their sense of acting as autonomous agents is erroneous, since they too are caught up in an interlocking web of multifaceted international relationships.

Wallerstein (1979) claimed that modern world comprises a single capitalist world economy. Nation States are not societies having parallel histories but are *parts* of the whole reflecting the *whole.* Some States are at the center of the system and some at the periphery, but all are defined by the relationship among them. From such a World Systems approach, development and under-development are not independent entities but two facets of the same process and cannot be understood in isolation from one another.

Earlier, Galtung (1971) had argued that these relationships are in fact the more subtle expressions of the inequitable patterns of international relations developed by western colonialism. Economic, military, and information relations all serve as the instruments of manipulation in order to maintain the central position of the former colonial powers. The line of reasoning suggests a radical perspective from which to think about international communication.

Dependency model can be seen as a more specific aspect of interdependency model. Nations who have come to think themselves as underdeveloped have done so because they have accepted the ideology of the highly industrial capitalist nations. The penetration of foreign advisers and experts (no matter how helpful they intend to be), imported technology, and the influx of information create an economic and cultural dependency on the developed countries.

One aspect of which is the acceptance of the definition of

underdevelopment as the ideology of capitalism, technological and personnel inequity perpetuate dependency. Free flow of information becomes code word for continued domination by the ex-colonial powers. In an economic environment, the transnational corporations and international trade tactics place smaller nations at pronounced disadvantage. Slogans of 'open markets' and 'free trade' are code words for perpetuation of the inequity.

Development theorists argue that the communication industry perpetuates an ideology that falsely identifies the problem of their countries as 'underdevelopment' and exacerbates existing social inequities. Mass media serve more to oppress than emancipate the people in these contexts.

Third Approach is Basic Needs Model. The basic needs model of development is an outgrowth of a specific aspect of the dependency model combined with the continuing concern of those in the international development community to know what to do to meet pressing human and national problems. Even if the underdevelopment is caused by the structure of international economic relationships, people in developing countries have to cope with over-population, unemployment, malnutrition, hunger and disease.

The continuing concern and efforts of underdeveloped nations to fight poverty and hunger, to provide basic needs to people and to improve quality of life for their populations create both national and international repercussions. It is a direct attack on poverty both absolute and relative. It advocated that development includes the improvement of quality of life for people by providing basic minimum needs and transformation of individual and social system.

It is conceived to create an infrastructure built around economic activities that depend on local manpower, material and energy resources. This process requires structural, social, and attitudinal transformation in order to overcome the inequalities within and between societies. Thus the process depends on the capacities of the societies to adjust to rapid techno-economic, socio-cultural, and the political changes and the collective capacities to generate, to reach out and to utilize vast amounts of information.

International community supports these concerns and efforts by providing monetary aid, food and other materials, technology and skilled manpower. The rich nations act from humanitarian as well political domination point of view.

Fourth Approach is Communication for Development. The communication perspective focus on how any form of social behavior expresses and (re) constitutes the social reality of the actors. It is a process by which persons collectively maintain and create 'social reality'. Human beings simultaneously live in a symbolic universe (social reality) and are engaged in sequences of interactions with their environments and with other people. They draw from the resources of their social realities and from the practices in which they are engaged with others.

In what way do development communication and other forms of actions express and constitute the social reality of the masses, planners and the change agents who deliver the messages? The phenomenon is best understood as 'enmeshment' in a particular system. A person is enmeshed in a system to the extent its boundaries comprise the horizons of a person's visions. Those who are enmeshed comfortably within a particular social reality, see its limits as the limits of the world. Analysis from communication perspectives discovers and articulates the limits of social realities and to show how these limits sometimes channel people into unwanted patterns of interactions.

The process of communication is an excellent means for coordinating interpersonal actions, but is a very poor means of expressing individual mentalities or for achieving mutual understanding. For a complete analysis, one must know what the actors themselves do not know about themselves and their interactions.

Communication has played significant role in all the approaches both in national and international development contexts. The evolutionary scenario of development communication globally in general and India in particular presents paradigmatic changes both in development and development communication. There have been several paradigms of development, each of which has slightly different notion of what development is, how it can be communicated and achieved.

But very soon models thus created led to models that were unique to particular developing countries. These models were functional for these countries' development needs and growth within the resources available. As the needs and resources have undergone change, so do these models have changed. These models also present the complexities of development, government and people's efforts, and the resultant consequences both intended and unintended and some unexplainable effects in each country.

The last six decades of research has revealed that role of communication in development is significant and it has changed with the change in development models. A historical analysis of development communication models since 50s provides insight into the changing development communication models and the role of communication that changed with these changing models. These changed with the changing dynamics of development, changing roles of mass media and interpersonal communication channels and the technological breakthrough in the mass media channels.

The *ideology* and *reality* of development as well as development communication through various mass media and interpersonal communication channels present social, cultural, economic, and political challenges.

The changes brought by information technologies by the end of century are of tremendous concern. The powerful flow of cultural commodities — information, news, and various television programs saturate the world markets, as they become accessible via satellite-broadcast. Communication technologies and interpersonal communication at various levels are essential for development both in national and international contexts. (For detailed discussions about development approaches refer to Narula Uma 1986).

International development theorists and practitioners have conceptualized development from various perspectives such as social change, modernization, progress and alternations in lifestyles. But all the perspectives have encompassed 'growth', the economic growth viz. industrialization, agrarian, and technological growth. The social growth is identified with structural and value changes.

In the second and third development decades, they argued and practiced that development implies commitment to social goals as well as to multifaceted interrelated sets of economic, social, political and cultural variables. Development includes the improvement of quality of life with programs of nutritional status, maternal and child health care, primary health care, and the transformation of individual as well as the social system.

The perspectives on development changed not only due to paradigmatic changes overtime; but also due to global changes in social milieu, economy, polity, technology and communications. These perspectives changed the notion of development, how to do development and why the development successes do not commensurate with the development efforts of the concerned.

The international community's concern with development in the developing countries and how to do development led us to examine how notions about development and ways to do development are communicated. Communication played a significant role in communicating about development *per se* and how to do development. Communication facilitated the development with its changing focus to fit in achieving these targets. The role of communication changed with the varied development models and thus communication played different roles in Development Communication Models of 70s, through 2000 decades.

In development contexts, inequalities in social, economic and political are important. Inequalities of access to communication technologies are to be considered also rather than technological change *per se*. Social structural considerations may impact these inequalities.

Exemplars of Dominant Paradigm model of 50s emphasized the role of mass media for information dissemination, for technological and social change. The high media exposure was necessary to make people participate to change their traditional beliefs and attitudes. Lerner (1958) and Klapper (1960), on the basis of empirical research advocated that media tends to reinforce attitude and behaviors that people already possess. It has no direct effect on people. Pye (1963) endorsed top-down communication in development and suggested that media should strengthen that influence in society.

Schramm, Lerner, Inkles and Smith and various other scholars in 60s observed that the task of the media is to alter people's psychological states and thinking ways; and important role of the media is to teach skills to people that are necessary for modern society. They argued that knowledge and skills could be multiplied rapidly and inexpensively by wide range of media systems. But they did not emphasize the role of media as educator and motivator.

In Dominant Paradigm the communication flow was one-way, top-down vertical communication from authorities to the people. The task of the mass media channels was to mobilize people for development and the audience was assigned a passive role; with little regard for the social structure.

Interdependent Model of Development of 60s suggested that the information that flows locally or internationally respond to the center of the power in the dominant states. The 'cultural agendas' of the world are that the worldwide hierarchy of power and values organizes a nation, and a community. The concept of 'new information order' was the outcome of these deliberations and aimed at de-colonization of the information conditions in developing countries. The communication works to advance the interests of the local and global ownership class by creating social environments in which these interests can prosper.

The communication pattern in dependency model is identified with the 'ideological domination' of and 'ideological oppression' by the developed countries towards dependent developing countries. Ideological domination is conveyed through commercial communication networks and transnational marketing corporations. The ideological aggression results when the transnational corporations penetrate the political sphere via their control over modern technology, education and by their own ideological and economic logic. By controlling mass media channels and its content, they create consumerism bias, aggravates dependency that unleashed frustration among the low earning level population and leads to collective aggressiveness as an escape valve.

The dependency theorists argued that communication serves the purpose of publicizing transnational interests only. If development has to occur then this role must change. The communication strategies should focus on educating people about the vicious nature of the stifling dependency relationships; and to mobilize national and regional support for the structural support of the society. They emphasize the use of interpersonal channels since mass media channels are caught in the dependency relationships.

The communication role changed in Basic Needs Development Model. The role was to create awareness among the masses about their basic minimum needs, its fulfillment and development. Interpersonal channels were advocated as important for development along with the media channels. As it was realized that poor people in the developing countries who needs development the most have low physical accessibility to media channels. Though government in these developing countries tried to provide community media access but there are information and social access blockages. Therefore interpersonal grid of communication is necessary.

The New Paradigm of Development in 70s emphasized the participatory role of people to achieve development. This communication model is interactive. It emphasized top-down communication from authorities to people, as well bottom-up from people to authorities and bottom-bottom, people to people communication. The audience is active and participatory. Thus there were many pathways to development and exact combination would be somewhat different in every nation.

The development communication models of the first three decades needed a changed perspective to make development effective. Developed countries had planned the earlier models for developing countries and a single communication pattern was being advocated for all developing countries. But the New Paradigm Development Model advocated that there should be country specific model for development and development communication. These models must be planned and implemented by the national government and people.

In 80s, thus the role of Development Communication changed over to the dynamic process of bringing development to the people for whom development is envisaged. It is conceptualized as information, education, communication within cultural matrix and motivation for participation in development (IECM). Development effort is defined as awareness about development, getting discontented with the current development, making further demands for development, motivation and participation to do and achieve development.

The varied development communication (devcom) approaches focus on extension, diffusion, mass media, development-support communication and planned strategies for devcom. These approaches facilitate actions for evolving effective communication strategy for development projects. (Discussed in detail in Part 3 Communication Strategies).

Development Communication Scenario has changed globally in the last six decades. There have been four-pronged major changes. The focus of development has changed, nature of development demands and issues have changed, new communication channels are available and the characteristics of the audience have changed.

The focus of development has undergone change during these decades because the international development community has become aware of the development needs of the people as well impediments to development *per se*.

People are becoming aware of their own local development issues because of planned communication strategies (by their own governments) to inform them and create awareness, and to involve people in their problem solving. People are demanding need-based solutions and they make participatory efforts to solve them within local and national framework. During these decades the focus has been on developing a well-informed, aware, motivated and participatory audience.

The new communication technologies of satellites, telematics, computer, and the applications of Internet have made it possible to communicate about development messages to a wider as well difficult to reach audience. The new electronic technologies including Internet have even changed the nature and scope of interpersonal communication.

The audience characteristics have changed because of more exposure to mass media and interpersonal channels and more exposure to development issues. The media exposure to global issues and problems has created an audience who is aware of global interdependent demands and development efforts of the international community in addition to their local development issues in the local and national contexts.

Globally, the emerging issues in political, social, economic and cultural areas have raised new development issues and demands. The development issues relate to alleviating absolute and relative poverty, and raising quality of life for people by the national governments. On the other hand, it is essential to keep pace with technology progress for greater productivity and employment. In addition to this, changes in social structure and values, both social and material innovations, new technologies and their applications have changed the nature of development demands of the people.

The development communication paradigmatic changes during these six decades from Dominant Paradigm to ICT Paradigm has been a good learning experience for the development communication community. They have learnt and are practicing an integrated devcom approach, multimedia approach and planned communication strategies to deliver and achieve development.

Compared to other decades, currently in 2000 decade the devcom efforts of government and people are more powerful and integrated. The constraints that were dysfunctional for development in the early decades are still posing psychological challenges for government and the people to deal with — though in renewed perspectives. What are not changed in development process even in the current decade are*: the dilemmas, the challenges, helplessness and the crunch of financial resources.*

Globally, on the development scenario, the major changes have been that the current development initiatives are now from the government and the people for whom the development is envisaged. The communication for development is also within their cultural, socio-economic and political realities. Earlier, the development initiative was not from within but imposed by an external authority, which was not well aware of people's needs, demands and communicative ability and threshold.

A livelihoods approach recognizes communication and information as essential components of the development process, to empower poor communities and inform development agencies and policy-makers alike, and for linking and informing decision-making processes at every level. Yet information and communication systems are rarely well integrated into development strategies and programs for livelihoods.

The Food and Agriculture Organization (FAO), Department for International Development (DFID) and the Overseas Development Institute (ODI) undertook a study in 2001-2002 to analyze the role of information in livelihoods. It made recommendations on how agencies can capitalize on and integrate the best elements of traditional communication methods and the ICT revolution technologies within the livelihood approach. The study was based on a literature review and field trips to three countries

It is universally recognized that educational development of a country is critical for poverty reduction, economic growth, better governance and citizenship. Governments in developing countries have long understood it; yet the public recognizes that the aggregate devoted to education does not commensurate with the recognized importance of education for development.

UNDPs Human Development reports have earned benchmark status among economists and policy-makers as an indication of a country's progress and highlighting sectors where it is lagging behind. At the same time, the idea of a Human Development report as a tool for identifying current socio-economic conditions and working out future strategies is spreading in the countries also.

In 2000 decade the development communication is predominately supported by participatory approach, ICT and Globalization in its various facets. The merits of ICT and

Globalization approaches as communications perspectives would be discussed in details in the following sections (Information Communication Technologies [ICT] Perspective in Part 2)

WIDER (May 2003) Conference in Helsinki on inequality, poverty and human well-being discussed and reports that the gaps in living conditions growing within and between countries, inequality, poverty, and human well being remain as the core issues for researchers and policy-makers alike. Rapid technological changes and growth has resulted in large disparities in the living standards within and between regions and countries of the world. Research emphasis has shifted from determinants of economic growth and convergence of per capita income among countries to the distribution of income. Regional disparities in the income, the incidence and depth of poverty, and health and education status is particularly high in large developing countries; reflecting such factors as historical differences in the pace of development, the uneven impact of economic reform, and discrimination in the provision of economic and social infrastructure. Thus National indicators of human development can mislead policy-makers when large regional disparities exist.

Measures of human well-being are used increasingly to monitor and evaluate performance within and among countries. Not only the numbers of indicators have increased appreciably in recent years but also these measures capture more fully progress in human well-being or development.

WIDER (March 2003) Conference in Tokyo discusses the rising income inequalities and spatial disparities. Spatial inequality is a dimension of overall inequality. But it has added significance when spatial and regional divisions align with political and ethnic tensions to undermine social and political stability. Spatial disparities in human development have attracted considerable interest from policy-makers. In countries such as China, Russia, India, Mexico and South Africa and most of the developing and transition economies, there is a sense that spatial and regional inequality (of economic activity, incomes, economic structure, social indicators, population, infrastructure and public expenditure) is sharply increasing. Also there is a perceived sense that increasing internal spatial inequality is related to the greater openness of economies and to globalization in general.

Despite these important policy concerns, there is little systematic and coherent documentation of the facts about spatial and regional inequality along different dimensions of human development. Consequently, there is insufficient understanding of the determinants of such spatial disparities in a globalizing world.

Development needs reinterpretation

The two discourses focus on Participatory Development and Good Governance (PDGG) model. The focus is on strengthening the partnership approach to participatory development and good governance. This has radical implication for world economy. The emphasis is on micro level action contexts, local resistance to change, community participation, and empowerment of people through participation.

Economic and political liberalism is necessary for PDGG model. It is necessary that there should be vital connection between open, democratic, and accountable political systems, individual rights, and effective and equitable operations of economic systems with substantial reduction of poverty.

Political liberalism aims at establishing accountable system of government through widespread participation of people and respect for human rights. The government is accountable to parliament and there is political decentralization.

The important dimensions of good governance are: rule of the law in the country, public sector is managed effectively and efficiently, controlling corruption, and reducing excessive military expenditure. Worldwide empirical evidence shows that corruption lowers economic growth. The explicit reasons for participation development are (a) empowerment of non-government actors on government and their influencing the public policy, (b) enhancement of efficiency, effectiveness, sustainability of concrete development programs.

Simple, moral, accountable, responsible and transparent (SMART) government is advocated for development. Debunking change i.e. pulling people down when they are trying to make progress is also part of the politics in many developing countries. Whatever the new initiatives party-in-power proposes, the opposition will inevitably pull it down.

In many developing countries including India the attitude of fatalism (let it be) of people towards development is their response to the manifest failures of its system of governance.

The misuse of state power creates serious credibility problems whose effects can be encountered long after the event. For example, it is hard to get foreign investors' credibility in Uganda now because of Ugandanian President Idi Amin misuse of power in throwing out people and businesses of foreign origin from the country and mistreating them in a dictatorial manner. Though this happened in way back in 80s. Credibility crisis also occurs if the national government has inconsistent economic policies overtime; as it happened in India in 90s. Foreign investors were reluctant to invest in infrastructure projects in India in 90s because of inconsistent economic policies; and they did put a hold on economic decisions due to political instability and frequent changes in national government.

Authoritarian governments spend loans and development aid on futile purposes. Sometimes such misconduct has created civil wars and destruction of attempts to find sustainable development. In India, in 90s the authoritarian political leaders have been misusing political power for personal gains and amass wealth and assets by jeopardizing the development of the citizens.

The PDGG model addresses the role of multinationals in developing socio-economic development; growing global disparities; and the importance of dialogue between government and civil society actors. In globalization of the world there is no symmetry and congruency between political and economic decision-makers, and political and economic decision-receivers. Thus there is widening of marginalization and deepening of polarization of world economy culminating in growing global disparities.

In globalization scenario, the national borders are of less significance than of before; national steering power is challenged, countries face legitimate problems but citizens' faith fades. Integration within and with the outside world puts greater demands on transformation of national societies. There are number of hegemonic nodal points in social transformation. Some of them are highly over determined and they may constitute points of condensation for a number of social relations and become focal points of multiplicity of total effects. The hegemony of the west is challenged and there is an attempt to denationalize the political and economic struggle of the globalizing world.

The major Paradigm of 2000 decade is *Technology Paradigm*. Technological advancements in the millennium and in 21st century are likely to shape our lives differently. Within this paradigm, the four alternative models (approaches) to development are: Country Specific Model, Decentralization Model, Sustainable Development Model, and Globalization Model. These operate effectively and efficiently within the framework of Technology Paradigm.

These models have a renewed perspective to development though based on various dimensions of the earlier development paradigms. These changed perspectives are shaped by the experiences and lessons learnt in the implementation of development programs and knowledge shared globally. In the present scenario some of the development initiatives in the developing countries could be: to move forward at the pace of the community, to let people speak their own voice, to learn from mistakes and generate new knowledge, and to focus on both localized and globalize community and communications. The changed technology and communication technology scenarios have further changed these perspectives.

Relations with technology and government can harness for positive social outcome and changes in public policy. Local community access to IT is vital for bridging the digital divide as well development divide — such as local owned and run radio stations, use of telephones, surfing the net, and access to other appropriate technologies give them platform for development. Sustainable development can occur by connecting communities to global resources, through training, consulting, and networking worldwide.

Development needs restructuring

New conceptual and practical demands on development and communications suggest reengineering and reinvention.

Development innovations, civil engagement, enabling environment, social accountability and participation, civil society in communication driven development, and self-regulation of civil society in development and e-government are some of the important factors in the restructured development scenario of current 2000 decade. This calls for mainstreaming e-development.

The goal of development innovations is to make the development more effective and efficient by disseminating innovative solutions to development challenges, contributing to an understanding of what drives innovation on the organizational and national levels, and providing tools for stimulating innovation on these two levels, or innovative approaches to improve society. We can define development innovations by four elements: novelty, effectiveness, significance and transferability. Does the innovation suggest a leap of creativity (novelty)? Is there evidence of tangible results (effectiveness)? Does the innovation address a problem of public concern (significance)? Can the innovation, or elements of it, be adopted by others (transferability)?

The innovations can be innovative ideas, policies, programs or practices. The efforts may be on adapting best practices in the focused areas of development, research on grass-root innovations, and technology enabled innovations. It is important to find funding for innovations, and find public and private partnerships for developing them.

Civil engagement is the participation of people both at grass root level and of civil society expectedly in democratic participation. The people and their organization network of people—civil society organizations (CSOs) influences and share control over priority setting, policy-making, resource allocations and access to public goods and services through democratic methods and public approval.

Enabling environment is a set of interrelated conditions —legal, bureaucratic, fiscal, informational, political, social and cultural that impact on the capacity of civil society organizations, and other development actors to engage in development process in a sustained and effective manner.

Social accountability is the extent to which institutions are attentive of their wider impact on society. It entails being responsible and even liable for actions taken for public welfare. It involves planning, tracking and reporting in transparent manner. Participation is the involvement of people and CSOs in government processes such as budget formulation and monitoring, government programs and policies.

Civil society in communication driven development (CDD) is the exercise of communication control over decisions and resources for poverty reduction. CDD implies community mobilization around public investment, community management of resources, creating partnership for community development through communication, strengthening of local government and empowering poor people.

Self-regulation of civil society in development is the institutional capacity and practice of CSOs to behave and act socially responsible without influence from the government. The adoptions of institutional norms such as code of conduct, peer reviews, public audits, are some of the good practices for self-regulation.

E-government is powerful strategy in e-development. The government initiative is to provide citizen services online for effective government. It reforms and upgrades both back offices and front offices and delivery system through it.

The various dimensions of e-government are: e-assistance that provides all services available by public administration and other government agencies. E-administration is managing on-line taxation, debt management, budget management and census etc. E-procurement is a tool to achieve transparency and efficiency and economic development via improved market penetration and increased investment on-line. Government utilize mobile wireless technology in specific activities of public administration such as citizens safety, interaction with citizens, gathering of salient information, payment to government, voting through mobile and use of this technology for transport, education and healthcare. E-local is promoting access to public information to citizens in different structures of government through transparency (anti corruption), good governance and social accountability. Most important is e-democracy. It harnesses ICT to enhance democratic processes and empower the citizens.

The strategies for e-government should be transparency, negotiation policies for contradictions; and balancing the needs of the citizens, concerns of government and macro-pressures of globalization

E-development (Nagy Hanna 2003) addresses the importance of mainstreaming e-development through integrating ICT into development agenda and utilizing it for development. How the concepts of 'e-development' and 'e-strategy' can make a difference operationally is the transition to the knowledge economy and information society. E-development is an outgrowth of our earlier efforts to introduce ICT into development projects and operations. The importance of it lies in the recognition that smaller components of (ICT) in projects do not create any strategic impact; that there is need to exploit ICT at a more strategic country level. This needs to be consistent with public sector management performance, private sector development, the overall poverty reduction strategies of a country, and its competitiveness agenda.

The key elements of the e-development are that it would address the larger information infrastructure issues: *connectivity* throughout society, human resources that would allow the country to exploit ICT in all sectors; and the broader applications of e-government that could transform the public sector and its means for providing the services to the citizens, the private sector and the civil society. It would tackle the issues of *diffusion* of ICT at private sector and towards e-commerce; the development of an enabling environment that could support such diffusion; and the building of *technological capabilities* particularly of software industry and of other sectors to allow information technology infrastructure to function effectively throughput the society and within government.

These are broad elements but they vary across countries. Some countries would emphasize on human resources, others on infrastructure if connectivity is low, or if there is a major divide between urban and rural areas. Countries, who want to export software services, may emphasize promotion of software industry. Or they may select some segments of ICT for participation at global level. This will depend on the initial conditions within a country, its comparative advantages, and aspirations in terms of participating in global knowledge economy.

A comprehensive and broader approach to e-development is needed to use technology for development. For example, India with its software industry is realizing the payoff from its vibrant high-tech industries and capabilities. Now they are looking within, how they can exploit the same for their own governments and for certain applications. Many East Asian countries focused on how to promote their software industries and how to participate in hardware production of ICT.

They are countries that are moving away from exclusively ICT exports to leverage other industries, revitalize other sectors of economy and to improve other government services (South Korea). Singapore started with the use of ICT as well as participation in ICT services. Many developing countries are moving towards a broader approach.

Now, e-development is becoming more comprehensive in e-government and other ways of enhancing the development and employment of people in knowledge industries.

The primary lesson learnt from these e-development initiatives is to integrate ICT potential within all sectors of economy. The more it becomes mainstreamed as part of development strategy for each sector, the more we will be able to leverage it in a more strategic manner and use IT to reform the way we do business in that sector, the institutions within that sector, enable new means of policy formulations and allow key stakeholders to improve sector performance.

The potential of ICT should not be ignored or isolated for the technical people, nor it should be idealized as panacea for all development needs. It should be rather integrated into the development agenda of each sector, and across all sectors. It should be an integral part of the way we think about development and achieving its goals.

E-development would assess opportunities to use ICT to

expand employment and earning opportunities for poor, marginalized groups, in rural areas and women. ICT may be used to increase access to market information and to lower transaction costs for farmers, traders, artisans, etc. E-development would aim to enable sustainable development by using ICT applications for clean technologies.

E-development strategies need to be shared by development community. Forums and other ways of accelerating the diffusion of knowledge within countries need development and encouragement. E-development can only be achieved in partnership. The partnership among the four — government, civil society, private sector and academia is important. None can take sole responsibility.

The government takes key role and takes a leadership and facilitative role. The private sector plays a crucial role not only in deploying ICT for specific applications but also in facilitating and outsourcing of some government services, and in co-investing with government in various public service modernization projects.

Civil society and NGOs can play vital role in using ICT to overcome the digital divide, for the rural sector and mobilizing and building capacity of the poor, women, youth and isolated communities to use ICT tools. The commitment of NGOs is important for articulating the needs of the community especially the isolated and vulnerable groups that would otherwise be disempowered in the society. Academic community has to be involved in this revolution. Reflection, monitoring, evaluation and analysis on the part of research community are extremely important. They are the one who are mobilizing new generation to utilize ICT. They would be motivating them to work with NGOs, civil society, the private sector and the government to generate new ideas as how to exploit ICT more effectively for development. They can be the change agents in society.

The World Summit on Information Society (Dec 2003 in Geneva) in the context of promoting agenda for e-development creates awareness and bring commitment at the highest levels of governments, civil society and the private sector towards some higher vision that enable all societies to benefit from ICT in two ways.

One is to build e-leadership in all societies to take advantage of ICT for development. This could be reinforced by building coalitions to empower countries to take advantage of ICT revolution, to set international policies and standards, and to facilitate learning across countries.

Secondly, by constructing practical mechanisms to translate these visions and aspirations of developing countries into realities. Aid agencies of all kind should look at ICT not as on add-on but as integral part of development agenda and comprehensive development strategy. It should put more practical emphasis on e-development mainstreamed into development activities. It should become a tool for achieving massive backlog of millennium development goals through innovative and strategic applications of these new technologies for development. ICT have profound impact on productivity, product differentiations, competing in time and accessing markets. Developing countries must use ICT to leverage their competitive advantage and participate in global economy.

An essential component of Summit outcomes should be practical investment programs and operations across countries at different stages of development.

Ethics and Development

The above discussion about development from various stances suggests that the underlying concern of development community is to deliver development products and services equitably and without discrimination. This is development ideology at its best. Faced with reality one confronts a different scenario.

Visualize this scene in a developing country (India), government runs public hospital: a diabetic patient, uneducated and from low income consults the doctor. At the same time another diabetic patient consults who is educated and from higher income group. Doctor does physical checks for both the patients. But he thoroughly checks the 2nd patient, spends more time in examining as well educating him about diet, exercise and medicine. Whereas, in the case of 1st patient, the doctor perfunctorily examines the patient, prescribes medicines without bothering to educate him about diet and exercise. The patient felt cheated when he compared the treatment meted to him. He lost faith and trust in government and its health care delivery programs on which government spends lots of money so that poor and uneducated specifically gets good health care. Dissatisfied, he consults a private doctor, pays hefty consultancy fee, that he could ill afford. But he is satisfied with the attention and the good treatment he got.

This poses ethical questions: why discrimination? Is government communication to poor for preventive and curative health checkups is wasted and a farce?

Take another instance, Indian Masses seem to have developed an "ethic of proportional efforts". This ethic holds that there is something wrong, perhaps even shameful, in exerting a *disproportionate effort* to accomplish a task that will have *equivalent benefits* for the whole group. This ethic seemed to be the context for the phrase often encountered when one ask the masses, why they do not engage in active participation. "Why should I"? When additional talk is elicited, they frequently refer to others who would benefit from their activity but who are not contributing proportional efforts. To put more effort, makes one seem foolish and exploited by others. This hypothesis of an ethic of disproportional effort in the social reality of the masses is significant.

There are numerous instances faced by population including poor and illiterate, where development meant for them is not delivered to them and that poses ethical challenges.

Development poses not only regional and contemporary ethical challenges for development project planning and procedures for policy-making but also for its delivery. Citizens all over the world are demanding that ethical quandaries and dilemmas (for development) be examined and taken into account.

Development community is faced with the questions: What values should be considered when drafting development strategies and public policy? How should they confront ethically charged problems such as poverty, sharp inequalities, discrimination and exclusion etc? What codes of conduct should be adopted by policy-makers and leaders? Ethical challenges and dilemmas need to be analyzed and discussed to ensure that chief decision-makers take them into account. In this context, how can a sense of community and social responsibility be promoted?

So far development has focused on human development through providing quality of life. But the society is posing impediments and ethical challenges for development delivery. Therefore, the major ethical challenge is to develop social capital.

Developing countries are awakening to the massive potential of *social capital.* The basic components of social capital are cooperative community, interpersonal trust and broad social conscience. International experience suggests that nations with strong social capital enjoy stronger economies and greater democratic maturity. Therefore, it is imperative to promote social capital in the development projects prepared and implemented by national government and international agencies. Further, growth of social capital can be promoted by adoption of ethical codes for the development capital in the specific region by the key social players.

In the context of development, political leaders, policy-makers, chief decision-makers and key social players must follow the ethical codes such as transparency and social accountability.

To sum up, the journey for development started since 50s. We have come a long way since then en route. Our concerns, strategies, and practices have changed. The information and knowledge has widened and is being shared. The communication channels have revolutionized beyond our imagination and made the world much smaller, easily accessible and with global ramifications.

It started with the efforts of the developed countries through one-way partnership. During the course of time, the outsourcing of manufacturing jobs to developing countries since 70s and the outsourcing of tech jobs since 90s have created economic boom in those developing countries and there is a two-way partnership between the developed and developing countries. This two-way partnership has created healthy interdependency for development.

Development has still to reduce poverty, helplessness of people, and provide basic needs to majority of the people around the world and to reduce the overall development gap among people in different societies.

It is an ongoing journey—you gain some, you lose some and in the end come wiser and stimulated to move on, and move ahead.

Summary

International development theorists and practitioners have conceptualized development from various perspectives such as social change, modernization, progress and alternations in life styles. All the perspectives have encompassed 'growth', the economic growth viz. industrialization, agrarian, and technological growth and the social growth identified with structural and value changes.

Development in developing countries *vis-à-vis* providing quality of life to people through modernization has been one of the major concerns of western countries since 50s. An historical analysis of development models since 50s provides insight into the changing development models. These changed with the changing dynamics of development, and the technological breakthrough in the mass media channels.

There have been four approaches to understand underdevelopment and how to do development. These are: modernization through dominant paradigm, Interdependency model, Basic needs model and communication for Development Model in national and international contexts. These approaches are exemplars of development and development communication.

There is a change, and since 70s the national governments and the people themselves have conceived the development for their own societies. Therefore all later models are country specific.

The last six decades of research has revealed that role of communication in development is significant and it has changed with the change in development models.

Development Communication scenario has changed globally in the last six decades. There have been four-pronged major changes. The focus of development has changed, nature of development demands and issues have changed, new communication channels are available and the characteristics of the audience have changed.

In 80s, the role of Development Communication changed over to the dynamic process of bringing development to the people for whom development is envisaged. It is conceptualized as information, education, communication within cultural matrix and motivation for participation in development (IECM). The varied development communication approaches facilitate actions for evolving effective communication strategy for development projects.

The major Paradigm of 2000 decade is Technology Paradigm. New conceptual and practical demands on development and communications suggest reengineering and reinvention. Development innovations, civil engagement, enabling environment, social accountability and participation, civil society in communication driven development, and self-regulation of civil society in development and e-government are some of the important factors in the restructured development scenario of current 2000 decade. This calls for mainstreaming e-development to shape our lives differently.

Development poses not only regional and contemporary ethical challenges for development project planning and procedures for policy-making but also for its delivery. So far development has focused on human development through providing quality of life. But the society is posing impediments and ethical challenges for development delivery. Therefore, the major ethical challenge is to develop social capital.

The key to development is access, empowerment of people and good governance. Moreover, integrating the dynamics of development and the dynamics of communication is the challenge of our times.

11

International Communication Perspective

I am merely a voyager, in search of insights, of greater understanding and of identity. —*Stephen Dachi*

A Framework

Globalization and International images are the two major approaches from which International communication perspective has been studied and researched. We have taken globalization approach as framework for International communication perspective. Both approaches are necessary for creating international understanding. From our viewpoint, International images approach by itself is narrow; whereas, Globalization approach encompasses international images approach also.

Globalization is the major focus of international communication in this era. The social process of globalization is the basic context in international communication. Globalization is being approached from diverse perspectives of political, economics and trade, migration, infotainment and communication.

Since from all perspectives, it involves communicating with diverse cultures and understanding of those cultures; and focusing on social phenomena and social theory of national identity. Thus intercultural communication is basic and important for international communication.

Secondly, International-relation theories are important. The focus is on economic and political relations. One must be well informed about social and political phenomena and ideologies of various nations to communicate with them effectively.

In 2000 decade the focus of International Communication is with multi-stakeholders both in the developed and developing world and with both high and low economies. This multilevel communication is to develop global solidarity and a global platform for various issues such as human rights and poverty eradication, population control, health care and disease control, environmental issues etc. since problems and hazards of these issues in one country affect worldwide. The solutions for these problematic issues also lie in worldwide collaborative efforts.

International Communication processes work through mass media and interpersonal communication channels focusing at social, political, cultural, economic and technological contexts of world community. These processes refer and upgrade from local, national to international contexts. Local and national communities transform into world communities' interests. Thus in International communication, we deal with local, national and international contexts, interests, and communication processes.

International communication may be through exchange of news, information, data and cultural products such as art, films, media programs, customs, rituals, ways of life and values, clothes and food etc. These factors have impact on practices of government, people's lifestyles encompassing education, leisure, business and work, scientific and technological innovations, military defense and warfare. Both mass media and interpersonal communication play important part in all these contexts.

History, politics, economy, science and technology, intercultural and cross-cultural factors at national levels affect the international affairs and international political economy and vice versa. International Communication plays a significant role in it. In these contexts, there is significance of the historical stance and politics in national and international conflicts, wars, negotiations and peace processes. International interests and communities are brought closer by scientific and technological breakthroughs in this information age. Interest and flow of migration all over the world not only brings intercultural and cross-cultural factors in interaction but also creates a world community in distant lands.

The logic of international interaction forces a high level of homology on the societies in today's world, meaning not only that they have to have structures of State, Capital and the Civil society with the Media influencing the three. But the parts have to have some similarities. The economic systems can be expressed in terms of the relative power of these three parts of modern society.

The basic thesis is that many of the problems of modern society derive from lack of communication among the three in bilateral relations: civil society – state, state — capital, capital – civil society. It must satisfy five criteria of dialogue, decision-making, having a broad agenda, be fairly regular, and be transparent. Can media fill the communication gap? Can multiple memberships fill the communication gap? (Galtung, 1999), "Tell me how State, Capital, and Civil society dialogues with each other and I shall tell you what kind of society you have". Civil society can use normative countervailing power. The essence of democracy is transparent dialogue as a prologue to decision-making for social transformation.

The significant facilitators for international communication could be directive or persuasive for bringing three types of changes: (a) creating awareness and disseminating information, (b) bringing attitudinal and behavioral changes for mutual understanding and (c) by educating and motivating people. The dynamic interplay of source, message, channels and audience is necessary for effective and successful communication.

Why do we need to communicate internationally?

Today, the world has become small in literal sense. Awareness, information, and knowledge about different people around us in different regions of the world through media exposure have made us curious to know them. Media and transport revolutions make us curious to know them well. We see around us people from different lands. We get instant feeling that they behave differently, they talk in different styles and languages, and they show different living styles. We feel the instant desire to know them better. We see TV shows and news. They tell us about different happenings on the world front, the lifestyles, and the political, socio-cultural and economic concerns of people from different lands. We get curious to know these dimensions better from our viewpoint as well from their viewpoints. Thus international communication is to know different viewpoints and different ways of doing. It does involve exchange of viewpoints, convincing or getting convinced about each other's viewpoints and ways of doing.

To communicate internationally, one way is to have exposure to the international ways through broadcasting channels and print. Another way is through other media technologies of telephone, computers, Internet and interpersonal channels of meeting people personally through traveling and in organized forums. *Interaction is important element.* The more we interact with others, the greater need is created for communication for co-operation, trade, development of arts and crafts, technologies, and even in lifestyles such as wearing apparels, food habits and tastes, and housing etc. All these call for constant and frequent communication. Thus both nature and frequency of international communication has changed in past decades due to advancement in communication technologies, transportation, and above all the growing political concern for a better world order.

Key factors to International Communication theories, strategies, and practice. International Communication has five major focuses. One, International Communication for conflict resolution and peace processes. This deals with war, political and military conflicts, and terrorism in national territory affecting the international interests and peace.

Second, international communication for development of developing countries and dealing with issues of development in the world at large such as issues of environment pollution, health, education, poverty, population etc.

Third is technological focus. This focuses on scientific and technological breakthroughs in various aspects of people's life and affecting the world community. The recent technologies of computers and computer chips, Internet, cellular phones, mobile communication and satellites have brought humanity closer to each other thus breaking the geographical, cultural, and language barriers. The information age has created information societies and knowledge economy.

Fourth focus deals with the international economic challenges and visions that the international communication through information age and knowledge economy has created.

The fifth focus — the cultural perspective focusing on intercultural and cross-cultural communications is significant in dealing with the above four mentioned focuses in creating a world community. This is the core of international communication.

People's interactions create political and military conflicts. People's exposure to different lands, and communities through mass media or interpersonal communication creates desire for different lifestyles, and for better ways of living and amenities and therefore need for development. The interactions, exposures bring people's interests, talents closer and they together search for technological innovations to benefit humanity. The technological innovations create *Economic Visions* and in turn pose *Economic Challenges* for people. The theory and practice of these five focuses for International Communication lead to theory and practice of globalization.

There are five contexts of International communication: Globalization, Inter-Dependency, Development Communication, Intercultural Communication and Technology. These pertain to the five focuses to international communication.

Globalization Context

Marshall McLuhan had a vision in 40s for a global village. A world connected with mass media. At that point his vision was that print media would connect the world. Since that was the main channel of communication at that time. He (1964) held that peculiar attributes of each medium help to determine the very meaning of communication. He argued that each historical epoch is characterized by the kind of media it uses predominately. Such as general system theories have led to the invention of computers and automation and as well fundamental changes in theoretical perspectives of social change.

50s experienced another form of globalization through the development models such as Dominant Paradigm, Interdependent Model, Dependency Model, and Basic Needs

Models. Dominant paradigm presented globalization perspective by modernizing the world, connecting it by media exposure and literacy on one hand and industrialization and urbanization on the other hand. They advocated that there would be global modernizing effect by trickle down effects from the developed world to the developing countries.

Interdependent Model in 60s advocated a global perspective for development. Developed countries wanted to be the dominating power both in business and values through ideological domination and ideological aggression. Ideological domination is conveyed through commercial communication networks, transnational marketing corporations. The ideological aggression results when the transnational corporations penetrate the political sphere via their control over modern technology, education and by their own ideological and economic logic. Their agendas were that the worldwide hierarchy of power and values should organize developing countries.

This interdependent approach implied that developing countries must develop in the context of political and economic realities of the developed countries. The offshoot of this is the dependency model where developing countries are faced with the problem of underdevelopment due to dependency created by the imposition of economic and political realities of the developed countries.

Dominating powers control the mass media channels and its content, create consumerism bias, aggravate dependency that unleash frustration among the low earning level population and leads to collective aggressiveness as an escape valve.

The dependency theorists argue that communication serves the purpose of the publicizing transnational interests only. They emphasize the use of interpersonal channels since mass media channels are caught in the dependency relationships. Later, these perspectives facilitated development communication models of 80s onward decades in developing countries to do development in their national contexts.

In 80s Basic Minimum Needs Model advocated by United Nations presented a global perspective on improving of quality of life for people globally by at least providing people with the five basic minimum needs of food, shelter, health, education and employment. This started with a global perspective on eradication of absolute and relative poverty.

Thus, earlier globalization perspectives had mixed concerns — development, power and cultural ideology domination, control of communication channels and the information disseminated through them and commerce controls. These concerns were more authoritarian in nature and moved in one-way direction — from developed to developing and poor countries. These had some elements of exploitation.

The current globalization perspectives have their roots in the early vision of 40s, and development communication models of 50s through 70s decades. The driving forces for globalization today are military and security, trade and commerce, technology, media, development and tourism.

Globalization Process

Globalization currently defined is a process that creates connectivity and convergence. It is understood from four contexts. One is cultural convergence. Second is political context, which is concerned about free flow of information. Third is economic context focusing on capitalism, consumerism, transnationalism, and globalization of western economic values. Fourth is media context focusing on media contribution to all the above-mentioned three contexts.

Information technology is important for the globalization process. It has impact on globalization process and vice versa. Importance and impact of information and ICT in the globalization process addresses three factors for rapid globalization: the liberalization of the market; encouragement of competition among different systems; and globalization processes in the context of third world.

The changes brought by ICT by the end of century are of tremendous concern. The powerful flow of cultural commodities — information, news, and various television programs saturate the world markets, as they become accessible via satellite-broadcast. The developing countries face serious challenges of whether to hook with the world telecommunication system or to avoid such integration in order to protect their culture from direct influence of powerful cultural commodity flows.

The convergence of telecommunication and computer is of recent origin. It suggests that distinctions are becoming less relevant as data can be moved across from one to other. The cable and the telephone network can now carry voice traffic, television signals and data; satellite systems can transmit to many points, computers can assist the information traffic, as well enhancing the value of information they can handle. These developments are further facilitated by digitalization; wherein all information is converted into digital signals and then capable of being processed by sophisticated electronic hardware. Such as text CD-ROM linked to computers can reproduce images and sound.

As boundaries between the different network systems are eroded, we can talk about wider electronic communication infrastructure rather than separate technologies, each transmitting different information system. Such changes are neither accidental nor positive fall-out of technological progress. They are by product of telecommunication policies in an era of rapid technological changes.

Existence of inequalities of access to communication technologies is to be considered rather than technological change *per se*. Though these inequalities may not be the product of technological change *per se*.

Globalization has followed three cycles. From 1800 onwards the transportation revolution through railways and roadways vehicles, steamships and in 1900 onwards the airplanes were bringing the different geographies closer. From World War I onwards the costs of these transportation modes have been falling and that had brought the different world geographies closer and that was Globalization 1.0, and it shrank the world from a large size to a medium size. The second globalization cycle lasted from 1980 – 2000 when the falling costs of telecom and Personal Computers (PC) shrank the distances among various geographies and the world became very small. The third globalization cycle is 2000 onwards which, is being driven by three factors: high-speed data connectivity pipes between geographies; the proliferation of PCs in all those geographies;

and the convergence of software that uses this infrastructure to create a genuine global work platform.

Global Communication is imperative these days to connect to people globally not only on just one on one basis but across many countries because of growing needs and demands on many fronts viz. political, economic, socio-cultural, technology etc. A network of communication across countries, inter-country and cross-country leads to globalization. An interesting example is holding summits. *Globalization follows a circular model of communication.*

Dominant Paradigm of development in 50s advocated that effects of modernization and industrialization would trickle down from developed to developing countries and from elite to the masses. Globalization model is different. It rather interconnects the parts. The frequent inter-country and cross-country interactions depend on their (each country's) needs and demand to interact. The force of globalization shifts power away from governments to private capital in whatever market it takes place.

Globalization Defined

Global has two meanings. One, is the traditional definition of international, which has messages, data, or people going across or through some kind of barriers, boundaries or constraints, whether it be the encoding or decoding process from one human being to other, or the artificial borders between nation-States. The other definition concerns issues that are common enough to group of people to transcend traditional boundaries.

80s produced Internet — the tool for global communication. This linked the international community that knew no boundaries of time and space. This does not know the traditional category of sovereignty. There is no international legislation besides the standards for interconnectivity and interoperability. No government can control the Internet, and no 'political qualification' is needed to enter the cyberspace. Internet is a new dimension, a new culture, and a new way of communicating internationally. The new technologies of Internet do not need heavy international infrastructure. A lighter more flexible approach is possible and is more competitive.

But Internet is not tool for open communication around the world. 30% of this is reduced to commercial activity and legally regulated activity. It has resulted in boom of advertising consumer goods. Satellite communication has facilitated it.

The communication revolution via cable TV, video, Internet and telecommunication, has brought the consumers in direct contact with evolving tastes all over the world. This has created a new class of consuming public who demands more value at a lower price. Success for any consumer company in such a demanding environment requires exceptional commitment to delivering value to every stakeholder. The paradigms of the past are not relevant to the future and successful organization would need to constantly reinvent itself to adapt to the evolving environment.

The global players participate in the flows of news, entertainment and education material, promotional messages, data flow, flow of voice messages, and text messages. These flows are organized around message producers, operators of networks, and manufacturers of technical equipment.

The significant is free flow of information through cultural industries and media entertainment based on free flow doctrine that influences the world. Super information highway has given better access to (a) change in international communication as consequences of communication technology such as fax, satellite, broadcasting etc.; (b) an emergence of corporate media systems as aspects of globalization; (c) cultural aspects of the process of contemporary globalization; (d) global culture as built into modern communication systems; and accessibility of technology with its wide angle reflecting cultural conflicts.

One of the curiosities of globalization revolution has been an accompanying inability to engage in constructive debate without choosing sides. The globalization is presented as a victory for internationalism over nationalism and victory for the free market. This approach has little internal inconsistency and the events of the real world contradict the general theory.

Globalization gets growing into *cultural convergence*

manifested in hardware and software transnational media products (telecommunication, video, TV), other commodities, business, banks, and advertising agencies etc. Others think of cultural convergence as evident in things people think about, the ways in which they think, and which things are expressed through everyday social practices. Other aspect of 'cultural hybridize' arises from play of global forces through immigration, in search of employment opportunities and global trade.

Technology is presented as a revolution that shapes society. The idea that society might have say in its shape is generally presented as ludditism. We find current technological tools of globalization turning themselves into tools of digital divide.

The deregulation and globalization that were supposed to lead to more capitalism and competition are leading to increasing number of monopolies and oligopolies. The result on the negative side is a frightened nationalism and on the positive side the rise of democratic-based regulations. Democracy is not the product of market place; rather democracy creates the conditions, which renders possible long-term market place prosperity.

Globalization process in its economic context can erode the autonomy of nation states when they have to follow the prescriptive policy of the world financial institutions from which they may borrow loan for development.

The current model of globalization has done very little to balance new economic structures with new social structures. We have worked hard to globalize the economic regulations and much of this has been positive but we have done almost nothing to globalize social and political regulations through enforceable treaties negotiated by the representative of the citizens at the nation state level. Not to balance social agreements with economic agreements sap the power of citizens. It has created imbalance within our societies and between self-interest and public good.

There is nothing wrong with globalization, the ugly nationalism or negative protectionism. It is a theory that can take many forms and pretend that internationalism can exist in a predetermined and inevitable form. A sensible use of ongoing technological revolution can be made; if the market place has long-term stability and competition to serve it and the societies out of which it grows.

The forces of interdependence of nation do create a close knit global economy. Trans-national Communication (TNC) is the primary agent of globalization through media and multi-corporate. The driving force is revolutions in Information Communication Technologies (ICTs). TNC with inter-linked interests in commodities, manufacturing, banking, finance, and its hold on technology can change international systems and can create a transnational world order — where national sovereignty will give way to TNC interests.

Trans-national Communication (TNC) is communicated through transnational corporations. Trans-border communication has changed due to technology advancement. The TNC media has been exposing different world communities to diverse cultural ideologies, lifestyles and artifacts thus creating globalization. The marvels of modern communication channels (TV., radio, video, films etc) have both negative and positive impact for the poor of the world. These bring to the poor the images of how the rich or even poor within the rich nations live. Poor are likely to feel frustrated and depressed on comparing to their (rich) living situations. But it has the positive effect when the poor are bound to exert pressure on their government to demand such lifestyle.

It is observed that media is losing its national communicative identity and its capacity to mediate in relation to the national social movements. Its technological developments are creating new *space* of industrial reconversion and a new *time* of realization of capital.

Broadcast media, satellites through deregulation have lost national control. It has enhanced political power of commercial media enterprises and shifted ideological balance from public emphasis to free market and commercial imperatives. Broadcasting is integrated into global market through different routes: One, through cross-border acquisition of interests in and control of program production and rights. Secondly, through Cable broadcasting facilities. Thirdly, through sale and rental of program stocks (movies and syndicated programs). Fourth, establishment and operation of satellite transmission facilities is established through technology equipment. These are functions of technological development, market growth, and opening of economic borders. These have created opportunities for media enterprises.

The TNC aim to diffuse the products, services, ideas and markets to world communities through multi-corporate and focus at creating international consumerism. Both separately and together they influence the world communities in many different ways.

Earlier, the role of transnational actor has been putting economic pressures with its negative effect on national behavior; dissocializing rationality of State; legitimization of the dissolution of the public; and confrontation with a civil society identified with market oriented private interests. But now the international scenario will be different because of multiple actors and nations involved in such communication; and such channels as Internet that knows no national boundaries. Multiple political, cultural and market ideologies will interact in the present scenario.

The TNC processes through ICTs, create new structures and recompose collective identities. It is paradoxical logic. The new ICTs are instrumental and have a role in making the State strong in its possibilities and tendencies to control and on the negative side making it weak by disconnecting it from the public functions.

TNC substitute the State as agent of hegemony and they make their private initiative as defender of freedom of creation and the only link between national and international cultures. The center of the society moves from politics to marketplace. This has brought a reconstitution of identities and a system of acknowledgements and symbolic differentiation of classes and social groups. It is here that new dynamics of culture tie in with the transformations in communications in its perceptive code of each community and the different experiences that make and recreate cultural heterogeneity through fragmentation and readjustments.

TNC dislocates centers of articulating the universe of each culture. The process of secularization and specialization of the symbolic world in a movement of segmentation and integration of world economy carry the dislocation. While the sources of production of culture are moved away from the community towards specialized bodies, communities' forms of life are gradually remodeled and replaced by patterns of consumption separated from the 'creative nucleus' that constitutes vital core of each culture.

The different cultural logics of the communities form new identities and reconstitute the meaning of national and local cultures due to this process. This happens through the abilities of the communities to transform through exposures to, and seeing and experiencing different ways.

The concept of TNC reduces communication to a set of strategies for cultural domination by giving new meaning to the knowledge and habits of each community and subordinating them to a complex transnational system. This implies rethinking about the interaction between the hegemonic message and the community.

A new international economic order, a new international technological order may emerge due to TNC processes. These may be equitable orders or leading to global disorder as the global commons of atmosphere, oceans, space, forests and genetic resources, bio-diversity are being regulated and privatized to become TNC property. The emerging pattern is seen as environmental colonialism.

The new ICTs reinforce TNC, assist integration of capitalist enterprises worldwide, it weakens authority of the national state, which is unable to cope with the power of these TNCs formally operating under their domain. Information does widen people's horizon but providers dominate them by their ideologies and images. Such as the unsolicited beaming of broadcast signals can be threat to identity of receiving nations.

TNC constitute both the driving force and the cutting edge of globalization. The economic space of their activities extends way beyond the geographical space of nation states. But there are no rules on what TNC can or cannot do.

Deepak Nayyar (WIDER study 2003) suggests creation of an international system of governance. There is need for discipline on restrictive business practices and for an international regime of anti-trust laws. Such a system can be built on the earlier work in UNCTAD, the experience of EU, and the initiatives of the OECD. The study concludes that existing arrangements for global governance are undemocratic in terms of both representation and decision-making. 'The reality is that all countries are not equal partners in the world just as people are not equal citizens in a democracy'..... the essential corrective then is to create institutional mechanisms that give poor countries and poor people a voice in the process of global governance.

WIDER research study notes that globalization has reduced the power of the national government without a corresponding increase in effective international cooperation or supra-national government that could regulate the market driven process. Without effective international coordination, international public bads (such as international crime, or international trade in drugs, arms, organs and people) are bound to increase while public goods (such as world peace and sustainable development) are most likely to decrease. An international mechanism for cooperation between nation states that facilitates coordinated action and cooperative behavior is needed.

WIDER (2003) study comments on the role of international institutions. The essence of the problem is the international capital flows without any international controls. Another failure is in promoting development, which is reflected in the persistent poverty and growing inequalities. The crisis of development has in fact accentuated in the era of globalization.

Nayar Deepak in this study notes that World Trade Organization (WTO) should recognize that development is the primary objective, so that poverty eradication, employment creation are just as important as trade liberalization and trade expansion. In the same mode it must be recognized that desirability of outcomes is more important than the procedural uniformity of rules. There is obvious need for an efficient system of representative decision-making in the WTO that is also democratic.

Nayyar emphasize that there are no international rules or international institutions that govern the cross-border movements of people. Yet illegal migrants, guest workers, and body-shopping is reality. There is a potential conflict between the laws of nations that restricts the movements of people across the borders and the economics of globalization that induces the movements of people across borders. It is necessary to initiate a process to set up a new institutional framework that would govern the cross-border movements of the people.

The Global governance initiative project of World economic forum (2004) assessing the level of effort and cooperation among governments, the private sector, civil society that includes non-governmental organizations, and international organizations in implementing the United Nations millennium declaration. It is unique that it goes beyond normal assessment of government efforts and commitments to other players. It has global reach, as it involves a network of 40 experts from around the world.

Globalization Theories

Tomilson John (1997) addresses theories of globalization and transnational cultural process for their 'iconoclasm'; that is their power in forcing us to rethink critical frameworks.

The Iconoclasm of globalization refers to rapidly developing process of complex interconnection among the societies, cultures, institutions, and individuals worldwide. It is a process which involves compression of time and space, shrinking distances through a dramatic reduction in time either physical or representational — to cross them, so making the world seem smaller and bringing human beings closer to one another. It is also a process that stretches social relationships from local contexts to global contexts.

Giddens (1994) suggests that globalization can be understood as 'action at distance'. The iconoclastic implications of the concept of globalization are that it challenges the familiar ways of describing the world. It threatens to destroy the images of the world cherished in so many intellectual and critical traditions, displacing or forcing reexamination of certain givens of social and cultural analysis.

(Giddens 1990, Mann 1986) point that the very idea of 'society' as a fundamental analytic category becomes problematic, once the complex interconnections of crosscutting of globalization's assumed societal boundaries are recognized.

It is the boundaries of the nation state that are traversed by the interconnections of globalization — by the global capitalist market, by global media flows, and cultural identifications. And this reveals social reality as comprising of 'structuring networks' of state, culture and economy, rather than on the basis of 'one master' or 'basic unit' concept of society.

McGrew (1992) argues, the process of globalization comprises four critical aspects of the nation state: its competence, its form, its autonomy, and its authority or legitimacy.

The iconoclasm of globalization lies in the implicit demand to re-envisage the world that arises once the nature of the complex global interconnectedness and the process of time-space compression and action at distance are recognized. Re-envisioning is disturbing and inevitably involves the destruction of shibboleths, many of which may be linked to political and moral commitments. But re-envisioning is not the same as revisionism.

New technologies present new possibilities as well as new threats. Satellite communication shrink distances. It is cost effective way to reach large population worldwide. But it can highlight problems of national sovereignty, cultural integrity, and deepening inequalities. The pattern of availability and use mirrors the imbalance of financial and political power.

Cultural globalization process rethinks about cultural power not as cultural imperialism but a process of cultural integration.

World is becoming one in technological sense but political, economic, social and cultural diversities will remain. The global village will also have the digital divide and the gaps of have and havenots.

The New World Information of Communication Order (NWICO) movement in 70s-80s began as a protest over the concentration of print and broadcast media ownership among de facto cartel, and developed into an argument about the cultural dominance of poor nations by wealthy ones. The basic premise of the movement was that an imbalance existed in the direction, volume, and types of information exchanged between adequately developed countries and the Third World, which was detrimental to development and systemic in nature.

Of equal importance with, and logically prior to this conception, is the ethical notion that information should be viewed as a shared resource or as a social good rather than as a commodity.

The situation is characterized by the dominance of information producing nations over those that consume cultural and information 'products'. The set of relations between these 'know' and 'know-not' nations has been described variously as a centre-periphery situation, as a North-South conflict, or as a relationship of neo-colonialism or neo-imperialism. Galtung's major contribution to this platform is his "centre-periphery" typology, which provided a perspective on cultural dominance.

"According to this schema, nations at the Centre... dominate a 'feudal network of communication'. The Centre owns the major news agencies and 'Centre news takes up a much larger proportion of Periphery news media than vice versa'... users in the Periphery come to see with Centre eyes." (Galtung 1979, 165-166).

(Centre-periphery perspective on cultural dominance is further discussed in section International influence on Media systems).

NWICO must take into account broad communication contexts and diversities of global cultures and what methods of accountability can be used to ensure defense of global public interest and world society at large. (More about NWICO in Part 1 Models Section 3, Notes 3.1).

Social dimensions of globalization: Amartya Sen (1998) points that globalization sans social welfare is counterproductive. People in developing economies (India and Pakistan) are not able to compete in the globalization. The problem arises when people enjoying protective environment are suddenly pushed into hard competition. A country may have globalization at the high speed but it creates problems for itself if it does not pay attention to lack of social opportunities, illiteracy, and lack of health care, land reforms, and micro credit. *The blame does not lie with globalization but on the policies to achieve it.* It needs broader contexts of social and economic policies. The countries where human development is low are threatened by globalization.

Further, he has linked the strategies of development to economic and social development. The solutions are healthcare, education, land reforms and empowerment to people. The developing countries do not need 'trickle down' from western countries but they can achieve development by developing their manpower. Human development is the main focus. It is necessary to bring into the public domain discussions about social deprivations and create a system for social opportunities. There is lack of initiative to focus on unemployment even in richer economies. The effort has to create a force so that benefits of liberalized economy reach the socially deprived.

Information society context: Information society presents a spirit of globalism with gradual disappearance of oral and traditional cultures and a quest for new cultural order, which goes beyond simple notion of information and communication.

The Monist mode of globalization of economic, political, and cultural global processes creates global integration by creation of coherent set of values and norms and discouraging divergent norms and perceiving deviance as threat to stability. But we require a pluralist mode of global integration that demands a global communication order that supports the creation of global civil society. It is a self-organizing civil society that transcends the national borders and facilitates people oriented communication to accommodate multipolarity of current world society and diversity that can be shared.

A serious discussion has started on globalization. World Bank development research director Paul Collier (2000) remarked, both sides are on extreme. At each end of the spectrum are ideologues that are pushing agenda unrelated to reality. Since the battle for market-driven economy has been won and the flaws of trying to force every country into the same template has become clear. It is time to forge a more enlightened consensus to take globalization to the next level.

***Cultural globalization or Cultural imperialism*:** Cultural imperialism scenario focuses on the model of center-periphery relationships, and historical patterns of domination. There is ubiquity of Western cultural goods. There is direct cultural imposition from the Western world.

Now-a-days the western cultural tastes and practices are becoming global ones; from clothes to music, food, films, television programs and architecture etc. The complex web of interconnections, crosscutting and overlay of communication paths and flows enmeshes and binds them in all cultures. The key aspect of this tradition is the cultural mixing, hybridization rather than direct cultural imposition from the developed world. The emphasis on transculturation, hybridize, and indigenization is important in understanding the hegemonic cultural influence. It also has a wider significance.

As James Lull (1995) puts it, the idea of emergence of monolithic global culture is implausible. Global culture is always 'meaning in motion' thus its space is between cultures rather than within cultures; and its essential nature is that of the hybrid. From the perspective of action at distance the locales are thoroughly penetrated by and shaped in terms of social influences quite distant from them.

Another conception of globalization argued by Hall (1992) ...driven by poverty, draught, famine, underdevelopment, crop failure, civil war, political unrest, regional conflicts, a very large number of the globe have taken the message of global consumerism at its face value. And they moved towards the places from where the goodies come and where the chances of survival are greater. In the era of global communications, the West is only a one-way charter ticket away. The political-economic impact of such migrations is ambiguous for Western nation states, at the same time offering cheap exploitable labor and threatening demographic invasion.

Globalization often draws attention to the more obvious cultural consequences of this process of migration — the commodification of the exotic and ethnic in the Western culture.

Globalization does not promise the techno-utopia of Mcluhan's global village but neither it is likely to produce the homogenized dystopia dominated by the same old power players. The globalization media technology may repeat pattern of political, economic and cultural dependency. But it will surely bring them the knowledge of global problems and sensitivity to global needs, acceptance and mutual recognition of socio-cultural differences and perception of needs of global community as more important than local communication. It needs broader context of social and economic policies.

***Globalism*:** Globalism discourse is based on three levels: values, knowledge and interests. The focus is on global understanding and global consciousness. It is awareness that local events have global consequences and understanding of global impact.

Globalism suggests a global culture of standardization of food, clothes, music, TV, films, business styles. The divergent values and norms merge. It is not true that these processes lead to global integration. The same processes propelling globalization can integrate as well disintegrate it. Disintegration occurs when value system that dominates globalization is refused. In a way this also protects weaker units. Interdependence does not merge nations into larger units. Global transactions can create more co-operation, competition as well conflicts.

***Global capitalism*:** Can globalism be made to work better? In the past decade, globalization—meaning the rise of market capitalism around the world has contributed to the new economy boom. It has created millions of jobs around the world. It has created phone service to millions of households in developing countries, and transfer of trillions from rich countries to poor nations through equity, investments and commercial loans. It has helped people topple dictators by making information freely available in once sheltered societies. And now the Internet is poised to narrow the commercial and cultural gulf separating the rich nations from poor even further in the decades to come. So it is little wonder that many poor countries are forging ahead in the boom. Foreign direct investment has soared in these countries to create better economy.

There is no one-size-fits all policies for development. There are no clear roadmaps for corporate behavior. Balancing growth with environmental and labor regulations is complex in countries where people live on the margin. At a time when image is paramount, corporations are besieged with activists, consumer boycotts, and their named smeared on the web. And as the costs of consumer boycott increase, companies and investors are likely to look for more uniform standards of behavior. Yet it is unlikely anyone will agree to global government to police corporations and capital markets. The new rules of global capitalism will evolve slowly and in pieces.

There are poor, strife-ridden countries, they neglect investment in its own people and have poor economic policies. In such countries the direct foreign investments have brought foreign exchange and more training but people want to work with dignity.

The problem of course is that leaders who pay attention to basics in work environments do not run down all-developing nations. If they are stuck with low-end sweat shops work. It is not the multinationals but they themselves are to be blamed. The basic requirements are smart policies and hard work.

Studies show that countries heavily dependent on natural resources tend to remain underdeveloped since governments have little incentive to nurture education or industries needed for growth. (e.g. Africa). Some 23% of the countries, which depend on exports of primary commodities, have military conflicts (Middle East). Countries with no such exports have less than 1% chance of conflicts.

Local people often do not clamor for foreign oil or mining companies to pull out. What they really want is more equitable share in the revenues and job opportunities. If they do not get the economic benefits as well as bear the environment consequences also, they are not happy (World Bank study).

Multinationals are facing a new era of accountability in the third world. Now the people's voices are heard globally and echo around the world through myriad web sites. Issues are more contentious where investment is concerned. Sorting out the issues gets complex. The developing nations need revenues for development.

The result is shaping up of corporate responsibilities. Multi nationals are hiring human rights advisers, drafting and enforcing codes of conducts, appointing monitors and improving operating practices. They are developing global standards of conduct. They are putting local people on board of directors and urging governments to adhere to international human rights standards. Acknowledging that too is a huge change. Until just a few years ago a very few companies were doing that.

World Bank shows that big oil projects can make money both for investors as well improve the lot of the poor. If the activists make the oil pipeline a centerpiece of their war against globalization, it is the poor in the region who would suffer the most (example Chad oil pipe-line supported by World Bank collaboration).

When governments commit to make guidelines work, then there is a good chance that the global capitalism of the 21st century will be guided by the rules under which everyone can prosper.

Economic context of globalization highlights that global communication industries study ways of customizing or innovating products suitable within geo-linguistic or geo-political regions. The local level producers are drawn on the global codes and conventions.

The information and entertainment products champion predominantly the western ways of life, and values of capitalism and individualism. But there is exposure to different lifestyles of the world people.

The enhanced and diversified trade and commerce markets usher countries into new economy. Unequal center and periphery relationships, hegemony *vs.* rivalry, upper and lower class structures, and uneven cyclical developments affect world economy.

The ideological categories and labels offer ideological self-satisfaction but impede and obscure the analysis of material real world, economic development, and real rather than ideal alternative choices it offers yesterday, today, and tomorrow.

There are three major trends that are shaping the future of the world. First, there is wide proliferation of the modern information and communication technologies. Second, there is increasing democratization of the social systems around the world. The third trend is the intensifying global expansion of mainly western-based corporations. Thus the convergence of these trends — communication technologies, political, and economic liberalization has transformed the way we live and communicate.

"Global Economic Prospects and the Developing Countries 2001" conference reviewed the global economic environment and its implications for the developing countries over the next decade, and examines how technological innovations and the dismantling of trade barriers over the past decade have contributed to an acceleration of growth in global trade. This year's "Global Economic Prospects" focused on international trade, and discussed policies that are required if developing countries are to benefit from global integration. It predicted that the global economy is likely to approach a cyclical high in 2000, boosted by a further acceleration of growth in the United States, the recovery in Europe and Japan, and the sharp rebound in countries affected by the global financial crisis. World trade volumes are likely to increase by the highest rate of growth since before the first oil shock of the 1970s. A moderation of growth in the crisis countries and slower consumption growth in the United States are likely to lead to a deceleration of output growth over the next year. There are prospects for long-term growth in developing countries.

Challenge of globalization: These days there is no way any economy can escape the rapid process of integrating with the world economy. Globalization is a vehicle for progress that we cannot ignore. However what we have quickly learned from globalization trend is that the economic fate of a country is not solely in its own hands. In the globalize world, events in one corner of the world can have immense effect on the fortunes of others in far away corners and not at all involved with the events.

UN Human development report 1999 points to the opportunities and rewards of globalization spread unequally and inequitably, concentrating wealth in a select group of people, nations and corporations, marginalizing others. It warns that when the profit motive of market players get out of hand, they challenge people's ethics and sacrifice respect for justice and human rights. The global indicators of inequality can be transferred to Individual societies and nations. In some countries with the greatest wealth, large pockets of poverty and penury can be found. We all live in global neighborhood and poverty need be eradicated for long-term benefits. The *challenge of next century is globalization of responsibility to eradicate poverty.*

In 2000 decade a new round of globalization is, America and Western Europe sending upscale jobs offshore to developing countries. They include chip design, engineering, basic research, medical transcriptions, medical diagnostics, accounting and even financial analysis. These jobs are being done in India, China, Philippines and the Baltic's and elsewhere. The cost savings to the US and European countries are enormous. These countries get good services since the workers are educated, skilled and productive. The outsourcing of jobs has meant more employment and booming economy and GDP growth in developing countries where the jobs are being outsourced (India, China).

It is globalization's next wave and biggest trend in reshaping the global economy. Two decades ago, there was exodus of jobs such as making shoes, garments, toys and cheap electronics etc. to the developing countries. After that, the exodus for simple service work like processing credit card receipts, medical transcriptions, writing software code etc. happened. Now in 2000 decade, all kinds of knowledge work are getting done from almost anywhere. There is explosion of work going overseas.

This also has a backlash from USA and UK where employees are losing their jobs because of outsourcing and where the economy is slowing. There have been employees' protests and efforts to call for legislation to bar outsourcing but without much success. It is a vicious circle. Economy is slow so jobs are being outsourced for cheaper labor to have profit margins. The economy slows down when jobs are being outsourced.

The trend of jobs moving to offshore is likely to grow. Until now the impact of free trade has been confined to blue-collar jobs but now white-collar jobs are hit. The outsourced white-collar jobs would contribute to the economic development of the developing nations, in low-wage nations especially where there are college graduates who speak Western languages.

Some suggest that the developed countries should look to outsourcing of jobs as *opportunities* and not as threats. The demands from developing nations for infrastructure, healthcare, education, and managerial and technical expertise can create enormous opportunities for developed countries.

In job sourcing, the developed countries' leadership is being challenged by emerging nations like India and China. What makes this challenge different is that these nations not only share rich educational heritages but they are also investing heavily in innovation and R&D to help drive the next generation of growth. Not only they are competitive but have knowledgeable work forces. (details Notes 3.2)

Participants in World Economic Forum (2004) in Davos have voiced doubts about the central tenets of global economic integration. Whether the increasingly global economy will produce many high-wage jobs in rich countries. Their concern stems from the free trade axiom that when a rich country sends blue-collar jobs overseas; it creates opportunities for back home workers to move up the skill ladder. The more recent corollary was that sending white-collar overseas jobs would do the same for white-collar workers back home. But the rising number of skilled white-collar jobs from rich nations to developing countries is raising fears for lack of well-paid jobs back home. Job-migration unsettles global economy and more so current economy in USA. Those in very senior positions with skilled, management, research and technical expertise have become effectively global-trotter to keep up their positions. The forum further worried that outsourcing could erode political support for free trade internationally. Some economists in Davos felt the fears over outsourcing are overblown. But in US it is increasingly becoming a political issue.

Media context of globalization suggests global media products and their implications for local cultures and media as vehicles of globalization (international news agencies were the first to communicate on global basis). Modern satellite technology facilitated media globalization.

Tehranian & Tehranian (1997) addresses the contradictory role of the media as a source of resistance to globalization, protector of capitalism, agents of democracy and vehicles for advertising and commodification.

Media-flow equals to international communication. It can result in media Imperialism, globalization and glocalization. Glocalization perspective appears as an alternative to media imperialism. Glocalization is composite of globalization and localization. It holds that the process of social change is union of both homogenization and heterogenization. It is interplay between local and global.

The media glocalization thesis holds that the process of media flow is the dialectic of global homogenizing and local heterogenization. The outcome of globalization and localization are cultural hybridize. Robertson (1995) suggested that media-flow studies spell out the ways in which homogenizing and heterogenizing tendencies are mutually implicative.

Media-flow suggests that we are dealing with the type of cultures that have definite geo origins and then have spatially expanded. Media-flow analysis is concerned with interaction between societies and not within societies. We study media as a form of communication and as a setting between cultures.

International influence on Media systems: Media peripheralism refers to societies and cultures reflecting a real and perceived dependence on transnational media systems. Both rich and poor periphery societies depend on media peripheralism.

In a periphery, links between the media and the power structures are close in a system that is predominantly based on private ownership. There are close links between the media and the politico-economic-power structures in a periphery disregarding ownership forms.

In poor periphery, countries may be dependent on transnational communication systems. But in these countries even the scant mass communication may represent higher degree of genuine locality and relevance and take strength from it. Moreover, local relevance is also brought by traditional and oral communication. Mass communication with interpersonal communication acts as 'buffer zone' in national building. They add traditional elements to urban oriented media. There are regionally and domestically operated mediations, formal or informal systems of news priorities, which cause selection of media content and cause reorientation. However, buffer zone tends to weaken in those sectors where mass communication is experiencing rapid growth such as entertainment and media experiencing commercial growth.

In wealthy periphery, the mass media cultures support mainstreaming with core culture but are indifferent to locality and spontaneous creativity especially in areas considered socially essentials such as entertainment. TV, video and cable depend heavily on exogenous and transnational markets. But book publishing does tackle locality to some extent. Even the richest cultural peripheries are dominated by big production powers. If content becomes too manufactured in mass communication, the audience creates their own spontaneous channels. This may be a quest for corpus.

Mass communication reinforces asymmetrical interdependencies with two different cores. One is the dependence for professional core. It links peripheral mass communication to international and transnational transmission networks and with transnational systems. Secondly, the rich periphery seldom uses its wealth to gain from pioneer developments in international mass communications. Most often mainstream networks are favored for it. Local media policies do not regulate these media organizations.

Media professionalism is a significant killer of genuine peripheral media culture, creativity and innovation. Professionalism implies standardization, homogeneity, and effectively denies cultural differences. Though Media professionalism is a deeply contradictory concept.

The 'preference spheres' of the different peripheries are different, reflecting shared past that increases news and media interest. Colonial practices lag in disappearing in media vehicles and also in production of culturally meaningful content.

Affluence and deliberate media policies have effect but legacy and history have strong effect. The professional ideologies have persistent effect.

Peripheral introversion is expressed in the high level of interest given to the periphery itself in relation to the other nations. Geo proximity is given to the next-door neighbors or those sharing particular history of each country.

Mass communication frequently operates as conservative societal force. All changes other than non-restricted growth of media volume takes place slowly. The particular legacy of the past can be read in the forms and operations of the media vehicles. The media vehicle easily adapts to rapid growth if no regulations are exercised and that limits the potential to control.

Non-restricted growth tends to asymmetrical development and media novelties do not concern with basic functions of the media or freedom of expression. Rather, they are offered in multi-layer network of mass media offering identical content preferences.

A pendulum movement characterized the debate on International mass communication flows. In the late 70s and 80s the great concern was the North/South imbalance and what was called 'Trans-nationalization of culture, Americanization, homogenization and cultural imperialism.' (NWICO debate)

In 80s the scientific discussion has been dominated by conceptualization of a global culture. This conceptualization has not been interested in homogenization, but signs and levels of quasi and true cosmopolitanism, diversity and richness in various discourses (Featherstone 1990, p. 2). This kind of polarization could prove fruitful but in actual fact it has not turned out that way so far. Inexpensive, universal access to telecommunication in most developing countries needs improvement viz. landlines, wireless and cellular phones, international links, radio spectrum and Internet.

To sum up, our highlights and insights about globalization, its impact in various fields, challenges and discontents since the last six decades may at one point of time, give us only an historical perspective, since we are facing a new trend, a new challenge in globalization very often. Therefore, whatever we have discussed may not be the update but gives us the insights to move ahead.

Summary

Globalization is the major focus of international communication in this era. The process of globalization is the basic context in international communication. Globalization is being approached from diverse perspectives of political, economics and trade, migration, infotainment and communication. Globalization contexts such as social, political, economic, cultural, information society, and media are discussed. International Communication processes work through mass media and interpersonal communication channels focusing at these contexts of world community. We have analyzed the international influence on media systems through trans-national communication (TNC). Theories of globalization are discussed.

Why do we need to communicate internationally? Awareness, information, and knowledge about different people and their concerns around us in different regions of the world through media exposure (and revolutions) and transport revolution have made us curious to know them and to know different viewpoints and ways of doing. International communication does involve exchange of viewpoints, convincing or getting convinced about each other's viewpoints and ways of doing.

The interaction of various world communities, exposure to world mass media and communication are the key factors to International Communication theories, strategies, and practice. International Communication has five major focuses: conflict resolution and peace processes, development of developing countries, technological and economic challenges and visions that the international communication through information age and knowledge economy has created, and intercultural and cross-cultural communications within the international framework.

12

Information Communication Technologies Perspective

The real danger is not that computers will begin to think like men, but that men will begin to think like computers.

—Sydney J. Harris

Information Technology (IT) simply means information or a new idea for doing something that transpired through technology. It is becoming an important factor in the new growth theory beside labor and capital.

Information technology allows information processes to be accomplished much more efficiently, and thus can be used to raise the productivity of information workers, and indeed of most work. As with any technological innovation, there will be winners and losers.

To-day, information communication technologies (ICTs) have significant role to play in all walks of life. They have been both evolutionary and revolutionary, and giving connectivity both in personal and professional life of people. The present scenario is that all technologies are integrated and converged which provides holistic information connectivity.

The social and economic repercussions of the advances in ICT will be so great that the term "information revolution" is probably justified. On the one hand, technological progress is so fast that basic ICT services may well become universal and pervasive even in poor societies. On the other hand, developed countries spend many times more per capita income on ICT than do poor countries. They spend more on the high end ICT. Thus while ICT offer unparalleled opportunities to meet basic human needs in poor countries, aspects of the digital divide continue to widen, offering new risks to those same poor countries.

In 14th century when paper and writing were discovered, they became the isolated technologies. But as inventions and innovations moved on from printing, broadcasting – radio and TV, satellites, telecommunication, and computer; the technologies were getting more and more integrated. The innovations of silicon computer chips, digitalization, and laser have added more integration, depth and breadth to communication technologies. People feel coming closer to the idea of global village and a network society.

The new ICTs model has made many old paradigms and theories of communication obsolete such as dominant paradigm, Lerner's model of modernity, Schramm's communication model and other subsequent communication models. The update model is *technology networking and technology convergence*.

The new ICTs accelerate process of cultural industries with social agenda and have impact on culture, infotainment, and governance. It also acts as powerful technology infrastructure for marketing the commercial needs of the national and transnational business systems.

Media technologies have evolved from conceptual moves in communications. The technological innovations overtime have supported the evolutionary process of media technologies. Development of new media technologies and technological advancements created Communication Revolutions.

The conventional electronic mass media channels comprise of print, broadcasting – radio and television, films, telephone. These conventional channels further expanded to supporting channels for these, such as VCR for television, audio players for radio and television etc. The electronic mass media channels further expanded to computers.

Over a period of time these basic channels have expanded in its different functional forms such as television expanded from black and white to color and from cable to satellites. Radio evolved in its frequencies modulates from its AM and FM modes. Films changed from silent to talkies, from black to Technicolor. These films are even presented on different kind of screens.

Multi media mix led to revolution in telecommunication from basic local telephony to regional, national and international and its quality is further facilitated by satellites. It matured from cordless to wireless and cellular telephones roaming across the national and international boundaries and with its varied features facilitating better connectivity.

Who could deny the Internet revolution through advancements in computers and telecommunications that created better connectivity, information and knowledge sharing globally.

Communications revolutions over the centuries created more and more of industrial products, consumer products and cultural products to develop and improve the living conditions around the world.

The six Communication Revolutions since early 14th century to date have exploded in information revolution and created new perspectives and contexts for media technologies, and their impact through changing media technologies over time. Different issues were brought on the forefront due to these technological changes. These focused on giving better connectivity to human beings through both machines and humans.

Innovations and technology advancement in printing, television, satellites wireless, cellular and mobile telecommunication, computerization, laser, fiber optics and quantum technologies have all enhanced connectivity in communication.

The ***first communication revolution*** evolved from oral traditions. Who invented paper? China and Egypt were the early inventors. Chinese were the inventors of Paper, Ink, and Writing. Chinese invented paper, writing and even early printing as early as third century. In the Han dynasty, 206 B.C.-A.D. 220, paper and ink were invented. In the T'ang dynasty, 618-906, the first printer was invented. In their writing, there were 80,000 different symbols. They were the first to invent books and had book-shops in every city by the end of the T'ang dynasty.

They manufactured three different important kinds of paper, the very first being silk rags. The cheap kinds were no more then wooden strips, and the most expensive was silk cloth. Although most of the kinds of paper were made from over 50% bamboo, some of the other things they were made of were silk, cloth, hemp, mulberry bark, and plant fibers.

About 1,800 years ago, during the Eastern Han Dynasty (25-220), Cai Lun improved China's papermaking technique using bark and hemp. Today, ancient papermaking has been replaced by modern means of production, but in some places in southwestern China's Guizhou Province, where many people of ethnic-minority groups live; this ancient technique is still practiced.

Grinding plant material into a pulp, forming it into thin sheets, and drying it in a form make paper. Ts'ai Lun, a Chinese official and member of the Chinese Imperial Court invented this process in 105 AD, about 2000 years ago; he originally used the waste from silk production. Early Chinese paper was made from the bark of the mulberry tree and other plant fibers.

Almost 5,000 years ago, in ancient Egypt, the papyrus plant was processed and used as paper. Papyrus paper was made from thin sheets of papyrus pith that were soaked in water, pressed together with the grains at right angles, and then dried - the sticky sap of the plant made the thin sheets stick together, forming a sturdy writing surface. Papyrus (*Cyperus papyrus* is its genus and species) is a grass-like aquatic plant native to the Nile valley of Egypt. Our word paper comes from "papyrus."

These early inventions of paper, ink and writing in one part of the world took many decades to reach other parts of the world due to transportation and communication difficulties. Even during this period people in other parts of the world were also making inventions of these quite unaware of these earlier inventions. These inventions were basic but revolutionary for the communication process.

The ***second communication revolution*** is Printing. Johannes Gutenberg, a German invented the printing press with replaceable wooden or metal letters in 1436 (completed by 1440). The press used by Gutenberg was a hand press, in which ink was rolled over the raised surfaces of hand-set letters held within a wooden form and the form was then press against a sheet of paper. The Gutenberg press with its wooden and later metal movable type printing brought down the price of printed materials and made such materials available for the masses. It remained the standard until the 20th century. During the centuries, many newer printing technologies were developed based on Gutenberg's printing machine e.g. offset printing.

Thus, intellectual life soon was no longer the exclusive domain of church and court in Europe, and literacy became a necessity of urban existence. The printing press stoked intellectual fires at the end of the Middle Ages, helping usher in an era of enlightenment. This great cultural rebirth was inspired by widespread access to and appreciation for classical art and literature, and these translated into a renewed passion for artistic expression. Without the development of the printing press, the Renaissance in Europe may never have happened. Without inexpensive printing to make books available to a large portion of society. Shakespeare, from rural England in the mid 1500s, may never have been inspired to write what are now recognized as some of history's greatest plays. What civilization gained from Gutenberg's invention is incalculable

The literary world was changed with the invention of movable type and its application to a series of known practices that were integrated into a method of mass production. Gutenberg's name does not appear on any of his work but he is generally accredited with the world's first book printed with movable type, the 42-line (the number of lines per page) Bible, also known as the Gutenberg Bible or the Mainz Bible (for the place where it was produced).

In three decades, printing spread across Europe where it became one of the chief means by which the Renaissance, the humanist re-birth of interest in learning and the classics, was transmitted from culture to culture. In time, the printed book became a means of political revolution, the necessary technological corollary for the rise of the vernacular (i.e. non-Latin) as a vehicle for literary texts, and the larger democratic revolutions of the eighteenth century.

In 1814, *The Times* of London introduced the first steam-press. Other technological innovations, such as linotype, invented in 1884 by Ottmar Mergentahler; and the monotype machine, first used in 1897, helped increase the ease with which a page could be type-set. Together, these new methods of mass production helped pave the way to the growth of a mass reading public, a public which finally wrested literature from the closed circles of the educated and wealthy. This revolution entailed not simply a change in the world of literature but, as Marshall Macluhan wrote, a change in consciousness itself.

Print media facilitated awareness, information and knowledge through Newspapers, books, magazines, brochures and other forms of printed material. Printed word changed the perspective about how information and knowledge was conveyed, processed and preserved for the coming generations. Writing and printing became the basis of worldwide literacy and education.

"Written language ended the monopoly of elders who preserved and handed over oral sagas and poems that contained the accumulated knowledge of generations. Printing challenged this monopoly of information, its monopoly of truth and changed the world for ever." The new mass media of writing, language and print through books, magazines and Newspapers being widely used in the society brought important changes in the human conditions.

Four factors made this new medium (print) far more efficient than the communication process of any earlier society. The new medium was more effective in terms of *expressiveness,* in that they carry a broad range of ideas and feelings; *Permanence* of record or the overcoming of time; *Swiftness,* or the overcoming of space; *diffusion* or access to all classes of people. The general character that Print medium brought is expressed in *enlargement* and *animation.*

Cooley (1909) "...the Age of Mass Communication would erode the barriers of isolation among people in the world and produce significant changes in the organization and functioning of society. It represented a revolution in every phase of life; in commerce, in politics, in education, even in mere sociability and gossip."

Third communication revolution: By mid century the telegraph became a reality. Although not a mass medium of communication, this device was an important element in technology that would eventually lead to mass electronic media. A few decades later experiments were being carried out successfully that were prerequisite to motion pictures and wireless telegraphy.

On 18th Jan 1903, G. Marconi sent a wireless message from Cape Cod in USA to England. This event was the start of the *wireless revolution that would transform communications, paving the way for radio, television, and today's cell phones*. Marconi based his inventions on the work of German physicist Heinrich Hertz, who first demonstrated the existence of electric and magnetic waves.

During the first decade of 20th century, motion pictures became a form of family entertainment. This was followed in the 1920s by the development of household radio and in the 1940s by the beginning of home television. By the early 1950s, radio had reached a saturation point in many countries of the world due to transistor revolution. In 1970s, television was progressing rapidly in the world from black and white to color television, from terrestrial to cable television, and the use of satellites for direct broadcast system (DBS). The invention of Space Satellites facilitated the communication revolution not only in broadcasting but also in telecommunication also in later decades. The invention of video technology and audio technology further supported the broadcasting revolution. Transistors played an important part in broadcasting revolution.

Further, broadcasting in third communication revolution focused on the innovative developments of radio in 40s and television in 50s. Radio developed from AM to FM modes and other high modality frequencies; from electricity operated radio sets to transistorized battery operated. The program content, functions changed overtime. Television technology developed in its various modes; changing from black and white to color mode, from Terrestrial to Cable and direct broadcast television, HDTV, Digital TV and Web TV, and from single to multi channels. Eventually 3-D television conventional may be created. At present 3-D television is not possible because of the enormous amount of memory necessary to store holographic pictures.

The entrance of the newspaper, the radio receiver set, or the television set into the ordinary citizens' home represented a technological change that had greater significance than our largest accomplishments in science. Mass Communication has become one of the most significant and inescapable facts of modern life. The Mass media is having impact upon the psychological, moral, economic, political, creative, and educational aspects of the ordinary individual's life.

The major milestones in the ability of the people to communicate show two major facts. First, communication 'revolution' has been occurring throughout human history. Each new medium provided means by which significant changes would be brought about in the organization of the society and the accumulation of culture. Second, in the recent rise of Mass media most of the major events have taken place within the lifetime of contemporary populations. Many people alive can recall a society without radio or television or motion pictures. Each of these media added to total daily availability of language-using opportunities for the average person. Moreover, these devices implied a dramatic increase in the pace of the communicative behavior for the majority of the people.

Broadcasting. The broadcasting sector in the whole world is redesigning its structures, operations, programming, and technology to adapt to change. The efforts involve diverse conceptual and strategic approaches as the industry confronts new communication technologies, expanding markets, increased competition, and changing audience preferences. It is a challenge for both private and public service (government) broadcasting to survive and thrive in this changing environment.

This poses two main issues and multiple sub-issues. First is to examine various strategies in managing business, competition, finance, programming, and technology in a diverse environments in broadcasting. Second, to define changing roles of public service broadcasting amid increasing competition from private services, and changing preferences of the audience.

Public service broadcasting is vital to promoting democratic rights and responsibilities of its citizens; and the social, cultural, and economic aspirations of their society. The major concerns are for fair competition for growth and expansion. Should public service broadcasters be more profit-driven then policy-driven? Should they have only pro-social program and not infotainment and entertainment? Should private broadcasters share more in addressing public service objectives or purely entertainment channels? Is autonomy the key for survival of public service broadcasting? What are the challenges and opportunities related to autonomy? Will public service broadcasters compete effectively given more independence? Is there a more effective system to ensure its growth? What challenges and opportunities the private operators will face with government control and audience demands vis-à-vis its growth?

Regulating the quality of commercial private services raises concerns about key elements of quality programming. Are they better achieved in a regulated environment? What financing strategies can be adopted to ensure program and business viability?

Governments' role is also important for regulating broadcasting programming, ownership, financing, and technology. The concern is whether less government control in broadcasting will enhance the quality of public life, empower individuals, and social groups to participate fully and equitably.

Broadcasters need strategies to address audience needs and their changing preferences. They have to decide whether priority should be given to local or imported programs in order to capture bigger audience share.

Digital age is further posing challenges and opportunities for broadcasting. The issue in which new digital communication technology is going to benefit broadcasting, impact programming, and manpower needs. Further, the multi-channel age creates competition.

Digitalization in broadcasting and the growing use of satellite communication technology has provided the opportunities to reach wider audience, and people in remote areas, in different regions, and internationally. It creates new markets, programs, and products in the regions.

There will be digital sets which are not HDTV capable, sets that are fully HDTV-capable (but require converter boxes), and HDTV sets which have built-in decoders and everything with them. The first two kinds will be available at relatively low price. In these, we are getting a far superior picture compared to any analogs, and one can use it with computer and other things because it is digital.

Interaction with one's television is going to be a way of life. How that interaction happens, whether it is web TV, or it is the Internet on TV. But it has got to be easier to use than what it is today.

Web TV is Microsoft's set-top device for accessing the Internet and downloading video-on-demand. It is fairly awkward way to access TV, but is not awkward when you take PC out of the equation for people. Web TV is a nice alternative when you are not computer-literate. The first generation of web TV is better than the second generation. It has evolved dramatically in the usefulness and functionality of that product. It has now a storage drive that can basically store video. With disk space being cheaper every year and compression technology being better every year. Web TV will be finding more and more uses and potentialities such as video-on-demand.

Every day there is change in finer points of this technology for better connectivity and affordable prices and that adds on more consumers.

Impact of Television

The impact of television is cultural, social, economic, political and overall globalization of values with its wider reach.

Satellite television and free trade have altered the once sheltered societies of Asia. Western influences foster youth rebellion in Asia. Across Asia, from richest country to the poorest a familiar pattern is folding - a youth rebellion, change of their values which is shaking the foundations of society. In the 90s whether borne by Satellite television or by free trade, the visions and values of an outside and largely western world has penetrated Asia's once sheltered societies.

Young people are spurning traditional Asian values of collective duty, filial respect. They are embracing sex, drugs, violence, materialism and MTV. It has distorted the way teenagers look at sex. Young people do not feel inhibited anymore.

Young people are beginning to sound, act, and even look more and more alike because of globalization of media. The young people in east are thinking more like their western counterparts. Fearing that a generation is slipping by, many civic groups and governments are fighting back with measures ranging from value education and national compulsory service to young protection groups.

There is equal concern for political propaganda and for imposing terrorism ideology by across border countries to the gullible public. Even governments in these countries control it, sometimes by censoring the channels by scrambling or controlling its program contents, and at times by counter propaganda.

Even the reactions to TV advertisement of world products are culture specific. Take instance of Chinese reaction to commercial ads on television. Recently since Jan 2004, on China television, Proctor & Gamble, 'whisper' brand of feminine hygiene pads and other ads of hemorrhoid medication, and athlete's foot ointment are banned during three daily meal times. Meal times are family times in China and decorum should be maintained. "What the ads bluntly said should be talked about between women" that is the general reaction of people. Viewers' complaint the ads are too graphic and frequent during dinner. Even the censors objected to a McDonald ad showing a man licking drippings from his juicy chicken burger off a magazine page. These are not socially acceptable.

The move highlights the difficulties facing China, home to the world's biggest television audience, as it tries to apply cultural and broadcasting standards without driving away deep-pocketed advertisers. China has become an increasingly competitive and important market for consumer goods over the past few years, advertisers are eager to push the limit of what is socially acceptable in order to get in their message across. Further, China's fast development is also creating cultural rifts between sophisticated urbanites and millions of rural farmers who are unable to understand or appreciate the commercials.

But advertisers and media buyers complain that the new rules are out of step with the country's quickly changing mores. Primetime TV is the main tool many marketers use to build brand reputations in China. But the new restrictions could potentially crimp the growth of the country's ad market because they limit the total number of ads shown at prime time.

But all is not negative when people are exposed to world events on television. On the positive side, people are exposed to other countries' lifestyles, happenings, concerns and viewpoints. These could give them a sense of global community. Such exposures could also be learning experiences.

Paradox concerning the customary concept of role of social and political national identity is less significant at present because of television. Though the very concept does shield people against foreign domination and protects national identity. It is also an instrument to repress people by national elite.

Cable technology has widened the scope of TV programs' reach through several channels and in even remote corners of the world and in rural areas. The programs can be beamed both nationally and internationally across the borders without losing any clarity of picture or vividness of sound. It may make *Internet* as accessible as TV. The Internet could never become a mass medium unless every user has access to high-speed, no-hassle connections that are always available without placing a call. One such technology is Cable Modem. Cable modem permits the users to receive the Internet over the same common TV cable already in homes and businesses without interrupting the normal TV reception.

Internet

Internet roots started with ARPANET in 60s for USA Pentagon's advance research project. In 1983 Internet for public use was born. It was in 1991 Timothy Berners-Lee created

World Wide Web; a system of Internet servers that supports formatted documents in CERN lab in Geneva. For people outside the computer science field, the key development was in 1994 invention of the Mosaic web browser, a forerunner to Netscape that combined text and graphics to make the Internet accessible to ordinary people.

Less than a decade and the technology has changed from being a novelty to integral part of everyday life. Its reach and applications are ubiquitous. It has become central to businesses, enabling real-time communications with customers, suppliers and partners. To some extent, the Internet is a tool that allows people to do things cheaper and faster. It is transformational. It allows you to do things you could never do before. The tremendous increase to information (and disinformation) generated by Internet has also resulted in Knowledge revolution and its attendant creation of virtual communities and disembodied publics.

The late 90s burst obscured the rapid progression of the Internet. But the current build-out marked by a proliferation of mobile Internet devices, the spread of Internet protocol telephony, and the emergence of spin off technologies will refocus attention on the Internet.

Despite such changes innovation remains at the center of computing and IT industry. Currently, *five technology themes are challenging the economy.* One is wireless and mobility through technology. Wireless networks including LANs have become more pervasive and they are changing the way individuals and companies access and use data. An array of new technologies and devices including PDAs and its applications are making it possible to tap into data including Internet anytime and anywhere. Two, enterprise infrastructure, enterprise resource planning (ERP) and customer relation management (CRM), procurement, logistics and supply chain management are becoming crucial to today's enterprises.

Third is Information security, The Internet and the increasing use of the digital data has fueled the need for a wide range of security solutions including virtual private networks (VPNs), firewalls, biometric devices, file encryption, and advanced network monitoring.

Fourth is Web services. The emergence of Web into everyday life has created opportunities for an array of new applications and services, ranging from weather reports and mapping to group collaboration software and file storage and backup, software-based automation tools and web service foundation platforms.

Fifth is emergence of digital lifestyles. Over the last few years, home networking, interactive TV satellite, radio MP3 players etc have created new ways to live and work.

Cable modems can be fast. It can deliver up to 10 million bits of data per second, nearly 350 times the speed of the fastest standard modem. Telephone modems on standard telephone lines can deliver 28,800 bits of data per second to the PC. With a special kind of modem-ISDN, one can get up to 128,000 bit per second. Moreover, cable modems are always switched on. It essentially combines the analog and digital systems in one single chip. A DSL (analog digital subscriber line) is faster for Internet and can be used for video-on-demand through subscriber telephone lines and for any other applications on the Internet. This modem will meet the demand for high-speed connectivity worldwide and for faster data download. The cost of modems will also come down overtime. So far Internet has three kinds of modem connections, dial on connection through telephone modem, ISDN cable modem, and DSL and wireless Wi-fi connection.

Ethnotronic Technologies

People from a variety of disciplines have produced a substantial body of research addressing the issues related to supportive-ethnotronic and advancement of a specific technology from a wide range of analytical perspectives. For instance, decades after their introduction, video systems (supportive-ethnotronic technology of TV) are beginning to realize their potential in supporting working from home, teaching and learning at a distance, conferencing, and interpersonal communication. In the face of upsurge of this developing interest in video technology - the questions are being asked: what functions does video really serve? What advantage does it provide over the telephone? How and why the video-mediated interaction is different from face to face interaction? How can we best configure video technology to support different kind of work at a distance? What is the future role of video technology? These kinds of pertinent questions are equally true for other technologies as they are advancing into many functions.

The focus of *fourth communication revolution* has been on computer through invention of silicon chips and telecommunication revolution through integrated technologies.

Computers

Computers in 80s revolutionized the communication scenario and changed media technology perspectives. Computerization converged with other technologies has created information revolution.

In computers the important hardware technologies involved are chips technology and Modem technology. Software technology develops on the use of various computer languages, software packages, and the services as Internet, Fax, e-mail etc.

Microchip innovations: The computer chips have come far ahead through research and development in the last decade. The chip innovations have been targeting at the size of the chip; smaller the chip better it enables software designers to put formerly separate functions on a single chip. Such feats of integration are allowing such innovations as digital cameras and advanced video games. Computer chipmakers use fine lenses and etching materials to miniaturize them. Designers can use smaller chips, expand capability, and cram more circuitry on each chip. The Wavelt based compression chips would work five or ten times more efficiently. MPEG-2 compression allows for faster processing. The next generation video-encoding method – i.e. compression algorithms that take snapshot of an entire image, then look at eliminating the redundancies across a much larger amount of data. With chip innovations, credit cards will be getting smarter with features such as touch-sensitive fingerprint identification. Chips are making many of our technologies work whether it is credit card, cell phone, your car giving voice directions for destinations, and many more. It is like the third revolution of transistors in 50s.

The computers and the consumer electronic industries are always looking for new storage media that can hold more software programs, data, and entertainment contents. The focus has been on producing computers with more memory, more storage and faster speed. Innovations in computer chips have facilitated that. The computer revolution evolved from bigger computers to desktop personal computers and on to laptops. Laptops are getting slimmer and less in weight. In less than a decade computers have become ubiquitous as the prices became affordable and become an integrated part of everyday life when its applications opened more opportunities for business, information and entertainment.

Intel discovery (2004) of using silicon to make optical components is a development that could significantly reduce the price in high-speed data communication. It has fabricated a silicon modulator – a device needed to send data down fiber-optic cabling that operates at a speed of one gigahertz; that is roughly 50 times faster than the devices made so far with silicon. Modulators encode data onto beams of light, essentially switching light from a laser on and off. These are typically made from materials using iridium phosphide, lithium niobate and gallium arsenide. These are costly materials to produce in large volumes. Researchers have been trying for years to replace these materials with silicon. This effort is called 'silicon photonics'.

Intel claims of reaching one gigahertz — which roughly translated in ability to send one billion bits a second down a single glass fiber provides evidence that eventually companies could use such components in commercial networking products. Researchers are confident that speed of 10 gigahertz could be achieved using Intel's techniques. Products based on Intel's research are at least several years away from the market.

Intel's Bulverde chip and Texas Instruments Wanda chip are about to be launched. They have showcased it in GSM World Congress at Cannes in March 2004. Its embedded software is being installed in handsets and PDAs waiting for air trials and other statutory tests prior to a commercial launch by the end of 2004.

The Chip has the wireless multimedia (WMMX) instruction

set, which means that one instruction operates on multimedia blocks allowing parallel processing. The PSS solution allows for higher processing speed while using lower MIPs, thereby using less power.

Computer software is the main ingredient — the integral component in the hardware computer to make it work. In the last two decades computer software technology has progressed variously in its applications. Newer software is written for tasks in different domains from business to medical facilities, to running e-mail to blocking the spam mail and anti virus protection etc. or even running the washing machine. Without our realizing computerization has become an essential part of our lives like pen and writing.

Software has always played a big role in getting voice and data from one place to the next. But the proprietary programs that were built into the networking hardware itself have now escaped those boxes and landed on computer servers running standard operating systems such as Windows NT and Unix. The first step in this direction came two decades ago, when services such as toll-free calling were first run through computers connected to the phone networks. But today software is more powerful because of change brought on by shift to Internet Protocol and data traffic. In essence the computing world – where software drives most functions – has invaded the traditional telecommunication landscape, and it is taking over.

The result is that the gear makers are able to add more sophisticated features to their products faster, and operators can upgrade their services without having to spend large amounts to change their hardware. 40% of telecom operators' expenditure is related to software as compared to 30% for hardware. Software has become the silent partner for everything. For instance, Swedish equipment giant Telefon AB L.M. Ericsson has shifted many of the features which used to be part of its AXE switching hardware, which controls the traffic on voice and data networks, to server-based software. Those systems include basic system-level call control and other services such as call waiting, call forwarding, and management of virtual private networks. Lucent Technologies Inc has recently put a product *Softswitch*. It is a software-based system that performs many of the functions of traditional hardware switches for IP networks.

The real interest of moving to software is that it lets telecom and networking companies quickly add new features that would have been impossible before. Unified messaging is a good example. The server-based system can route wireless and fixed lines voice calls, e-mails, faxes, and wireless-data messages to wherever a user is located. These systems employ sophisticated computer technologies to pull off high-tech tricks like dialing a user's mobile telephone and reading urgent e-mails to him when he is away from his desk.

The equipment makers think new server-based e-commerce features they are planning to integrate into their networks will be even more impressive. The analysts predict that the shift to standard software will allow start-up developers to get their own innovative products into the ring and let them work across different manufacturers' gear.

The economic argument for software-based features is also powerful. The cost of new switching hardware has not dropped nearly as quickly as the prices of the computer-servers and software. So in order to save money and hassle the telephone companies would rather hold on to the old switches when they can add new functions by upgrading their software. This is true, given the breakneck pace of technology advances these days.

In addition, the shift to server based software and IP standards is opening the door for newer, smaller entrants to compete with the equipment makers on their own turf.

There is move to add on Linux open source software in addition to windows software by Microsoft. Linux does not cost much and it can reduce the cost for many computer applications not only for businesses but it also make many of these applications affordable for poor developing countries. Versions of Linux have already become commonplace in products such as handheld computers and cell phones. One of the main promoters of Linux for consumer electronics and industrial applications has been MontaVista software Inc in California whose investors include Intel Corp and IBM. Linux's underlying programming can be customized for different uses.

Hardware markets also like Linux because it comes in versions that do not require them to pay continuing royalty for each device they sell. They need to pay royalty if they use Microsoft software.

Unlike Psion which produced Palmtop organizer in 1980s; the Microsoft entry into the world of Palmtop computing began only in 1995. Following the huge success of palm-pilot — the tiny organizer that uses a plastic pen instead of keyboard; Microsoft enlisted another eight manufacturers to make a competing version of a similar unit. Other supportive devices for computerization such as floppy disks and CD for storage data, and Mouse for operations have also gone through innovations and have improved functionality.

As computerization is advancing in its applications, computer security is posing problems by fraudulent e-mail. The efforts are intensified to find software solutions for it; and explore ways to thwart data theft and span. There is one rapidly spreading scam known as 'phishing', computer users are fooled into revealing credit-card numbers and other confidential information by e-mail that appears to come from legitimate banks or Internet-commerce sites. Corporate users are also targeted by bogus e-mails that may appear to come from internal security administrators, asking them to reveal password information. This could allow hackers to crack into corporate computer system.

Safeguarding computer information is becoming a hotter topic. In this context a few solutions are being proposed (2004). One proposed solution dubbed SPF — sender permitted form is based on publishing the Internet-protocol numbers of computers that have been authorized to send mail in their names. That way recipient can check mail against those numbers, known as IP addresses to check for falsified identities. Another approach called 'PassMark' security uses images to help identify legitimate web sites. Users are assigned a random image the first time they come to a site that uses the PassMark system; and would be shown that image on subsequent visits before entering their user name and password. If users do not see the right image, they know the site is false. Microsystems Inc is suggesting use of smart card or special security tokens that can help protect web sites and better identify senders of e-mail to reduce spam and fraud. VeriSign Inc has offered technology to help protect e-commerce transactions; is announcing technical guidelines to make it less costly to use smart cards and other strong forms of identification. It is working with IBM, BEA systems Inc and Gemplus international SA on 'open authentication system — OATH', to help companies create online identification products that work with each other with little extra programming.

Another solution proposed help to mange the way users log on to multiple corporate applications and ensure that they can tap only certain files. Another solution helps screen corporate e-mail to prevent company insiders from sending confidential information, a capability not including in conventional 'firewall' programs that companies use to block external attack. Other companies are now offering technology for protecting instant-messaging from eavesdropping. These solutions are being tested and would be available soon.

Computer has become an integrated technology for other technologies to usher. Without it many of the newer technology applications, devices, and innovations will be handicapped.

People have been concerned about the impact of television, video, Internet and even calculators in schools. These or any other technologies have positive and negative repercussions. Much depends on the extent of their utilization.

Soni Tara (2004) from her interview protocols of parents and school kids surmise that there are some legitimate concerns also about the use of computers in schools; where the school kids are exposed even at the age of five years. True, kids thus exposed are sharper and more knowledgeable than their parental generation. They are exposed to global ways and happenings through Internet and search engines.

There are three concerns:

Concern 1: The concerns are whether too much exposure of kids to 'virtual world' will turn them into couch potatoes and opting for less reading and minimal socialization. Also there is concern if kids rely on computers for their search to solving problems they may not sharpen their mental faculties.

Even they may shun writing with hands! These concerns were true for calculators and television exposure at one time.

Concern 2: The computers have changed the way we live and work. They have become vital part of our lives and work, schools and businesses. Now every one uses computer technology on a daily basis. Many people think this is good thing and computers have made our lives and jobs easier. Others believe that computers are not so great. That is because in some industries computers may be taking jobs away from people. Workers are concerned that someday robots will replace them. Do you think computers should replace people, or they are just a valuable resource that we can all work with?

Concern 3: Expression Vs Regulation. We have the right to speak our minds, even if the words are hateful or distasteful to some. The freedom of speech is guaranteed by Constitution.

The Internet raises new questions about our right to 'free speech'. People post words, pictures on line to exchange information and seek response. These words and pictures are stored in huge databases, available to anyone who has the technology and is able to find them. Parental concern about what is found online and the ease with which children can find inappropriate material are very real.

Although the Internet service providers reserve the right to disconnect people who abuse their services, some people feel that controls on language and topics are too loose. These people want tighter controls and more government regulation. Other people argue that free speech should apply to the Internet just as it does to newspapers, television and other media.

With which position do you agree?

Fourth revolution focused also on telecommunication that was stimulated and advanced by advance wireless and cellular technology and advancement in computerization. Telegraph, telephone and cell and wireless technology and computer are the four main pillars of telecommunication.

More than a century ago a seed was planted in the spirit of bringing world closer together. The seed prospered - growing to shape the way people interact with each other in global telecommunication. Telegraph and telephone gave people means to communicate and help people stay in touch. People were exposed to landline telephones a century and halfback after its invention. It took many decades to develop variety of features and applications both in hardware and usage. Also lots of efforts have been put since then to increase the telephone density all over the world. Landline improved in its many services including long distance within the country and internationally which provided world-wide connectivity. It also added many technical features to improve on voice quality and products — from rotary to push button phones, and delivery of services. Initially, landline telephones were concentrated mainly in the urban areas particularly in developing countries. Rural areas had no telephone connectivity. In decades of 80s India made efforts to develop rural telephone exchange but it was not implemented in majority of the villages. It only remained at experiment stage.

In developing countries including India the landline telephone density has been very low till 90s. The copper wire telephone system invented by Alexander Graham Bell has gone through tremendous innovations. During the past few decades these innovations have changed the Graham Bell system to fiber optic cables, satellites, wireless telephone technology, cellular technology and now to Internet telephony — VOIP (voice over Internet Protocol) technology. Though the decades of 90s and 2000 have been the fastest in innovations in telecommunications. It is still an ongoing process. Decades of 80s onwards have been the revolutionary period for telephones. People are enjoying Wireless and Cellular telephones. As part of global activities, the advanced global telecommunication network is bringing people closer together.

People's needs for reliable means for communicating over long distances increased as society grew in complexity. Hudson (1997) writes that four major technological trends — capacity, digitalization, ubiquity, and convergence are driving the current telecommunication revolution, which parallels the emergence of a global economy. Investment in telecommunication revolution itself can contribute to economic, social, and political development. Reliable telecommunication could improve agriculture, industries, and social services.

Various research studies of World Bank, and the Maitland Commission (1994) have all pointed out to the telecommunication-produced benefits across the spectrum of development activities. Hanson & Narula (1990) endorsed these benefits for developing country of India.

The wireless and cell telecommunication technology has been revolutionary and the development of its infrastructure as well the hardware and software components of telephones have been revolutionary. In the following sections we have intentionally presented an expanded scenario of innovations in both these areas to familiarize the readers with the ongoing fast changes and also to give them ideas about how price wars and competition have been stimulating the new products and services world-wide. Further, this helps them to assess the revolutionary impact of these technologies on people's life style and businesses.

Wireless and Cellular Technology

The first automatic analog cellular phone was made in the 1960s. Commercial models were introduced in Japan by NTT on December 3, 1979. They were introduced in Scandinavia in 1981, in Chicago, USA, on October 13, 1983 (by Motorola), and in Europe in the late 1980s, and in late 90s in India. Early mobile FM (frequency modulation radio was invented by Edwin H. Armstrong in 1935) radio telephones had been in use in the USA since 1946, but since the number of radio frequencies are very limited in any area, the number of phone calls was also very limited. Only a dozen or two calls could be made at the same time in an area. To solve this problem, there could be many small areas (called cells) which share the same frequencies. But when users moved from one area to another while calling, the call would have to be switched over automatically without losing the call. In this system, a small number of radio frequencies could accommodate a huge number of calls. A team of researchers at Bell Labs devised this cellular phone concept in 1947, but there were no computers available to do the switching. As small inexpensive computers were developed, cell phones could be produced. Motorola holds the US patents for the cell phone. Henry Taylor Sampson and George H. Miley hold a 1968 patent on a "gamma electric cell," which is not a component of cellular phones

Brace yourself for a New World. The communication may never be the same. It is wireless. The cord is cut; there are no wires. In New World, the invisible communication-network grid in every metropolitan area, link workers inside office buildings and warehouses, surround the earth via flotillas of satellites. It is a world in which wireless devices combine the functions of telephone and computers, sending and receiving voice, text and graphics and sifting through rims of information on behalf of their human masters. In this New World, we are reachable any time ——— any place. The cellular phone is on the scene. But before this, cordless telephone was the first application of wireless phones.

The changing communication scenario gives a sense that telecommunication revolution is a volcano ready to erupt though in some ways it has already erupted.

The wireless vision is possible because of advances in technology of microchips and software that helps in building wireless networks. For years, the technology and costs have conspired to ensure that most communication flow through wires and the gadget that we communicate through such as phones, faxes, computers etc. were tethered to wires. The advance technology is making wireless technology vision come true and is proving the achievement of cellular phone, worldwide wireless satellite system, and personal communication services etc.

Microchips and software technology developments have allowed miniaturization of the cellular phones, driving down prices, and driving up performances. Another breakthrough is the moving cellular technology from analog to digital. This greatly speeds up the traffic and it is also free from static interference and transmission errors.

Everyday in decade of 2000, more and more new features of geo mobility and message access are being provided on cell phones. There is stiff competition even in developing countries both for its hardware and software. This has brought down the prices of both cell services and cell phones and increasing consumers. Thus cell phones are becoming an essential part of life of consumers and they are ubiquitous rather than status symbol in these countries. SMS messages on cell are useful, cost effective and are boon to the hearing disabled.

The Internet on cell phone is likely to have a huge appeal; but surfing the Web on the phone is impractical on the tiny screen. So designers have come up with a micro browser that let the users surf for information by pressing a number on the dialing pad instead of fumbling with a computer mouse. Typing e-mail (on phone screen) is a hassle even with the latest technology; voice recognition software will enable users to dictate directly to their cell phones.

Cellular technology has great telecommunication potentialities. Cellular phones are expected to grow worldwide usage to nearly 100 millions by the year 2000 and increasing substantially in years in developing countries because of accessibility and affordability. More and more developing countries are introducing cellular phones with new features suiting to their consumers' indigenous needs. They could bring down to affordable prices and accessibility and thus add on millions of consumers and with stiff competition from many players in the field due to liberalized government telecom policies in these countries and less restrictions for import of technology.

Cell phones have added applications from sending SMS to e-mail. It is keyboard, camcorder, TV, videogame, MP3Player, camera, and etch-a-sketch and GPS (providing location information for emergency calls). The new software development has exploited the possibility of video, sound, messaging, and color screen technology. Even with these new applications cell phones are becoming smaller and smaller in size.

Pagers blanket the world in many places as a substitute for inadequate or non-existent telephones services. About more than five millions are in use in China and India currently and consumers for cellular telephones and pagers are likely to go up day by day because of better connectivity and affordable prices and easy availability. This can be evidenced by explosion of cellular phones, pagers, portable computers, e-mail users, and Internet subscribers. Market researchers and people in general have spent a lot of time thinking about all other possibilities of powerful networks and powerful devices. But the uses are limitless. (Narula Technology revisited: India case study 2003).

Consumers are ready to pay great deal of money for these; for people want mobility and access to messages and data. This can be evidenced by explosion of cellular phones, pagers, portable computers, e-mail users, and Internet subscribers. Market researchers and people in general have spent a lot of time thinking about all other possibilities of powerful networks and powerful devices. But the uses are limitless. A corporation may track 40,000 trucks via satellite constantly monitoring their locations and even engine conditions or a wireless system for vending machines to talk to a computer at headquarters ordering more goods or reporting vandalism.

In fact the big Corporates (Motorola for one) worldwide plans to sell the idea to the masses that anything that has a switch including car engines can be turned off and off by wireless network.

At the same time wireless world may create hostile environment for those who have invested billions in outmoded technology and now must invest billions to convert to digital transmissions or take over the PCs Networks.

Similarly retailers, distributors, store services will be outmoded when 'virtual stores' can be shopped on a wireless device through e-commerce. What need is there for a film distribution company when it can rent a space on a satellite network to beam a new movie to 3000 theaters?

Eventually the devices and networks will be ubiquitous and the ultimate effect will increase the pace of the society, liberating people from physical constraints of time and space. Wireless servants and alter egos will do much of the communication that we do now while we are doing something else somewhere.

Telephones. In 1874 the first transatlantic cable was laid between Ireland and USA. It could carry 22 messages at one time and it carried the world into new era of communications.

Siemens Corporation first manufactured this cable. In 1994 the digital telephone switch (also manufactured by Siemens) handles 1000000 calls an hour. It can even carry data, text, and voice simultaneously on a single line. These voice and data solutions help both large corporations and small businesses improve productivity.

The smart phone allows Web surfing, e-mail access, faxing and even includes a speakerphone. Smart-phone era has dawned. Nokia began selling 9110 Communicator to Europe in 1998. It is a second-generation device about the size of a large mobile phone with a flip-top computer screen, capable of composing faxes, sending and reading e-mail, and accessing the Internet. Alcatel, the French company is already marketing the 'one touch Com' which has taken all the functions of a palm-size organizer installed in a mobile handset and small enough to slip in a shirt pocket.

The landline phones that plug into your walls are also getting snazzy Internet features. The iphone from Cidco features a 6'' by 4-1/2'' screen which users can use to check e-mail, and surf the web without ever booting the personal computers.

Despite offering cool features, the makers of smart phones have yet to figure out the exact combination of features, size, and price that will make millions of users see the new devices as must-haves.

Nokia and other companies are trying to create devices that synchronize easily with PCs. With Nokia's 9110 communicator in Europe and in USA, users will be able to move information between phone and PC by simply dropping the phone in a cradle on the PC and pressing a button. Qualcomm Inc with 3Com Corp the maker of palm-pilot is developing a phone that combines the functions of PDA and a mobile phone in a single gadget. Nokia communicator 9500 Wi-Fi (wireless local area) network compatible will be available in 2004.

The perception that devices need to be cheaper has driven several phone makers for less expensive models. The phones use a special browser developed by Unwired Planet Inc Calif. It works on 40 or so sites which pair down their data to run with the browser. At the moment standard websites are virtually unreadable at that size. A new version of the browser expected soon would have technology that will make these pages easier to read.

Currently phone companies have an interest in promoting other services such as caller ID, call waiting, and three-way calling. Special electronic commerce phones are proving popular. Nortel is testing it in conjunction with several Canadian banks and international smart card companies. These phones allow consumers to access their bank accounts and add money to smart cards from homes.

Geowork Corp which make software for Nokia 9000i says studies indicate that 85% of the consumers use mobile phones for making calls, eschewing address books, and other useful features. All the other functionality is too difficult to use. Our aim is to develop easier-to-use phone; it is not changing the functionality but giving people a graphical. In the beginning cellular engineers aimed for too much channel capacity at the expense of voice quality. They were compressing speech too soon, looking to grow capacity over conventional networks by a factor of 10 instead of 5. The first generation cellular phones miscoded background noise in a car or in a street corner. The phone would actually turn the noises into voices that led to 'warbling'. First generation digital cellular used eight-bit technology, while newer systems today used 16 bits or higher. The more bit of computer code used, the more information calls can transmit for full faith reproduction. The most critical mission is to synchronize various components of sound reproduction so that high quality multimedia transmission will be possible by phone or computer network.

The joint venture called Symbian (joint venture of Nokia, Motorola, Ericsson) intends license Psion's software for new generation of smart devices ranging from mobile phones that receive e-mail, surf the Internet, and even pay for transactions; to laptop computers that can go online automatically without anyone having to open the carrying case. The battle between Symbian and Microsoft is not who will make next era's cool gadgets but who will control the next era of personal computers.

European companies have triumphed over American for mobile phones. Whereas the European computer maker such as Britain's Amigo, France Bull, Italy's Olivetti are crushed by American competition. Also European use more of mobile phones and Americans are hooked more on computers at home and in offices. One reason is Europe's more cooperative approach to technical issues: In 1991 manufacturers, network operators, and regulators all agreed on a single digital standard called GSM (global system for mobile communications). It spread quickly to Hongkong, Australia, etc. This gave Europe a competitive edge in the global market place. The US companies chose a variety of incompatible standards that made it hard to use a single phone while traveling from New York to Los Angeles or from Boston to Bombay. The fact that European companies have the volume benefit of a standard applied in more than 100 countries gave a kick to the whole industry and lowered risks.

Two other marketing innovations have helped boost demand in Europe. Phone companies there quickly realized that people would leave their call phone switched on longer if the cost of the call was paid by the caller and not by the receiver of the mobile call. The opposite of the system is common in USA and India. The US economists realize that the US business model - subsidizing the cost of the phone handset in order to lure customers to sign up for the service is less appealing to consumers than an approach by which customers pay full price for the phone set but get cheaper talk time.

Once the preserve of business users, cell phone has become everyday consumer appliance — even a fashion accessory, a status symbol in Asian countries. Alcatel claims to have 10% of the world phone market with cheap handset available in rainbow colors. Nokia reports half of its (Finland's) population about 5.1 million uses mobile phone to manage their daily lives in 1998. It is assumed that 100% market penetration will be achieved in the next five years.

Since 2000, cell phones by many big players in the field connect India heavily. It has added many indigenous applications and features in the cell phone services. This has made cell phones affordable and useful in India. Even a roaming real estate agent or a car mechanic or a plumber would own cell phone since it would give them better connectivity with their customers. They find it cost effective and useful. Even rural areas closer to the cellular range use cell phones. In many of these areas even landlines are not connected. Cell phones have become so ubiquitous that landline is pushed into the background for household or for businesses. The roaming (within the country) feature on the cell has greatly facilitated the connectivity for the businesses.

The prepaid calling cards, both for domestic long distance and international calls and cheap mobile phones, have made markets grow worldwide. In Israel children have got some 200,000 units of a phone known as 'Mango'. It can only ring one specific phone number. Sven Christer Nilsson President of Ericsson observed (1998) that it has taken 120 years from Alexander Graham Bell's invention of the conventional telephone to wire up one billion customers worldwide. Current estimates of mobile operators suggest same number to be achieved by 2005 for mobile phones.

Symbian a joint venture of Nokia, Ericsson, and Motorola are planning to use Psion operating system EPOC as the basis for the smart phones. So far only Philips has licensed Psion software for smart phone. Ericsson Vice President Jan Ahrenbring (1998) adds that Microsoft operating system was not actually applicable for mobile. But Microsoft maintains that its software is modular and can be customized to suit customers' needs.

In addition to Symbion, telecommunication industry has formed two other alliances to improve the usability of wireless devices. One of them WAP forum (wireless applications protocol) is designing special browsers to being Internet data to mobile phones. The second group Bluetooth is trying to set a universal standard for radio communication between smart devices like palm computers and mobile phones. Microsoft has not joined either group.

Finland offers some interesting insights into some of these devices sideshows. At the Helsinki airport, a coke-wending machine has a mobile number instead of coin slot — dial up the machine and a coke drops out with the charge appearing on your phone bill. Similar practices are spreading across

Europe. In Italy, operator Omnitel let users call a special number while standing in front of designated piazzas; the computer figures out where you are and plays back a recorded discourse on the art and history of the location in one of the five languages. Soon an advertiser like McDonald will be able to send a data message to every mobile phone at football stadium urging their owners to eat a Big Mac at half time. Or a pedestrian walking past a car showroom might receive a message inviting him inside for a special deal. Though people feel some of these features will intrude on their privacy.

The third generation of mobile phones will switch on around 2003 resulting in real sprint for technological superiority. For this, European and Japanese have agreed on a technical standard called Wideband Code — Division Multiple Access (DMA) as the successor to GSM. Probably Qualcomm USA will adopt different standard from Europe and Asia.

The vision of the future may be: Hand-held computer makers could offer machines made with Symbian's software in the hope of making them more appealing to consumers with mobile phones. Or the mobile phone industry could adopt Window CE to ensure that their devices link easily with existing desktop PCs. That depends how the battle between Microsoft and Symbian is resolved. But likelihood is Europe will be communicating with a single standard.

"Watch out Bill Gates: Europeans are getting a jump on the next information revolution. A British company Psion is giving brains to new mobile phones that receive e-mail, surf the Internet, and can even pay for transactions".

The satellite phones - The super cell phones. The Iridium Consortium and rival joint ventures are closing on their goal of making sat-phones into multibillion-dollar mainstays of the Info-superhighway. (Material is based on — High Flying phones by Charles P. Wallace, *Times,* Sept. 28, 1998).

In consequence to Nokia's 9110 communicator, Nokia is bringing into the market Communicator 9500 - Wi-Fi (wireless local area) compatible handsets. The Wi-Fi chips are built-in the handsets. It will be able to bypass conventional cell phone networks, but still access the web and even make phone calls using the Wi-Fi (wireless local area) network. Key to its operation are 'hot spots' within 300 ft of a Wi-Fi base station connected to the Internet by a fixed line. Its limitation is that people will be able to use the Wi-Fi function within a hot spot. At present consumer needs a specially equipped laptop or a personal organizer to use these hot spots. Communicator 9500 set will be a threat to other cell operators who were trying to sell data wireless services such as web browsing and e-mail (March 2004).

Wi-Fi uses unlicensed spectrum meaning any property owner can offer wireless Internet access in the proximity of their premises. Today cell phone operators can largely access the content delivered over their networks. But media companies using Wi-Fi networks can sell video clips and music to mobile phone users without any intervention by an operator.

Nokia and other cell phone manufacturers hope that this feature would spur consumers to replace handsets and that would boost the cell phone industries. Nokia faces competition from Motorola and other cell phone manufacturers to get Wi-Fi compatible sets in the market by year-end. Nokia intends retailing it for $1013. It would be several years before they are commonplace.

Airplane phone: The airplane phone is an incredible concept. They have the constraints of poor connections, poor sound quality, lack of privacy, and exorbitant rates. There are potentialities and promises for air phones in the next generation. There may be service where through calling a central number in the plane will locate you and the phone at your seat will ring. Eventually air phones will be cheaper than today.

In the 'virtual office' in the sky where business fliers send and receive faxes, plug in their laptops and select and watch videos. Even some of the airlines provide TV monitor in front of every seat; not only you watch video but you can surf the Internet also on these monitors.

Analog ground stations used by most airplanes installed in 80s are outdated in its capabilities. Analog calls are full of interference of air whooshing, noise, and getting disconnected when moving away from the range of one ground station to the next. Now in-flight phone companies are converting its analog system to digital or going directly to digital system skipping the analog phase.

Digital phone systems will translate sound into electronic pulses that register in ground station computers as zeros and ones. A 'call hand off' will pass the pulses from one ground station to another. A 'Doppler effect' detect when the signal is weakening, the system than begin phoning the next ground station to transfer the call when the airplane gets close enough. The most important is before the calls get disconnected; this sophisticated technology can switch calls back and forth between ground stations when necessary.

A second big advantage of the digital technology is its ability to screen out background noise. The ground station computers are programmed to recognize voices as opposed to things like static and whooshing. Similarly ground computers are programmed to recognize word patterns. If there is a blip, they will fill in synthesized voice thus making up broken conversations whole again. This brings up two concerns about digital: synthetic voice gives a metallic quality and the technology causes the kind of voice delay that makes many users uncomfortable.

The concept of global cellular communication using intermediate-circular-orbit, and low-earth-orbit offer a hope for rural communication for rural areas in developing countries. Four mobile satellite operators — Globalstar, odyssey, Iridium, and Immarsat ICO are developing such systems to offer a global system by 2000. (The APT yearbook 1997) the current cost of such global cellular is beyond the reach of rural folks.

Personal Communication Services (PCS). This is another kind of micro-cellular digital network, which use low power and high frequency radio waves. Current cellular transmissions move from cell to cell geo unit. Each of which is equipped with high-powered transmitter. Micro cells will be much smaller, allowing phones to use less power and smaller batteries thus reducing the size and cost. Low power also means the ability to use the entire frequency all over again in each micro cell transmission area. PCS networks will be twenty times as efficient as existing cellular analog systems and provide much better services and quality.

In the 2000 decade another feat of integration of technologies will occur. Cellular phones and pagers will exist on single microchips making them extraordinary cheap and capable, being built into a single device. This will be possible when the functions and capabilities of cellular phones, pagers, faster microprocessors, color screens and more powerful batteries are blended together.

World wide wireless satellite system. This system would beam voice, data, fax, or physical location from a small handset, anywhere in the world to anywhere (Motorola Iridium phone). Transmitters as small as bricks are developed that can be hung from utility (electrical) poles, creating wireless networks inside buildings, on campuses, and in downtown areas. Soon there will be credit size wireless modems that will easily slip into handheld communicators and portable computers.

Tech-savvy consumers have 'an affinity' for the benefits that advance products provide. Technology related multinational companies come up with the offerings. This approach is categorized in two. First, is the repositioning and repackaging of the existing technology to cater to individual needs. An example is prototype-messaging center IBM is working on, which lets consumers' access computer information in the kitchen. The second part includes technology that does not yet exist, but consumers have expressed interest in that, such as the transmission of high-speed data on power lines.

It is advocated that development and deployment of open-source software should be encouraged, as appropriate open standard for ICT. 2004 year can be a true broadband era. Broadband is through analog, DSL and cable modem. Internet is being casted as multimedia platform with a flexible data expecting maximum connecting through broadband.

Internet telephoning is a bright spot in the telecom world because it is more cost efficient method of transmitting voice calls. Earlier, users needed to speak into microphone attached to a computer to make an Internet call, but today most of these calls originate from ordinary phones. Many phone companies sell Internet based services and sell pre-paid phone cards also. Though the sound quality of the Internet based calls do not match that of standard calls but the service is growing and improving. It is still (in 2004) in infancy mode and is being protected by governments to encourage it.

A new Internet based phone technology known as VOIP or voice over Internet protocol is available since early 2003. Telecom expert says, most business people will convert to VOIP for cost saving and wide range of new features the technology will offer, such as improved conference calling, and combining voice and e-mail messages on one directory and eventually video phone. This technology could make dramatic changes the way businesses operate comparable to those by the Internet and the PC.

VOIP works by transforming voice into data and then transmitting over the Internet or some other data network in the same way text, photos and e-mail are sent. Introduced in mid-90s, this new technology overpromised and underdelivered creating frustrations for early adopters and huge losses for investors. Some of the earliest businesses that installed VOIP were critical of the sound quality. Enough improvement has been made now to let businesses install it now as a way of increasing efficiency and productivity and cutting costs.

VOIP can make a wide range of existing phone features easier to use because when voice turned into data, it is essentially another application on the computer. Features can also be combined with other data applications. For instance voice mail and e-mail can be combined in a single directory. Another plus for VOIP is their portability. VOIP phones with a particular number can be taken anywhere, connected to a broadband connection and still receives call at the same number. Moving employees from one location to another can use this efficiently. There are savings on the long-distance calls for businesses, given VOIP calls between the offices cost the same as sending e-mail. VOIP phone systems are proving useful for businesses that rely heavily on roving employees like a hotel, or a warehouse. VOIP is also making big changes in call centers. In some cases enabling companies to replace big centralized facilities with virtual operations.

Businesses can expect a wide range of new features. Major telecom companies and startups are busy developing new software that will incorporate videophone, voice recognition, wireless technology and other applications in the VOIP system.

A battle is heating up in phone industry over the growing number of voice calls sent over the Internet, pitting local phone companies against long-distance providers. Issue is whether long-distance companies pay the local phone companies access fees. Since the carriers generally do not own the lines that go into homes and businesses. They are not ready to pay for transmitting Internet calls to customers. It will be potentially more destructive to the Internet to charge full access fees on basic Internet voice calling, particularly when the technology is in its infancy. The other questions are: whether these new services need to pay to local telephone companies to complete the calls to conventional phones? Whether such calls should be subject to the same fees as regular telephone service? The feeling is that this new technology should be lightly regulated.

There are ongoing debates for legislation of VOIP. The questions posed are:

1. Should local government regulate and tax any communication between two individuals?
2. Should we discourage the use of broadband networks for fast, reliable and cheap communications because a new technology does not fit into existing regulatory slot?
3. Should regulations discriminate between two data files simply because one carries instant messaging and other someone's voice?

Today these issues have become practical, substantive questions that will make or break the implementation of VOIP. It generates significant network efficiencies, reduces capital expenditures, and produces considerable cost savings.

Supporters of VOIP to protect this new technology advocate that it should be treated as an information service. The broadband cable, DSL or high speed line that you are using does not care whether data packaged using the Internet protocol is spread sheet, e-mail, instant message or voice traffic. There exist no sound basis for discriminating among different types of data. Would anyone argue that e-mail, power point presentations should be differently taxed than VOIP. Secondly, it will be costly and unnecessary burden on a country's communication network to regulate a global network that transcends country's boundaries. Thirdly, VOIP as a data service should be protected from taxation.

Other innovation would offer high-speed Internet access over electrical power lines. Web's new outlet is household power line. So far we have dial-up, cable, DSL and broadband outlets. The idea of using power lines has been around for years. It is based on the fact that electricity travels at a far lower frequency than the Internet signal, so the two generally do not interfere. But earlier results were disappointments because of equipment needed and technical issues.

Two years ago there was a breakthrough for the modem called Home-Plug. This has to be plugged into the wall sockets to bring the Internet into homes. Another technical issue has been how to get the Internet signal through the transformers that step the power down from the medium voltage, which runs along the street, to low voltage that goes into homes. Current communications have solved this problem with a 'bridge' that skips the transformer, allowing the signal to go through uninterrupted. The technology is ready for prime time. This outlet is being offered initially in early 2004 as an experiment to wrinkle out the product and service problems and would be available at a larger scale at the end of year. This innovative service could help spread high speed Internet in rural and inner-city areas of the country that are not wired for Internet.

We observe that modes, types of channel are the same. The concept is the same but it is getting complex and more people oriented and adding further interaction complexity of non-human communication process, form, and focus.

In the 2000 decade Internet telephony – VOIP is being marketed.

Can optical chips replace telecom gear? The goal is to replace bulky telecommunication gear with devices the size of a quarter that combines lasers routers, receivers, and other devices commonly used in fiber-optic networks. Simple optical chips are in the market but they are not as nearly sophisticated as chips inside a personal computer whose processor contains billions of transistors. Still the technology is advancing fast and in five years mass-produced versions can slash the cost of voice and data networks and could eventually become a new gateway to deliver high-bandwidth movies, music and games directly to homes. The possibility of miniature optical circuits has drawn interests from computer-chip manufacturers. If telecommunications components can be manufactured from optical chips than computer-processor performance may double. Developments in optical chips may add intelligence and reduce cost.

Optical chips are not a new idea. In 1969 Bell Lab engineer Stewart E. Miller envisioned, 'guiding laser beams on miniature transmission lines' using the same manufacturing methods as for integrated circuits. But due to technical challenges, his ideas were goals rather than accomplishments. Today, many of those issues are solved but still real product is still challenging.

In 90s the world was going through *fifth communication revolution* of digitalization supported by computerizations resulting from the convergence of communication satellites. It exploded the information revolution and changed media technology perspective in information, entertainment and business by introducing new devices and new modes of communications.

Digitalization

Digitalization converts all information — text, sound, and pictures into binary codes that can promptly travel through a global network of computers linked by telephones, fiber optics, and satellites. Miniaturization has been the driving force in the digital revolution, yielding faster, smaller and better computers every year.

Digital Media: Entertainment plus Technology

The technologies have changed the way we act and interact. The growing integration between digital devices and the widespread use of Internet and wireless communications have altered the way we view personal computing, entertainment, shopping, gaming, banking and financial services, information access and much more. The threads of information technology reach us through our society and across globe. Both desktop and laptop computers, PDAs (personal digital assistants) and smart phones are everywhere. Today, it is tough to imagine a world without e-mail, web pages, wireless communications and on-the go presentation.

We had VCR since 70's and CD in early 80's, and digitalization began with CD. The other products are DVD (digital videodisk), Web TV, digital television, and Dolby digital sound system. DVIX (digital video express) is a DVD player with additional encryption technology in a 'modem' that allows you to buy disk whenever you want and when you want to watch it. For years CD or compact disk both in its common audio format and CD-ROM variant used in personal computers have been in the market. The new type of storage disk is called DVD which first meant Digital Video Disk now relabeled as Digital Versatile Disk. They also come in two forms DVD for consumer electronic playback and DVD-ROM for use in PCs. Unlike videotape both formats are digital. They store text, graphics, video and audio in the formats computers can read. DVD are constructed and encoded differently and can hold material seven times more than a CD. The technology permits with two layers of data on them, totaling 8.5 gigabytes, and even greater capacity in the future.

Both DVD players and DVD-ROM drives for personal computers are also designed to be backward compatible. That means they can play music CDs and CD-ROMs so consumers need not discard their old collections. DVD offers many viewing options than videotape. Each movie is divided onto sections or chapters and you can move around according to your choice. You can view the movie in several language options. You will be able to see scenes from various angles. DVD disks do not wear like videotapes and does not need to be rewound. But you cannot record on it. The latest DVDs have more storage space. Earlier computer CDs is read only but now newer CDs allow you both read and write (editing) functions. Digital photography is on the anvil. Digital cameras are in the market. Digital pictures are stored in the camera itself. Its printing is computerized. Interesting point is one can play around with these pictures with background colors and other details the way one wants and original pictures may look different when these are moved around. The printing gives them life like painting quality. These cameras are still expensive for everyone to own.

Digital is setting aside the old analog ways. It may be more efficient. It may allow all sorts of gadgets to do all sorts of tricks. For starters, the wonders of digital come at the expense of clarity and depth. Digital describes things that rely on computing technology to operate. Digital is also the language that unites chips, software, and all computing devices. The ones and zeros of digital codes allow engineer to pack more calls into a radio channel or a beam of light; to record and manipulate sounds and images; and to store all that data into a computer file, on a disk, or chip to replay later. It is efficient, but not enough to satisfy those who work with the technology and many of those who use it.

Take the problems of integrating digital technology into communication networks. Such networks with computerized switches, laser-driven fiber optics and signaling systems, have replaced the old electro-mechanical gear that once required larger number of maintenance and technicians to run the system. The newer digital gear is more efficient, able to handle more calls and data traffic. Digital communication is tough to tap with cell phones and other security features.

Two *driving forces* for digital came about in 60's and 70's as methods were developed in turning information — a sound, a moving image, an odor into binary or digital language of computers. Now much of the discussion about digital technology advance is about how to make connections happen.

Most of the today's advances in digital in consumer electronics are done with an eye towards more connections in the future. Digital technology will change the face of consumer electronics in near future — and the obstacles that each of the products has to overcome.

Just as in the 90's the Internet has changed the ways companies behave internally, and with customers and suppliers. It has changed from relatively obscure network being used by government agencies and colleges to a global library and business tool used by millions.

Digital media are still in their infancy. But the early efforts are beginning to provide hints about what will and what won't work. Soon the digital media from the World Wide Web to 3-D video games, to popular digital technology responsible for popular innovation in audio i.e. separation of sound among five or more speakers, which drive consumers to turn TV watching rooms into home theaters. The personal computer is the product most associated with digital wave. It first brought new productivity and educational tools in the home. Recently, it has become new portal to connect people to Internet. There are still-to-come digital technologies that will exercise a force as pervasive and powerful in our lives as films and television today.

Soft Corder PSS (Pace Soft Silicon) solution is a camcorder application for mobile devices including PDAs and handheld devices, which captures video and audio, playable on devices ranging from mobile phones to windows and Mac personal computers. PSS has optimized the computational efforts, quality of video, network bandwidth, and power consumption of its embedded software product. The soft Corder allows the user of the handset to optimize it, since it allows other functions to run in parallel. For instance if the camcorder is in use, the other functions of phone, browsing does not stop.

These new media will bring us drama and diversions unlike anything we have known. They will change the way we think about entertainment and leisure. But what will this entertainment look like? In short, what will make digital media work?

There is disagreement among broadcasters, cable companies, and computer industries as how to use the extra transmission or the bandwidth that is being allotted for digital signals. Digital channels can be used in multitude ways. The broadcasters can use that space for one channel to give an ultra clear picture and CD quality sound. Cable companies are worried; they have to sacrifice the variety of channels they offer in order to squeeze in the fatter digital channels. Cable companies' capacity difficulty may provide an opening for satellite program firms to win more customers.

In 2004, RFID (radio frequency identification) is another technology making new headway. RFID involves tiny computer chips that transmit radio signals that can be read by a scanner. RFID chips are already common, such as being used by drivers to zip past toll-booths and in the ID cards that employee use to open the office doors or for using hotel room doors by the customer. But in its new use, the big retailers are using them to tag all sorts of product to make inventory tracking more efficient and help prevent theft. Because of its higher cost, RFID will be initially used in warehouses and back of its stores and not at cash registers.

The fifth revolution might shift the national and global power structures in different ways.

Sixth Communication Revolution of 2000 Decade is the Quantum Computing. Other technologies, such as laser and quantum are facilitating information revolution. Taking a quantum Leap researchers are now harnessing the bizarre laws of quantum physics to make computers out of single molecule. Will molecule-sized computers revolutionize the world?

In classical computing, a computer can store one piece of data, either a 1 or a 0. In quantum computing the qubits can be both 0 and 1 at the same time meaning that they can specify numbers simultaneously. In quantum computers, researchers can use atom nuclei to store information. If mixed up together, in quantum physics, an object's attributes can be linked or entangled with another object.

Seth Lloyds, MIT professor (2000) is experimenting with Quantum computing, a completely new way to crunch numbers and process data. If quantum computing can be perfected, it will revolutionize everything we know about computers.

Sometimes around 2020, researchers reckon, each transistor will shrunk to the size of a single atom. The magnitude of data storage at this scale is unprecedented. "If you could put a bit of information on a single atom, you could store way more than the library of congress" Lloyd said.

If new rule of quantum physics can be mastered by new generation of computer scientists, the payoff would be astounding, allowing hard secret codes to be made and broken and instant searching of incredibly voluminous databases.

This extraordinary power is possible in the counter-intuitive world of quantum mechanics, the physical laws that govern microscopic things like atoms. Unlike our everyday existence, in quantum mechanics you really can be in two places at once.

Even qbits can exhibit a totally bizarre property called entanglement. This purely quantum effect means that all qbits in a quantum computer are hooked together — entangled, so that a computer operation on qbits can influence other qbits.

It is this strange communication among qbits that allows huge amounts of quantum data to be searched and manipulated simultaneously.

The experimental challenges are incredibly difficult. Quantum computing is still in its infancy. Issac Chuang MIT professor, Peter Shor at Bell lab, David Cory (MIT) are into 'quantum computer building' (For details see Notes 4.1).

A general-purpose quantum computer (like desktop PC) is decades away. Nonetheless the interest is high in its applications like ultra-secure communications, cryptography and other infotech applications.

Laser Technology

The word Laser is acronym, which stands for Light Amplification through Stimulated Emission of Radiation. Light moves in waves, and sunlight or artificial light contains a mixture of wavelengths. By contrast, laser is a beam of light that has a single frequency or wavelength.

The laser is created by subjecting a substance, such as crystal or gas mixture, to energy in the form of strong light, electricity, or a chemical or a nuclear reaction. This excites the atoms of the substance, which emits light of a particular wavelength.

The advantage of a laser is that all the photons or particles of light have the same wavelength, so they are the same color, unlike a flash light which gives off a whole range of wavelengths. With a tight energy-rich beam you can do useful things like cutting metal.

A light's wavelength — the distance between the tips of two successive waves determines the color that our eyes perceive. Wavelengths are measured in nanometers. The spectrum of rainbow runs roughly from 400nm for the violet end to the 750nm for the red. Below 400nm are ultraviolet light, then X-rays and gamma rays. Above 750nm is infrared, then microwaves, then radio waves.

At present the commercial devices use infrared lasers and red lasers. Currently (1999) the hottest research in laser is finding a way to harness the power of a blue laser, which could lead to vastly increased storage capacity of CDs and DVDs, faster laser printers, and a better way to identify cancerous cells with blue light.

Most semiconductor diode lasers — those in CD players and printers are infrared, their beams invisible to the naked eye. The ones that you can see at the checkout counter and laser pointers are on the red end of the spectrum and have been around for years.

Red lasers are tiny chips of crystal, the size of a small, square pebble. They put out bright single-colored light a few thousandth of a watt in power. But lasers that shine blue have much shorter wavelength and are difficult to make. A decade ago researchers could make crystals that would emit blue light, but that would only work few seconds and would fade. Scientists say they can improve the laser if they can find a way to turn it from red to blue.

Infrared lasers capacity is 650mb (such as in CD). Red lasers capacity is 4,700mb (as in DVD), and Blue lasers capacity will be 16,000mb. Lasers with smaller wavelengths can read smaller pits in a disc. Comparatively red lasers have shorter wavelengths than infrared, blue lasers with smaller wavelengths would greatly increase the amount of data stored in a disc.

Light's different wavelengths correspond to different colors: red at one end of the spectrum has a wavelength nearly twice that of blue at the other end. Lasers emit light only in one frequency, all parallel and aligned so their peaks and troughs are synchronized.

LEDs (light emitting diodes) are less powerful cousins of lasers. The green light that says computer is on is an LED.

Shuji Nakamura of Nichia – a company based in Japan in 1994 made marketable blue LEDs. He is the leader in Blue laser development through gallium nitride. What silicon did for computer chips; gallium nitride is doing for blue laser.

Making the Blue lasers continues to be a challenge because gallium nitride is very hard, very strong, but difficult to synthesize. It takes temperature of 1000C to grow gallium nitride crystals. Nakamura could find a way to reduce the temperature to 500 or 600C by working in a nitrogen-hydrogen atmosphere. This way defects did not spread throughout the crystal. Nichia is expecting to start selling samples of high-power laser diode in October 1999. Nichia's laser lasts 2000 hours. It is necessary that a laser have a lifetime of 10000 hours to put in a commercial device.

Since the Laser invention in 1960, researchers have been hard at work looking for more useful applications of the technology — mainly for the good of the humanity. Today, lasers are familiar part of everyday life, used in everything from surgical instruments to supermarket checkout scanners to compact disc players. Laser is creating information revolution. It has the ability to send billions of telephone calls along beams of light using fiber optics. Beside telecommunication, laser has created and revolutionized laser printing, laser CDs, laser surgery, and laser diamond cutters and other metal cutters for the industry. They are also used by Military in designing weapons of destruction. The next generation of lasers may open new realms, as they become microscopic as well as gargantuan.

As you get to the shorter wavelength, you get a big increase in data storage. For example, the blue lasers would give Xerox the ability to print with smaller dots, and to cluster more individual lasers together giving better resolution and faster speed. The blue diodes can aid in the building of new medical devices. Already dentists are using blue light to harden the fillings or whiten teeth. The blue laser under the right wavelength can find cancerous cells. The military would like shorter wavelength lasers to apply similar fluorescence techniques for detection of chemical and biological weapons. The light blue-green color allows underwater communication between submarines.

Despite difficulties still to overcome, scientists believe the widespread manufacturing of blue diode laser will take only a few years more (material is based on, Lasers — the thin blue line of laser research, Boston Globe Oct. 18, 1999).

Micro-lasers are the key link in optical computers. There are X-ray lasers. A great deal more information can be packed on them. X-ray lasers can etch fine lines onto silicon microprocessors. X-ray lasers may be able to illuminate the world of bacteria and viruses in greater detail, giving us the atomic structure of these living entities because they have short wavelengths.

The quantum revolution will give us new material, new energy sources, and perhaps ability to create new forms of matter. Other areas being developed for ICTs are nontechnology and fuel cells.

These new perspectives in mass media technologies ushered *Information society* to a *Technology society.* In the technology society the applications of advance technology are used for well being of humanity primarily. Therefore, we find the same technologies covering a wide range from information, knowledge, entertainment, network, medical applications, genetics, drug development, space applications, to war weapons and nuclear advancement. The focus is entertainment, wealth, health, prosperity with speed, efficiency and connectivity; shrinking time and space.

ICT initiatives

The ICTs are on the scene. We have discussed and highlighted in the earlier sections of the chapter the development of ICTs through six communication revolutions of the last many decades and even some spreading over a century. These highlights provide background for ICT initiatives in multiple domains. The current integrated ICT are revolutionary in their development and applications. The benefits that people, a country, and the world reap from these commensurate with their efforts and initiatives.

In the context of a particular communication medium, there is an incubation period, *i.e.* the early stage of initiating the medium. During this period, the medium faces hardware and software problematic issues and social issues of acceptance or rejection of the medium. At this stage there is experimentation and adaptation with various modes of the medium. The innovators, adapters and administrators and early adopters are at the helm of medium during this period. This period may spread over to about 10-15 years according to the resources and Political Will of the country. The next is the rapid growth period that is revolutionary period for the medium and may catch up within five years. Quite likely more developed and technologically advanced countries may have already passed over that particular revolution which is making headway and ripples in the developing and less technology advanced countries. Analysis and observation show that passing of the specific Communication revolution will impact and revolutionized the other less resourceful countries.

A significant point in setting up ICT initiatives is setting up Infodev incubator initiative (2000). It established the first common repository of knowledge, best practices, experience and services — specifically targeted to address the challenges and opportunities facing technology and business incubators in developing countries. The ICT incubator support center would provide information, organization and technical support to incubators from developing countries during the implementation of the incubator initiative.

People are exploring creative business approaches, public-private partnership, and other sustainable ways to bridge the global digital divide and create lasting economic, social and environmental benefits. ICTS for development are seeking convergence between IT have and have-nots. By weakening the influence of geography on development and opening opportunities for countries to leapfrog stages of development, ICTs are challenging some aspects of conventional wisdom in economic development theory.

What are the main issues in international assistance related to the use of these technologies in developing countries?

Katherine Sierra (2000) advocates that the information revolution are opening tremendous new opportunities for developing countries by promoting foreign direct investment in emerging markets, contributing to better governance, improvement of public services, amplifying the voices of the poor. But the digital-divide necessitates a response that encompasses fibers, computers, and the switches but also the development of the soft infra-structure required for building knowledge economies including education, cyber law, and modern regulatory institutions. Developing countries have to face the new challenges and opportunities offered by information revolution particularly Internet. The regulators, entrepreneurs, donor agencies have to go through the 'cultural-revolution' to fully tap the potential of new economy.

Some emphasized the dangers of technological determinism and the need to maintain a human development focus in ICT efforts and supporting Information Development's (InfoDev) proposed initiative for promoting incubators designed to foster Internet-centered start-up companies and social applications in emerging markets.

Rural Information Networks

Another necessary and significant social applications of ICT are 'Rural Information Network'. These need to be created using Internet technology for employment, education and empowerment of the villages in India particularly and other developing countries in general.

It is fundamental to service industries as well as to rural economic diversification strategies. Internet can help to overcome the geo-boundaries and isolation of rural communities and promote their participation in rural economy. Access to sophisticated databases, information services and value-added networks can improve the efficiency and productivity. It can provide communities an opportunity to compete in the fast growing service sector and increase productivity. Rural businesses and citizens can participate directly in national and global economies. It allows urban-based industries and customers to access rural products, services and markets more easily. Without Internet the rural communities will be denied the economic opportunities and quality of life that new technologies have created. It can provide rural people connectivity to the outside world, facilitating information exchange and development.

Unfortunately, rural areas are at disadvantage because they do not receive the technologies as quickly as urban areas. There is reluctance on the part of the technology providers to take interest in the comparatively small rural market. As a result, people who live in rural areas may be unable to reap the benefits of the advances in the information technology and Internet access. But we should not let them 'fall through the net' and be have-nots.

Electronic Networking for Rural Asia/Pacific (ENRAP) covers eight countries Bangladesh, China, India, Indonesia, Nepal, Pakistan, Philippines and Sri Lanka. It initiates knowledge, networking and Internet applications development at local, national and international levels. Special focus is on methods and practical solutions for fostering participation at the grassroots level.

Countries are able to benefit from training material, documents and database available on its web site and technical advice provided electronically. There are three distinct but interrelated levels of ENRAP support activities. The first helps them to get connected to the Internet including training and developing a web presence. The second focuses on identifying and documenting knowledge and experience generated within projects and activating exchange between them. Third engages with project needs at the field level where the Internet can offer some solutions or support.

ENRAP builds capacity for the knowledge age by helping project stakeholders: to adapt using the electronic communication as part of problem solving process; to incorporate the electronic venue in the organizational structures; to develop an understanding of the electronic networking potential in the social processes; and to participate in information and exchange of information and knowledge sharing via Internet.

Foundation of occupational development India (Food) is experimenting with e-commerce to improve the economic conditions of rural women and NGOs by marketing their products online using the Internet and training e-marketers.

Telecommunication offers a unique opportunity for rural development in developing countries. In rural areas cellular telephones are useful as landlines are not available since rural telephone exchanges are not set up in most of the rural and remote areas. Cell phones give them connectivity.

The conventional electronic media of radio and television has been on the rural scene for decades for entertainment and pro-social messages from national channels. Cable technology available to rural areas has further enhanced the potentialities of TV medium for exposure to international news, views, life styles, behavior and attitudes and multitude of events that directly or indirectly impact their lives.

ICTs Perceptions, Visions

The decade of 2000 onwards is the era for consolidating and updating advancement being made through the six communication revolutions. The media of print, radio, television, telecommunications, computers are all forging ahead in its varied advance forms. Even the oral traditions are benefiting through these advancements. The oral communication through various modes of telephony, online communication through Internet have given new perspective to interpersonal communication

This is the global communication scenario. Many countries including India fit their communication scenario within the framework of these contexts.

Gore (1996) emphasized the five core principles that global community must ensure to accommodate the best information network that is prerequisite to participate in communication revolutions. These are private investment, competition, flexible regulation, open access, and universal service.

Irving (1996) says that developing countries can and must become a part of the information age and have robust telecommunication and information industries. The developing countries have the potentialities to leapfrog into sophisticated technologies such as satellites, and wireless. The governments can create a structure that would enable its citizens to use these technologies to improve their quality of life. Knight (1996) endorses Irving's views and asserts that those countries that fail to embrace the revolution are bound to become further marginalized and left out. Knight contends that developing countries must build new learning systems, mobilize international resources to create massive programs, community information, and learning centers.

A review of the arguments of the utopians and dystopians on the current communication revolution suggests that countries have no alternative but to join the current communication revolution/s to compete in the world material economy.

Countries must weigh the utopian and dystopian views on informatization when they plan to expand their computerization, and telecommunication infrastructure to compete in the world material economy rejuvenated by third communication revolution.

The utopians believe countries can best achieve open access and universal service by competition, flexibility, and private enterprise. The global village offers vast opportunities to solve national and local problems. It enables people to access knowledge through multi layered electronic libraries along the global information highway. Investments in telecommunication would produce multiplier effects and lead to economic, social, and political developments. New information technologies will undercut monopolies on information, curtail censorship and promote citizen-based democracy.

Dystopian argues that the economic arguments for new communication technologies must be balanced against the social, organizational and administrative aspects. Countries must protect their security and sovereignty; and citizens must be concerned about their privacy and surveillance. They point the negative effects of commercialization, privatization, deregulation, and internationalization. They point that new communication technologies will not democratize communication. These technologies will disempower people through new forms of dependence.

Communication, through gaining information, knowledge, and its preservation was the key objectives when writing and paper and ink was invented in China 206 B.C.-A.D. 220. About 1,800 years ago, China's papermaking technique using bark and hemp was improved. Today, ancient papermaking has been replaced by modern means of production. Printing ushered in 14th century. Invention of Telephone provided connectivity to people. With broadcasting — radio, television, satellites the entertainment dimensions were added. Further, telecommunication advancement, computerization focused more on connectivity and a network society.

These new perspectives in mass media technologies ushered *Information society* to a *technology society.* In the technology society the applications of advance technology are used for well being of humanity primarily. Therefore, we find the same technologies covering a wide range from information, knowledge, entertainment, network, medical applications, genetics, drug development, space applications, to war weapons and nuclear advancement. The focus is infotainment, wealth, health, prosperity with speed, efficiency and connectivity; and shrinking time and space.

In the present scenario people are interacting with multiple forms of communications simultaneously. For instance, a person is using Internet for chat, instant messaging, e-mail, virtual conference, telephoning. In multi virtual conferences, it is interpersonal conference, but the interaction is so complex that at one point you are interacting simultaneously with more than one participant in the virtual conference.

ICTs can bring many benefits to developing countries and to the process of socio-economic development. It is important to assess the role and applications of ICTs in *key development institutions* such as government and private sector organizations, NGOs, communities and international organizations. Further, ICTs role and applications in *key development sectors* such as health, education and infrastructure and to assess ICTs in relation to *key development targets* such as sustainable development and environment, gender equality, poverty alleviation and realizing human rights. ICTs and various *aspects of development* such as rural development, urban development, small enterprise development and social development can be targeted. Moreover there are *ICT specific development issues* such as digital divide, northern domination of ICT models, products, agendas and policies.

Digital empowerment through (Digital Empowerment Foundation) is a program organized to make information technology and Internet available to those who do not know English and, in general may not have access to the technology infrastructure that would allow them to utilize ICT. A bigger aim is to help these people flourish economically and connect them with others around the world. The target audience is non-English-speaking people in countries that are aligned with the South Asian Association for Regional Co-operation (SAARC); countries that have access to PCs and Internet but are unable to use them given the lack of applications or operating systems in vernacular languages of the subcontinent.

The rush to develop Internet access in developing countries needs to be adjusted to the context of already established and effective communication systems. Attention needs to be paid to bridging the digital-divide for the rural and between those who can afford access to the new technologies and those who cannot.

In 21st century we expect superfast and revolutionary pace of innovations in science and information technology and their applications.

Our world and our lives are being shaped by the conflicting trends of globalization and identity. The information technology revolution and the restructuring of capitalism have induced a new form of society — the network society.

Cultural Impact: The media technologies have crossed the barriers of space and time in the present decade which tantamount to crossing the cultural barriers also. People are assuming multicultural identity on one hand; on the other hand they assimilate good or the bad points of other cultures in their culture when they are exposed to international perspectives through media technologies. People do have anxieties and fear about loss of their cultural identity. But the good point is, other cultures are brought closer through radio, television, films, Internet, telecommunication etc. Awareness is created about other cultural resources, values, life styles, technologies and other innovations.

Diffusion of both technological and social innovations is facilitated. Images, stereotypes, and prejudices about other cultures undergo change thus creating better international understanding.

Information communication technologies in this decade stimulate intercultural and cross-cultural communication at its best. Exposure to media technologies can refine understanding of the complex roles that cultural processes play in the development of ICTs in various sectors of society and the challenges of social technology.

Impact of ICTs in Practice

Media scene: We face certain questions to review and assess recent trends in communications, their social and business implications in practice.

What information skills citizens must possess to participate responsibly in modern society? How do we spread media literacy and the grammar of the new media? What are the new services and applications in the convergence process and their effects on business and people?

How do we balance the needs of analytical or social sciences and professional education amidst the new media, globalization and organizational restructuring?

How do we reinvent newspaper in digital age? What will be tomorrow's print products? Should the newspaper for mass or niche marketing adopt single or multimedia approach?

As more channels become available to the TV audience, the race for contents heats up. What products will be available, who will produce them, and what will it cost? How will producers monitor and assess audience needs and program preferences when TV audiences are global; and at the same time there is demand for culture specific programs also.

The status of a society depends on what is the above-mentioned media scenario. It keeps changing as how these trends are handled and how it impacts the specific society.

Network society is on the scene. Globalization gives Internet connectivity to majority. A network society where everyone is connected may take few centuries to evolve. As such, technology may leapfrog for some but still many are even on the first stage of technology in developing countries, where the resources of government and people are limited for the reach.

It is presumed that for years to come people have to depend on network society for economic survival. The direct impact of networked society is expected to be less travel and less polluted cities.

The success of Internet has been triggered by the technology rather than by human endeavor. The speed at which people have adopted the Internet is at far faster rates than adoption of previous technologies such as telegraph, radio, television, video and fax. Fast adoption has been driven by rapidly improving technology in all the key areas—telecommunications, computers, storage bandwidth, digital cameras etc. This is accompanied by equal fall in prices in real time.

Digital-divide has become a common term to describe gaps between the rich and poor in the effective access and use of information technology. Most policy-makers, researchers and practitioners could at least agree on one point that reaching the poorest of the poor is going to be the most difficult of challenges. Even reaching the so-called 'ordinary' poor would entail challenges of electrical power, telecommunications connectivity, human resources infrastructure, and the like. A major barrier to the use of IT tools today is limitations of human skill competencies.

Digital-divide is the pervasive theme of 21st century. Can it be bridged? Most social problems of this magnitude are debated openly after the event. The conscience of the world is stirred and remedies explored when the global developments produce social chasm in health, wealth or gender. Therefore, digital divide is not unusual. A solution is being sought in real time while the revolution is being unrolled.

Attention needs to be paid to bridging the rural digital divide and digital divide between those who can afford access to the new technologies and those who cannot.

Actually there is no single digital divide but lots of overlapping ones; between old and young, men and women, rich and poor, rural and urban blacks and whites, northern hemispheres and southern hemispheres, and above all between developed and developing nations. Yet the creation of a vast new underprivileged *digitariat* seems inevitable unless dramatic action is taken. (More about digital divide in section ICT and education in later section).

E-commerce is spreading rapidly world-wide, more than US $1 trillion-worth of goods and services are likely to be traded electronically by 2003, covering b2c (business to consumer) and the far larger b2b (business to business). It is expanding in the years to come. In the North, impacts on both business and trade have been uneven but rapid, particularly in certain sectors. Possibilities exist for both existing enterprises and new entrants: new supply-chain models are emerging around both dis-intermediation and re-intermediation of existing firms. In the South, e-commerce is also present and expanding, albeit from a far smaller base. In the short-term, international trade will be the main focus for development of e-commerce.

Most of the business opportunities in the next few decades would either be the creation of digital goods or application of the digital and Internet techniques to old economy products. All this will doubly hit those developing countries where the Internet has bypassed. They will not be making any new economy products that people want to buy. Their traditional markets will be squeezed by the price deflation brought by electronic marketplaces on the Internet. International investment will be directed to exciting interrelated projects generated by the information-rich countries.

Not having electricity or a phone in a rich society are fewer handicaps these days than not having Internet access because of all pervasive nature of the new revolution. Not to have access to information in an information-driven age is to risk exclusion.

Narula (2003), IT professionals are seeking new roles and exploring new ways to help tackle India's poverty through ICT. The strategy is to link high-tech entrepreneurs with social entrepreneurs and empower the latter to use IT in appropriate ways to enrich the lives of the poor. There is a demand and need for such market. The first step is to facilitate the development of localized content that would be useful and relevant to the poor. Companies can make money by serving viable products and services to the poor.

In India there is digital divide, yet there are tremendous opportunities. There are national and state efforts to promote e-governance and rural access through IT. India has a great talent pool of IT expertise. Indian expatriates in the USA are at the forefront of IT revolution and are spearheading this effort in India.

In a country that lacks power and telecom infrastructure, how will IT be used for poor? Already India is developing very innovative technologies to provide telephone and Internet accesses to the rural poor. For instance, there is the Microwave loop technology developed at IIT Madras. Similarly the Indian Institute of Science in Bangalore has developed a hand held computer called 'Simputer' which will be available at low price of Rs. 9500 (less than $200). Such efforts need support because these can solve some of the infrastructure needs in this area. Technology by itself cannot solve poverty-related problems. But creative adaptations of the technology by those who are already working with the poor can tackle poverty-related issues.

Narula further advocates that adaptive use of technology should be promoted at a large scale across the country. Initially the specific initiatives planned are to support education, health care and micro-enterprise. Village information centers can be set up where IT support can be given for education programs, healthcare information and management, and to improve the process of giving micro-loans.

ICT and Education

The joint efforts of Australia and World Bank to bridge the 'digital divide' — the growing gap between the information-rich and those who are information-poor; by taking education and knowledge through ICT to developing countries. In March 2001 they embarked on a joint study to assess the opportunities presented by ICTs and identify specific education and knowledge needs of developing countries and particular Australian skills, materials and expertise that could be responsive to those needs. The study also examined the technological, policy and regulatory aspects affecting the flow of education and knowledge services. The key findings of the study were:

- Developing countries want to capture the opportunities offered by ICTs to leap-frog in the development process;

- Access to knowledge has been severely limited in developing countries;
- Education and access to knowledge are increasingly important building blocks for development in the age of ICT revolutions;
- ICT can improve the delivery of education in schools and broaden the range of options available for distance education. The policy and strategy must be tailored to local circumstances, and locally appropriate technologies found to maximize the benefits and minimize the costs;
- The affordability and sustainability of ICTs will progressively and rapidly increase in developing countries; and
- Along with the right policies and access, widespread basic IT literacy will be essential to tap the opportunities.

Through joint initiatives and expertise, Australia and World Bank intend to deliver through ICT better basic education for children and youth, higher education, knowledge infrastructure for better access to global knowledge, knowledge dissemination and new learning opportunities for policy-makers. These will be addressed through virtual Colombo plan operative in 2004. Since 'one size fit all' VCP model will not work, these activities should align with priorities of the developing countries.

Narula (2003) suggests that such social-technical revolution would need a dynamic set of IT entrepreneurs, business leaders, highly placed government officials, international donors, social entrepreneurs and leading academicians. In collaboration and coordination with one another this Network will find trigger points where IT can become a catalyst for development and shape public policy related to IT. More specifically, through the virtual and live forums, it can develop innovative approaches for the use of IT to benefit the poor and create new funding mechanisms to support such efforts. It is necessary to form an advocacy group that looks at important public policy issues that impact IT. Finally, it is important to visualize how to integrate various ways into current development strategies to benefit the poor.

Women and ICT

ICT are clearly powerful and capable of serving both men and women. They can be important tools for those seeking to promote gender equality and empower women. However, the technology has potential risks as well as benefits. Optimism is justified about the potential of ICT for women. But caution is needed to assure that benefits are realized and risks averted. On occasions, those seeking to profit from the exploitation of women have effectively appropriated it.

Communication technology allows information to be transferred across distances without face-to-face contact. As such it offers possibilities to engage women in distance education, e-commerce, and e-government, thereby overcoming barriers to women economic advancement. This aspect of technology can also exploit women over distance when misused. Social institutions will determine the gender distribution of gains and losses. In some societies, ICT will empower women in the work force, in others; they will surely benefit men over women.

Relatively few technologies will be planned to achieve gender goals, but indirectly ICT may have profound effects on gender roles, gender equality and women empowerment. It may be that most countries will maintain the policies and build the institutions needed to utilize the technology to promote social and economic development. The improvement of status of women will be part and parcel of the resulting modernization and development. However, it may be that pre-existing inequalities will be reflected in the differential abilities of men and women to appropriate the technologies, and that the information revolution will see a continuation or worsening of gender inequality. In some countries, a reaction to modernization and threat to the *status quo* is posed especially through ICT.

Will ICT empower women? There are two aspects to this issue. ICT may empower women directly or indirectly. The development in affordable information services and women access to them will facilitate their participation in ICTs. The trends are, a roll out of basic ICT infrastructure and services. Mobile and fixed line services are expanding in developing nations and are becoming more affordable. Computer hardware will be more affordable especially low priced devices developed for markets in developing countries. Software will be more affordable as the markets are expanded for commercial products and as more 'open source' software becomes available. Telecenters and other approaches for providing community access are being invented, business plans for shared access services are improving and helpful telecommunication policies are promulgated more widely. Together, these trends will encourage the continued expansion of Internet. Community radio offers new local radio service, and television reaches larger audience in rural areas including women.

These trends will empower women with more information services, with more information and with more voice in public affairs.

While ICT infrastructure will be more affordable and available, Will women have access to them? Hafkin Nancy *et al.* (2001) study indicated "women are 22% of all Internet users in Asia, 38% in Latin America and 6% in Middle East". Another Study (2001) found that fewer than 20% of people cited in media in southern Africa were women. In some countries women have limited physical access to telecenters and other shared facilities. Even where social and cultural practices allow access to expanding ICT infrastructure, women access may be limited by preexisting inequalities in income and education. The cost of ICT is often less affordable to women than men. In some countries, rural women do not have access where ICT infrastructure is sparse or non-existent. More often they are limited in their use of national or cosmopolitan languages and thus more limited in their access to text content. A review of World Links Programs (2002) noted that, "domestic chores, culturally-imbued feelings of shyness and traditional rules forced many girls to have less access than boys to computer labs".

In some cultures women are not permitted to have face to face contact with men other than those in their own families; or are expected to stay at home or isolated in restricted living facilities. For such cultures, communication technologies may empower women. Telephone, radio, television, and the Internet allow women to interact with men without being in the same place, and without face-to-face contact. Especially distance education and e-commerce may be important in this respect.

Another study (2003) done for Bolivian women suggests technological approaches to overcome these limitations. Thus PRODEM in Bolivia is rolling out ATMs for their microfinance women customers that allows transactions 24/7 days in local languages and can be used by people who are illiterate.

A Brazilian project (2003) about strengthening women leadership in community development illustrates a related phenomenon. A large number of Brazilian women spend most of their time within their homes, engaged in child-care, food preparation, and other tasks. Such women have little access to information provided formally in schools or in workplaces. So a network of women has been formed to broadcast information they need via radio. The radio mass medium reaches homes, is affordable and serves as an effective means of communication with the homebound listeners. The Internet allows the 'network' to provide programming and content to local programmers and stations.

ICT and Millennium Goals

World Summit on the Information Society (WSIS) in Dec. 2003 in Geneva provided central role for governments, private sector, civil society, and international organizations to engage in dialogue about the vital role of ICTs in development and opportunities offered to policy-makers and practitioners in efforts to achieve the eight Millennium Development Goals that were identified in the United Nations Millennium Summit in 2000.

The discussions focused on the practical ways of translating information society visions into concrete and operational plans for e-development projects and related activities. It specifically addressed the development opportunities offered by the Information Revolution.

At the United Nations Millennium Summit in 2000, the global community adopted eight Millennium Development Goals (MDGs) to guide and measure the development efforts by various stakeholders. These are: (1) Eradication of extreme poverty and hunger. (2) Achievement of universal primary education. (3) Promote gender equality and empowerment of women. (4) Reduce child mortality. (5) Improve maternal health. (6) Combat HIV/AIDS, malaria and other diseases. (7) Ensure environment sustainability. (8) Develop global partnership for development.

MDGs provide a vision of development — one in which development reduces number of poor and specifically targets the worst aspects of poverty.

A commitment was made to achieve more progress in these directions and in less time. ICTs have important role to play in this development endeavor. It crosses all sectors bringing increased efficiency and new opportunities to areas from small enterprise development to international trade, to education and healthcare. It also facilitates sharing of experiences across organizations and geographic areas, furthering collective learning and the ability for organizations and countries to build on one another's advances.

Daly John (2003) argues that ICT infrastructures and its use has been growing explosively even in developing countries in the recent decades. This growth has contributed for progress in meeting MDGs. Technology is one of the factors in achieving these goals. *Technological innovations open possibilities but social and economic factors control the development of technological infrastructures, their use, and distribution of their benefits. Social, economic and technological systems are highly interconnected.* ICT innovations in one place have wide repercussions through society. They are occurring globally and influence each other. He further suggests that MDG are interrelated and there is *complexity* and difficulty in predicting the *emergent effects* of the information revolution on poverty and development. An enormous number of innovations (in ICT) are taking place but there is *complexity in diffusion* of those innovations. Moreover, powerful forces unleashed by information revolution will have both positive and negative effects.

No country utilizes ICT solely to achieve MDG, since in all countries different groups seek simultaneously to achieve their objectives. Because of this competition, limited ICT resources are allocated in patterns that favor one ethnic group over other, male over female, rich over poor, and urban over rural.

ICT, Economic Growth and Poverty Reduction

In recent decades it has been recognized that technological improvements, increase in economic productivity are important for long-term economic growth. Old economic theories of economic growth emphasized land, labor and capital as determinants of economic productivity. Recently, economists emphasized that better organization and better technology are responsible for significant growth in productivity. "Total Factor Productivity"(TFP) is the keystone to study the effect of technology on economic development.

Restructuring and reengineering are needed to effectively utilize the potential of a new technology; the technological innovations are the most easily visible markers of the changes being made.

Easterly Williams (2001) argues that technological determinism is just one of many single-factor theories. It seems clear that technology with many interacting factors affect the course of social and economic development. Good policies, institutions and human capital are important factors. Harrison *et al.* (2001) emphasized the role of cultural institutions in this context.

ICTs will have potential effects on both social conditions and economic conditions. ICT related large-scale changes in culture, political systems, communities, and families are important.

There is interest in reduction of both *economic and social poverty.* Lack of wealth and income are the common markers of economic poverty but social aspects of poverty are crucially important. These include poor health and early mortality, many forms of physical disability, ignorance, lack of information, lack of voice, political powerlessness, and other forms of cultural deprivations. Efforts of ICT to reduce economic poverty are easy to quantify but it is difficult to quantify reduction in social poverty.

Solow Robert argues (2003) 'that a very small investment in ICTs should not be expected to produce large social and economic impact'. It is paradoxical for developing nations. Poor countries are constrained to spend less portion of their GDP on ICTs as compared to rich countries. Therefore, the impact of ICTs is delayed and smaller than in rich nations. While basic ICT services and infrastructure are being rolled out in developing nations; the digital-divide in high-end ICT is increasing between rich and poor nations. Rich nations tend to spend a greater portion of their GDP on ICT then poor nations. Since in developed nations the market in many of the basic ICT is essentially saturated, so they are spending their ICT budget on high-end ICTs while poor nations are still struggling to provide basic services.

The ICT technological revolution has high and improving total factor productivity in ICT industries — ICT infrastructure and producing ICT goods and complementary services. The growth of these raises a rapid increase in the TFP of the economy. As technology is put to work, efficiency in primary and other manufacturing and service industries is improved. This encourages employment of labor and capital. There is economic growth if TFP is improving, and there is increased investment in capital and labor. Growth is enhanced in sectors that are able to increase TFP utilizing ICTs.

Some developing nations built export-oriented ICT industries to have significant micro-economic impacts. Costa Rica stimulated its economy by attracting Intel facility for production of microchips. India is developing a software industry and exporting a significant portion of its products. It is developing ICT based industries producing 'back-office' services such as customer services, accounting, medical transcriptions, radiology etc. for foreign and international corporations. These are outsourced from home countries. These provide jobs. Thus there is interplay between ICTs and economic development.

ICT innovations have triggered complimentary innovations in society. For example, microchips in automobiles and other manufactured goods. The effective utilization of the potential of ICTs restructure the markets and other institutions in which those enterprise function. For example, efficiency of transportation combined with ICT innovations has enhanced the efficiency of the manufacturing enterprises.

Cairncross *et al.* (2001) address the importance of clusters for ICT innovations in Silicon valley in USA and Bangalore in India. They have been successful in using ICTs for development. Dunning John (2002) talks about the geographical advantages of the so-called Asian and Celtic tigers. Regional markets are enhanced by the new information infrastructure. Globalization is clearly enhanced by the information revolution. It has affected the economies of the developing nations as well the spread of the knowledge-based economies. In short, both physical and cyberspace geography clearly matters in the distribution of the effects of the information revolution and adequate effects of ICTs on development.

In some countries, initial exploratory investments in ICT may lead to reductions in economic growth as they may give low immediate economic yields. Even some bad investments in ICT in fads related to Internet, e-commerce, telemedicine, distance education etc. through incompetence may lead to malfeasance. Corrupt and coercive regimes, uncaring and greedy businessman and others may use the technology in ways that will exacerbate poverty and underdevelopment. So it is a powerful tool in the pursuit of both bad as well good ends.

The comparative advantages of nations *vide* economic growth and reduction of economic poverty depends on the relative productivities in different economic sectors. Sectoral productivities will change according to the degrees that different sectors are successfully harnessing the ICT to increase productivity. Thus the pattern of comparative advantage among nations is likely to change as a result of the ICT revolution.

International trade in ICT and high technology products is increasing. Rich countries are trading ICT and high tech products for labor-intensive products from poor countries. Some developing countries are developing ICT exports but most have not.

ICT and Social Poverty. Let us consider three areas of ICT for development: (a) Development of ICT physical infrastructure for telecommunication, computer, radio, television and print media. (b) Development of ICT industries. In developing nations, there is focus on export oriented ICT industries (software, microchips etc. (c) IT enabled services.

Developing nations need to develop ICT industries for domestic use, wholesale and retail distribution of ICT products, ICT maintenance, consulting and Internet value added services and utilize ICT in all productive sectors of society. These include telemedicine, distance education, e-commerce and e-government, but also applications of telephone, mass media, and computers to business, government and people in general. These three areas should develop in parallel since they are interdependent, and create a virtuous ICT for development cycle.

People are impoverished not only because they lack money but they are impoverished by ill health, by denied knowledge, by hunger, by failure in the systems through which other basic needs are met, and by the lack of effective voice in their own affairs and in their communities' affairs. This is social poverty. Applications of ICT industries must reduce this. Therefore it is necessary that ICT industries must be developed for domestic use.

Rolling out ICT infrastructure is important but equally important is how it is done. Shared connectivity is required to provide ICT to the poor. The providers would need regulatory requirements or incentives to extend their services to the poor and rural areas. Poor people do benefit from ICTs when they have access. For example, people spend more time with radio and TV not only for entertainment but to inform themselves in socially and economically viable ways. If they use telephone, they get more benefit of saving on travel cost, getting information in important and emergency situations and social connectivity. If farmers have Internet connectivity, they benefit from market information of commodities etc.

Building ICTs is also important but it is equally important how they are built. Focus on building export oriented hardware and software industries are important but such industries will provide little direct employment or service to the poor. On the other hand, ICT enterprises can be developed and that would provide services and even employment to the poor. For example, community radio and Grameen (rural) phone approach.

Developing applications of ICTs is appropriate to the poor and for poverty reduction. Appropriate ICTs can make small and medium enterprises more productive, and help creating jobs and benefiting the poor. E-government applications can help the poor to access government services, and influence government. It is important to utilize ICT for improving health through telemedicine, improving hospital services and primary health care services for poor; and improve primary education and skills training programs benefiting the poor. The poor will benefit much more from the ICT directly meant for them.

If the poor have to benefit from the information revolution, there must be simultaneous efforts for national economic growth for rolling out the infrastructure, building appropriate ICT industries and utilizing them in many sectors of economy. Not only there need to be pro-poor policies and institutions for ICT revolution but also pro-poor policies to assure that ICT and its progress is shared by poor. Empowerment of poor through access to ICT is important and indirectly this may help in development and poverty reduction.

ICT and Improvement of Health

ICT can be powerful tool for improving health given the right policies and institutions. Improving health involves; social, economic, medical and other factors. Improving health significantly depends on improving income and reduction of poverty (Goal 1), improving education including health education (Goal 2), empowering and educating women (Goal 3), and improving water and sanitation (Goal 7). Partnership and in cooperation with pharmaceutical companies provide access to affordable and essential drugs in developing countries (Goal 8). These are millennium development goals.

The use of low-cost, hand held computers for collection of medical information, and use of telephones by auxiliary health personnel can significantly improve the quality of services. Smart cards and ICT based diagnostic devices, automated lab devices and medical equipment may improve primary health care.

Lack of information about health protection and wide spread misinformation about health is major problem in developing countries. Doctors do not often educate poor people. Appropriate and affordable ICT can educate the people in schools and health facilities. Knowledge, attitude and practices of people in health can be changed through communication media.

ICT applications (many developed in business and government) can improve the administrative efficiency and quality in health sector. Such as, maintaining medical records to access information for medical practitioners, updated village maps, creating e-procurement for medical supplies and equipment and even e-government platform for health agencies. Health services need staff, equipment, money and supplies that must be served by infrastructure of power, communications, roads etc. ICT can improve the efficiency, production and distribution of these resources.

ICT can be applied in training of health professional and paraprofessionals. Many applications can make such training efficient and of higher quality and also manageable for geographically dispersed health workers. Not only university training is required for the professions but also continuing rapid advances in medical knowledge and technology requires strong programs of continuing education. ICT can be applied to the entire operation of medical schools and related training institutions serving entire health sectors. ICT can be applied to improve the 'labor markets' for health professionals, facilitating the efforts of the health facilities to hire professional staff and of health professionals to find employment.

Health care finance system typically comprising of consultation fee, insurance, charitable contributions, public financing etc. is complex. For efficient handling, it can be ICT intensive and extraordinarily dependent on computers and telecommunications.

Modern industries dominate the production of medical equipment, pharmaceuticals and other supplies. These industries are invested with ICT. The products are marketed and distributed through variety of channels. By appropriate ICT applications they can even benefit the poor countries.

ICT is essential in health research. Bioinformatics is increasingly fundamental to the development of new drugs and vaccines. Genomics, proteomics and other emerging fields are based on automated lab equipment and powerful computer analyses. The research work is planned, tracked and analyzed *via* ICT. Developed countries are doing much of this work but some developing countries are entering the field. Even applications of ICT in bioinformatics done in developed countries may be critically important in meeting the MDG. Epidemiological research ranges from geo tracking of epidemic or emerging diseases, to the incrimination of the source of an outbreak of a food-borne disease, to analysis of long term trend of diseases, morbidity and mortality. ICT can facilitate these researches in all its forms.

Health policy should be evidence-based, informed by epidemiological research and health service statistics. An understanding of public concerns and attitude of key stakeholders — including the public health workers, employers, government and civil society organizations, should also inform it. The policy-making process is broadened *via* ICT, and it becomes indispensable in compiling public information for determining the public health policy and its options. Communication media can be extensively used for public debate on health policies, and mobilizing public support. Targeted groups can use specialized interactive media such as telephones, e-mail etc. for effectively communicating their views to the policy-makers.

Health facilities serving affluent populations will have more and better ICT than those serving poor. Often the pattern will reflect social barriers in the society such as distributing technology to benefit rich rather than poor, men rather than women, urban rather than rural populations, and dominant rather than peripheral ethnic groups. Even powerful politicians may better equip their constituencies. Generally military health facilities are equipped well in developing countries than public facilities serving civilians.

Our discussion suggests that a huge variety of ICT applications can affect the health services. The applications are growing rapidly worldwide. The most salient point is resource constrains about diffusion of these innovations in developing countries. There are not enough ICT experts, not enough ICT-literate health professionals and not enough money to introduce ICT at every cost-effective point of application. The pattern of ICT and its diffusion are constrained by policies and institutional capacities in every country and even by lack of general understanding of best practices in its applications in the health field.

In short, where will the information revolution lead? According to the experts, by the year 2020, the information revolution would have altered life on this planet even more dramatically than in the last 20 years. Even if they hesitate to specify exactly what the technological changes might be over the next two decades, the experts offer even more intriguing insights into how those technological changes could, in turn, change us as people, as nations, and as a global web of human thought and action.

With regard to technological breakthroughs, the fear of forecasting the future is forgivable. Back in 1980, a mere 20 years ago, almost no one could have predicted the explosive growth of the World Wide Web. In 80s, there was still no hypertext language for navigating from web site to web site, still no graphical interface, nothing like today's chat rooms, no laptop computers, and no cell phones, let alone cell phones that could deliver e-mail *via* satellite. Conversely, predictions that once seemed reasonable now appear naïve in retrospect. With regard to overall technological trends on the other hand, an effort to anticipate the future is more than exercises in futility. While it is risky to predict the future in detail, it may be even more foolish not to prepare for it at all, especially when the future promises to bring changes as swift and pervasive as those made possible by the information revolution.

Summary

IT is becoming an important factor in the new growth theory beside labor and capital. Information communication technologies (ICT) are important. They have been both evolutionary and revolutionary, giving connectivity both in personal and professional life of people. The present scenario is that all technologies are integrated and converged and that provides holistic information connectivity. The social and economic repercussions of the advances in ICT are so great that the term "information revolution" is probably justifiable. The new ICT model has made many old paradigms and theories of communication obsolete. The update model is technology networking and technology convergence.

Technological advancements *vis-à-vis* development of new media technologies created six Communication Revolutions: in Writing, Printing, Broadcasting, Films, Telecommunications, Computer and e-technologies and Quantum computing, nanotechnology and fuel cell technology of 2000 decade (the last one yet to be revolutionized). These technologies introduced at different decades of the centuries revolutionized communication because of advancement in technologies over a period of time; and that expanded their different functional forms and supporting-ethnotronic technologies. It further changed their program contents and functions tuning to the audience demand.

The six Communication Revolutions since early 8th through 14th century to date have exploded in information revolution and created new perspectives for media technologies, contexts and impacts through changing media technologies over time. Technological changes brought different issues on the forefront. These communication revolutions focused on giving better connectivity to human beings through both machines and humans.

Social equity and public policy challenges of transformative technology are being faced by developing countries — understanding the social and public policy dimensions. The focus is how social equity and the human condition is being affected by the emerging technologies (both ICT and other technologies) as well as what mechanisms and learning processes are in place or have been developed to be in place to assist government and public stakeholders groups engaged in the decision-making processes associated with these new technologies.

We recognize that new knowledge is not neutral and is embedded in specific social contexts, it can offer opportunity, but can also constrain human activity.

Communications revolutions over the centuries created more and more of industrial products, consumer products and cultural products to develop and improve the living conditions around the world. Computer has become an integrated technology for other technologies to usher. Without it many of the newer technology applications, devices, and innovations will be handicapped.

The explosive growth of the World Wide Web through Internet in 90s, its burst in late 90s, obscured the rapid progression of the Internet. But the current build-out in 2000 decade marked by a proliferation of mobile Internet devices, the spread of Internet protocol telephony, and the emergence of spin-off technologies will refocus attention on the Internet.

The ICTs initiatives are to handle digital divide, create rural networks for development, knowledge economies and e-development mainstreaming. Internet may be a great facilitator.

There are perceptions and visions about how ICT advancement will benefit the developing countries. We discuss about the impact of ICT in practice on the media scene, the network society, digital-divide, health improvement, economic growth and poverty reduction, empowerment of women, and in achieving millennium development goals.

Such techno-social revolution would need a dynamic set of IT entrepreneurs, business leaders, highly placed government officials, international donors, social entrepreneurs and leading academicians. In collaboration and coordination with one another this 'network' will find trigger points where IT can become a catalyst for development and shape public policy related to IT.

The fourth, fifth and the sixth communication revolutions have been the harbinger of convergent technologies suggesting that different upcoming technologies of computer, telecommunication, laser, quantum, fuel cell technology and nanotechnologies; all have to work in unison and are interdependent on one another to develop myriad applications.

13

Intercultural Communication Perspective

Whenever my journeys take me, to dwell or to visit, I search for the essence of the people and the cultures.

—Stephen Dachi

The Framework

The fifth perspective — the cultural perspective focusing on intercultural and cross-cultural communications is significant in dealing with the above four mentioned perspectives in creating a world community. This is the core of international communication and globalization. Intercultural communication is basic and important for them.

Communication among people across nations, countries, and cultures is important. Since from all perspectives, it involves communicating with diverse cultures and understanding of those cultures, and therefore focusing on social phenomena. Thus social theory of national identity becomes significant.

Cultural ways are our resources and when we communicate within our psychological and cultural milieu, through our particular resources, we create explicit or implicit mutual understanding. Cultural diversity can create new opportunities as well as stress and strains in a society. Therefore, the efforts are made to manage cultural diversity by valuing it and integrating it.

Intercultural invasion, domination, and cultural diversity in a society pose dilemmas. Influences by other cultures can be both subtle and direct. Cultural influences are determined by social structural values, culture specific values, and opportunities within a culture. These are reinforced by interpersonal contacts and media technologies. The powerful influences of new media technologies rather create invasion and domination by other influential cultures and globalization of cultures. Globalization of cultures does create international understanding but also anxieties about their negative influences. Many cultures censor content of media technologies to protect their own cultures.

The theoretical conceptual framework of Culture and Communication is critical to understand and research the process of intercultural communication, acculturation, and the development of intercultural communication competence to optimize these processes and develop a Practical Analytical Framework (PAF). The PAF is based on theoretical cultural postulates, ends, and means from a practical point of view that contributes strongly towards culture learning for acculturation. Communicating across cultures highlights the diversity of global cultures and cultural ways. The ambition of mankind has always been to migrate to unknown places and cultures in search of better life and economic opportunities. Such an endeavor is bold, risk taking, enterprising, and ambitious.

In the process of acculturation to the unknown and novel cultures, people as immigrants, sojourners, and tourists put their cultural resources at risk. However, they also draw on those resources, inappropriate as they may be in the new culture, by using *transclusion phenomenon.* Transclusion phenomenon suggests bringing a great change in appearance and characteristics of cultural traits by building on the basics. The new cultures are diffused and assimilated through the process of adaptation and culture learning by internalization of the particular culture.

The culture and communication phenomena have two aspects: acculturation and cross-cultural comparisons. Acculturation focuses on the assimilation, diffusion, and cultural experiences of individuals from a culture to 'other culture' of host society where the acculturation contexts may be multiple other cultural groups or a single culture. Cross-culture comparison contexts focus on culture universals and specifics in different cultures in their native environments. Cross-culture research in Imagery and Stereotypes enables us to understand a specific culture as well comparisons with other cultures. Moreover, cross-cultural imagery research can facilitate or impede cultural and international understanding.

The migrants and the host societies face issues and constraints that have changed with the development of complexities of human existence over time. The physical and technological means of communication have brought human beings closer to each other with a universal outlook for solving these issues. At the same time, it has become critically important to the political, economic, and social realities and to the vitality of the world's multicultural and mono-cultural societies to describe, understand, predict and control diverse cultural behavior across the world.

Communication competence is important in managing the intercultural communication process and cultural diversities by the immigrants and sojourners in any culture.

The journey through diversity of cultures, and the human endeavor to acculturate in novel cultures in unknown lands with unknown people facing individual and social constraints is unique. The issues of cultural identities, multiculturalism, cultural dilemmas, and influences perhaps pose far more reaching practical concerns. An integrated perspective for intercultural communication through dynamics and challenges for cultural diffusion is significant.

The cultural uproot willfully or forcefully create dilemmas, cultural identity crises and transculturation. The technology and media connectivity not only *exposes* people to global cultural ways but also *diffuse* the same to a global audience. It also stimulates people to migrate to attractive cultures. Somehow, the cultural globalization does not create a 'monolithic culture' but unique cultural ways are shaped through the process of diffusion.

The pragmatics of cultural diversity and the phenomena of cultural invasion and domination by other cultures through media and technology create cultural dilemmas, crisis of cultural identities and related tensions. Technology and media are the ideological apparatuses through which *cultural invasion* and *domination* may take place.

Communicating across Cultures

The basic human need is to communicate to self, among ourselves and to others. We express about ourselves, project about ourselves (Self-Image) and we desire to know about others (Other Image). We interact in this process. We live in a community, a society, a nation, and a country. This forms *A Broad Cultural Spectrum.*

A nation and a country may further comprise of sub-cultures within this broad cultural spectrum. The world has many communities, societies, and nations therefore many cultures. Intercultural communication occurs when we have the desire to interact across other cultures. In intercultural communication, we assess and project *intercultural imagery* i.e. self-image and other-image in interaction. Culture and communication are inseparable. The differences across cultures are the different ways in which people communicate.

A cultural image is specific to a culture — it is their worldview. The intercultural image is specific to multi-cultures that interact among themselves. They carry a worldview about each other that facilitates or impedes the inter-cultural interaction. The intercultural image is different from the cultural image.

Culture and communication are the two basic components in cultural communication. It is important to see how these two concepts are defined. Cultural imagery and intercultural imagery are the basic components in intercultural communication. The cultural variables are languages, attitudes and beliefs, values and ways of life, religion, artifacts, rituals and festivals. These are our *cultural resources* with which we interact within our cultures and with others.

A few sensitizing concepts have been the focus of recent research in inter-cultural communication. Sensitizing concepts convey a sense of reference and orientation grasped through personal experiences. William (1973) argues that the major problem with such concepts (value orientations, assumptions, set of expectations) is that they are discussed in isolation and never directly related to the process of communication. Scholars have recently been making deliberations in conventions and workshops to construct a theory of inter-cultural communication. There is an ambivalence among the scholars as to whether it is desirable or possible to develop a theory (theories) of intercultural communication.

What is the function of theorizing in intercultural communication? There are possibly three functions — to explain, to control or to predict. Research evidence is that generalizations have not been possible and therefore none of these functions have been applicable. Scholars have also been deliberating about the need for developing conceptual frameworks to give directions to the diverse research within the area and the need for theory to understand the process of communication between and among people of diverse cultures. Intercultural communication is still at an 'aparadigmatic' stage. This implies that it is an immature area that has not even gone through the development of its first paradigm.

Scholars of intercultural communication warned that intercultural communication was not sufficiently distinguished from other areas of research to justify its existence for independent area of investigation. The basis of their argument is that there is little consensus about what constitutes intercultural communication situation. For some, the critical attributes in intercultural communication are precisely identifying observable features of ethnicity and history of behavior etc. Others find intercultural communication occurring in all interactions between the two cultures or among different cultures.

Intercultural communication is a unique phenomenon. Its approaches differ depending on the perspective. In immigrant society, the significance of inter-cultural communication is important from the point of view of how people are acculturating to the host culture. The acculturating process has its own dilemmas, paradoxes and counter-paradoxes. In the acculturation process, the dilemmas may further develop the *transcultural perspective* of intercultural communication where the pull and push of both cultures suggests co-existence of the two cultures at a certain point of time.

In *enculturation communication,* people interact with different cultural resources among sub-cultures (or regional cultures in a country) in the broad cultural spectrum but there are still a few integrating cultural resources such as the political system, broad social structure, a common nationality, and a country that binds them culturally. This stance may present different intercultural dilemmas, paradoxes and counter paradoxes.

Earlier, culture, intercultural studies and research have been the domain of the anthropologists. The anthropologists looked at the evolution of the cultural resources in different cultures and across cultures. Later, in the 1950's the sociologists got interested in cultural and intercultural studies and research. They looked at social structural dimensions of the cultures and developed cultural social theories of modernization through a comparative approach of different cultures. These cultures included traditional and modern cultures as well as eastern and western cultures. Modernization theories developed indices for intercultural communication across these cultures and societies.

In the 1960's, the psychologists developed an interest in cross-cultural psychological studies and research. Cross-cultural psychology is the empirical study of members of various cultural groups that have had different experiences that led to predictable differences in their behavior. Cross-cultural psychologists used psychological concepts and theories developed in Western countries (mostly in the USA and European nations) and investigated them in non-western countries. These concepts included those from Piaget's developmental stages, Freudian's positions and Murray's needs. The investigations were often concerned with behavior associated with the antecedents and consequences of the behavior associated with these theories. Other studies involved replication of west-based experiments in other cultures, often with modifications to solve potential procedural difficulties. West-based experimental studies of leadership, stereotyping, perception, learning, and conformity have been replicated in other cultures. Psychological tests material designed and standardized in one culture have been administered in another. These are tests of intelligence, personality, interests and so forth. Later research evidenced that these have culture-bias and could not have given you the same reliability and validity and qualitative content that they had in western cultures.

Discovering differences is one of the most exciting parts of cross-cultural research. Psychologists have the goal of incorporating the behavior of many cultures into one theory (etic approach), and they must understand the behavior within each culture (emic approach). Cross-cultural research does face constraints and limitations in research issues and research methodology even from the point of these two approaches.

Communication has been the central and significant dimension in intercultural and cross-cultural research undertaken from anthropological, psychological, and sociological perspectives. However, until the 1970's, communication theorists, researchers, and practitioners did not show much interest in undertaking inter-cultural or cross-cultural research from a communication perspective in order to delineate a different set of research issues, research methodology and research models.

From the point of theory, research and practice, communication — whether interpersonal or mass media always has cultural contexts, in which it is presented, received, reacted to and acted upon. Thus utilization or effectiveness of communication is placed in cultural contexts and is therefore culture specific. The major players in the communication-culture-contexts (CCC) are national and international government, people and the media community. These specific CCC activate us for intercultural communication contexts. Communication is a vital link in the intercultural scenario.

Culture and communication are basic and necessary components for intercultural communication. The cultural models in both homogenous and heterogeneous cultural societies highlight the cultural diversity, influences, and contexts. These create multi-culturalism and related tensions.

The processes of diffusion, assimilation, adaptation, culture learning, and internalization of the host culture pose dilemmas, and challenges. The cultural uproot willfully or forcefully create dilemmas, cultural identity crises, and transculturation. These will vary according to the objectives of cultural diffusion to the host culture in a continuum of being an immigrant, sojourner, or a tourist.

Concept of Culture

Culture is defined in various ways. Some people define culture in terms of what people produce and know i.e., focusing on artifacts and their cognition. Others define culture in terms of the resources on which people may draw to conduct and make sense of their activities. The cultural ways are their resources. Culture is a part of our social world.

Culture is an integrated system of learned behavior patterns that are characteristics of the members of any given society. Cultures refer to the total way of life of any particular group of people and therefore include the customs, material artifacts, shared systems of attitudes and feelings as well as ways of thinking, saying and doing. Culture is consciously or unconsciously learned and then taught and handed over by one generation to another.

Culture is defined by shared manners, customs, beliefs, rituals, ceremonies, laws (written and unwritten), ideas, thought patterns, arts, tools, social institutions, religious beliefs, myths and legends, knowledge, values, concept of self, morals, ideals and accepted ways of behaving. It involves the social acquisition and transmission of patterns of customs, beliefs and behavior through symbols and widely shared meanings. It enables people of a given society to adapt to each other and to their physical and social environment. It involves learned responses and a system of ready-made solutions to the problems people face. It is the way we do things. It is constructed. Members can and do change cultural ways.

Culture manifests itself both in patterns of language and thought and in forms of activity and behavior. These patterns become models of common acts and styles of expressive behavior that enables people to live in a society within a given geographical environment at a given state of technological development. The modern concept of culture suggests a number of sub-cultures within the larger cultural spectrum.

All these definitions are not mutually exclusive. Actually, there is no single definition of culture. We learn culture by participating in it. As we grow we learn certain given roles in a particular set of relationships and learn to act in set situations. We learn through culture-specific language.

We find it advantageous to use the concept of culture as 'resources'. These resources are embedded in an individual's logic for meanings and actions. Conceptually, cultures can be compared in terms of their resources for compatibility or incompatibility. Procedures for repair, when these resources are negated or violated, and different configurations of these resources suggest different interaction settings within a culture and between different cultures. Interaction settings differ in the degree to which members draw upon culturally shared (as opposed to personal or inter-personal) resources to obtain coordination and coherence.

We live, do things, think and act in varied ways. These practices are particular ways that give us an identity. These are our cultural ways and give us cultural identity. Cultural ways are our resources and when we communicate within our psychological and cultural milieu, through our particular resources, we create explicit or implicit mutual understanding. The prime dynamics of culture are a unique social perceptual set with co-ordinated meaning and action, and cultural variance.

The differences in communication performance and the diverse forms of communication can create diversity among various cultures. People who live in various cultures and historical epochs communicate differently and have different patterns of thoughts.

Pearce (1989) presents three forms of intercultural communication: Co-ordination, Coherence, and Mystery; whereby we experience different ways of being human. The particular forms of communication shape the social institutions, and cultural traditions through which people interpret their environments and experiences. Human communication presupposes the existence of a vast reservoir of cultural habits and practices and derives their communicative power from them. The Coordination occurs by intervention when (intercultural) communication patterns break down. We interact with fellow people and interpret our culture and the world around us by Coherence. There is 'Mystery' that reminds us that there is more to life than the facts of daily existence. All human beings everywhere, and always, communicate by coordinating, achieving coherence, and experiencing mystery, although everyone may not achieve these in the same way. These are important differences and comprise of distinct ways of being human and culturally different.

Culture, Communication, Intercultural Communication

We see the world according to our world-view. Our experiences can greatly impact how we interpret what we see. We put our cultural resources at risk when we interact with others who are in our geographical milieu but not in our psychological milieu. The interaction of various cultural resources among diverse cultures is *Intercultural Communication.* The outcome of such interaction may be amalgamation, integration, adaptation and negotiation of certain cultural resources. Other outcomes may be coexistence of other cultural resources, and giving up yet other cultural resources as outdated. A convergent (novel) culture is thus created which could still be understood within the original cultural contexts, meanings and intentions.

There are *six basic axioms* about intercultural communication. First, the perceived differences among the cultures motivate people to interact. Second, personal styles of interpersonal communication such as cognitive, social, and communication styles affect it. Third, it has both content and relationship. Fourth, communication system symbolizes culture. Each culture has its own communication style and communication is central to culture. Fifth, intercultural communication reduces uncertainty level about other people. Sixth, intercultural interactions facilitate intercultural effectiveness.

Nature of Intercultural Communication

Intercultural communication use multi labels such as cross-cultural, inter-racial, inter-ethnic, and transcultural communication. These cultural groups may be other ethnic or racial groups, other nations or specifically defined groups with different socio-economic characteristics within the same ethnic or national group e.g., elite, middle class, lower class, youth groups, etc. Since these particular groups have a specific culture of their own, the communication is across these specific cultures and across these groups. Among these multi labels, intercultural is the best label for this form of communication.

Intercultural communication occurs whenever a message producer is a member of one culture and the message receiver is a member of another culture. Both assign meanings to the messages according to their perceptual sets in order to reach an understanding of the message produced.

People live in global vicinities and closer to diverse cultures due to advancement in media technologies. They experience the diversities and similarities of different cultural groups through exposure to media technologies and interpersonal contacts. These cultures have become more visible and vocal through these media technologies. Therefore, though people may not have a chance to visit these cultures or interact with them personally, they feel they know them well. Thus developments in media technologies facilitate intercultural communication *vis-à-vis* international communication.

Traditionally, perhaps the intercultural communication could have taken place within a few social groups. We are seeking something other than this traditional force with increased mobility and awareness of the new technological phase. There is a pragmatic interest in inter-cultural communication as cultures must be known and understood in the right communication perspective for wider political, social, educational, commercial, and technological ramifications.

To sum up, the principles of intercultural communication focus on effective understanding, and positive feelings between the targeted culture and host culture. The functional skills are developed to deal with the new phenomenon. Therefore, *the model for intercultural communication effectiveness is*: to develop functional communication styles that allow us to develop positive relationships so necessary for adaptation to the alien culture. The communication content should be clear and precise without any ambiguities as far as possible.

Dynamics of Intercultural Communication

The dynamics of intercultural communication are building intercultural climate, social perceptions and intercultural variance.

The pattern of intercultural climate building is social acceptance of our thinking, feeling, and acting as much as possible to know the ideal role and cultural behavior in the alien set up. This is created through three dimensions that occur in intercultural encounters. One, these are the positive feelings that we have about our own and other culture. Two, our beliefs i.e. our expectations and uncertainties and accurate understanding, actions and skills such as non-verbal and verbal communication, performance, survival skills, and interfacing with systems and institutions in the new culture to create social perceptions. Three, when we bring these two factors to intercultural encounters with other people from another culture we create variance.

Social perceptions have been the moving force for intercultural communication. Social perception is how we perceive the social events and objects in our environment and what meanings we attach to them. In intercultural communication act, both perceptions as well as ascribing meanings to the message received are important. Cultural environments condition our perceptual acts in such a way that we develop culturally determined perceptual sets.

Intercultural variance occurs due to the social perceptions. People may be living in the same geo areas, speaking the same language, following the same religion but may be very different in 'culture.' Why it is so? They differ in their cultures because they do not share the same life styles, beliefs, attitudes and values such as the culture of elite or middle class; of younger generation *Vs* older generation.

The focus on different cultures has made us realize that intercultural communication is inevitable as well unsuccessful. We realize that communication across cultural boundaries is difficult even if we cross the language barrier between one culture and other. We could still fail to understand and be understood. These failures in both the international arena as well as on the domestic scene give rise to the study of, and importance of Intercultural Communication as a field of study.

Process of Communication is an essential component of intercultural communication. We cannot share ideas and feelings if we do not communicate. In intercultural interaction, communication is a dynamic process whereby verbal and non-verbal human behavior is perceived and responded to. Communication is a dynamic process since it is ongoing and active and there are series of interaction patterns before and during the communication process, and after the cultural encounter. Communication is a symbolic behavior both verbal and nonverbal, to encode our internal notions and feelings. Waltzlawick *et al.* (1967, p. 48) advocates that 'One cannot not communicate.' Communication elicits response. We transform others' verbal and non-verbal behaviors into meanings in the context of our experiences. From these past experiences, we attach meanings to the observed behavior. It is eventually the receiver of the message who must determine what the behavior symbolizes.

Communication is complex because it contains many variables. There are many aspects of human personality among these variables that each person brings to the cultural encounter, such as, message form, the diversity of environments, channel of communication, and the influence of contexts on communication. The communication process of encoding and decoding is culture specific but it is a process that creates intercultural interaction and understanding.

There are films and media programs intended to increase intercultural understanding, to sensitize young people for tolerance, dialogue and peace. Some of these projects are within the UNESCO frame-work to create content and initiative to intensify the dialogue among the communities, cultures and civilizations.

The impact of Information technologies does facilitate cultural identity but they create cultural tensions also by exposing people to multicultural and global perspectives.

Cultural Variance, Diversity, Communication Effectiveness

Culture is extremely complex. Cultural differences vary along a maximal-minimal scale. The amount of cultural differences between the two cultural groups depends on the social uniqueness of the two groups. For example, there are maximal differences between western and eastern cultures; fewer variations between two western cultural groups or two eastern cultural groups; and low variations among sub-cultural groups within the same culture. Cultural variance occurs when the cultural groups do not share the same experiences and perceptions. Their worldview is different. Their life styles, beliefs, attitudes, and values differ.

There are variations in *subjective culture.* That is, the fundamental way in which people in different cultures perceives and cognitively experiences their physical and social environments. There are cross-cultural differences in patterns of message decoding in interpersonal communication.

Hall (1976) differentiates between high-context and low-context cultures. He argues that individuals in high-context cultures tend to rely more on subtle implicit contextual cues such as relational and social context, knowledge about the other person, non-verbal cues, and situational characteristics. Compared to low-context cultures, high-context cultures readily accept and value intuitive, holistic and direct modes of thinking. Individuals in high-context cultures have stronger group orientation, more explicit in-group and out-group distinctions, more intense involvement with intimates than do people in low-context culture who have strong individualistic orientation. Therefore, it is difficult as well it takes long for individuals from low-context culture to develop accurate understanding of perceptual and cognitive patterns of an alien from high-context culture. India can be an example of high-context culture and America of low-context culture.

Cultural Variance Variables. There are eight variables that create cultural variance within a culture and between cultures. These variables are only convenient categories and do not exist or exert in isolation rather they interact with one another and overlap to affect our intercultural communication behaviors and communication effectiveness. These variables are attitudes and beliefs, patterns of thoughts, language, non-verbal expressions, social organizations, role prescriptions, use and organization of space, and conceptualization of time. These variables are culture specific.

Individuals and the social setups are the focus of cultural communication hence interpersonal communication rules, social interaction and networks, and various other factors affecting it are broadly applicable to intercultural communication phenomenon. It is important to know and understand these since it is necessary to know and understand the cultures in right communication perspective for wider political, social, economic, educational, business and technological ramifications.

Cultural Diversity in meaning and action is created by cultural variance variables. Understanding of cultural diversities, facilitating cultural understanding, and communication effectiveness depend on knowing these variables in the right perspectives.

The interaction of various variables among diverse cultures is *Intercultural Communication.* Our cultural resources give us cultural identity. Culture specific images interact in multicultural settings and create inter-cultural images. Another way through which intercultural images develop is through our stereotypes and prejudices. Moreover, some time knowledge through inter-cultural communication helps in changing these images.

Ideal global culture is where voices of all cultures and people are heard with equal clarity, where no one culture should over-shadow another and where pride in one's own culture only increases respect for the cultures of others; and the diversity of cultures would express different visions of the world. But in reality, among various global cultures, the cultural ways and values of the predominant cultures dominate the cultural scenario.

We are not the same. Our diversity is our heritage, our strength, and our unique speciality. Why not take pride in these differences and celebrate, not subvert them. They nurture, define and sustain us. They give us roots and a sense of belonging. They make us feel special; and in this mammoth and indifferent world special is what we all yearn to feel. But in real world, diversity can have advantages as well disadvantages; depending upon how the cultural group is placed.

Cultural diversity may be in region, ethnicity, neighborhood, life styles, age, gender, mental, and physical abilities; or in professional goals, and learning styles. Our similarities allow us to come together in a common effort.

Working together from the perspective of diversities takes us to new levels of creativity and innovations. Our differences represent the greatest value as well as the greatest threat. These differences are both as a result of our individuality as well as our association with, and belonging to a cultural group. They have impact on us how we see the world, and what we see in the world.

We believe, that in general, people from different regional, ethnic, and racial backgrounds, and men and women from different educational and professional groups can and often do bring a different set of assumptions, beliefs, attitudes, and expectations to and about the life styles, work environments, and overall cultural environments.

The differences represent a richness and heightened source of energy, which when managed well lead to better development. These differences have impact on the effectiveness of individual and group performances. But because of differences, they need enhanced or new set of skills to enable them to optimize social and professional performance.

Research reveals that there is significant level of tension between and among the cultural groups both in social and professional set up. This tension exists just below the surface of outward interaction, yet has a major impact on the way in which people do interact with each other, and with their assigned roles in society, and work place. In any cultural environment, unless the differences we represent are appreciated and valued, those differences will tend to hinder rather than help the performance. Therefore, to manage diversity well whether in a social set up, or in work place, it is necessary to recognize, value, respect, and utilize differences to the benefit of the host cultural institutions.

There are six goals to 'Valuing Diversity Programs':

- Emphasize that valuing difference is an issue.
- Encourage mutual respect and trust by helping establish authentic relationships.
- Let people recognize the significance of valuing diversity for personal and professional productivity.

- Create a forum for examining stereotypes and assumptions.
- Create a shared vision of the society and workplace that value differences.
- Provide insights, tools, skills and techniques for change.

The diversity programs should focus on individuals to enhance awareness, explore impact of behaviors, modify limiting behavior, learn practical skills, and increase interpersonal effectiveness. The organization focus should be to enrich climate of workplace and decrease exposure to critical events. We can plan to achieve these diversity goals by looking at valuing diversity from three perspectives: (i) how we can and do limit ourselves when we interact with people who are different from us? (ii) how we can and do limit others from our untested mental models? (iii) how our behaviors both verbal and non-verbal can confuse and contradict our intentions?

Valuing diversity starts with managing diversity. Management of diversity not only recognizes that differences exist among people but it recognizes that these differences represent the potential strengths for host cultures. In an environment, where we value diversity, and view differences from the perspectives of productivity, creativity, and innovations, there is bound to be better intercultural understanding. We also believe that the products we create, the services we provide will diminish if there is lack of diversity input.

Cultural diversity is a major and immediate concern for humanity today. The right to live in one's own culture is among the most basic rights of life. Even UN charter in 1948 Universal Declaration of Human Rights acknowledged this as a fundamental human right. The forces of modernization have put devastating pressures on traditional cultures. The forces of ideology in this century repeatedly seek to impose uniformity across a range of differing cultures. There is need to integrate the issues of cultural diversity into all aspects of intercultural global communication.

History bears witness to the central role of culture and cultural diversity. In the colonial era culture was use as a tool for oppression and fragmentation. As many cultures of the world began to emerge from the shadow of imperialism; a new and troublesome phenomenon appeared — an explosion of micro nationalism. It took place in reaction to pressures of modernization, globalization and cross-cultural communication. Ethnic, religious, and cultural separatism threatened a return of the some of the worst problems of the past: intolerance or antagonism towards other cultures; opposition to practices unlike one's own; and an inability to conduct productive dialogue across the global range of diverse cultures. The cause of cooperation and progress on a global scale is set back by sterility and antagonism.

It becomes imperative to build and develop cultures in global contexts. Joint cultural programs such as freer travel, cultural exchanges, mutually beneficial youth and educational projects can bring down the barriers among nations.

The cultural universals of human behavior comprise of biological, psychological, and social needs. The cultural variability of the contents occurs within these universals. We do not need a new set of values to understand other cultures. What we need is new ways of expressing familiar ideas and values. In immigrant societies there are many distinct ethnic groups coexisting, speaking various languages and dialects of the world and having diverse 'own' cultural ways as well as acculturating to diverse cultural ways of others. They seem to be comfortable with their heritage and culture despite of endless differences, problems, conflicts and concerns in their home countries.

The '*Transculturation Model*' assumes that the assimilation and acculturation of minority groups into the culture of majority groups is an evolutionary and unilinear process. This would result into disappearance of the minority group is a facile generalization applied to all immigrant societies. But this is not the social reality. The 'cultural pluralism' prevails within a particular society and is accepted by it. Cultural pluralism may be plural ethnic groups in an immigrant society or plural regional sub-cultures within a country. There is assimilation of certain cultural characteristics from various cultures/ subcultures into the host culture. The 'Melting Pot Model' works to this extent. But beyond this, the plural cultures and subcultures hold on to their own cultural resources fitting these into Mosaics (Mosaic Model). They pass that on to their coming generations by word of mouth, ethnic media use (print, film, music, myths, stories etc.), artifacts, food and contact with own cultural scenarios by visits to and from home country.

Fukuyama Francis (2004) argues that America is assimilation 'powerhouse'. Europeans have only recently begun to confront the problem of assimilation, and continue to suffer from a stifling political correctness in talking honestly about the issue of immigration. Germans thought about accepting immigrants if they in turn accept certain German cultural values. In France, recent policy of banning of headscarves by Muslim women is not to crush religious freedom but to promote assimilation.

The ultimate success of assimilation depends not just on policy but also on the cultural characteristics of the immigrant group being assimilated. The speed with which an immigrant group assimilates in second and third generations after their arrival depends on group's rate of outmarriage. In US rates of outmarriage correlates strongly with both assimilation and upward social mobility on the part of different racial and ethnic groups. Assimilation of culturally distinct immigrants will be the greatest social challenge faced by developed democracies over the coming decades.

The '*Media Exposure Model'* shows that the host country media also show sensitivity to multi-cultural stimuli and respect cultural differences among the ethnic groups. Media has to re-examine the ways to deal with diverse cultures. Can media continue to play homogenizing role of mass culture? Media has to address them along their cultural and racial identities rather than to address as part of the melting pot. In this process media do reinforce diversity in a positive way. Cultural diversity does create new opportunities as the immigrants bring different cultural traditions. Some may see the cultural diversity changes as problematic creating stress and strain, others may take this as an opportunity for developing new learning ways. This is an effort towards intercultural understanding.

At international level in immigrant societies like USA, the Melting Pot Model, Transcultural Model, Mosaic Model and Media Exposure Model may create integration in cultural diversity.

Cultural Determinants: Cultural Experiences

Our cultural experiences are different and therefore our ways of acting and thinking are different. Such diverse cultural experiences do affect our ways, forms, and content of communication, as well as communication effectiveness. We do try to minimize 'not knowing the culture' by acting in different ways. One such way is to know the various cultural determinants that affect our cultural experiences. There are four cultural determinants that influence our cultural experiences:

Social structural values are one such determinant. The family institution among the social structures plays predominant role in molding the cultural experiences. The forms of family, such as nuclear or extended, authority in the family, child rearing practices, gender preference and roles in the family, inheritance, marital selection, sanctity or disintegration of marriage and sex mores are culture specific social structural values.

The second important determinant is *the philosophy of life* in a specific culture. The culture specific philosophy will mold the culture to be. Such a philosophy characterizes a culture as fatalistic or achieving; traditional or modern; orienting to technology or not; and socio-economic development oriented or not.

The third determinant is the *values and experiences* that are unique to sub-cultures within a society. For example, attitude towards education, authority, and life in general among sub-cultures of poor class, middle class or the elite class within the same culture will differ.

The fourth determinant is the *opportunities available* to its members within the cultures such as social and geographic mobility, technological exposures to other cultures, visibility to other cultures both geographically and through media technologies.

We interact with diverse cultures with background of our own culture-specific experiences, and adjust to their culture specific experiences.

Intercultural Communication Effectiveness (ICE)

Communication style, and personality of the interactants, ability to function efficiently, and a pragmatic approach to issues in the novel culture are central for being effective in work place, and in social and political relationships. ICE is composite of abilities: (i) for professional competence and actual job performance, (ii) to interact with clarity, friendliness and appropriateness, (iii) to adjust well by coping effectively with culture stress and dealing with adaptation, (iv) facilitate adjustment and manage stress for self, family, and significant others, (v) to see the others' point of view and react positively to it, and (vi) competence to minimize the negative judgment effects particularly in political situations.

Effectiveness is an integral part of skill development for intercultural adjustments. The variables related to develop intercultural effectiveness skills are:

- To develop a cultural fit between one's interpersonal style, one's corporate culture and the culture in which one is working.
- Tolerance of ambiguity, fluidity and flexibility in attitudes, openness and flexibility in personal communication styles are important in building intercultural relationships.
- To develop cognitive complexity. It refers to the ability of a person to perceive wide variety of things about another person and make finer discriminations. A cognitive complex person experiences less cultural stress than cognitive simple person. They make better and more accurate judgments about developing impressions about others. They can see situations in larger contexts, come up with more differentiated descriptions, and they see more possibilities about people and situations.
- To develop attitudes, and skills to feel comfortable in interpersonal relationships. As research has shown, it is significantly correlated with maximum intercultural adjustments.

- The amount of immediate and personal control we have about our communication environments is significantly correlated to ICE. Personal control (remaining confident) facilitates intercultural adjustment and performance. It has significant impact on adaptation to new culture and being interpersonally effective.
- Innovativeness to develop, and accept new ideas within a context of social acceptance; and willingness to experiment new approaches, and learn new things help in ICE.
- To develop self-esteem i.e. confidence in one self is necessary for ICE.
- Communication apprehension (i.e. personal anxiety) in groups, in public, and in interpersonal situations has impact upon intercultural adjustments and effectiveness.
- Excessive self-praise or self-blame, showing disinterest in other cultural groups is not functional for ICE.
- Ethnocentrism and prejudice disrupt ICE.
- Some of the other variables that correlates significantly with ICE are acculturation motivation, interactive skills, language competency, positive expectations from the host culture, degree of similarity or differences with the host culture, age, occupation and intercultural training etc.

Cultural Dilemmas

Cultural variance evokes curiosity about the origin of human difference viz. cultural ways, resources, artifacts etc. The cultural variance curiosity (CVC) is evoked when there is personal as well media mediated contact with many other cultures. CVC not only adds to the information, and knowledge about various cultures but a mix of cultural influences gives a hybrid dynamism. The expansion of dynamism depends on the number and extent of cultural contacts, and receptivity of the people. This produces a kind of cultural critical mass.

Cultural Influences: People when influenced by other cultures do not look for total assimilation rather they seek adaptation of certain other cultural ways that they find attractive or closer to their own ways.

Cultural influences can be both subtle and direct. Therefore, initially, the positive cultural aspects of any other culture influence people. Later, they may be drawn to the negative aspects too. 'Other cultural influences' can be thus both positive and negative. Four determinants such as social structural values, culture specific values of life, values and experiences of subcultures, and opportunities within the cultures have impact on cultural influences.

Interpersonal contacts, and living in that culture reinforces cultural influences but such experiences are not widely possible. Now-a-days, cultural influences reinforced by mass media are stronger than through interpersonal contacts. Mass mediated influences have two added advantages. One, mass media such as terrestrial television, cable television, satellites, and direct broadcasting (DBS) through satellites, VCR, telecommunications with it's added dimensions of (LAN, ISDN, voice mail, fax, Internet) books, Newspapers etc., and other advanced new communications technologies have brought us closer to other cultures. It is thus paving the way for a global culture. Two, we are strongly exposed to political, social, development, economic, religious philosophies, values, and ways of living of both masses and elite of number of varied cultures simultaneously. This provides us the opportunities to study closely the various cultures, to inter-mix the positive and negative cultural philosophies and resources, and to be selective about what we like about other cultures. *We try to incorporate the selective cultural life styles and cultural resources in our own culture.*

Many societies label these direct cultural influences as 'Cultural Invasion'. Cultural invasion suggests predominance of other cultural values whether it is consumerism or democratic values etc. through communications technologies. Governments in traditional developing societies try to protect their cultural values from western media influences, and from such cultural invasions by scrambling the media channels or censorship of media contents. The penetration and exposure of these communications technologies are getting so stronger and deeper day by day that varied cultures are either losing their boundaries or their boundaries are overlapping. Therefore, it is not possible to protect one's own cultural values from extraneous cultural influences.

Globalization on one hand presents few scenarios. The diverse cultural resources are integrated. The expectations of world are coming closer both through visual and personal contacts. These two factors create international understanding. On the other hand, there is anxiety, that dominant cultures may impose their cultural values, life styles, political, economic, technological, social, and educational systems.

In olden days, the cultural influences occurred through interpersonal contacts by explorers, missionaries, and visiting dignitaries. Since the 'contact influence' used to be over a period of time, and therefore subtle; it never seemed to create stress and anxieties. Only immediate rejections of the interpersonal situations were part of the scenario those days.

The new communication technologies both electronic and ethnotronic have currently changed the entire scenario as far as cultural invasions and ensuing threats are concerned. The extent and intensity of media exposure, as well exposure to other communications technologies; and the interpersonal contacts through these technologies have brought diverse cultures closer to influence one another more speedily and simultaneously; and both with positive and negative impacts.

There are political and social impacts of cultural invasions. Some cultures handle it by censoring the media program contents, and by scrambling the media channels. They may bar the interpersonal exchange of people so that they are not exposed to the alien cultural influences. Other societies may make efforts to counteract by giving more healthy mix of their own cultural resources in order to create interest, achievement, and preservation motive for their own cultural identities. They also try to counteract the alien values by presenting their own cultural values in the right perspective and aggressively promoting their own cultural values.

India presents an interesting case study. In late 80's Cable Television started in India by STAR TV Network that is being operated from Hongkong. The program contents of channels of STAR TV were (are) different in two ways. One, it was (is) presenting the global happenings from an information and educational focus. Two, the Indian audience were (are) being exposed to entertainment oriented media programs that were (are) a mix of Indian, western, and other alien cultural values. Over and above, it offered (offers) round the clock and multi program channels to select from. The Indian TV a terrestrial television service — 'Doordarshan' is run by government. During 80's, it was being operated only for a few hours, and had only two program channels. Further, it did run educational and information programs but offered programs low in entertainment focus.

The government of India at that time felt that it was virtual cultural invasion by STAR TV. They talked about banning its operation in India. But the audience groups had the upper hand and government could neither ban it nor scramble the channels. But it did create impetus for Doordarshan to change and grow with the times. As a result, since 1994, Doordarshan has started multi program channels, has improved and introduced new kind of program contents to attract the audience. They also produced programs to counteract the values that they did not want STAR TV to propagate. This was a healthier step to take rather than to totally ban the operations and shut people's exposure to STAR TV.

In another instance, India does not want its people to be exposed to the political culture and ideology of its neighboring country — Pakistan by being exposed to Pakistan TV. Not only its beaming is banned in India but the Pakistan TV channels are also scrambled. This is done off and on according to political correctness. Pakistan also does the same to Indian television channels. Geographically and culturally, these countries are so close that they can have very good reception of their programs both technically and culturally.

In an era of satellite communications and other advance technologies, to what extent, and how long it is possible to be a close society and shut its people to intercultural influences from world media exposure? It is also not favorable and possible to minimize personal intercultural exposures in a shrinking world made possible by all the advanced technologies.

International Image: Familiar images make false and lasting impressions. Certain images are so familiar and so deeply embedded in the consciousness of human beings that they have become cultural icons. Unfortunately many of these images — and the understanding they convey — are seriously misleading and creating false impressions of those cultures. They are remarkably difficult to correct.

A typical image widely copied and embellished can shape impressions that nearly become universal. And when such images convey information supposedly based on science they can enhance human understanding perhaps more profoundly than words could ever do. Visual images have amazing power of depictions, either to clarify or distort our understanding of scientific concepts.

We remember through images but we understand through words. But because of the amazing power of the images to shape the way people remember and think about important concepts, we have to be careful in what images we expect to become icons and make sure we get them right.

Cultural identity is the symbol of one's essential experiences of one self as it incorporates worldview, values, attitudes, and beliefs of a shared cultural group. As such it is an interpretive frame for experiences. It is an image of self and culture intertwined in the individual's total perception of reality. Different domains of self-conception, and different social groups have sub-cultural and inter-connected identities. Cultural identities vary along three inter-dependent dimensions of scope, salience, and intensity. Contextual parameters of participants' interactions influence them.

Beyond cultural identity, *Multiculturalism* emerges from human interactions in global perspectives. Multiculturalism is practicing an international frame of reference while living within one's own cultural society or in a multicultural immigrant society. It has its own charms and dilemmas. Multiculturalism perspective takes the position that no one culture is better or worse than the other. All cultural systems are equally valid as variations on human experiences. Every culture provides identity, regulated behavior, and a sense of personal place.

Globalization of cultures through media technology exposures, and interpersonal contacts lead to multiculturalism and vice versa. Media exposure, Information technology, and Information society are influencing factors in preserving multiculturalism and cultural identity. Communication and cultural exchanges are preconditions to global cultures. Multicultural societies do face the problems of diversity management, as various cultural identities have to be addressed and managed separately.

The government of India at one time was concerned with the cultural invasion by foreign television channels but in 2000 decade there is cultural invasion of a different kind from out sourced jobs from abroad. Young people are spurning traditions as foreign goods, and foreign outsourced jobs flood the country. For India's youth new money through outsourced jobs in call centers and other areas fuels a cultural revolution beside consumerism.

The social shifts go hand-in-hand with huge economic change such as the young like to spend and not save, and arranged marriages are outdated. They are also creating a young, affluent class absorbing western attitudes at the office. Earlier, young girls who worked at night were presumed to be call girls and not call center workers. Now they enjoy working at night with confidence and freedom. The outsourcing gathers up more upwardly mobile young people who are gaining confidence and social freedom.

The cultural transformation is more intense among call center workers. Mostly, in their 20s, just English speaking graduates, they earn more money than their mothers in academics would have earned. Along with training in foreign accents and geography they are also absorbing new ideas about family, they do not want to live in extended families. Their social and cultural outlook is changing.

Arundhati Roy (2000) an Indian activist sounds a broader concern about cultural transformation. Call centers strip young Indian workers of their cultural identities by using American names on the phone. 'How easily an ancient civilization can be made to abase itself completely. The girls will never be able to live the life of their mothers — the meek and quiet role of housewife in an extended family.'

This can be the best example of acculturation to the host countries ways while being in your social set up. They can go through tensions, stress and anxieties because of the push and pull of cultural values.

Cultural identity, multiculturalism, and acculturation create intercultural tensions. It is a challenge to preserve one's own cultural identity. People go through tensions, stress, and anxieties on three counts to preserve it. One, when integrating plural sub-cultures in a homogeneous culture. Two, when there is push and pull towards globalization of culture and multiculturalism. Three, acculturation process in a host culture, where there is conflict, as to which cultural values to assimilate and practice, and which ones to preserve for coming generations.

Multiculturalism and globalization of cultures create unique tensions and strains on three counts. One, there are no clear and secure cultural boundaries for a multicultural person to develop relational identities. Two, persons develop 'diffused personality' where configuration of loyalties and identifications are in constant flux and constant exposure to, and overwhelming demands of messages and stimuli from diverse cultural groups overwhelm them. Three, one looses sense of integrity and congruity because of practicing multiculturalism.

Culture and Development

We noted in our earlier discussions from Development communication perspective that development follows a culture specific model and cultural dimensions enriches development. In 70s, the development practitioners learnt from the experiences that culture specific models are necessary for successful development. Since every culture has unique demands for its development and related actions. These in turn have to be in tune with its material and non-material cultural resources. Certain cultural dimensions will affect the course of development and its areas. Many times, threat to cultural identity may block some development programs.

The key issues that needs focus in this context are: culture and economic development, culture and digital divide, cultural management (for development) focusing on management practices in cultural enterprises, culture and governance focusing on cultural policies, civil society and government support for cultural enterprises, cultural identity during periods of stability, and economic growth in political conflicts or war.

Culture and sustainable tourism is another issue, which focus on promoting and protecting cultural heritage sites. The tangible and intangible cultural elements are heritage, historic, and natural sacred sites; museums — handicrafts and oral traditions; languages and literature; performing arts — music, songs, documentary, cinema and digital heritage; festival and events — rites and beliefs; traditional — sports & games, medicines, and cuisine.

Raising awareness and action for culture of peace is equally important in development context. This involves a specific set of values, attitudes, traditions and modes of behavior and ways of life. Peace is precursor of social, economic, political and cultural growth and the overall development of the people, society both nationally and internationally.

Culture: New Communications & Information Technologies

Cultures have become more visible, vocal, and global through exposure to media technologies. Therefore, even though we may not have a chance to visit people in other countries and cultures or interact with them; but we feel we know them. Such an interaction is facilitated by development in media technologies. ICT have facilitated simultaneous interpersonal and intercultural communication. Innovations and refinements in innovations in media technologies (TV, VCR, audiocassettes, telecom, computers and its networks) have brought people into potential contacts.

Communication media and information technologies have important role to play in sustaining and developing the world cultures and languages. The implementation of this principle requires support for a plurality of means of information and communication and respect for culture and language diversity.

The focus is on cultural changes engendered by the ICT within the technological base of developing societies. Cultural issues are central to the research questions whenever research is done about appropriate development of information literacy in developing societies; and even these cultural issues permeates findings.

Buses, automobiles, trains, airplanes, have created linkages within and between local, regional, national and international levels of human organizations. Human connections through communication have made possible the interaction of goods, products, services, and more significant exchange of thoughts and ideas. Growth of human communication has brought down the barriers that separated people throughout — historically, geographically, linguistically, and culturally. Such openness is likely to modify our basic perspective of one another.

Simultaneous events in the world, overall awareness through mass media, other international information technologies, and close interactions with diverse cultural groups for business or otherwise create awareness of changing world realities. These world realties pertain to change in social structures, values, politics, and in human relationships. Technological connectivity in both international and domestic environments; and changes in every pattern of life demand human adaptability within the culture or with diverse cultural groups.

As stated in earlier sections, Innis Harold (1950) through his theory of Technological Determinism propounded that the fundamental breakthroughs in technology are first applied to the process of communication. The forms of social organizations, stages of society, and the characteristics of the society are determined by the *medium of the time.* In current times, the computers, Internet, telecommunications with their advance functions, cable television, and satellite communications are shaping societies differently and giving more intercultural and inter-societal connectivity.

Marshall McLuhan (1964) sharpened the thesis *that medium is the message,* and that dominant technology of the communications shapes the culture and the cultural ways. If we apply this in present contexts, the personal and work cultures, entertainment, and leisure activities are shaped differently by the dominant communication technology of broadcasting, computerization and telecommunications in different times. It is further argued that there is impact of media on cultures, and cultures have impact on shaping of the media systems. Therefore, there are different and varied media systems due to cultural diversity at present.

The political economy theorists argue that dominant ideas in a society are those of the dominant class. The class that is the dominant material power of the society is also the cultural and spiritual power. From intercultural and international communication perspective it is necessary to know the dominant cultural power of any nation for better relations.

We continue to see more of international and domestic conflicts despite the fact that people know more of one another across diverse cultural and sub-cultural groups. We do see many different ways in which people try to cope with these complexities and changes of life. It becomes easier to cope and adapt to these complex and changed ways — if we understand the intercultural aspect of our international and domestic realities. Moreover, it becomes still easier if we understand the dynamics and direction of change of the contemporary world where diverse cultures interact. In order to develop intercultural perspective, we must be sensitive, understanding, and possess social skills of our own cultures as well of the diverse cultures with which we may interact. Media and information technologies play significant roles in these contexts.

Hanson & Narula (1990, p. 14) argue that cultures determine in part, the types of communication we engage in and the appropriateness of the information and technology models. Many of these models evolve into social institutions that have powerful social effects and act within the cultural contexts to reinforce existing values, norms or practices while at the same time introducing the potential for change. Communication whether mediated or interpersonal is always in a cultural context. The effectiveness of a particular technology depends on the dominant cultural ideology of a country. For example, in India, the cultural ideology towards technology is pro-social; and its application favors the medium of television as a purveyor of this ideology. Therefore, the effort is to develop more television technology rather than other technologies that enhance the cultural goals. In the United States the dominant cultural ideology is labor saving devices (such as computers), which indicates that there may be more flexibility and incentive to develop computer technology than to develop more of television.

Though at present in 2004, India is leaning towards giving more connectivity to people more so in rural areas, so focuses are varying: cell phones and Internet to some extent, increasing telephone density also in the country, and computer software development because of economic gains through its export though its not utilized so much for domestic gains.

Narula (1988) research suggests that cultural determinants are necessary along with technological and economic determinants for successful implementation of technology. The cultural determinants identified are cultural values of both elite and the masses, the cultural policies of the government, societal values, media structures its controls and practices, and work ethics. Moreover, homogeneity of the cultural ways and languages can facilitate or hinder communication technologies. The cultural effects of the technology will depend on the nature of technology itself. The social component of the technology must be culturally relevant for low resistance to the particular technology itself.

Narula (1990) argues that we face communication technology challenges and cultural challenges simultaneously. It is twofold. First, cultural challenge concerns the communication medium and the technology related to it. Second, cultural challenge addresses the way and means in which technology is accepted into the individual's lifestyle and social system; as well as how the communities relate technology to their life styles and national identities. Further, new communication technologies pose cultural challenges for societies for preserving cultural identity and values of the particular society. Technology choice is within a system — never in a vacuum.

The communicators in developing countries identify development and expansion of media technologies with pro-social roles. They are perpetually concerned whether media technologies will be preservers or destroyers of cultural values? Will these technologies encourage a breakdown of traditional values, and support mediocre and substandard alien values?

While preserving cultural identity, will these technologies erode cultural vitality, internal diversity, and intercultural understanding? Erosion of cultural vitality is identified with a process of stereotyping, a breakdown of cultural forms, and reduction in opportunities for minority cultures.

Hanson & Narula (1990) present 'culture specific' viewpoints of the use of media technologies especially in pluralistic societies rather than taking a global perspective. They argue that function and gratification of media technologies are not applicable the same way universally though the medium may be available universally. Media technologies must be adapted to the needs of the different cultures, and they must be acquired and introduced with a concern for levels and regions with different variations.

They further argue that some people assume that people live in 'split level' cultures created by media technologies. What matters is not the abstract potentiality of media technologies but the value that is attributed to them locally. Technology is not 'constant' but a political, economic, cultural acquisition, with short-term and long-term effects and consequences. There has to be a positive relationship between technology and cultural development enriching the cultural resources and respect for cultural diversity.

Noshir *et al*. (1986) advocate that five value orientations, such as regard for human nature, relationship of man to nature, time orientation, orientation towards activity, and types of relationship among people vary along cultures. These cultural orientations help or hinder the implementation of technological innovations in the first as well in the third world.

Introduction of any new communication technology will have important implications for the culture and the system of social relationships in that society such as, new social roles, ability and readiness of the culture to absorb the new technology, and the work ethics to make that technology work. Further, the technology also affects the psyche of the people. This in turn effects the way people think and act. It alters sense ratios and perceptions. Generally, the effects of technology on culture do not occur at the level of opinions or concepts but instead affects the sense ratios and perceptions steadily without resistance.

The performance demands of the technology must fit the social roles. Therefore, we need social competence to deal with communication technology changes. We can expect a twofold impact: impact of communication technology on cultural values and vice versa.

It has been observed that modern communication technologies create a cultural-lag phenomenon by running ahead of the some parts of the culture of these societies. Thus it takes some time for the culture to adjust to the demands of the new technology. In third world countries, the cultural lag between the material and non-material cultures is quite pronounced particularly when the material culture is from a foreign country. Further, culture lag occurs when disparities are created among the information rich and information poor within the society itself. Hanson (1988) suggests that cultural lag may occur in two forms: the disparity in material possessions (possession of technology receiving sets) and the disparity in information.

People are ready to accept the technological challenges when they are ready to put their cultural resources at risk; thereby suggesting that they are ready to change conventional values and lifestyles to match the technological changes. The performance demands of technology require a change in values.

MacBride Sean (1980) observed that however confident any society may be of having grasped the historical and contemporary essentials of problems in communication; it may well discover in the next decade, or at furthest in the next century that other technological advances have produced unforeseen effects, uncertainties, and imponderables.

However, the global perspective of the Information technology cannot be overlooked. Information technology relies on a global grid for international use. We can see that any one nation's desire, decision, or trial with ICT inevitably link that nation to *a system.* The changes within one nation could ostensibly have ramifications for the rest of the world.

Important criticisms and considerations for areas of technology transfer, content exchange, and experts' training in the technology systems and designs pertain to cultural domination. The host (technology producing) nations produce more than technology, software, or instructions; these exchanges bring with them the dominant ideology of the producing nations that affects the cultural context of the receiving nations (mostly developing countries) by infusing alien concepts into the traditional cultures. Cultural domination can also take place through imposition of 'experts' who are put in charge of (usually) indigenous workers and of the social technologies that come from these organizational components. The policies for enhanced technological opportunities and development creates cultural dependency, and reinforces economic power and domination.

Jussawalla & Hughs (1984) emphasized that a few information systems qualify as the indigenous media to preserve people's traditions and culture. It will be up to the policy-makers to find the path by which indigenous media can best serve the people and strengthen the heritage in the forthcoming technological age.

Hanson & Narula (1990) conclude that the information society is not a utopian society, nor it is a global village, or capitalists' convention in which information is a commodity that is bought and sold. The real information society represents and celebrates diversity within cultural contexts. It acknowledges that powers influence dynamics within and among nations; but it does foster *communication and a relationship of interaction among people of a nation and among nations of the world.*

Information is a tool for change, and technologies create that change. The cultural challenges involve a determination of what change can, will, and must take place. The 'Internet' connections through the information technologies are expanding the global intercultural connectivity though creating some positive and other negative issues and challenges in the process.

The cultures in developing countries are faced with the dilemmas that ICT may pose. They are in paradoxical situation, ICT are necessary for cultural development and ICT must not be an instrument for destroying the culture. Issues concerned with this paradoxical situation are widely debated in world forums.

UNESCO (2003) research report for World summit on information society, addresses the social and cultural changes engendered by the introduction of ICT within the technological base of developing societies. Attention is paid to the ethical dimensions of the issues and to the importance of freedom of expression, and cultural and linguistic diversity. An inclusive approach is taken to specific groups such as women, youth, and seniors, disabled and indigenous people.

Another UNESCO research report (2003a) investigated the understandings of schooling of students, teachers, parents, and other community members. The research is concerned with the impact of technological change on these understandings and the implications these might have on development initiatives. The study explored the possibilities and problems afforded by ICTs as educational tools in rural Africa. The study locale was a Ghanian village. A broader goal was to generate knowledge about the appropriate development of information literacy in developing countries. Cultural issues were central to the research questions and permeate many of the findings.

Eminent political and intellectual world leaders debated at the UNESCO symposium at WSIS (2003), about the main implications and challenges for the construction of knowledge societies. Some of the questions they debated are: how to achieve pluralism in knowledge societies — cultural and linguistic diversity, and pluralism in content? How ICTs can promote and safeguard both tangible and intangible cultural heritage? How to enhance intercultural dialogues and exchanges in knowledge societies? What are the new dimensions for culture in knowledge societies and how to ensure universal access to information? The outcomes of these discussions will contribute to building a holistic and comprehensive vision and a clear developmental perspective.

Kochiro Matsuura Director General of UNESCO (Nov 2002) while inaugurating preparatory meeting for WSIS 2003, commented on cultural diversity and the technological divides. He emphasized the critical importance of cultural diversity and multilingualism by focusing attention on preservation and promotion of cultural diversity and multilingualism. *The access to ICT infrastructure should be full access to society but more than this; it is about the capacity to influence the kind of society being generated by large-scale technological and economic forces.* He further commented that there is conviction that the specific social outcomes of technological change are not given or inevitable but are subject to ethical choice and public preference. Different forms of knowledge are embodied in technology itself and in the uses to which technology is put. Therefore, WSIS debates in Dec 2003 must give recognition to the several types of knowledge and understanding that are involved in formation of knowledge societies. This can give a perspective on how ICT might best be harnessed so that education, science and culture are advanced in inclusive and equitable ways.

He further commented that vital social, political, cultural and institutional aspects of change must be seriously considered. This requires that issues of human rights, social inclusion, intercultural dialogue, cultural diversity, and gender and youth be accorded a central and not a marginal place. Inequalities between different societies must be examined and also the ways in which these societies can enter into meaningful dialogue with one another so that cultural as well technological divides are narrowed.

Communication media and information technologies have an important role particularly in sustaining and developing the world's cultures and languages. The implementation of this principle requires support from a plurality of means of information and communication and respect for cultural and linguistic diversity.

In context of UNESCO's universal declaration on Cultural Diversity, it is suggested that the evolution of information society must be founded on the respect and promotion of the recognition of the rights of the indigenous people and their distinctiveness as outlined in ILO convention 169 and UN Draft Declaration on the Rights of Indigenous peoples. Indigenous people have fundamental rights to protect, preserve and strengthen their own identity and cultural diversity.

Information technologies should be used to support and promote those rights.

World Social Forum (2004) provided an open platform to discuss strategies of resistance to the model for globalization formulated at the World Economic Forum (2004). World social forum discusses alternatives to dominant neo-liberal strategies, for sharing experiences, and for strengthening alliances among mass organizations, people's movements and civil society.

WSIS (Dec 2003) addressed the issues of local languages and the impact of ICT on cultural identity in local communities. It highlighted the role of libraries in promoting the safeguarding of intangible cultural heritage, as well as building cultural (local and national) identity.

At the dawn of the new era, a vast expansion of human communication is profoundly influencing culture everywhere. Revolutionary technological changes are only part of what is happening. More than ever before, ours is a society focused on communication and civilization centered on images. Ultimately society is communication. Communication technologies have developed audiovisual languages and new forms of rhetoric. The very concept of an audiovisual culture is now commonly accepted. Recent technological developments in a unique manner bring artistic and cultural achievements within the orbit of a great part of the human race.

To sum up *culture* as understood from its varied standpoints is pragmatic, alive and effective when understood, experienced and practiced within the framework of intercultural communications. Development of societies and ICTs applications facilitate cultural and intercultural development.

Summary

The intercultural communication framework addresses the significance of images — self-image, other-image and inter-cultural image expressed through our cultural resources both tangible and intangible.

In context to this framework the focus is on cultural identity, multiculturalism, cultural experiences and influences, and the cultural diversity. These variables create dilemmas and tensions. Cultures make efforts to achieve intercultural communication effectiveness despite these limitations. Therefore, the model for intercultural communication effectiveness is to develop functional communication styles that allow us to develop positive relationships so necessary for adaptation to the alien culture.

Communication among people across nations, countries, and cultures is important. Since from all perspectives, it involves communicating with diverse cultures and understanding of those cultures, and therefore focusing on social phenomena. Thus social theory of national identity becomes significant.

The outcome of interaction of various cultural resources may be amalgamation, integration, adaptation and negotiation of certain cultural resources. In such interactions, communication is a dynamic process whereby verbal and non-verbal human behavior is perceived and responded to.

There is a pragmatic interest in intercultural communication as cultures must be known and understood in the right communication perspective for wider political, social, educational, commercial, and technological ramifications. The dynamics of intercultural communication are building intercultural climate, social perceptions and intercultural variance.

In intercultural interaction, vis-à-vis cultural diversity, in any cultural environment, unless the differences we represent are appreciated and valued, those differences will tend to hinder rather than help the performance. Therefore, to manage diversity well whether in a social set up, or in work place; it is necessary to recognize, value, respect, and utilize differences to the benefit of the host cultural institutions. Our differences represent the greatest value as well as the greatest threat. At international level in immigrant societies like USA the Melting Pot Model, Transcultural Model, Mosaic Model and Media Exposure Model may create integration in cultural diversity.

The development practitioners learnt from the experiences that culture specific models are necessary for successful development for its unique development demands in tune with its material and non-material cultural resources. Many times, threat to cultural identity may block some development programs.

The key issues that need focus in development context are: culture and economic development, culture and digital divide, cultural management (for development) focusing on management practices in cultural enterprises, culture and governance focusing on cultural policies, civil society and government support for cultural enterprises, cultural identity during periods of stability, and economic growth in political conflicts or war. Culture and sustainable tourism is another issue, which focus on promoting and protecting cultural heritage sites. Culture of peace is precursor of social, economic, political and cultural growth and the overall development of the people, society both nationally and internationally.

The impact of Information technologies does facilitate intercultural communication but they can also create cultural dilemmas and tensions by exposing people to multicultural and global perspectives.

14

Communication Management Perspective

Communication is an important component in every human activity. It is effective when it is managed well. Therefore it is important how communication is managed in various streams for effective delivery of ideas, products, and services. The management could be of both human and non-human communications (computer, telecommunication etc).

Both human and non-human communication is used in managing communication in the focused issues and areas supporting each other to manage the communication effectively. Thus both management and communication strategies are incorporated.

Management approach calls for holistic approach to communication in any particular area be it business, information technology or development. The necessary conditions for such a holistic approach is IECM strategies; linkages between civil society, administrators and communication channels, and good governance.

Communication management operations depend on number of factors that must be managed efficiently and effectively. These are organizational or individual goals, audience profile and analysis, economic and social trends and issues related to specific areas, planning decisions, appropriate actions for solving issues and research strategies appropriate to the scope and nature of communication situation. The management education and practice do focus on different areas for communication management as an expertise area.

To specify few areas that we have discussed in this section are: *Management of business communications and managing knowledge economies, health care communications, intercultural communications, development communications, information communications, conflict management and knowledge management.*

It is necessary and important to manage both human and non-human communication per se in all sectors of activity and communication situations. Effective communication is well-managed communication.

The focus of management of human communication is essentially the five dimensions: creating awareness, disseminating information, delivery of services, ideas and products, coordinating linkages for both human and non-human communications and better administration of campaigns, services and linkages. Communication competence is needed to manage these five dimensions. Narula (1984) argues that communication competence varies in different environments: of work, professions, social setup and family. The focus of communication relationships in these environments is related to communication skills and behavior of the individual/s. Even within these environments, different sets of relationships are developed according to the communication competence of the individual/s.

Non-human communications focus is on conventional mass media electronic communication channels, information communication technologies in general and particularly computers, Internet and its applications and telecommunications.

Management of Non-human communications channels depends on the availability and accessibility of communication channels. Let us take computer technology for instance. The questions we face: Is it available in 2000 decade in advance forms in a developing society of India? Whether it is imported or indigenous. Will it help managing its information, people's life style, trade and governance better?

Yes, for India computer is an advance communication technology capable of many significant tasks but it will be effective in the areas where it will be managed well by professionals, administrators and people to their advantage. If they fail, they do not make progress viz this technology.

If this technology is accessible only in urban areas then they are the people who will benefit and not the rural areas. If it is only the rich who can buy it then poor will be deprived. If it is the educated who can have computer skills then uneducated will suffer. So computer technology will be effective to the extent how its availability and accessibility is managed. How the digital-divide is managed to the benefit of different segments of society.

The focus of communications would vary with different sectors of human activity such as health, education, knowledge, development, economy and business, conflict and war etc. Though the basics of management would be the same for varied sectors; but different management strategies would be necessary to deal with different foci of these sectors. These strategies would differ according to the demographics of targeted audience, the nature and extent of program itself, people's demands and discontents and motivations for the programs. Moreover, these above mentioned dimensions must be managed well in order to make the communication strategies and the programs delivered effectively to the targeted audience.

In short, communication management encompasses the coordination and management of communication components as well other essential dimensions of the particular sector of activity.

We will discuss the above-mentioned areas in communication management context.

Health care Communications Management

Doctors, pharmaceuticals' responsibility is to provide information to consumers about the side effects of medicines, what they can cure, and what is only preventive and not curative. In addition, the development planners communicate health care plans for the people. The development administrators inform, educate and motivate consumers about taking care of health and providing health care facilities. Such health care initiatives need efficient management in order to provide effective health care.

Health care communication also focus significantly on doctors-patient relationships, paramedic and patient relationships and the administrators' role at the health care facilities such as hospital, primary health care centers, nursing homes and doctor's clinics.

Health care communications through intensive and extensive campaigns through media and interpersonal channels are important. These campaigns focus about diseases (HIV, cancers currently), immunizations, health and hygiene etc. to give people facts about the diseases and suggest the preventive and curative steps to be taken. The campaigns focus on communicating with different age groups such as children, youth and old; male and females, since health needs are different for each group. These address health needs and problems of different geo areas such as rural and urban and urban slum.

For instance, geriatric health care and communication needs urgent attention. Not only doctors need expertise about the old age problems and diseases but the old people themselves and other health care providers need awareness and knowledge about the old age problems. The expertise in geriatric communications facilitates planning awareness and knowledge for changing attitudes and behavior towards old age health. It facilitates better management of geriatric health care. This three pronged approach calls for management of health care for old from a new perspective to deliver better health care to them by doctors, paramedic, pharmaceuticals, care providers, communicators, family and old people themselves.

Communication competence and communication management is correlated with better health care delivery.

Intercultural Communication Management

Communication competence is important in managing the intercultural communication process and cultural diversities by the immigrants and sojourners in any culture. Even within a nation, regional cultural diversities if managed well can create national integration and social and political cohesiveness.

Valuing diversity starts with managing diversity. Management of diversity not only recognizes that differences exist among people but it recognizes that these differences represent the potential strengths for host cultures. In an environment, where we value diversity, and view differences as potential strengths, communication competence and management are significant.

Multicultural societies do face the problems of diversity management, as various cultural identities have to be addressed and managed separately. Globalization of cultures addresses the importance of managing cultural identities efficiently.

Equally significant is managing cultural conflicts both national and international through conflict management and peace process (for more details refer to conflict management section).

Development Communications Management

The information and knowledge for development is not met adequately by current initiatives. There is gap and inefficiencies among policy makers, national governments, development administrators, development functionaries and people. It is important that the efforts of all the stakeholders in development are managed effectively.

Development is a complex process of negotiations over meanings, values and social goals within the sphere of public actions. Therefore, development communication management is managing these three dimensions and not just project-based interventions or quantifiable inputs or outputs.

Development programs can increase levels of knowledge, skills, technical know-how and productive capacity of population for all the stakeholders. Participatory empowerment of the various stakeholders builds capacity and a framework enabling social forces to contribute and develop a new paradigm of knowledge about development dimensions in the network age; and thus managing new solutions for the old problems and issues.

Communication strategies to disseminate information and knowledge to do development are necessary condition for effective development. Therefore, it is necessary that information and knowledge for development should be managed well. Knowledge management is through knowledge generation, sharing, and applications.

Key tools of development are information and knowledge of needs of different development stakeholders and development participants. Development stakeholders are national, local and international governments, policy makers and people. The participants are development administrators and functionaries and academicians. The information and knowledge 'needs' varies for all.

People at grass-root level need awareness about their self-needs and needs identified by others; their demands for what needs to be done, and their discontents with others' efforts. Their participation in what is being done at their own level, at the levels of development administrators, development functionaries and government. They need information about what indigenous or external resources of self, governments, development functionaries or international development community are available to them to provide for their needs. They need knowledge of best practices, solutions, and how to implement and build their development capacity.

Development administrators need information and knowledge about operating development projects say in the health and nutrition for different socio-economic strata of society and different geo areas such as rural, urban and slums. They need to know the training needs of the functionaries and train them according to the requirements of the projects. The information and knowledge regarding the project is well managed when the development functionaries are able to coordinate development functionaries and people's efforts in these programs.

Development functionaries should have information and knowledge about the projects that they will deal, about geo area and characteristics of the people that they will deal with. They must be well versed with their roles in this context and training and knowledge about how to coordinate people's efforts, development administrators' efforts and their own efforts.

Key information and knowledge needs of the policy makers are to identify needs of the people, identify resources available, both human capital and materials at local, state and national government levels, and at the levels of international development community. They must also be well versed with the tools for implementation.

Civil society needs update information and knowledge of needs of people, resources available, and those that can be generated and required; both media and interpersonal implementation tools; and about the political will of the government.

Government needs local, national and global information and knowledge about the health and nutrition program as a contextual framework for action, creating policies and political will in this context. They coordinate efforts of local, national, world organizations and development community

Thus the effectiveness of the health and nutrition development programs depends on how the information and knowledge of all the stakeholders and participant is shared, coordinated, applied; and how these efforts are managed.

The development community must listen to the voices of multiple stakeholders through their feedback loops to address the needs of users and protect interests of the civil society by the government. Guidance and support is necessary from all the stakeholders. They should work together to overcome the knowledge and digital gap. There should be right to communicate, freedom of access to information, content, and knowledge. Together they must frame issues and discuss the concerns. They should share ideas in individual and group forums to develop connectivity. They must supplement and strengthen other initiatives. *Such efforts will facilitate the way to manage knowledge for development.*

The development community among themselves and at different hierarchy must share the latest research, best practices, and new ideas and evaluate them for effective dissemination of research products. Knowledge sharing is through development of ideas and practical implementation and improving connectivity with sources of knowledge. Analysis and evaluation of information should be shared. Access to intervention and local voices should be facilitated.

We need both local and global information and knowledge for development in any sector area such as health and nutrition, safe water, sanitation etc. Let us for instance take health and nutrition program. Local information is needed to create awareness among the targeted audience about the specific needs for the health and nutrition etc. It is necessary to seek knowledge for solutions and actions. It is important to first look for solutions and best practices that are indigenous in nature. Indigenous actions are also needed to solve the issues.

We need global information and knowledge as second step for knowledge led and knowledge based development. We need global information and knowledge to create awareness about what is happening about those specific needs in health and nutrition in other developing and developed countries. What issues and problems they are facing regarding these? Development stakeholders including the people need to share global knowledge about best practices, issues, solutions and actions taken in health and nutrition programs in other parts of the world.

Development community as a group is a significant 'social capital'. Managing their enrichment, and strong stakes in development is putting social capital to work.

Communication and management services act as a neutral, and informed provider of services for building the capacity of the development assistance agencies and partnerships within the development community to use ICTs more effectively to achieve their objectives. This they could do while helping the participating organizations to learn how to use these tools as part of the organizational change.

Information Communications Management

The focus is on IT portfolio management, applications, outsourcing, content management for IT effectiveness. There is need to manage efficiently IT infrastructure solutions, high availability servers, critical management services and resource optimization solutions.

Technical assistance is geared towards, the best use of ICTs; to create and manage web sites and information management tools and to develop new applications for the use of specific partnerships.

Further, technical assistance is managed towards creating Web-based working environment, web sites with links to discussion groups, hosting electronic discussions and conferencing etc. Document management tools helps in managing online database. Information management helps in planning integration of ICTs into implementation of particular projects and providing ICT program strategy.

The common element is using ICTs for creating awareness of linkages between organization and human dynamics on the one hand, and technical tools on the other hand. Both have to be coordinated in order to be managed well.

Beside technical, the other aspects, to be managed are 'Information' and the 'humans' who generate, use and share information. Both strategic and practical options to improve information and information related changes needs to be coordinated with the existing information. These changes must be managed well so that it is efficiently applied in various sectors. The information environment must be created for the humans who need information; and professional skills must be imparted to those who generate, use, and share information with others. Thirdly, the information (development) organizations must be strengthened so that they interact efficiently with the communities they serve.

In short, managing e-readiness and k-readiness is important. E-readiness is managing the quality of physical ICT infrastructure and the skills of the population to utilize this infrastructure; initiatives from government, and degree of Internet based efficiency in businesses. K-readiness (knowledge readiness) includes other systems such as education wide range of vocational skills training, business research and innovation.

Discussion of ICT perspective in earlier section highlights communication management in specific areas.

Business Communications Management

Economic productivity and economic growth also depends on how the communication component in business and knowledge economy is managed.

The focus of business communication is on diverse dimensions of businesses such as business communications in general: various perspectives in business communications, negotiations, management, product-cycle, advertisement and public relations, globalization, information technology, training including intercultural training, and specific aspects of different business sectors. This also includes corporate governance encompassing employee relation management (ERM), customer relation management (CRM), product relation management (PRM) etc., business regulations, trade and development, privatization, and foreign direct investments.

Further focus of communications is on business and economic intelligence and analysis, economics of business communications, business models and value management and market research for product, services and innovative ideas. It is further suggested that effective management of communications in the above-mentioned various dimensions of businesses can enhance economic productivity.

We are stepping into knowledge economies such as e-commerce etc. through newer technologies of Internet etc. These various modes of mobile communications have facilitated global business and globalization in business.

Communication through various mass media channels and interpersonal channels facilitate management of various dimensions of businesses. Some salient conceptual moves such as business culture, business intelligence and its social intelligence model, and communication plans highlight the importance of communication management for businesses. We discuss these in this context.

Business Culture: Every business has its distinctive focus and culture like societies. These are the norms, beliefs, values and work ethics that regulate the behavior of individuals and groups within any corporate. Many may not be aware of their distinct cultural characteristics. Culture of a business is influenced by the culture of the country of its origin and the nature of its business.

For example, Japanese automobile companies are an amalgam of Japanese business culture with some of the distinctive features of the global automobile industry and with the business culture of the particular country in which they are operating. American oil companies may essentially retain their American culture along with the common practices of the world Petroleum industries and the business culture of the Middle East businesses. Indian companies would find it necessary to combine their distinctive ways of doing business with the global practices of the businesses in which they are involved.

This coordination of business cultures calls for effective communication strategies as well management of those strategies.

A business culture that is constantly changing and evolving is vibrant and thriving. Progress occurs when they change. It is not the success but the threat of failure that compels businesses to reinvent themselves. Changes in a business occur when its leader provides ideas that challenge traditions. Successful businesses have leaders who revived, changed the culture and the course of business. In most cases, such changes are based on retaining and developing what is good in the existing culture and adding it to new elements that will stimulate the progress. Total rejection of existing culture is devastation. Therefore, the skill in reinventing the culture is to identify and retain what is good and what is to be rejected and modified. The exercise starts with review of existing cultures, with its strength and weaknesses by its senior managers and outside consultants in organized and formal discussions.

To effect receptivity to change, the top management team and the layers below them must be stimulated to examine issues and implementing changes, and accepting challenges associated with it.

How fast an organization should attempt to modify its culture? The wise thing is to change as fast as practicable but not that slow that organization becomes stagnant and people lose motivation and incentive for achievement.

Business intelligence Model and its social model are in tune with changing dimensions and areas of businesses and the new and wider applications of ICTs. These create technological challenges such as technology management for cost effectiveness, competition and reaching new markets. The new market environments could be local, monopolistic to global. Technology and market environment together pose challenges for product and service quality, upgraded technology, cost competition, cost effectiveness, motivated customers and personnel.

Communications is the core of managing business culture from various perspectives and dimensions whether initiating the change, reinventing the culture, leadership roles and receptivity to these. The success depends how effective is the communications in various contexts. Both interpersonal and media channels can be used for effective communications.

The businesses need *Communication Plan,* which could be both short-term and long-term. The communication plan encompasses communication strategies to create awareness and knowledge, acceptability, marketability, and adaptability (AAMA) about the corporate product, services and technology worldwide. It is essential to relate both short-term and long-term communication plans with both short-term and long-term business plans. Coordinating both the plans is effective business management.

Managing Knowledge Economies

Knowledge and its use has always been a critical ingredient to economic success. However, in recent times its importance is increased. The rapid globalization of economic activity, incredible increases in the science and technology output, and massive growth in the importance of networks and connectivity — all are driven by knowledge and its use, and knowledge is power. In emerging economies, knowledge has become the driver of economic competitiveness and success. The applications of new technologies and new ideas and also new applications of existing knowledge have brought revolutionary change to all markets and sectors. Thus both new knowledge and indigenous knowledge is highly relevant to knowledge economy. Therefore, better ways should be developed to capture, codify, apply and protect indigenous knowledge also for economic productive use.

E-readiness is the extent to which market is conducive to Internet based opportunities ranging from factors like quality of IT infrastructure, government initiatives, and degree of Internet based efficiency in businesses.

Knowledge economy (is an economy that) creates, disseminates and uses knowledge to enhance growth and competitiveness. It is not necessarily about high tech or IT but rather applications of new techniques. How an economy uses appropriate knowledge to improve its productivity and increase welfare. The new techniques and practices (which were not hi tech) created the food abundance through green revolution and milk abundance through white revolution in India.

Knowledge economy and knowledge management are different and connected to an extent. Knowledge economy defines the process whereby a country uses knowledge and converts it into economic gain and welfare improvement. Whereas, knowledge management defines the tools, techniques and processes used by sectors, organizations and individuals to achieve these.

Information society and knowledge economy are different. Information society is focused on information and not on knowledge. It is concerned with the broader context of society as a whole as opposed to 'knowledge economy' that is concerned with knowledge applied for economic use.

The knowledge for development (K4D) program of the World Bank Institute (2003) has developed the following framework to help countries articulate strategies for their transition to knowledge economy.

- An economic and institutional regime to provide incentives for the efficient use of existing and new knowledge and the flourishing of entrepreneurship.

The incentive regime describes the framework within which society and economy works. In the context of knowledge economy, does this provide a context that encourages and stimulates the creation, sharing and applications of all sorts of knowledge? Does it encourage the right level of education and training to support the economy and society's needs? Does it ensure that access to financing is not an obstacle to innovation and there is sufficient rule of law and appropriate intellectual property rights to ensure that creativity is not stifled?

- An educated and skilled population to create, share, and use knowledge well.

Education is the fundamental enabler of the knowledge economy. Well-educated and skilled people are key to creating, sharing, disseminating and using knowledge effectively. The knowledge economy system requires an education system that is flexible — starting from basic education that provides the foundation for learning, to secondary and tertiary education that can develop core skills, including technical skills; that encourage creative and critical thinking for problem-solving and innovation and to a system of life-long learning. Lifelong learning system encompasses formal training, non-formal on-job learning, and informal learning from family members and people in the community.

Education encourages exploration of new knowledge. ICT provides the mechanism to exchange knowledge and reduce the transaction costs associated with communication and exchange of knowledge.

- A dynamic information infrastructure to facilitate the effective communication, dissemination and processing of information.
- An efficient innovation system of firms, research centers, universities and consultants to tap into the growing stock of global knowledge, assimilate and adopt it to local needs and create new technology.

Innovation consists in the design, development and diffusion of technology (or a practice) that is new for the society concerned. In order to take shape innovation requires: (i) climate favorable to entrepreneurs without the hassles of bureaucratic, regulatory and other obstacles, and ii) appropriate interactions between the local business world and different sources of knowledge. Those knowledge sources include 'classical' establishments such as universities, public labs and research centers, and users and indigenous communities. Innovation systems are made of interactions among those actors. They are complex and sophisticated depending on the level of development. The role played by domestic research capabilities increases as an economy develops. In low-income countries, innovation is much dependant on foreign technology and its adaptation to local contexts.

In developing countries, innovation systems do not take shape easily because the groups and organizations are more concerned with the day-to-day survival issues, or the defense of vested interests, or because they are lacking the necessary technical culture. This affects communications and exchanges of information. Therefore, innovation policies in developing countries primarily deal with the building of an appropriate technical culture and with the establishment of incentives to stimulate cooperation and entrepreneurship.

Derek H. Chen & Carl J. Dahlman (2003) research highlights that stock of human capital, the level of domestic innovation and technological adaptation, and the level of ICTs infrastructure exert significant effects on long-term economic growth.

Developing countries do learn from other developing countries as well from developed countries. They learn the lessons both from success and failures. Lessons learnt must be contextualized to local contexts. They can leapfrog their performance by using knowledge and experiences of others coupled with their own knowledge of local circumstances.

E-readiness is concerned with physical ICT infrastructure and the skills of the population to utilize this infrastructure. K-readiness (knowledge readiness) includes other systems such as education, wide range of vocational skills training, business research and innovation. K-readiness is the ability to create, access, share, and apply knowledge across a wide range of sectors; it may or may not involve the use of e-technologies. K-readiness is necessary condition for knowledge economy and e-readiness is sufficient condition for it.

Knowledge assessment methodology (KAM) developed by World Bank Institute (WBI) measures a country's readiness for knowledge economy. KAM consists of a set of 76 structural and qualitative variables that benchmark how an economy compares with its neighbors, competitors and the countries it wants to emulate.

WBI provides policy services to the client countries consisting of, detailed analysis on critical issues relating to their transition to the knowledge economy (KE) and concrete recommendations on how to address these challenges. The program offers different levels of assessment and policy advice to meet the needs of the countries at different stages of development. Different levels of KE assessment are: benchmark assessments, enhanced sector assessments, and comprehensive assessments.

This program also offers policy-consulting advice on aspects of KE such as providing clients insights into policy development experiences related to various aspects of KE. This work is demand led.

During year 2004 the WBI is undertaking several policy studies to bring together global learning and experience on the knowledge economy. It will also be working on country case studies on KE; such as, role of Diasporas in knowledge economy, various pieces on innovations, linkages between KE and growth, and work on the knowledge divide. It is undertaking two significant global policy reports. First, the development of conceptual framework and toolkit for promoting innovations in low and middle income countries. Second, report on lessons and experiences of knowledge economy policy work to date.

Other learning events during the year include a global symposium on Knowledge economy and policy conferences to facilitate exchange of knowledge, information and experiences among interested client countries on knowledge economy. (information based on K4D program of WBI).

Conflict Management

Understanding the conceptual analysis of conflict, conflict process, variables of conflicts, conflict resolution and role of communication in managing conflict facilitate our understanding about management of conflicts in war and peace, political conflicts, social conflicts and business conflicts.

Conceptual analysis of conflict: Whenever a person meets a conflicting situation, he has two basic considerations in mind. One, that people are in disagreement i.e. in conflict of interests. Two, producing results i.e. getting resolution to the disagreement. The *political conflicts* are created by twin factors: exploitation of the masses and political leadership rivalries. The international *war conflicts* erupt by political conflict of interests as well striving for power and ego inflation of the political leaders. In general, people are in *social conflicts* when the pull of traditional values and push for modern values are in social change context. Conflicts of business interests and disagreements on business issues create *business conflicts.*

Conflict process: The discourses of local, national and international political and social leaders, bureaucrats, scientific-technical persons have twin roles. They create political, social-cultural, and religious conflicting environments in the country. On the other hand, these discourses also aim at resolving conflicts by negotiations, mediation and third party interventions. Media facilitates these roles. Interpersonal communication through discourses and mass media communication plays significant role in the conflict process.

The conflicts could be national as well international. Within the country, the regional and local disturbances may bring such crisis because of deprivations, lack of opportunities for growth and identity. Political unrest, political alienation, and the lack of basic needs and quality of life for the people may cause discontentment among the people. Political unrest is identified with social, cultural and economic exploitations, deprivations and discriminations. The political alienation is identified with loss of political, social and human identity.

For example, the national conflicts in Pakistan may occur due to unstable government, disturbed political environment, and perverse attitude towards other country (India). Pakistan national conflicts are protracted socio-economic and religious conflicts. Political leadership rivalries and roles further trigger them.

National conflicts create international conflicts. The socio-economic deprivations, political unrest and alienation within the nation create national conflicts. The causal accounts and conceptualization of national conflicts, value judgments of the leaders, socio-political environments and the two or more countries (parties) involved in the conflicting situation cause the international conflicts. These national conflicts trigger into international conflicts on two counts: One, to distract people's attention from national conflicts and two, to motivate leaders (social, religious) and bureaucrats to negotiate their demands.

The recurrence of social conflicts in the same situation suggests protracted conflicts, which are deep rooted in the lives of people. Sources of such conflicts are lack of societal needs such as security of cultural and value relationships, distinctive identity in the political process and social recognition of such identity, and lack of effective participation in the development process. In social protracted conflicting situations; the identity group such as racial, religious, ethnic, cultural become more powerful than the nation state.

Social conflict theorists advocate the role of conflict in arousing and maintaining citizen participation. Clash of values and ideas between competing groups may be sign of vitality and creativity. Conflict within a system can lead to revitalization of old norms and emergence of the new ones. Conflict with an external group may in addition strengthen internal cohesion. Conflict and information diffusion are basic variables in community change and there is functional relationship between the two.

Political scientists noted the relationship between intensities of political conflicts and having information about political policies and objectives. Research supports the view that opinion intensity, political understanding and political participation are correlated.

Peace is deep-rooted commitment to the principles of liberty, justice, equality, and solidarity among all human beings. Peace is also harmonious relationship of human kind and environment. It is a mode of behavior. There is interrelationship between peace, human rights, development and environment. All of these imply certain forms of communication. In most analysis, conflict is considered as dichotomous condition rather than a variable.

Events are interconnected but environments and situations around us prevent us from seeing total reality. For instance social justice, ethnic race or gender equity are not treated as issues of international relations or conflicts. Once these are bypassed *conflict resolution* becomes essentially *conflict management* by force. The real issues behind the conflict remain unapprised.

Variables of conflict: There are five types of actors who create conflicts. These are the national leaders in political, social, cultural and religious fields and the activists involved in social movements. These actors are the major variable in any conflict. Other variables are issue fields, tensions and actions that are targeted to escalate, resolve or manage the conflict.

Conflict behavior has both positive and negative connotations. When it is positive and mild; it can increase motivation, energy, create innovation, and highlight diverse viewpoints. It can increase understanding by articulating and supporting arguments. When it is negative and intense; it can rigid the system and distort reality.

Political unrest, political alienation, and lack of basic needs and quality of life may cause discontentment among people. Lack of interactive communication among the people and biased communication perspective can lead to low development, backwardness and mass violence at times. The political conflicts are created by twin factors, exploitation of the masses and political leadership rivalries.

Both external and internal peace issues for national and international community differ from country to country. They also differ in strength of peace disturbance at different points of time. Both, the cause of crisis and ensuing tensions are also country and culture specific. Moreover, the heuristic solutions that these countries will find from time to time will also be culture, country and time period specific because of the unique problems that a country faces through its cultural bindings and at a particular period of time in the conflict generation and resolution.

Variations in attitudes provide basic condition for conflicts. As the number of different attitudinal positions on social, economic, political issues change in a community, higher level of conflicts is likely to exist.

Conflict Resolution: Conflict resolution exclusively has the objective of resolving the conflicts *per se*. Controlling or resolving the conflicting issues can manage conflict. The conflicts need control where they are amenable for resolution.

Misunderstandings in a society are inevitable and it is a challenge to express differences and find reconciliation.

Expressing differences increases our chances for finding the best solutions to the many dilemmas that arise while living. A person has autonomy to make decisions when it may be possible for a person to make choices among several solutions without infringing on the other's freedom or requiring his cooperation. But in many situations in life this does not happen. One has to cooperate and coordinate in conducting life in family, community, business, government, and politics at local, national and international levels. When differences arise, it must find reconciliation. A solution must be agreed upon and those involved should confirm their behavior to the solution.

There are five classical solutions for resolving the conflicts. In a society we rely on four major formal and structural arrangements for resolving differences. They are scientific methods, politics, organizational hierarchy, and law with its associated police powers.

Through scientific methods a well-designed experiment confirms which of the several alternatives are the most valid basis of explanation (of phenomenon) while simultaneously demonstrating the unacceptability of the remaining explanations.

Political mechanisms provide resolution of differences according to the weighting approach and the basis is usually that majority prevails.

Legal mechanism applies in resolving differences when questions of law are involved and other means of reaching agreement have failed. Police powers are associated with it when there is violation of law. But this is severe solution to the problem.

Use of military force is used in times of war and civil conflicts to bring peace and order.

Within society's formal institutions such as business, government, education and family, organizational hierarchy can and does permit the resolution of differences. The boss takes the unilateral decision. While this arrangement does help in avoiding indecision and impasse, it has adverse affects on future creativity and undesirable consequences of sacrificing the support of those affected by the decision.

But the fifth and the best approach is the problem solving approach. People (group) must understand the roots of conflict. Resolve the differences through their insights to the problem and apply human skills to reach at mutually agreeable and committed solutions and implementations.

The three components of conflict resolution are: an open attitude to mutual compromise on terms and conditions, readiness to see the other parties' point of view and to take action, and create environment for such action to be successful. Both the parties must contribute equally. Therefore, this process significantly includes the efforts of both the parties concerned and the efforts of the mediators if any.

The political, social, cultural situations can be conflicting. They need to be resolved for everybody's advantage. Conflict resolution process should involve those who are affected; since they know where the shoe pinches. But they have to make efforts to suggest the solutions for resolving the conflicts; and implementing those solutions. The leaders, policy makers, those in governance must be ready to involve the people, listen to their suggestions, and cooperate with people in taking actions according to the consensus. Consensus building is important in this context

In larger pluralistic communities, conflict may be a force for social stability. Open conflict may be a negative force for cohesion in a less pluralistic society. Conflict should be an accelerating factor for communication, until, because of the nature of the conflict and community, a tension reaches at a disruptive point. At that point resistance to formal mass media communication is likely to occur.

Management of conflict becomes necessary, when conflicts cannot be resolved and they remain in fluid state, and when they escalate the situation. Communication management of both media and interpersonal channels, and management of specific event and situation can facilitate managing the conflict.

Different styles of conflict management may be used depending on the issues, parties, and situations arousing conflicts. *Intuitive styles of conflict management* are used in managing cultural conflicts. In this context, direct conflict communication management style is used by individualistic cultures and indirect communication style and communication avoidance is used by collectivist cultures. 'Face-saving' negotiations are also used in managing cultural conflicts. Intercultural understanding and such related strategies are necessary to manage these conflicts.

Ting-Toomey (1985) support these stances and takes the position that conflict is a normative behavior. It is a form of social action but regulated by norms of the particular culture. She extends the cultural influence and regulation notion to high and low context cultures. For instance, in high context cultures, the individuals find the causes of conflict important, are sensitive to norm violations, are generally indirect, and are likely to *use intuitive styles of conflict management.*

Later Ting-Toomey (1989) extended the cultural theoretical point of individualism-collectivism as an example of cultural variability that can explain conflict. She observed that individualistic cultures use *direct conflict communication management style* but collectivist cultures use *indirect communication style and communication avoidance.* She argues for a 'face-saving' negotiations in cultural conflicts that have implications for ethno-linguistic identity, impression management, interpersonal bonding and validation of personal identity.

Further, cultural researchers have focused on the implications of negotiation style for conflict resolutions. The assumption is that understanding of culture is illuminated through intercultural negotiation. It suggests a number of communication behaviors including decision-making and other strategies for conflict resolution.

Consensus building approach may be seen as mode of resolution of tension in different social systems. In smaller communities the conflicts are handled by consensus approach where a few individuals may play the multiple leadership roles behind the scene and conflicting issues are not reported in mass media. Conflicts can be often managed by presenting ideas for better forms of communications in conflict situations. *Mediation, public issue facilitation and empowerment* help in political conflict management. *Negotiations, third party* *intervention* and *organizational hierarchy* intervention may manage business conflicts.

Narula Uma (2000) researched culture-related tensions. She takes the position that issues of multiculturalism, cultural identity, cultural diversity, and the process of acculturation create tensions. These tensions are liable to create intercultural and international conflicts. *Intercultural understanding and such related strategies are necessary to resolve and manage these conflicts.* The implications of this position are discussed in Communication strategies Part 3.

Role of communication can be significant in managing, controlling and resolving the conflicts. The communication perspective can be analytical, supportive and developmental. Various media channels both media and interpersonal play IEMC role in managing, controlling and resolving conflicts.

Narula Uma (1998) analyzed the role of Indian media in political conflict between India and Pakistan. Kashmir issue is the focus. Her research highlights the role of media in political conflicts:

- They inform and educate about conflicting situations by creating awareness and opinion among actors about such situations.
- Mobilize actors' opinion about conflicts.
- Motivate actors to resolve, manage and negotiate conflicts.
- Creates analytical, supportive and developmental communication perspective.

The role of Media channels both print and broadcast is significant. The role is both positive and negative. They create awareness about the issue, set agenda for public discussions and inter-communication of five actors of the issue. Media role is limited to IEMC role, whereas the implementation of strategies and solutions suggested through media depends on the actors.

There are three media cycles escalating the various stages of conflict. *Media blitz cycle,* when the issue is initiated and is hot. A lot of coverage is given to the issue during this time. *Media plateau,* when issue is under discussion, it studies tensions and actors' strategies to escalate, de-escalate or manage conflicts. Medium media time and space coverage is given during this period. Comparatively *low media* coverage is given when issue is still pending. Low media attention may occur because, either shifts of the issue have changed, or people have lost interest and they are indifferent, or the issue is at status quo. Low media attention may not necessarily mean low saliency of the issue.

Again these three stages of the media coverage will be repeated when the issue is reactivated. Will media be responsible for the reactivation of the issue? Or which actor will reactivate the issue and why?

Interpersonal communication channels play implementation role in addition to IEMC role. But media support is necessary condition for its significant role. Both can play supporting roles to escalate or de-escalate the conflicts.

Various empirical communications patterns helps to manage conflicts. These could be:

- Surface harmony is maintained for peaceful coexistence by ignoring the disagreements.
- Compromise, bargaining and middle class position is accepted so nobody wins or loses. Accommodation and adjustment lead to workable rather than the best solution.
- Neutrality is maintained by withdrawal from social responsibility.
- Conflict is suppressed through authority-obedience approach. Win-lose power struggles are fought out decided by the highest boss or through third party intervention.
- Valid problem solving with varying points of view is objectively evaluated against facts. Problem solving is creative and challenging in finding new and better ways to replace outmoded.

Conflict and conformity are interdependent. When people conform to the expectations of others and patterns of their institutions, this readiness to conform reduce conflict and permits regularity, order and predictability. Non-conformity leads to conflict.

In conflict resolutions and conformity, flexibility of behavior is important. Flexibility calls for alternative in options and alternatives. It sets up a climate that permits people to move back and forth and in and out from one situation to other, but based on facts, data and logic of the situation. This is creative problem solving that creates opportunities, anticipate threats and risks when people fail to react. Thus through flexibility, adjustment to differences and altered circumstances can keep peace and show better results.

Flexibility in communication calls for communication competence. Convergence model of communication and circular communication is necessary in resolution of conflicts. Feedback loops are significant for identifying and implementing the solution/s, and strengthening their own capabilities and skills for coping with the conflicts.

Mass media messages become entangled in conflicts, disputes and disturbances at the local, national and international levels. Communication is impaired by extremely intense conflicts.

The relationship between social conflict and communicative activity in a system may take a number of empirical patterns depending upon the structure of the system. In some systems it may be linear, in others it may take several forms of curvilinear. When conflicts reach an intense level, communication changes in form and shifts from one set of actors to another. Certain types of communication may be inhibited in conflict situations.

In a maximal conflict situation, communication through mass media may be restrained or shifted entirely from mass to interpersonal channels leading to 'communication breakdown' which may actually be 'accommodation to the intensity of the conflict. For example, when negotiations between formal organizations become so conflict-ridden that participants cease talking to each other (and thereby cease being quoted in the mass media), the negotiations at this point shift to different representatives of the organizations. This turning point occurs when the conflict itself becomes the focal point of concern, taking priority over the initial issue. In such a situation, inhibitions to distribution, acquisition and assimilation of information through mass media may become as part of new mode of adjustment to the heightened conflict condition.

Media channels create significant communication effects of national and international policies for managing and resolving tensions and conflicts in a region. They cover policy analysis and policy implications in conflicting situations and its impact on masses. The media coverage of conflicts occurs in Media blitz, media Plateau, and media low.

The media maps the national and international communication patterns, contexts and strategies, heuristic solutions and actions in conflicting situations. The media highlights the perceived socio-political reality in conflict contexts. It identifies peace issues and challenges, and crisis factors. It is assumed, whether as media imperialism or otherwise, because of satellites and cable channel worldwide, broadcasting especially television with its visual effects is mostly used as propaganda instrument in foreign policy.

High level of reporting of social conflicts in the mass media may stimulate attention to an issue among socio-economic strata who otherwise are unlikely to become aware of the issue.

As the level of mass media coverage of a social conflict issue increases, there will be higher level of knowledge, and perception of conflict regarding that issue. There is likely to be no difference about knowledge and perceptions about the conflicting issue among the higher and lower socio-economic groups if they are equally exposed to the media.

Mostly interpersonal communication channels in negotiations and third party interventions manage business conflicts. Media attention is given to it when such conflicts impact the economy and the interests of the public.

Interpersonal communication channels whether it is the neighborhood community spreading rumors or the leaders with vested interests instigating people to conflagrant race or religious riots cannot be underestimated.

Management of media, its control and censorship of

contents, unbiased presentation of the conflicting situations and solutions is important. Equally important is that larger sections of the people have access to these unbiased opinions. Effective management of the media and other communication channels including interpersonal channels can, not only avoid escalation of social and political tensions but also can help resolve the tensions and conflicts to a greater extent.

Management of conflict becomes necessary, when conflicts cannot be resolved and they remain in fluid state, and when they escalate the situation. Management of both media and interpersonal channels, and specific event and situations management can manage the conflict. Different regions of the world are facing conflict situations and ICTs have been used by NGOs effectively as tools for learning, sharing and coping with conflicts.

Knowledge Management

The great end of knowledge is not knowledge but action.
— Thomas Henry Huxley

The major components of knowledge management strategies pertain to knowledge generation, knowledge organization, knowledge applications and knowledge codification; and co-ordination of these dimensions. *Knowledge Management is effective use of knowledge in an appropriate way.* Organizations manage knowledge for individuals, and by them in context of certain programs and projects.

Communication plays a significant role in managing knowledge since it depends on how information and knowledge is disseminated and used by the senders and the receivers and in what context.

Generation and organization of Knowledge

Data, information and knowledge are the main components for Generation and organization of Knowledge. Let us differentiate the three.

Data is a set of discreet and objective facts about events. In organization context, it is structured record of transactions. Data by itself has little relevance or purpose. Available data in the organization can be identified through its technology system. Quantitatively data management has to be in terms of cost, speed and capacity. Qualitatively measurements are timeliness, relevance, and clarity.

Information is a message in the form of document, or an audible and visible communication. Information is meant to change the receivers' perceptions and has impact on their judgment and behavior.

Information moves in and around organization through hard and soft networks and identifying available information. Quantitative measurement of information management is connectivity and transaction. Qualitative measures are being informative and useful thus creating insights and solutions.

Information has relevance and it is organized to some purpose. Data becomes information when its creator adds meaning to it. Data need to be contextualized, categorized, calculated, corrected and condensed for it to become information. McLuhan stated, 'medium is the message'. But the information management believes that medium strongly affect the message depending upon how medium is used.

Knowledge is a fluid mix of framed experience, values, contextual information, and expert insight. These provide a framework for evaluating new experiences and information. It is structured also. Knowledge is an asset if it is accessible, and its value increases with the level of its accessibility.

Knowledge creating activities takes place within and between human beings, through books and documents and structured media. These activities could be focus-specific information: (1) Comparing information in different situations; (2) assessing the consequences of information i.e. what implications will the information have on decisions and actions; (3) connecting various pieces of information and relating to each other; (4) how people would react to various pieces of information; (5) would people converse about particular bit of information and what do people think about it?

The key components of knowledge are experience, ground truth complexity, judgment, rules of thumb and intuition, and values and beliefs. These human characteristics make the job of minimizing and maximizing knowledge as a challenge. Applying insights and managing practices of knowledge is first step towards long-term success.

Experience, i.e. what we absorb from formal and informal learning. It provides a historical perspective from which to view and understand the new situations. It makes connection between familiar patterns. When hiring experts, they buy experience-based insights.

Ground truth, managers recognize the importance of real life knowledge or ground truth than theories and generalizations.

Complexity, experience and ground truth in knowledge indicates knowledge ability to deal with complexity. Knowledge is not a rigid structure that excludes what does not fit. It can deal with complexity in a complex way.

Judgment. It can judge new situations and information in the light of what is already known. It judges and refines itself in response to new situations and information.

Rules of thumb and intuition. Knowledge works through flexible guides to action that develops through trial and error and over long periods of experience and observation. Heuristics (rules of the thumb) are short cuts to new problems that resemble problems previously solved by experienced workers. Those with knowledge one can see familiar patterns in new situations and can respond appropriately. Internalized experience (intuition) labeled scripts or 'compressed expertise' are efficient guides to complex situations.

Values and beliefs. People's values and beliefs have powerful impact on organizations as well organization of knowledge. It influences their thoughts and actions. The power of knowledge comes from values, beliefs, and commitment in an organization and to the programs.

The above-mentioned key points and powers of knowledge are needed for knowledge-based technical know-how, product design, innovation and personal creativity. Effective use of knowledge is necessary in this context. Knowledge can provide sustainable advantage. Knowledge assets increase with use, ideas breed new ideas, shared knowledge stays with the giver while it enriches the receiver. The knowledge-rich and knowledge managed organization moves on to a new level of quality, creativity and efficiency.

Knowledge Management is effective use of knowledge in an appropriate way. Organizations require quality, value, service, innovation and speed to market for business and social success. They will differentiate themselves on the basis of what they know, how they know to do things well and efficiently. In search for effectiveness, the knowledge based activities of developing products, ideas and processes are becoming primary internal functions and for competitive advantage.

Knowledge management techniques: Communications, business change, organizational behavior, people's behavior and technology help in knowledge management

Organizational knowledge is highly dynamic. It is moved by variety of forces. In an organization, knowledge moves slowly or rapidly, bought, exchanged, bartered, generated or applied to programs. The objective is that it should move and be utilized effectively.

The organizational behavior manages knowledge by giving data and information accessibility. It gives openness to shared knowledge with co-workers and give knowledge sharing incentives. Management provides support and resources for it. Knowledge originates and resides in people's minds and draw people out. Knowledge-sharing needs trust. Knowledge is creative and should be encouraged to develop in unexpected ways and incentives should be provided for it. Technology enables new knowledge behaviors. Management support and resources are essential for it. Quantitative measurements for knowledge sharing are cost effectiveness and increase in productivity. The qualitative measurements are participants' enthusiasm, creativity and innovations.

Social, political, and economic realities govern the *knowledge market.* Four factors exist in knowledge market: reciprocity, reputation, altruism and trust. Trust is of vital importance, knowledge sharing must be trusted and not exploited. There should be knowledge sharing not hoarding and sharing must be rewarded. Informal knowledge networks such as informal interactions and gossiping updates the internal knowledge of the organizations and its concerns.

There are *knowledge buyers* who are seekers of knowledge looking for insights, judgments, and understanding to accomplish a task efficiently. There are *knowledge sellers* such as consultants, lawyers, bankers and other professionals who provide specialized knowledge outside the organizational knowledge. There are *knowledge brokers* who make connections between buyers and sellers of knowledge. Even corporate librarian acts as covert knowledge broker. They may make people to people connection or people to text connections. Thus librarians are key players in creating efficient knowledge market and connecting buyers and sellers.

Knowledge management of various public programs involves mapping and modeling knowledge. This is important for communication strategies, identifying issues, best practices, solutions and actions. Knowledge categories are simple and generic.

Knowledge mapping is of skills and knowledge of employees and expertise they require for particular jobs. A knowledge map shows **where** important knowledge in an organization is available, such as the people, documents, and databases. **Where** do they go when they need expertise? It is a kind of an inventory of what exist and where it is located.

One can create an organization's knowledge map by combining individual's 'mini maps'— where individuals go when they seek expertise. Internal surveys are used to assess employees' knowledge and their sources and channels when they need expertise for their jobs.

Map-makers follow a trail of recommendations, talking to knowledge sources suggested by one person, then another and following with people they mention and then with people they suggest and so on. This has snowball effect and thus six steps trail leads to information from within and outside organization. Pooling the resources creates critical mass of knowledge that helps in planning communication strategies for identifying issues, best practices, solutions and actions.

***Knowledge transfer* is twofold**: a) transmission i.e. sending and presenting to the potential audience and absorption and use by that audience. b) Knowledge is applied when it is available and accessible. Thus these two put together leads to knowledge transfer and change in behavior. Though initial resistance to change is always there. The new ideas are sparked by access to the existing ones. The adoption and application of new knowledge is slow and arduous process.

Local knowledge transfer takes place within organization. This is informal knowledge transfer of technology and ideas. Conversations within the organization are the most important way of creating knowledge. Through it, they discover what they know, share it with colleagues and in the process create new knowledge for the organization. Thus knowledge exchange can be through informal 'talk rooms'.

Hard and Soft aspects of knowledge transfer are: velocity (speed), viscosity (richness), and access to attention and documents for discussion. Hard skills of knowledge are structured knowledge, technical abilities and professional experience. Soft traits are sense of cultural, political and personal aspects of knowledge.

Applications of Knowledge

Knowledge manager's role demands unusual mix of technological, psychological, and business skills. Knowledge asset management approach involves activities such as:

Calculating knowledge valuations, negotiations with internal and external holders of intellectual capital.

Knowledge management needs to design, implement and oversees different forms of knowledge infrastructure including libraries, knowledge bases, human and computer knowledge networks, research centers and knowledge oriented organizational structures. The external providers of knowledge such as databases, academic and professional partners are to be managed. The critical input to the process of knowledge creation and applications are as new product development, market research, business strategy and development. Further it involves designing and implementing codification approach. The value of knowledge is measured and managed by financial analysis or anecdote management; and application of knowledge per se to development of key approaches in various sectors.

Impact of Globalization on knowledge management

With globalization and increased speed of technological change, generation of knowledge and access to it is seen as source of advantage for business or whole economies. In fact the power of science and technology through ICT revolutions now allow access to wider information, knowledge, and communication at lower cost, and promises solutions to longstanding problems of diseases, health, sanitation, safe water, environment and crop production etc which has deluded science in the past. It facilitates leapfrogging in development process and supporting human capital for financial capital as key factor for production.

But there is also the danger of exclusion of poor countries and people because the prerequisites for the effective generation and/or use of knowledge are not yet in place in certain parts of the developing world. Globalization of knowledge may be even threat to valuable sources of locally produced knowledge. Developing countries may be adversely affected; relatively or absolutely by a higher premium on knowledge.

The role of public sector nationally or internationally should be to provide the framework and incentive for generation and use of knowledge to promote pro-poor growth policies, social inclusion and to stimulate initiatives to widen access to information and knowledge.

The principal objective must be to develop the capacity of the developing countries to generate, use, and absorb knowledge to foster their own development. Not all countries need to develop capacity equally for research. But all countries would need the capacity to be intelligent customers of knowledge, wherever generated and the ability to put that knowledge for effective use. Therefore, there is need to use the power of ICT to help meet international targets in health, education and poverty reduction. Secondly, how best to utilize ICT to aid learning in all spheres most effectively.

A self-sustaining knowledge and research infrastructure has proved difficult to create. Too often managerial and financial obstacles have frustrated efforts to create sustainable institutional capacity through human resource development. Highly skilled become disillusioned.

World Bank has taken a lead in developing its own capacity to manage knowledge and communicate it effectively. UN system also has an important role in creating the right environment for the development of knowledge systems and effective strategies for knowledge and research in various sectors. In order to build capacity in developing countries they (UN agencies) should focus on, reorienting knowledge and research in its programs and their effectiveness, focus on issues of client orientation, access and relevance of knowledge to client's programs and make efforts to promote skills for development. The private sector also has an important role in developing knowledge relevant to the problems of developing countries.

In fact, our discussion in the above section suggests that knowledge management is the significant component in communication management per se and in various other sectors of health care, business, development, and information technology and in conflict management in war and peace.

Summary

Communication is an important component in every human activity. It is effective when it is managed well. Therefore, it is important how communication is managed in various streams for effective delivery of ideas, products, and services. The management could be of both human and non-human communications (computer, telecommunication etc). It is an expertise area. The focus of management of human communication is essentially the five dimensions: creating awareness, disseminating information, delivery of services, ideas and products, coordinating linkages for both human and non-human communications and better administration of campaigns, services and linkages. Communication competence is significant to manage these five dimensions.

Management focus is addressed to health care, intercultural communications, development communications, information and communications technologies, business communications and managing knowledge economies, conflict management and knowledge management.

15

Communication Research Perspective

There is the world of ideas and there is the world of practice.
—Mathews Arnold

Communication research has been ongoing for the last six decades to set up communication as a discipline. Since 60s there has been research for newer perspectives in theory, research and practice to enrich the discipline. Researches also advocated, supported and developed different perspectives from which communication has been studied and applied overtime.

Communication research methodology has evolved and developed overtime with the changing communication priorities, functions, audience demographics, media consumption, advancement in ICT and the need and significance of supporting role of both interpersonal communication and media channels. Communication research has facilitated these changes.

The early researches and confrontation with new communication situations stimulated communication research scholars in specific areas of source, audience, message, channels and effects (both mass media and interpersonal), communication rule and contextual research. In fact communication research perspective encompasses the various other perspectives from which communication is being practiced.

Communication research does operate within the broad framework of social science research. But in this section we are exclusively addressing about communication research.

Narula & Pearce (1990, p. 4) argue that decades of research has proved the point that research itself is a human enterprise that occupies a particular place within the social order and occurs within specific situations. Rather than being the operators of objective research methods, researchers are embroiled in the human process of communicating often between groups of people dissimilar in temperament, education, and interests. The continued research points practical problems that are debilitating.

Narula & Pearce (1990, p. 7) suggest that narrowly technical presentation of research methods is insufficient and dysfunctional for contemporary researchers. The developing countries have undergone a transformation in terms of their research communities and research sites. They have created a strong indigenous research community sufficiently self-confident to say that research models from the west do not fit their cultural, social and material circumstances. For example, the methods of sophisticated scaling are irrelevant when the subject population is illiterate or does not share the conventions of continuums underlying social judgments.

Rosario Braid (1983, p. 84) points that the old models which have been developed in the west have been linear, one-way static and culture bound....and many of the traditional communication theories have been inadequate in explaining environmental realities of the developing world.

Research has also established that practical problems in research are constitutive of research methods as they provide information about the situations in which research operates, therefore they should be considered part of the data and not impediments to research.

Penman & Sless (1990, pp. 232-233) points that the very idea of identifying practical problems in research raises the fundamental question that the most critical problem any society faces is in what sense they understand the idea of communication. The prevailing descriptions offered for the communication process and the role that communication is commonly expected to play in public life determine the agenda of communication issues addressed.

They further argue and support the viewpoint of Pearce and Cronen (1980) that when we propose a conceptual framework for making sense of the world, we are making a contribution to how we understand our world. Thus the traditional view of the theory as an objective explanation for how things work has changed through empirical research. We generate ways of making sense of our world. In fact, we provide framework for our actions. The range of action possibilities is as narrow and as broad depending on the interpretations available.

Narula & Pearce (1990, pp. 238-239) points that much of the information is available but not used when there is low 'communication density'. Communication density suggests low linkage among researchers, decision-making groups, planners and policy groups; and between researchers and research institutions.

They further argue (1990, p. 242) if research is seen as a special form of activity in which preconditions for better communication are created within a cultural and political context then the results are understood as part of the evolution of those contexts.

Foley (1979) argued that diversities of findings rather than unified body of theory mark the mass communication field. Thus communication scholars are faced with continuing expanding set of variables calling for further investigations. The more the set of variables grows, more complex it becomes, and less we know about the relationship among the variables.

Communication research has significantly impacted the communication theories and its essential variables such as source, audience, channels, messages (content), communication patterns and networks, individual differences, social categories, social relations, communication effects and overall communication consumption.

As evident from the above discussion, the main focus of communication research is the changing *communication patterns and networks*. They impact the expanding set of variables. The other focus is the *communication research methodology* that may need research and updating to study the change and impact for improving communication *per se*, communication situations and communication density.

Communication research over a period of time has supported or refuted or improved upon various assumptions, constructs and other factors that have impact on changing perspectives on communication theory and practice.

But the major contribution of research perspective is the realization that there are practical problems in research, the world over, and those practical problems differ in cultural, social and political contexts.

Theories: The early general theories of mass media and interpersonal communication, of 40s and 50s were researched and developed as base for the theories of 60s to meet the need for changing communication situations and to set up the identity of the communication discipline. At that point the research studies pointed two significant points. One, that special theories were needed to explain the diverse communication perspectives. Second, that some of the research findings do not hold good for all time, for all situations and for all segments of the society. Therefore, there is need for special and specific theories. This led to great fervor in research in 80s and special theories were developed for effective communication.

Research has impact on some of the salient communication theories and it has changed some of the dimensions.

Two-step flow theory: In 60s, the researchers began to probe systematically the role of informal contacts — the personal influence on other people as an important set of variables to assess the effects of mass media. The research was supporting that informal social relationship play a significant part in modifying the manner in which given individuals will act upon a message through mass media.

In fact, research suggested that a very few have first hand exposure to certain messages through media. Research further suggested movement of mass media messages through two stages. First, information moved from media to a few well-informed individuals who have access to media. Second, from those persons it moved to others who do not have direct exposure to media, through interpersonal channels. This communication process was labeled *Two-step flow theory.* Those who had more exposure and contact were called *opinion leaders.*

Further, it also revealed that opinion leaders were selective in passing the information intentionally or unintentionally in order to have media power and control. Moreover, some of the messages would get twisted in the process and the intended pro-effect would get lost.

Two-step flow theory lost much of its fervor in 70s onwards as a larger population was having physical and social access to mass media information. Radio and TV have become inexpensive or government was providing community sets. Literacy was also increasing.

Narula (1984 and her later researches) point that many of the development planners in developing countries in India particularly were concerned about the pro-social messages in development in rural areas. The messages won't reach the intended audience as opinion leaders would block the messages or twist them due to vested interests of caste and village factions. To counter it, two steps were taken. One, the community radio and TV sets were provided so villagers have access to mass media messages regularly. Two, the development administration set up a village hierarchy though block development infrastructure, where an official village level worker (VLW) for every village and another for cluster of villages were responsible to convey and explain the mass media messages on daily basis. This 'personal influence' of official opinion leaders was the intervening variable between communication message through the media and the responses made to that message. Thus even feedback loops were set up between the VLWs and villages. The feedback was conveyed back to the development administrators. Such set up helped in doing development more effective and timely.

Even research studies were pointing to the influence of informal social relationships in adopting farm technology and farm innovation messages. Though further research overtime revealed that women were blocked from these messages.

Thus it was through research that two-step flow theory had undergone change and lost its credibility and through further research only another dimensions were added to make it effective.

Significance of informal social relationships and personal influence activated the interest of communication theorists in Opinion leadership theories and diffusion theories.

Theory of Opinion Leadership: Research also validated that on the positive side, the opinion leaders not only passed on the information to others but they were influential and significant in shaping the opinion of others. As along with passing the information they would add on their own interpretations of the communication content and clear their doubts. People turn to opinion leaders for information and advice for which they have less information exposure through mass media or informal social relationships. They are influential in adoption process in diffusion of innovations by passing on information and acting as mediator through informal social relationship. Opinion leaders can be different for different human activities.

Narula (1984, p. 94) advocates that communication research has revealed that village opinion leadership is essential for development communication (in India) and encouraging people to participate in development. Opinion leadership in villages is a significant communication link for development information and feedback. These links are missing in urban areas. Her research further revealed that in opinion leadership theory the leader bridges and sanctions of the leaders have lost their importance. This is due to the fact that both mass media and organized interpersonal infrastructure (block development infrastructure) are having wider reach to the rural areas in India. Therefore, more and more people are having direct access to these communication channels. These channels are enjoying the credibility.

Narula further contends those opinion leaders and their sanctions are losing importance and credibility because, as stated earlier, these leaders would block information at times because of vested interest. They are selective in passing selective information and to selected persons. Even they may pass misinformation by adding their own misinterpretations to the communication content from both mass media and interpersonal channels. These factors limit the effectiveness of opinion leadership as well two-step flow theory.

Communication research did refute certain assumptions of the *Trickle-Down Theory* in its early years in 60s and research in the later years of 80s and 90s.

During the Dominant Paradigm period of the 50s, Tickle-down theory was an important contribution in communication field. Schramm, Rogers (1962) and other supporters of this theory argued that there would be so much economic gains of industrialization and high technology in rich countries (developed countries) that they would trickle down to the poorest (developing country). Even the social gains of urbanization, literacy and mass media would trickle down.

Subsequent research in 60s rather established the facts that both material and social gains did not trickle down to the poor in society rather it created wide gap between the rich and poor.

Further researches rather showed that trickle down theory is invalid for development. The developing countries have to follow their own models of development of technology or social structures and values. This led to the New Paradigm of development of the 70s.

Even the researches in 80s and 90s reveal that communication technology does create digital divide between the rich and poor countries as well between the rich and poor within the society. This does affect the economic growth of the countries. Economic growth or technology growth invariably has to follow the path of self-reliance and indigenous efforts. Though in this era of globalization, developed countries may lend its material and social technology to developing countries by way of import, transfer of technology or international aid. These are collaborative efforts of the countries and no trickle down.

Thus Trickle-down theory has no place in the present set up and it is only through researches that we could refute its validity.

Diffusion of innovation communication theory identified the diffusion of technological ideas for development. The role of communication was to transfer the objects of technology to the masses as planned by the authorities and policy-makers. Rogers (1962) advocated that the linear communications model: S—M—C—R—E was appropriate for diffusion of technological innovations.

In later years diffusion communication research changed perspectives for communication theory and practice. Rogers felt that development cannot be explained within the present framework of diffusion communication. Rogers (1976) argued that for diffusion of innovations (material), it was necessary to diffuse social innovations also. Moreover, later in 1980s Rogers and Adhikarya suggested that the role of communication in diffusion of innovations has to be multilogue rather than linear. People will accept and adopt, or reject an innovation through the process of knowing more about it. And that can be done only through multilogues and feedback loops.

Communication research also set up that Dominant Paradigm emphasized individual diffusion decisions; whereas heavy top-down vertical communication in developing countries implied authority diffusion decisions that are made by the authorities for the people in collective interest. The research has also suggested the pro-innovation bias and diagnostic stage in the diffusion process, which was missing earlier in the diffusion communication model.

The communication research has changed the opinion that laggards (slow in adoption) may not be slow necessarily due to being slow in receptivity but rather due to the lack of exposure, opportunities and accessibility for a particular innovation. This often happens in developing countries.

Innis theory of technological determinism: Innis Harold (1950) through his theory of Technological determinism propounded that the fundamental breakthroughs in technology are first applied to the process of communication. The forms of social organizations, stages of society, and the characteristics of the society are determined by the *medium of the time.* In current times, the computers, Internet, telecommunications with their advance functions, cable television, and satellite communications are shaping societies differently and giving more intercultural and inter-societal connectivity. Since 90s diffusion of technological innovations whether in information communication technologies or biotechnology has created globalization.

Marshall McLuhan (1964) sharpened the thesis that medium is the message, and that dominant technology of the communications shapes the culture and the cultural ways.

The personal and work cultures, entertainment, and leisure activities are being shaped differently by the dominant communication technology of telecommunications, broadcasting, and computerization in different times. It is further argued that there is impact of media on cultures, and cultures have impact on shaping of the media systems. Therefore, there are different and varied media systems due to cultural diversity. The political economy theorists argue that dominant ideas in a society are those of the dominant class. The class that is the dominant material power of the society is also the cultural and spiritual power. From intercultural and Inter-national communication perspective, it is necessary to know the dominant cultural power of any nation for better relations.

McLuhan further contended that the nature of media technology prevailing in a society at a given point of time influences members of that society. How they think, behave and communicate. From the technologist determinist perspective, the most important characteristic of media-audience encounter is the technological properties of the medium. He elaborated Innis thesis and characterized television as cool medium because of its capacity for rich configuration. Audio-visual stimuli elicit high but passive participation.

Empirical communication research has been contending the impact of new communication technologies on audience and society. Computer, telecommunication, Internet, radio and television and the international nature of these technologies have made people think and behave globally and have global connectivity.

But research has rejected the single factor theory of Innis and McLuhan. There is research evidence that technology, economy, psycho-social factors and encounters with mass media and interpersonal communications affect the communication behavior, relationships and experiences. The technological characteristics of the medium are one of the factors to be accounted for. Moreover, research has also refuted McLuhan assertion that 'Medium is the message' thus giving importance to medium only whereas research has evidenced that the content of the medium is important. Research created 'total factor theory'.

Rule theories of communication explain, control and predict communication behavior. Research has shown that this has utility for development communication theory since this approach is heuristic and rules have important place in human communication inquiry. Rules research is concerned with explicating symbolic regularities in communicative behavior.

Development communication approaches, practice and its research methodology have undergone change with the changing development theories overtime. Earlier, people used to be the focus of communication. It was linear from top to bottom. But now in addition to being the focus, people voice their demands and discontents and plan developments for themselves by participating. This suggests planning development through the voices of people and not treating them as naïve. It also suggests horizontal, bottom to top and circular communication.

Therefore, the researchers and development practitioners and theorists need to know the communication strategies of the people and their concerns through dialogue with them to assess development communication.

Communication functions. Priorities and functions of communication theory, applications, and practice also keep changing. The changing communication scenario over the world creates demand and priorities for changing communication perspectives and conceptualizations. The communication scenario differs in developed and developing countries and even within these countries.

Communication research has asserted why these functions change. What factors impact it? For instance Internet has given us, instantaneous global interconnectivity. The cell phone has given us mobility, in addition to connectivity. This has changed the connectivity function. Internet and cell phones have strong influence on the communication behavior of younger generation of 2000 decade. The exposure to world cultures through cable TV and satellite and other media technologies has changed the cultural concept and resources of many cultures. In many developing countries including India the priorities of media control and censorship may change and become futile to some extent as Internet or cable TV facilitate access to International media. Globalization contexts not only in media exposure but also in economic, political, social, cultural and international contexts; and the multiplying arrays of economic, social and technological forces acting on our lives have changed communication functions extensively. Such change will be an ongoing process because of speed of change in ICTs. These changed functions have impacted the communication process, various perspectives, and developing new models of communication.

Audience: Audience is an important component in the communication process. The decades of audience research has pointed out that receptive and effective communication depends on the characteristics of the targeted audience, which should be compatible with the type of messages and the communication channels selected. The perception differentials of the different audiences and the effects of the media or interpersonal channels depend on the selected stimuli. This is important for the power of the communication. Research has shown that changing demographics of the general audience and sub-audience (many publics) have brought significant impact on the various perspectives, in which communication is being practiced, applied and studied.

Operational communication policies should be formulated on the basis of audience — its individual and societal needs and expectations assessed both by the audience and the policy-planners. Since audience needs and expectations undergo changes and complexities due to variables over time; the communication policies should be reviewed and monitored periodically to fit the policy goals. Empirical research helps in assessing the change and complexities, and policy research helps in reviewing, monitoring and revising communication policies to fit the change.

The media policies also are culture specific since communication needs are culturally anchored and uniquely responsive to specific societal expectations and norms. And that vary from audience and sub-audience within that society; in a particular society and also for the targeted audiences in broad issue sectors such as health, education, employment etc. Therefore, differential communication strategies and policies are formulated within the broad policy to deal with the different societal needs and communication perspectives to deal with them (targeted audience); such as, health issues may be communicated differently to rural people than to urban and urban slum people. Or communication policies may be gender specific. Communication research is a pointer for these differentials.

The communication channels. Communication research sets up the changing communication scenario comprising of various mass media and interpersonal channels.

The role of both mass media and interpersonal communication channels is significant for all the above-mentioned communication perspectives. Research plays a significant role in setting up the priorities of particular channels for specific programs, audience, and geo areas. Research also sets up the agenda to what extent a particular channel is significant and essential overtime.

For instance, Interpersonal channels in villages of India (block development channels) may get priority for health related persuasion. Research may also suggest that informal interpersonal networks of family and friends may be significant in specific health programs of family planning etc. But research may also set limitations of this channel as there are number of villages and even far spread out; so for wider reach of the health messages, mass media channel of radio supported by interpersonal channel may be used. It is research that sets up the agenda, which channel will be suitable for which audience: according to accessibility and availability of the channels.

The communication contents (media) are also molded by the demands of the targeted audience, society and the controlling authority (political will). Therefore, the media content is always culture and society specific. But it does changes with the demands and needs of the society and the political will in the country. Role of the media could be both agenda-setting and reinforcing the agenda. Government controls and even censors the media contents to fit in with its communication policies. Media content is planned, projected and filtered according to its social, economic and political policies. The ongoing communication research is important so that the content does not stagnate; rather it should inform, educate, and entertain people according to changing times; people's needs and demands and according to the dictates of the government. It also reflects the changing life styles, and values of the society however censored it may be. Ongoing research is used to evaluate the media content.

How to approach people (message) through both formal and informal Interpersonal channels is planned and conveyed. Research facilitates the appropriateness of the messages (differently) to the targeted audiences in context of several programs; and to change the messages when the saturation points come and the plateau effect results.

Communication patterns and Networks: It is important to understand the communication patterns and networks in a society to understand it, its issues, and its communication density.

Research has highlighted that various communication perspectives affect communication patterns and networks. Individual differences, differences in social categories and social relations define the differences in communication patterns and networks.

Individual difference in individual personality and traits such as their physical, psychological and material environments, their exposure to opportunities and accessibility to communication channels define the individual differences in communication patterns and networks. These are also affected by social categories of the geo areas viz urban, rural, urban slum; and also by various social stratifications within a society. Further, age, gender, income, occupation and social status also determine these. They focus on group relationships in interpersonal communication in large and small groups and in opinion leadership.

Research has also highlighted the cultural differences in these patterns and networks. They also develop according to the needs and demands of various communication programs; such as women networks for child and mother health programs, or for their self-employment efforts (in low income groups); professional support networks and cancer support groups. Virtual communities may develop because of Internet.

Further, research addresses the intended and unintended consequences of these networks, which may facilitate or hinder communication over time.

Communication effects can be assessed in terms of creating awareness, knowledge, attitude and behavior change through relationship between communication channels, targeted audience and society.

Media effects address the dependency of audience on media. It is key variable in understanding why and when media will change their beliefs, attitude, and behavior and maintain a sense of connectivity with social reality.

Media effects research is a pointer to 'effects changes' in High cultures Vs Low cultures suggesting that media effects are contextual. Since these are contextual, it changes with socio-economic, cultural, political and technological changes. It also points to the changes of functions of media and interpersonal channels overtime such as knowledge, information, motivation and development in the wider sense; in addition to global connectivity, it does create different communication effects for the segmented audiences; who are receptive according to their communication threshold. Thus research itself has highlighted communication effects gap.

Interpersonal communication effects: The research is a pointer to show the significance of this channel on the communication scenario. The importance of persuasion through personal influence is suggested. Further, it suggests the mutually supportive role of the interpersonal communication to mass media channels and vice versa. Research overtime suggested the necessity of feedback loops of both positive and negative feedback loops for communication effects.

Component of 'effects' in communications suggested the need for impact studies, evaluation research and monitoring.

Communication Consumption (CC). It is only through research that we find the changing patterns and extent of media and interpersonal channels' consumption. It also points to the factors responsible for the changing patterns and the impact it has on people's personal and professional life styles, changing societal values and political effects and concerns both nationally and internationally.

Communication consumption is instrument and reflector of change. The changing patterns of CC impact the changes in communication channels, content, functions and effects. It reflects the changing demographics of audience.

We are able to plan communication strategies and policies based on this change as assessed by the communication research.

Communication Models: Evolution of communication models in the last six decades has been possible because of communication research in its various dimensions: source, message, channel, audience and effects. Other corollaries such as feedback component, diffusion, and segmented audiences were added because of ongoing research.

As we have discussed, some of these models were exemplar of their times. These were basic models and subsequent models developed according to the demands of communication both human and non-human in the last six decades — whether it was the demands of modernization, globalization or technology paradigm. But the most significant meta-model (New paradigm) that developed in 70s was (the need for) several culture-specific models in various domains. This happened through research; the development community gained insights and learned experiences from failed communications in development.

Most of the developing countries in 50s decades have been focusing on a single model of communication research for rural, urban and urban slum areas. Subsequent researches have highlighted the need for diverse models.

In the 50s India experimented with various research models to handle development and development communications (see Narula 1984). The researchers were mainly preoccupied with developing a rural model because 90% of population at that time and less later on lived in rural areas. Thus rural model remained a top priority.

During the ongoing decades, the urban slums grew in three tiers — slums within the urban areas, slums in shanty-towns, resettlement slum colonies on the periphery of metropolitan towns (the third planned by government).

The urban areas during these decades ushered into towns, cities and metropolitan (getting more commercial and cosmopolitan). The three geo areas and its people posed different communication issues. But a single communication model has been applied in all the three geo areas.

The nodal points in this model posing problems were: communication networks and patterns, opinion leadership and cohesive nature of rural society. Urban slum and urban areas specifically lack the interpersonal communications networks of Block development hierarchy (formal), and opinion leadership (elected or informal) or any other interpersonal contact points. However, these areas have the higher accessibility to mass media channels.

North and South regions in India have cultural and language diversities and the fact that the social, economic, and political realities are diverse in these regions. This suggests the need for two 'regional communication models'.

Research addressed the necessity of having three separate research models for three geo areas, and regional models in developing countries.

90s decades onwards, ICTs have been overcoming the geographic, regional and national differences. Further communication researches have been highlighting a 'Technology Paradigm' for all. But this 'Technology Paradigm' has its own shades of differences and diversity of models within this paradigm (see detailed discussion Technology Paradigm, section). Ongoing research supports it.

Part 1 through its seven sections discusses the evolution of communication models. Some of these models have been revolutionary. Research has facilitated such an evolution and revolution.

Research Methodology

We find that research methods are also culture specific. The rigorous western sophistication does not work when dealing with rural folks in eastern societies such as India or even less developed societies such as Bhutan, Nepal etc. or Middle East societies with different cultural and religious modes and values.

Narula & Pearce (1990) has pointed that there are practical constraints in field research in different societies since the societies differ in their cultures and even the findings of one society cannot be universally applicable to other societies. Though the basic methodologies may remain the same. The major point is that differences in these countries are not merely obstacles to be overcome but constitutive of research practice. An assessment of research methods that does not take into account culture and politics into account will be as misleading as a research plan that ignores these same factors. There are ample stories about the horrible fates of culturally and politically naïve. Rather current decades are focusing on what more culturally and politically perceptive researchers might do and how the results of their research might be evaluated. The research projects are always completed under conditions of local feasibility rather than ideal desirability. There is no ideal site for research.

A considerable body of accumulated wisdom about the ways in which research is actually being done exists in the form of folklore and anecdotes. There are results of 'experienced sophistication' in research. Though these experiences are not readily accessible and codified.

The empirical research itself has sharpened and sophisticated certain methodologies, rejected some for its non-effectiveness and suggested new tools.

The major focus of communication research has been the changing communication scenario in the past decades and currently vis-à-vis communication issues that have been changing overtime. These issues raised are different in developed or developing countries and very country and culture specific. The other variables of socio, economic, political and technological in specific context of cultures and countries have molded as well impacted these issues. The changing communication issues and the changing variables also impact the other essential components of source, message, audience and channels. Ongoing researches highlight these.

Thus the needs, demands, and credibility of the source and audience are the major focus of communication research. The communication channels — its contents, its consumption and effects are other focus. Research methods have also gone through change, and add-ons (for being culture specifics); since the issues, nature of source, audience and channels have been changing in specific cultural contexts.

There are also practical constraints faced by changing methods.

It does focus on communication strategies and policies and who controls the communication scenario — the public, the national government, the national political will or the international media or international community. Role of communication research is significant in determining the roles of above-mentioned factors.

Communication research reframes the understanding of practical problems in research; from *impediments* of research methods to *constituents* of the research process, and from *threats* to *validity* to *information.* It facilitates the 'experienced sophistication' in researchers, which we believe is a necessary part of research methodology.

Practical constrains in communication research. What we mean by this term is that there are problems encountered in conducting specific research projects. Sometimes these problems are derived from cultural contexts in which the research takes place, from the logistical arrangements required to conduct the research, from the availability of channels through which to disseminate the research results and so forth.

The developing nations have undergone transformation in terms of their research communities and research sites and issues. Earlier after the Second World War, these countries were in political disarray and these were frequently the research sites for western investigators, using methods that emerged from western traditions and served western interests. They did set up the standards of training and research methodology. Even for years local researchers trained in west brought home the same western methodology. However for the last three decades there is awareness among the developing countries that western models of research do not work in developing nations. Over a period of time, they have created a strong indigenous research community, sufficiently confident to say that the western models of research do not fit their cultural, social and material circumstances.

In 70s and 80s the western research community has turned to non-traditional research methods: ethnography, ethnomethodology, participant observation, focus group interviews, unobtrusive measures, rules analysis, critical analysis, cultural studies and so on. The important strand in this emerging consensus is the attention to the particular instances of social action, appreciation of unique features rather than universal characteristics of which is being studied. This emphasis of human activity both by the researchers and those studied reframes the understanding of the 'research problems' in research.

Every research project face practical problems, this may seem impediments to some researchers; but we argue that practical problems are constitutive of research methods. From this view point there is no such thing as 'pristine' method since all research is situated and every local, historical, temporal situations produce practical problems in research. We reframe the status of practical problems from *impediments* to *constituents,* and from *obstacle* to *information.* They provide information about the situation and that should be considered as part of the data.

Let us see what are the implications of this neat conceptual reframing. There is willingness to innovate and adapt to particular situations and a commitment to the belief that there is no single best way of doing research. Experienced sophistication gives a chef mastery of culinary techniques. Same way a researcher through experienced sophistication develops intensive and extensive knowledge of the particularities of many specific situations rather than by a formal description of one ideal model. Experienced sophistication can be learned but not taught. Learning about researches and their practical problems in variety of culture specific situations and wide range of communication issues and potential ways of dealing with them provide us knowledge about best practices and solutions. This is learning from experienced sophistication of others. The communication scenario of the world changing constantly, with every new foray into the field, the communication researcher undertakes a discovery for the self as for the others.

Narula & Pearce (1990) highlight that every country in the world developing or developed is facing practical problems in social/communication research and its status. There are problematic issues in pre-research, during research and post-research. Communication research contributors in the above study talks about communication research status in diverse countries. Their in-formed views are quoted and it familiarizes the readers with status of communication research in these countries. More than a decade has elapsed since this study and viewpoints expressed but it does give insight into the research reality at a particular point of time.

Enrique Sanchez-Ruiz *et al.* (p. 85) sheds light on the Maxican communication research status: "It is marginal, poor, centralized, dispersed in thematic, theoretical and in methodological terms. It is pretentious, authoritarian, anti empiricist, and fashion prone. Most of the scholars within it lack adequate training and work under unfavorable institutional support and there is scarce diffusion of their work".

Aggrey Brown (p. 39) talks about communication research in Caribbean: "The researcher discovers that within Caricom (Caribbean countries) regionally meaningful research in the region has to be collective and collaborative undertaking and that highly developed interpersonal skills are essential to success. At the level of scholarly community, written report, papers and articles are universal 'media' for transmitting findings. However at the popular level, given the 'orality' of the Caricom society, audio and visual media are appropriate and preferred media for publishing research findings. The use of these media helps to ensure positive impact on public policy of research outcomes. Caricom 'reality' is the reality of its people — not of the government, not of the bureaucrats, not of intellectuals. It is therefore to the people of the region that social researcher/communication researcher looks for a definition and understanding of the region's reality".

Kwame Boafo *et al.* (p. 60) talk about communication research status in African countries: "A greater interaction at a mutually comprehensible level among researchers, policy-makers and practitioners at the pre-research and post-research stages can contribute to orienting research endeavors most appropriately to national development and better integration of research findings into development policy and planning. As a corollary such research efforts need to be encouraged by policymakers, planners and practitioners through manifested utilization of findings. There have been critical questions about the social research process in African countries and there is need to modify the methods to suit the conditions in those countries".

This is not peculiar to Ghana but has relevance for many African countries. There are other diverse views expressed about the status of communication research and practical problems in research in other countries both developing and developed at this point of time by countries of Japan, Australia, Argentina, Great Britain, India and other developing countries which suggests that every one of these countries would have gained during the ensuing period of time an experienced sophistication for best ways to deal with the practical problems in their own societies.

There are practical constraints at three stages: pre-research, during research, and post-research.

Pre-research issues that sets the agenda for research in many countries particularly developing countries is rural-urban dichotomy, heavy concentration of communication infrastructure and social facilities, high illiteracy rate, poverty, low employment rate, unstable political system, low economic growth spawned by high cost of living. The general consciousness, socio-eco, political, and cultural climate prevailing in the country can affect the quantity and quality, and type of social research encompassing communication research in many of the countries.

There are other pre-research issues of economic interests, authoritative and intellectual interests and training of researchers for particular research project. The other pre-research constraints show that planning for research is mostly poor, inconsistent and uncoordinated.

Serious problems arise when doing communication research in conventional scientific frame where communication is not taken as process but a single factor. Communication is a dynamic process whose character arises from the joint action of the people in relation.

The intellectual atmosphere of the country, the interest of the people in communication research does affect the organization and topics of research.

Even some countries believe that the political stance of the major researchers does affect the communication research.

During research issues may be the particularities of culture and society, communication density, and project research logistics. The field research constraints in sampling, measuring techniques and gathering field data points to the need for culture specific approach to research and methodological techniques. Such as theoretical sampling techniques, greater use of non-probability sampling, group and circular questionnaires for gathering data, use of diverse research models such as nodal models, rather than using one single research model for studying all communities and subcultures. For example, in developing countries, there is little systematic attempt to assimilate research findings into universal theoretical conceptualizations or to develop culture-specific concepts through empirical research.

Inadequate access to communication channels especially blockage of channels intentionally pose problems. The manner in which communication is conceptualized creates research and post research constraints

The post-research issues may be about dissemination of results. The questions posed are: To whom these results will be disseminated? Will it be accessible to people who are affected by it? And will there be interaction among the people involved i.e. practitioners, clients and researchers? Will there be 'action' component of the results? Will there be coordination between research findings and implications?

Further, basic characteristics of the society pose post research constraints. These could be basic social structural conflicts of class, casteism and social distance; the close and evasive society facing the pull of traditions and push of modernization and technology. The basic conflicts between the bureaucracy and the masses such as the bureaucratic attitude of 'trained incapacity' towards the masses suggesting that masses are naïve and incapable of deciding what are their development needs; and thus creating learned dependency and distrust binds among them. These create constraints among governance, and communication bureaucracy; and the conflicts between practitioners and researchers.

There has been a three-way communication gap between the practitioners, clients and researchers. Clients create practical difficulties for the researchers to assess the real problems and work out solutions. If researchers pose those problems and solutions to the practitioners and they do not respond well and are indifferent to their suggestions then the clients are likely to distrust them.

Further, low applications of the research as well low credibility of research applications create constraints. There are weaknesses and biases of applied research in developing countries as a problem-solving tool. The practitioners point that only a few of the findings from the research are applicable to the practice. From their point of view the findings are more academic. Then there is confirmation of theories in single variable terms with little applications to the complexities of the real world.

There are other problems, which are not obvious to the practitioners or the conventional researchers. Serious logical contradictions may invalidate many of the questions that research addressed. Particularly problems of method not appropriate for the subject-matter.

What should we make of the fact that research never ends? "More research needs to be done". It is phrase that summarizes the conclusion of virtually all research programs.

If research is designed to answer questions, validate theories, to establish the facts, then this never ending quality presents a problem. But if alternative concept of research is envisioned; and if research is seen as a special form of activity in which preconditions for better communications are created within particular and cultural contexts than the *results of research* are understood as part of the evolution of those contexts. Of course more research should be done, but as part of the cultural and political structure of the society, not as an *objective* (whatever that might mean), *report* (to whom), for what purpose about that society.

Summary

Research has been a significant and essential component in developing the Communication discipline. Both empirical and theoretical researches have helped in ironing out the wrinkles as well developing more insights, new dimensions and components in the discipline. In this context, we discuss, the communication source, audience, channels, consumption, effects and evolution of its models; and its strategies and policies; and various socio, economic, cultural, political, technological and international factors which have been conducive or non-conducive to it; and the practical problems that it faces.

Communication research methodology has evolved and developed overtime with the changing communication priorities, functions, audience demographics, media consumption, advancement in ICT and the need and significance of supporting role of both interpersonal communication and media channels. Communication research has facilitated these changes. Other perspectives presented in earlier sections highlight the research and development in those specific areas as supported by the basic framework.

Researches also advocated, supported and developed different perspectives from which communication has been studied and applied overtime. The impact of ongoing research is clearly evidenced in the six perspectives that we have discussed in Part 2 through six chapters.

What should we make of the fact that research never ends? 'More research needs to be done' is a phrase that summarizes the conclusion of virtually all research programs. If research is seen as a special form of activity in which the preconditions for better communication are created within a particular cultural and political context, then the *results* of research is understood as *part* of the evolution of those contexts.

PART 3

COMMUNICATION STRATEGIES

16

Communication Planning, Policies, Strategies

I have often been struck how planning, policies and actions
Let you define achievements harmoniously.

—*Annonmous*

Part 3 discusses Communication Planning and Policies, and Communication Strategies. The role of positive and negative communication strategies is discussed in the context of earlier discussed seven perspectives in Part 2.

Communication Planning and Policies

The focused area of activity is identified, the general and specific objectives for the activity project are spelled out but to implement it, communication planning is necessary. Communication planning involves: communication strategies, media planning (channel planning) and resource management culminating in communication policies.

Communication policies are sets of principles and norms established to guide the behavior of the communication systems. Their orientation is fundamental and long range although they may have operational implications of short-range significance. They are shaped in the context of society's general approach to communication. Emanating from political ideologies, the social and economic conditions of the country and the values on which they are based. They strive to relate these to the real needs and prospective opportunities of communication.

Communication policies exist in every society, though frequently they may be latent and disjointed rather than clearly articulated and harmonized. What is proposed as communication policy is nothing new but deliberate prospective formulation of practices already established in society. We cannot plan in any meaningful and realistic way without a clear analysis and articulation of existing structures in a society and their influences upon communication.

The rationales given for communication planning and policy are associated with two broad perspectives. One, the techno-economic perspective and second is the political economy perspective. In the first case, the focus of attention is on technology assessment, innovation, utilization, techniques for increasing effectiveness of communication, and economics of communications i.e. technical and economic efficiency and cost effectiveness. The second perspective encompasses broader socio-political factors that include public needs and participation, access, equity, power and dependency; and changes in power relations in society.

Further, there is need for communication policy and planning due to concerns about inequality of access and utilization of information among different social classes and groups in the society. A vicious circle persists in communication: the well-informed have more access to knowledge and information and seek more information; the ill-informed and socio-economic disadvantaged have less access and do not regard information as particularly important. The pattern of distribution of information is dependent on media (and other channels) policies, planning and production levels. A wide range of factors such as material living conditions, socio-economic structures, ideological and cultural factors determine these in turn.

Communication policies proceed from the analysis and acknowledgement of existing practices and formulation of new principles, and norms for realizing the set goals. The communication policies are reoriented and redirected when analysis of communication policies reveals structures and pressures against individual or even collective goals.

Conceptually, the indicated stages in policy formulation are: policies (existing or planned), planning strategies, operational planning and budgeting resources. In reality, planning and operational action can precede the formulation of policies.

The emergence of new communication technologies and initiatives, and the immediate needs of the communication networks though considered within a limited context to achieve immediate ends may determine the future of communications for decades. Other realities of technology transfer, market forces, interplay of information, ideas and expertise also enter directly into the policy-planning framework.

Communication planning both long range and short range is efficient and equitable use of communication resources for the realization of communication policies. It identifies the priorities, possibilities and pressures.

The policy planning by objectives is to determine needs, set goals and targets, frame objectives, devise strategic plans, devise operational plans, implementations, evaluation and feedback, modifications and extensions. The policies can be at national, regional and at local levels. The infrastructures involved are: organization of data, communication systems planning, implementation and evaluation.

Identifying sectoral goals and policies, social attitudes and aspirations, economic, societal and developmental goals, assessment of organizational capacity, assessment of technical capacity and regulatory constraints establish goals and targets.

Organization of data is through social research about social and cultural attitudes, demographic data and market and commercial organizational infrastructures. The informational storage and distribution, media structure, production and distribution, and its sectoral policies are essential. Research also focuses on educational plans and structures, economic and societal development goals; and science and technology plans to organize data. Political and government infrastructures and regulatory provisions, and urban and rural plans further facilitate the organization of data.

Communication systems planning involve interpreting policies and devising systems and subsystems for implementation. The aim is to frame strategic plans through alternatives and then approve strategic plan for overall operational plans. These are further classified into sectoral and institutional operational plans.

The recent trend of *formative evaluation* is in keeping with the whole trend of communication planning, where many checks are run on the system performance in advance. The critical task at this stage is not only to evaluate prototype version of the communication system plan but device the evaluation framework to run parallel to and feed into the system for implementation. The overall objective is to evaluate and refurbish the system on a continuing basis. It is important that change should be accommodated in system design as early as possible and those planning frameworks should be flexible enough to incorporate shifts of emphasis. Evaluation involves continuous monitoring and evaluating at different stages of the project against the set design, planning and policies and specific targets and goals. All the tasks are inter-connected, allowing and reformulation of the system as it expands and its experiences are assimilated.

As mentioned above communication planning involves: communication strategies, media planning (channel planning) and resource management. Practice of communication planning is differentiated into horizontal and vertical planning. Horizontal planning is coordination, integration and cohesion of the different tasks of planning. Vertical planning is through participation.

In Horizontal planning, coordination among various tasks, various agencies, and team members is necessary. Coordination difficulties of different planning tasks arise because of lack of identification and value sharing among those involved as to the significance and overall priority of the overall task. Identification demands a common goal structure, a shared perception of priorities in the communication-planning task. It can come only from a deep and sustained interaction among the parties. Second problem arises when there is lack of information and communication exchanged among them. Though these needs are less value oriented. There is sufficient sharing to allow parts of the overall system to function both independently and in unison. These difficulties can recur throughout from policy formulation to implementation.

Integration is needed at the fundamental stages of policy and planning. While implementation depends on coordinated arrangements, identification correlates with integration. The resolution of these needs require different kinds of administrative and management frameworks and cohesion. Cohesion is needed to forge links between the two continuums of integration and coordination. It means imposing the sense of an overall policy plan upon all parts of the system particularly when implementation stage is reached. *Communication planning in fact becomes like reconciling the whole of communication system, its component parts, with the social system that it serves.*

A small professional unit at the central level and then going down to regional and local levels may undertake communication planning. The regional and local levels can provide feedback of information and opinion to the central level for further modifications. These two levels will disseminate about the overall plans and priorities and the rationale on which they are based. They will also promote them. Promotional needs for communication planning are needed at all levels of, and stages of planning and implementation. Much of its success at these levels depends on the creative energies of people involved.

In communication planning there is a continuous interaction between functions (of planning, research and decision-making), between agencies and institutions, and between processes (i.e. the phase planning and implementation sequence).

A communication planner is forced to take account of number of fields and differentiated policies and many inconsistencies of approach. But he/she will not be welcomed for externalizing these contradictions. Therefore, the planner must work with sensitivity through the maze of sectoral approaches, synthesizing their aims without opening up hostilities.

Vertical planning has two focuses: One, participation of member groups responsible for communication planning and policies by sharing common goals and perceptions. Two, participation by people by interacting with these member groups. In developing societies, the patterns of participant planning carry a basic potential for greater participation in communication planning. In many cases there are local mechanisms for discussion, administration, for organization, for decision-making that could be expended to move both the upward movement of ideas and representative participation in planning activities. For instance, there have to be more cohesion in the way development work operates, extension activities tend to be sectoral in approach, and to reflect elements of interagency rivalries in planning for village development communication policies.

When we descend to regional and local levels, there need to be good deal of latitude and flexibility. Theoretical models of organizations are unlikely to work, since they must deal with residual factors of local culture, social organizations, special interests, status and local innovations threshold. Moreover, a highly decentralized structure would be necessary, giving maximum identity to each level of the chain including the ability to be accountable for its own affairs. Goal sharing and the common perception problems demand participation in the early stages of policy formulation.

Since communication policy-making involves the process of communication planning. Before public policy can be formulated on any issue, it needs to be recognized as a 'public issue' i.e. that it needs to be put on the action agenda of the official policy-makers. Policy-making has to be based on reliable database that allows for an inventory for locally available resources, a projection of needs and a scenario for resource development. Problems, issues and directives of a policy nature and decisions or actions are needed in this context. All policies must be reviewed constantly and raise salient points needing attention and intervention of the policy-initiators and policy-makers concerned. Old policies should be reviewed and related to present-day situations, trends thinking and technologies.

The emergence of policies comes out from a gradual process of attrition and compromise. This participation is needed at number of levels: among the planning team, among related agencies, and among cadres of researchers, planners and decision-makers.

If these conditions are not met then a *conflict of criteria* will result. It reflects differing and contradictory judgments in various circumstances. The decisions may be made arbitrarily responding to immediate political pressures. Faced with conflicting pressures, the decision-maker opts for the choice that intuitively he/she feels has the higher priority and most immediate reward. Mutually inconsistent value frames are likely to coexist, and any number of factors can destroy the integrity of the planning process.

The second set is methodological. This affects planning tools and the planning process. Here planning problems are those of organization and structure. The constraints are of diffusion (when it is thinly spread out, not concentrated, and not concise), inflexibility, and dysfunction. Diffusion and inflexibility arise from defects in the original planning design, from inadequate preliminary task analysis and from overly incomplete phasing. Dysfunction refers to uncoordinated activities among members of the planning team. Therefore, attention should be paid to team selection, group dynamics, and emergence of consensus. Successful coordination can help in overcoming the constraints.

Communication planning and policy processes in different societies are important and equally important are the factors influencing those processes. Both the substance and the methods of their formulations and implementation are legitimate concerns of policy and planning.

Communication Planning Constraints

Constraints experienced by communication planners are of two kinds. One set is related to the status of the communication discipline itself. This relates to the value that is placed by politicians and decision-makers, the attention that it receives from other planners, and the contradictory positions and assessments that result sometimes about communication planning *per se.*

There is qualitative need for well-informed planners with vision. Since this is likely to have impact on the final outcome. For example, communication policies in India are paradoxical. On one hand, they emphasize about self-reliance, on the other hand everything has to be tailor made by the government for the people and thus inducing learned dependency. Secondly, there is no integrated communication policy. They are sectoral policies such as for TV and radio and its various aspects, print, films, and folk and oral traditions and telecommunication etc. Some of these policies are well developed but others may not. Some of these are reviews of old policies and related to present day situations, trends and thinking. But these sectoral policies if not integrated into *a communication policy per se* could be an impediment for efficient communication framework.

Further, the status constraints could be time, finance, administrative and technical support and access. Time is important when planning is stimulated by a perception of crisis, when time is needed for planning tools for particular functions. It needs fair share of finance, administrative and technical support. Access to people and information can be a problem both for decision-making and research. It is important to get access to relevant information. Authentic field and secondary research is necessary to assess people's needs and expectations and provide reliable database. It is necessary to identify the correct levels of competency of decision-making and have access to them at pre-determined times or at critical times. Financial resources and technical support, and status of update communication technology can affect the communication planning process.

Strategic planning determines the alternative ways to achieve long-range goals and sets the frame of reference for short-range operational planning. The strategic plan is broken into many operational plans. The various components of operational plans are: technical components including designs at macro-level, organizational infrastructures, existing and projected institutional framework for implementation, construction components designs at macro-level, finance and personnel including training needs, operational framework and networks on both time and systemic frames, and coordination and relationship with other projects and phasing.

Strategic planning is necessary and important for communications viz. technologies of the media channels and for interpersonal channels, the communication infrastructures and its development in update time frames and technologies within the local, national and global contexts, the trained personnel including administrators, functionaries, researchers and even training people for interactive participation. Most important is coordination of different aspects of communications for achieving the specific project goals. The operational plans in the strategic planning are coordinated according to different communication perspectives. Therefore, these operational plans would differ in respect of the seven perspectives we discussed earlier within the broad framework of strategic planning.

We will discuss communication strategies and media planning (channel planning) in later sections.

Communication Strategies: Framework

The communication strategy framework comprises of communication needs, communication resources, policies and operational principles. Communication strategies are based on field experiences and theoretical analysis of focused activity areas. The nature, forms and types of communication strategies are planned accordingly.

Varied communication strategies are used (planned) both by government and people to communicate to their targeted audience. These strategies would differ according to the demographics of targeted audience, the nature and extent of program itself, people's demands and discontents and motivations for the programs. Moreover, these above-mentioned dimensions must be managed well in order to make the communication strategies and the programs delivered to the targeted audience effectively. There are spontaneous (unplanned) communication strategies also pertaining to our mundane activities. However spontaneous these may be, even when we converse or communicate otherwise, we do plan at the back of our mind at conscious or subconscious level what we want to say to whom and with what effect.

Nature and forms of communications strategies: Nature, forms and types of communication strategies suggest *who* would use these strategies, with what *objectives* and with what *effects.* These strategies could be both positive and negative. They are focused on media and interpersonal channels. They are vertical, horizontal and circular in nature.

Singhal Arvind (2003) talking in the context of health care communication strategies suggests that there are differences in communication strategies applied to developed and developing countries. He advocates that the differences should be the function of the differences in culture. The cultural differences are not between developed and developing countries but within a country also. Each communication strategy should ideally resonate with its own socio-cultural milieu. The cultural differences in relation to social norms, prevailing practices, local policies, availability of health care and other local factors should guide the communication strategy for health care.

Lack of noise (hype) politically, in the media and in the public discourse could be problematic. When a communication strategy does not make the high level noise and there is no coherence, it will have low impact or no impact on the issue. The challenge really lies in taking up health issues as they exist, turn them around in ways that they become useful for your communication strategy.

For example, in HIV/AIDS communication strategy in India, the mistakes have been: not acknowledging that there is a problem, not doing that early enough, denying it, being silent about it, thinking that it will go away; and lack of mobilization through political unity, media and resources.

The communication discourses in this context has to be engaging, involving and enlightening.

Positive communication strategies. Some salient positive communication strategies are information, education, communication and motivation (IECM) strategies, development communication strategies, public dialogue and dialogue action strategies, media control, role model and demonstration effects, ethics in communications and non-violence as a strategy.

IECM strategies are used to create awareness, information, knowledge and motivation about varied issues current and historical. The government uses this strategy to get across their viewpoints and policies, and implementation activities across people. People use this strategy to make government aware of their issues, which are uppermost in their minds, and government might have sidetracked them. They disseminate information and their own knowledge about these issues and that becomes a good resource for government. They motivate government to give priority to those issues. People use this strategy also among people; to create awareness, information and knowledge, and motivation for other people.

Thus this strategy can be used for communicating both vertically — from top to bottom, and horizontally from bottom to bottom. These are horizontal strategies when used by people to people, and from authorities to authorities. These are vertical when they are from government or other authorities, and to people.

Though the modern mind is ruled by technological advancement, we still depend on human emotions. Therefore, a thorough study of people's insights is a must before chalking out awareness strategies. Product can be a success if it appeals to the emotions of the people along with rationale for those products. We need good tools and techniques to understand these insights.

People, government and other agencies base IECM strategies on assessment of needs, demands, and insights of the people who are the consumers of products and services.

Development communication strategies. The focus of development communication strategies is generating knowledge about development and sharing it; to have access to good ideas and best practices among development professionals, practitioners, policymakers and other stakeholders at all the three levels: local, national and international. At local and national level the initiatives are by governments, NGOs in many development areas, and people.

Internet and web gateways are such channels to connect international community for these modes for knowledge generating and knowledge sharing. Since the year 2000, many such gateways sponsored by World Bank and other international organizations attempt to share development concerns from global perspective. Global gateway by World Bank, Indev sponsored by British Council to connect developing countries for development information, IDRC for developing countries are some good examples.

In international development communication, different development stakeholders are exposed to IECM strategies.

The power of media control and word power is used. Thus Information Communication Technologies (ICT) and interpersonal communication models address the international development issues.

The strategies of development can be linked to economic and social development. The solutions are health care, education, land reforms and empowerment to people. The developing countries do not need 'trickle down' from western countries but they can achieve development by developing their manpower. Human development is the main focus. It is necessary to bring into the public domain discussions about social deprivations and create a system for social opportunities. There is lack of initiative to focus on unemployment even in richer economies. The effort has to create a force so that benefits of liberalized economy reach the socially deprived.

Strategies and tools to help empower individuals and communities to improve their lives at every level — economic, social, cultural, and political need to be identified accordingly. Ways should be explored in which new technologies can enable more efficient, transparent, and participatory forms of governance locally, nationally and globally.

Knowledge and information as tools for development at local, national, and global levels need to be harnessed and impediments to these would need solutions. Building knowledge for development capacity in developing countries is essential. The contexts could be the key issues and challenges facing the development community and the world's poor with a particular emphasis on learning from the experiences of those who face these challenges in their daily lives. Information and knowledge needs in developing societies are not met adequately by current local, national, international initiatives by traditional media or ICTs because of lack of accessibility due to cost, technology, and ICT literacy and exposure to it; and other social constraints.

There are varied development communication strategies to deliver development. The development communication approaches focus on extension, diffusion, mass media, development support communication, planned strategies for Devcom and dialogue strategies. These approaches facilitate actions for evolving effective communication strategy for Development projects (discussed in detail in Development Communication perspective Chapter 2 Part 2). Development strategists play significant role in evolving pertinent development communication strategy.

Development Strategists (DS) are policy incubators and policy think tank that would focus on continuing policy reforms in the areas. They plan strategies, develop action plans and implement action plans. Development Strategy (DS) focuses on organization, empowerment, motivation, aspirations, and achievement of targeted groups.

Development strategies need to be different for different targeted groups. There is need for specific DS for Absolute poor, and for lower income groups based on need requirements and based on social principles. These have to be tried in smaller groups in different geographic areas. These need more attention.

Development Strategists focus on particular targeted groups to organize people and empower them. For example, the need is to organize people for shelter, food, work, skill-training and functional literacy. It is a combination of strategies through which empowering people may achieve this goal. One strategy is to empower people by employment that increases their purchasing power. Second, by education, that creates awareness in them about their needs, and how they can procure them. By providing health care, by giving them information, knowledge about preventive measures, personal and environmental cleanliness, civic sense, nutrition etc. access to curative medical facilities, it inculcates motivation and aspiration for better quality of life. Empower them by making them learn about societal values and judgments and participation for self-development, self-reliance, trust, and credibility as member of society.

Strategy implementation dimensions can be identified through dialogue action strategies, both multimedia and interpersonal IECM campaigns, multistage video and audio productions, and docudramas. Further, role model and demonstration effects strategies can be used for implementation by providing positive role model and success stories.

It is demonstrated further to reinforce the implementation. Thus multi communication strategies can focus on organization and empowerment process.

Diffusion approach to Devcom focuses on adoption of technological and social innovations through diffusion of new ideas, products and services. Diffusion of both material and social innovation is necessary for development. Material innovations refer to technical and economic innovations and social innovations pertain to social needs and structure.

The individual and community decisions about the acceptance and rejection of innovations depend on what is communicated about innovations and how it is communicated. In Devcom context there are three important stages for diffusion of innovations: reorientation, refocus and reinforcing. The innovation is reoriented with changed elements; the reorientation necessitates refocusing of the individuals and communities on the innovations. The innovative ideas, products and services have to be reinforced intensively and extensively by media and interpersonal campaigns. Both mass media and interpersonal communication channels are used for diffusion.

Mass Media and Extension approach for Devcom. A well defined mass media and interpersonal approach (extension) infrastructure is necessary for development communication. These infrastructures should be both socially and physically accessible to people. The messages should be need-based, appeal to people, be relevant to them, and also aimed at the specific targeted audience — rural or urban, urban slum, rich and the poor, educated and the illiterate etc.

Localized approaches to devcom: Communication scholars argue that mass communication produces demonstration effect and such information stimulates for new ways of doing development. Thus there is correlation between media exposure and development variables. Other scholars have expressed that mere availability of any kind of mass media messages is not likely to be useful for innovative changes. The information transmitted must be locally and functionally relevant and relates to patterns of content presented to the audience.

Information must be perceived as useful, applicable, timely and specific in given situation.

The development programs must meet the local needs that vary widely in different regions and sub-regions in developing countries, as there is plurality of cultures and languages. The localized approach would enable the communicators to design messages that will be relevant in terms of utility, timeliness, applicability and specificity. Such an approach would facilitate greater involvement and participation of the audience in the communication process.

Planned development communication strategy is a communication plan for changing human attitudes and behavior through transfer of new ideas. It is a systematic framework for action for effective communication. It focuses on four specific lines of actions.

First, the contextual and contemporary needs of the targeted community must be correlated to the focus of the specific development project. Second, identify the communication patterns within the community, the movement of communication in each community-network whether it is vertical, horizontal, circular or multiways. Identify the decision-makers, potential agents of change in the community. This will help in constructing a pattern of interpersonal communication within the community. Patterns of mass media for the community can be constructed by considering media availability, media credibility and cost effectiveness of media channels, literacy and understanding of media messages by the people.

Third, the attitudes, beliefs and prejudices of the people should be assessed so that communication contents and techniques give adequate consideration to them. This calls for systematic and periodic research in the socio-psychic life of the community. Fourth, find out the communicative ability of the communication support material available such as posters, brochures, documentaries, audio-visual aids etc. for the specific development project. Material should be pre-tested and its distribution system should be evaluated for maximum efficiency. These are the basic lines of action and several more can be added according to the communication environment of the project.

Such Devcom strategy could ensure wider reach and lasting effects of development. The focus of such strategy for implementation is: multi-channel Devcom approach and a team approach. The team one, should consist of team of development planners, consultants and administrators and other development agencies. Team two comprises of communicators, subject-matter specialists and researchers. There should be coordination, consultation and collaboration between the two teams for implementation of the project. Further, there should be coordination between multi communication channels, between both the teams, and development agencies.

Development Support Communication (DSC) addresses development planning and the plan of operation for implementation; whereas Devcom focus is on IECM role. DSC emphasizes on widespread understanding of development plan for public cooperation and participation. Understanding of the priorities that govern these plans would enable people to relate role of plans for development purposes. Therefore, the development plan messages to people must be in the language and symbols that they would understand. These must address their common needs and problems.

DSC continuously emphasizes the appropriate motivation for the ongoing support to the sectoral development programs. It is used as a vital instrument for social and political change associated with sectoral development programs beside its IECM role.

Any effective Devcom strategy could ensure wider reach and lasting effects of development. The focus of such strategy for implementation is: multi-channel Devcom approach and a team approach. Yet information and communication systems are rarely well integrated into development strategies and programs.

Public Dialogue (PD) Strategies

We envision a world in which communication in public sphere is humane, constructive and benefit all. We believe such communication is possible by trust and respect. We can focus on ways that make it possible. The ways of working Public Dialogue strategy is to approach a situation, as complex network of relationships among people and messages.

The PD techniques are designed three ways: one, to bring to light the various social worlds created within communication systems. Two, to find the positive resources within the system for making a better world and three, to elicit ideas on how the system might move forward in new and productive ways.

Community building is necessary for developing public dialogue in communities. The community is viewed as a complex of interconnected relationships; the community contains many social worlds and the residents need to be involved if community building is to take place. Initiatives for public dialogue must come from the bottom. But there should be support from the top. Most residents are not interested in 'just talk' but they want to see the connection between their ideas and the community initiatives, support and initiative from government agencies and action steps. It is crucial for (e.g. local) government to recognize and support residents' involvement and for residents to feel heard. This often requires quality communication to occur between residents, community leaders and government agencies.

It is important that the issues are framed and discussed in effective language since that would affect the 'outcomes as well as level of trust and respect among the various stakeholders'. It is important to work collaboratively with the community.

This entire process is a series of dialogic conversations. We think of dialogue as the ability to state your perspectives, values, and desires while remaining open to the perspectives, values and desires of others. We think engaging in this form of communication creates the conditions for trust and respect and open up possibilities for enriched actions.

To promote constructive communications on public issues we focus on: innovative public meetings, organizing focus groups, resident association groups, and sponsoring dialogue groups, framing issues and organizing deliberations, assisting community planning efforts, facilitating vision to action workshops and action research protocols. These steps are essential, parallel or together for working through difficult public issues.

This needs collaboration with other groups — clients and participants. We emphasize connections and patterns of interaction within the larger systems; instead of positions, personalities or proposals. It encourages individuals and groups to pay attention to their relationships and to find new and better ways of interacting.

Public dialogue and participatory communication model is important. Another corollary of PD strategies is open public debates on specific issues through various forums. For example, in India, government at one time banned use of polythene colored bags because its disposal was creating environment hazards. They were planning to adopt this as an environmental policy law later on. It did not work as an effective deterrent. Why? Since this was never debated in the public to make them aware of its hazards or to look for suggestions for alternatives from the public. Public felt ignored and continued using and disposing the bags in the manner convenient to them. In many other instances of public laws when issues are not debated and public is not consulted; there are public agitations, demonstration and violence etc. Thus public energy is wasted and issues become controversial and implementation on them is delayed.

E-development Strategies

This strategy has two foci. One is development of Information Communication technologies both hardware and software and its various applications. The particular emphasis is on development of Internet and its applications. This is a global communication strategy and within this framework national, regional and local frameworks are developed.

The strategy is to develop applications of electronic communications such as e-mail, e-commerce for online business transactions, e-governance for transparent and accountable services to the public, build e-leadership in all societies to take advantage of ICT for development and many other online applications to facilitate data services, business, knowledge management, and knowledge economies etc. to the maximal benefits of its citizens as well reducing the geo distances. The essential feature of this strategy is to facilitate physical and social availability and accessibility of the ICT and its applications for effective communication among various segments of society. The digital divide of information, knowledge and learning practices does happen and the efforts are made to bridge the gaps.

E-development applications and strategies are discussed in detail in our discussion of ICT perspective and it has bearing on other perspectives also discussed in the section on Perspectives. E-strategies impact education, information, knowledge, economic growth and productivity. The aim is to reduce physical poverty and social poverty and thereby developing social capital through ICTs and improvement of health. It gives social and cultural connectivity and global connectivity.

Second focus is developing ICT strategies for development. E-development strategies need to be shared by development community. E-development can only be achieved in partnership. The partnership among the four — government, civil society, private sector and academia is important. None can take sole responsibility. The government takes key role and takes a leadership and facilitative role. The private sector plays a crucial role not only in deploying ICT for specific applications but also in facilitating and outsourcing of some government services. Civil society plays vital role in using ICT to overcome the digital divide. Engagement of academia in reflection, monitoring, evaluation and analysis of the needs, situations and tools for e-development strategies, and planning of such strategies is important.

The potential of ICT should not be idealized as panacea for all development needs. It should be rather integrated into the development agenda of each sector, and across all sectors. It should be an integral part of the way we think about development and achieving its goals.

E-development would assess opportunities to use ICT to expand employment and earning opportunities for poor, marginalized groups, in rural areas and women. E-development would aim to enable sustainable development by using ICT applications. This is a powerful development communication strategy.

Non-violence communication is positive protest strategies. They are varied among different cultures, different segments of society and even different socio-economic levels within a society and culture. Non-violence positive strategies are planned to attract attention, to register their demands, discontents and causes, and to create awareness among the larger segments of the society about their demands and causes. These could be planned, unplanned and spontaneous.

General strikes by not working are a common strategy among a vast population of the world societies. In some societies they will be vocal by raising slogans for their cause and against leaders involved. In others they may move silently with demands on the placards that they carry. The silent protests are other positive strategies to suggest that they are ready to sacrifice themselves for their cause and good of others. Hunger strike by abstaining from food is one such strategy. It is a kind of non-violent threat to opposition—'acquiesce to my demands or I die'. Observing silence (*maun vrat*) is a silent protest by the leader for registering the demands of his followers to the opposition leaders, it is against the defaulting leaders. One puts forth tolerance by tolerating violence without being violent. These kinds of strategies are attempt to demonstrate physical and mental torture to oneself for the common good of others. Civil disobedience, political and social rallies and grassroots activism are other forms of non-violent positive communication strategies

Negative Communication Strategies

The most salient negative communication strategies are violence in its various forms. It is one of the most crucial strategies. These could be both planned and unplanned to achieve its objectives through verbal and non-verbal power. Another negative strategy is *Punishment* in its varied forms. Some of the positive communication strategies can be negative also depending upon its usage, motive and targeted audience at a certain point of time.

Violence as a strategy for communication is used widely. Broadly, violence can be categorized in two types — physical and mental. These may occur in mild or severe forms. Further, social, political, and moral violence falls within these two broad categories.

Violence is focused as individual strategy, group strategy and social strategy protesting against the norms of these three. It is used both vertically and horizontally. Government expresses violence against the public to check lawlessness, and to deter wrong doing. People are violent against the people, and government. They express it by protests, anger, hatred and helplessness to draw attention, to reject and to show superiority. Verbal violence is expression in abusive language, hurtling insults and varied objects, and entering into angry debates and arguments. Action oriented violence erupts in violent acts.

What is conveyed through violence is assumed superiority, assertiveness, aggression, hatred, frustration, unhappiness, and even helplessness against the society, systems, and self. It is expressed through media, communication acts, interpersonal communication and campaigns both verbally and non-verbally. It is expressed both symbolically and in written words.

Violence is much more prevalent today. Number of firearms has doubled to millions, many of them are high powered and with logical functions to kill human beings. The levels of prosperity (in affluent societies) mask society's failure to come in grips with the underlying causes of crime. Crime has been aggravated by vast and shameful inequality in income, wealth, and opportunities. Violence is expressed in individual, group and social actions and its form varies from political, social, to domestic violence.

Political violence is expressed in national conflicts, wars, civil war, communal riots, religious violence, terrorism and political coups. National conflicts erupts when different political parties within the countries have in-fights, when they are corrupt, when the governance is not transparent and accountable and people are deprived of their basic survival needs and legitimate rights.

Many a times the civil unrest, because of inequality, causes strife and political violence that culminates in political assassinations. A few examples from India, Mahatma Gandhi was assassinated in Jan 1948, when people felt they could not tolerate his propagating about secularism and pro-Muslim attitude when Hindus were being killed during Partition Holocaust in India-Pakistan in 1947. Indira Gandhi, the Prime Minister of India was killed in 1984 when Sikhs (a community in India) felt religiously offended by Blue Star Operation attacking their holy shrine of Golden Temple in Amritsar. Though this operation was actually meant against terrorist attacks believed to be based in the holy shrine. This was also a reaction of people against the political and administrative 'Emergency' imposed by her (India Case 1). Another Prime Minister of India, Rajiv Gandhi was killed in 1991 when the LTTE terrorist group (based in Sri Lanka) felt he was not sympathetic to their cause but siding with Sri Lanka government (India Case 2). These two cases discussed in the following paragraphs show how political violence can be disruptive.

Long drawn conflicts with other countries erupt in wars to find solutions. Sometimes war is fought to gain political power, to satisfy the ego of the political leader, and that of the country. Sometimes war is fought for an ideology. Rather than finding solutions, war brings untold misery, destruction, social, political and economic instability. This aftermath has more repercussions than war itself. Recent examples are (in 2002-2003), war in Afghanistan and Iraq. In Iraq it took flicker of a time to bomb and destroy the thousand years' old heritage when they bombed National Museum in Bagdad.

In political coups there is large-scale arrests of politicians, political elite, bureaucrats and businessmen. This is set against threats to the ruler/dictator. Often there is victimization and vendetta against them in the garb of political cleansing. These result in international reactions and opinions and a greater pressure on economy.

Racial violence is expression of racism and hatred set against stereotypes and negative images. Religious violence is indulged to prove fundamentalism, and religious superiority and bigotry. Take the case of Kashmir (a State in India). Pakistan and India are fighting over it (who should have territorial occupation) not only in the battlefield but guerilla warfare and terrorism occur because of religious bigotry and fundamentalism. The religious violence among the civilians creates more unrest and complicates the political issue of territorial occupation of Kashmir.

Two cases mentioned below show how political violence can be disruptive:

India Case 1. Communal outrages and violence against Sikh community were provoked in 1982. In early 80s Jarnail Singh Bhinderwala headed the Sikh national party Akali Dal and asked for more autonomy for Punjab. They threatened to stop paying taxes to the Central government and stop shipment of grain from Punjab to rest of the country. Indira Gandhi attacked Sikh fundamentalists and ordered troops to attack Bhinderwala's headquarters at Golden Temple in Amritsar in June 1982 for 3 days. Bhinderwala and his armed supporters were killed and temple complex was damaged. In the process Gandhi made even moderate Sikhs sympathetic with the radicals. In October 1984 her Sikh bodyguard assassinated her. He sought to avenge the insult to Sikh people, since it was advocated that entering the holy precincts of the temple by the military was sacrilege.

India Case 2. If leadership cooperates for political reasons, they pay heavy price. For instance, Rajiv Gandhi (the Prime Minister of India since 1982) government tried to solve the problem of LTTE (an alleged terrorist group of Tamil Nadu India based in Sri Lanka and India). They have been fighting in Sri Lanka for autonomy for Tamilian origin Sri Lanka citizens. Rajiv Gandhi was killed by a human suicide bomb of LTTE on May 21, 1991, when he was addressing a political meeting in Tamil Nadu in South India. The anger of LTTE was directed against him because of his cooperation with Sri Lanka for solving LTTE problem.

In this context, Indian government is extremely sensitive in attacking the sensibilities of any community outside the country lest it provokes communal outrages. It learnt its lesson after the assassination of Indian Prime Minister Indira Gandhi and moved rapidly to defuse any fall out on the Tamil speaking community in New Delhi in the aftermath of Indian Prime Minister Rajiv Gandhi's assassination.

Social violence is expressed in domestic violence, angry activism and moral violence.

In domestic violence there is gender violence and women—young or old are mostly subjected to it. It is both verbal and action oriented. It expresses in abusive language, insults, and physical assaults. Even at times resulting in killings. The root causes are economic frustrations, spouses being incompatible, low management of stress resulting in children being the scapegoat for anger and frustrations. Unemployment, poverty can also activate violence as reaction against helplessness and frustrations. This may be directed against the family or the social system through crime. At times alcoholism can result in violence.

Women experience a multitude of violence, from infanticide to abuse of older women. We see that they are victims of violence at every stage of life. In Indian domestic situations, social evils like Sati, demand for dowry (bride money) and crime against women such as rape and even socially approved gang rapes, murders to save honors of the family when they marry inter-caste, inter-religion or unwed pregnancy, killing girl fetuses or babies can result in social violence.

A woman is burnt alive along with the funeral pyre of her husband. Normally this should evoke horror, but numbed by custom people cheer. There is grand celebration with flowers, red chunri (scarf) in festive atmosphere celebrating *Sati.* By twisted logic they are celebrating the macabre death of woman and glorifying suicide. While she was alive, villagers refused to accompany her to the cremation ground to cremate her husband who was suffering from tuberculosis. They were afraid to contact the disease. Now after death she has become icon of worship; shunned when alive, she acquired status of goddess when dead! Frenzy of religious rituals and activity, myths and superstitions overtook rationality and humanity. This practice is linked to socio-economic backwardness, dismal status of women and where social reforms for women have not made dent.

On the other hand, she burnt herself on *Sati pyre* to get rid of poverty. Being a widow is social disgrace but Sati culture is glorified; she did not want to go through social disgrace and suffer but rather be glorified in death. At times women are forced by in-laws to be Sati to get glory for the family! Force is not the weapon to fight such mindsets. They have to be educated about the ills.

By not satisfying the demands of dowry many women are physically and mentally tortured and in extreme cases burnt alive by husbands or in-laws. Many times when a married woman is helpless and has no support system she expresses violence against self. Sometimes this she expresses by torturing herself by living in open hostile environments; and depriving herself of legitimate demands and rights. She may even commit suicide when overwhelmed.

Gender violence crosses every racial, ethnic, and socio-economic boundary. It is centuries old problem. There is recent explosion of interest on this. That demonstrates the need for analysis of the theoretical, methodological issues in research, about types of violence, prevention and direct intervention, ethical issues, and continuing and emerging issues in both domestic and international public policy on gender violence.

Angry activism is expressed in protests, strikes, demonstrations, and disruptions in normal life, hostile attitude, violating human freedom and burning public properties like buses, public buildings, sabotaging trains; and even kidnappings for ransom and hijacking can take place.

This kind of activism is anger expressed against the social order, some of its evils, and unmet public demands and oppression of the poor. Religious violence occurs to prove superiority over others and due to fanaticism. To check this kind of violence, police may impose curfew, use tear gas, peppery spray and rubber pellets etc. and even at times shooting takes place.

Positive activism for an issue or a cause may be expressed in public litigation petition, addressed through consumer courts, human rights commission, and mediation courts.

Moral violence is expressed in tortures, rapes etc., and communicated in mild forms when debating over moral issues. Human rights abuses occur when freedom of speech and expression is censored, when freedom of media is censored, women are degraded, burnt and tortured for dowries, poor are oppressed and child labor abuses take place.

Risk factors in violence: Violence of any kind is degrading to self-esteem of an individual through a nation. It is damaging and demoralizing to the social tenets of any society whether it is domestic violence or social violence or political violence. Public properties like buses, trains and public buildings are burnt and destroyed. The sabotaging not only destroys and mangles the buses and trains but it kills many of the innocents. The recent example of bombing destroy the thousand years' old heritage when USA bombed National Museum in Baghdad, Iraq in April 2003. The sad part was when the Iraqi civilians were violent and they destroyed the precious heritage by looting and burning it. The destroying of ancient Budha Stupas in Afghnistan a few years back by religious fanatics arguing that it is symbol of Hinduism and thus communicating hatred for this religion. They never identified these Stupas with piece of ancient art and object of tourism for which they should have been proud of. The art of thousands years was destroyed through violence. Though this is not new, history is evidence that temples, mosques, forts have been plundered and destroyed by greed, religious hatred and intolerance. Still people world around do communicate pride in ancient art, monuments and heritage sites be it be Moghul architecture (Taj Mahal in India), Roman architecture (Vatican in Rome) or Hindu architecture (Konark temples, Khajurao temples in India).

Despite the fact that violence results in risk for life, values and property, this strategy is widely used globally to communicate hostilities, anger, power hunger and domination, egotism and competition.

Punishment is second negative strategy. It may be used to communicate hostility, revenge and get power over others. As positive strategy it is posed as deterrent for wrong doing, stimulus for corrective behavior and attitude; and to respect rules and regulations of institutions and both legal and social laws of the society.

There are few communication strategies which are both positive and negative depending upon their applications. Angry activism, punishment can be such strategies. Both verbal and non-verbal words, and media are powerful strategies. They can acts as both positive as well negative strategies.

Power and Control of Communication depends on strategies of power of words and media power and control. These can be both positive and negative strategies when applied in different situations and with diverse objectives.

Power of Words — Verbal Power may be used as negative strategy to deflect attention from real issues. The politicians may use bombastic speeches to deflect real issues from the public. This may happen when they have feelings of low self-worth, and lack of control with focus. People may react to such speeches with sarcasm and criticism. If public is helpless they may face punishment. But if they are powerful, there follows a verbal power sea-saw between the politicians and the public. The efforts should be to make the point and get the message across without engaging in verbal power struggle.

It can impede communication if one uses denial or self-protective statements without investigating the issues.

As a positive strategy, verbal power is used to give information, understand the situation and act against unacceptable behavior. People use verbal power for expressing their discontents and demands for development or even when their human rights are abused. People can make effective use of verbal power in dialogue strategies. Poor are voiceless and silent majority without the verbal power and have negligible control on communications to improve their lot. Verbal power is also used effectively for information, knowledge and persuasion through mass media channels of radio, television, films and telephones etc.

Non-verbal power: The expression of silent reactions both positive and negative is used as communication strategy. It may be bodily gestures, or actions like walking away from the scene when you want to avoid it. The demonstration of protests may be expressed silently in violent manner such as burning the buses when there is fare hike, or non-violently like hunger-strike to call attention on a particular issue. Thus it can be use both as positive and negative communication strategy.

Power of Media depends on media planning and media control. Media is planned to implement the communication strategies. They are planned according to the targeted audience, the focused activity and the availability of the channels. Media planning emphasize the societal objectives through social and individual needs of the masses, dimensions of human communications problems and resource availability.

What type of media and content are best suited to what kinds of tasks and how can media confer the greatest benefit at the lowest cost? These questions are concerned about realizing the societal objectives and ways of realizing those objectives.

Various media technologies — telecommunication, the press, radio, TV, Internet, Mobile phones and other electronic media technologies have powerfully influenced the communication scenario.

Media control is a vertical strategy. As negative strategy it may be used to communicate hostility, revenge and get power over others. As positive strategy, it is posed as deterrent for wrongdoing, stimulus for corrective behavior and attitude, to respect rules and regulations of institutions and both legal and social laws of the society.

The waves of privatization and pressures toward liberalized trade that have marked the world economic order at the turn of the 21st century have also shaped the world media order. But the media industry is not only affected by these trends, it is also a potential instrument to combat the poverty and inequity that continues to plague so many of the world's people.

Mass media can be the ideological army in support of globalization, but can also become the grassroots weapons to fight its impact. As coalitions and activists around the world demand that sustainable development becomes a priority in the world's changing political and economic systems, many civil-society advocates are urging the use of mass media to help communities find local solutions to economic, political and social disempowerment.

Research studies have evidenced that media policies are challenge in the context of actors, its goals and issues involved. Media policies are predominated by economic, political and pro-social goals. Generally, issues posed are: breaking the monopoly of service institutions, commercialism i.e. ideological *versus* consumerism, deregulation of media within cultural contexts, foreign culture predomination, pro-social and national development.

Ethics in Media is challenging. Transparency, accountability, responsibility, morality, truth, in what is being communicated to public; by media, governance, politicians, activists, and other members of the civil society is very important in national, societal, and international contexts.

It is the responsibility of press and other media to project the salient public issues unbiased to both national and international communities when communicating to society and families. This is important for credibility. Sometimes media does report the events but underplay it for the fear of arousing the tensions. Sometimes it does not report the events because the government and other authorities censor it. Sometimes media overplays the events and it's reporting is subjective to create sensationalism, to sell well and to be the mouthpiece of a particular political or social party. Media reporting should be objective and investigative to give facts and to lower the tensions. These are some of the challenges that media has to face.

Media is reality check on activities of civil society and of politicians, and of politics. It gives alerts both to the government and to the public when a culture of intolerance is developing against the public issues and eruption is likely to occur. Media through its empowerment; does empowers the institutions and individuals.

National governments use, manipulate and control media technologies to channel their own viewpoints and policies and to set political and social agenda for people's thinking.

People use power of media to express their demands, viewpoints and set their own agenda. This public agenda sets the government for interaction with the public's viewpoints and opens way for public discourses on many issues.

The International governments, organizations and communities control and influence the media to set political agenda with the national governments and social agenda for people. Media in combination with information, education, communication and motivation (IECM) strategies work on international community programs.

Media, word power both verbal and non-verbal are used nationally and internationally as both positive and negative communication strategies.

Summary

Communication planning, policy and strategies are important for effective communication. Role of development strategist, vision of political leaders, administrators and functionaries is significant in this context. The positive and negative participation of people is not an ignored factor but equally significant.

Communication planning both long range and short range is efficient and equitable use of communication resources for the realization of communication policies. It identifies the priorities, possibilities and pressures. We do face communication-planning constraints such as the conceptual framework of communication in a particular society, political will and the vision of its leaders. Further, the status constraints could be time, finance, administrative and technical support and access.

Practice of communication planning is differentiated into horizontal and vertical planning. Horizontal planning is coordination, integration and cohesion of the different tasks of planning. Vertical planning is through participation.

Communication policies are sets of principles and norms established to guide the behavior of the communication systems. Their orientation is fundamental and long range although they may have operational implications of short-range significance. They are shaped in the context of society's general approach to communication. Policy-making criteria, strategic planning and communication strategies are important in this context.

Communication strategies are based on field experiences and theoretical analysis of focused activity areas. The nature, forms and types of communication strategies are planned accordingly. Some of these are planned others are unplanned and spontaneous. These communication strategies could be positive, negative and mixed i.e. used both as positive and negative strategies according to the situations and objectives.

Some salient positive communication strategies are information, education, communication and motivation (IECM) strategies, development communication strategies, public dialogue and dialogue action strategies, media control, role model and demonstration effects, ethics in communications and non-violence as a strategy. The most salient negative communication strategies are violence in its various forms and punishment. Both verbal and non-verbal words, media-power are powerful strategies. They can acts as both positive as well negative strategies. These strategies control communications.

Concluding Chapter

All said and done — I reflect — the rise and fall of
Individual, Society, Technology
I move ahead for Innovative solutions

Afterword

Communication scenarios are ongoing, changing fast and moving ahead. The communication scenarios in all the perspectives, and outlook for planning and strategies are advancing fast. We do not want and cannot conclude what we have said earlier since it is ongoing. But it will be more satisfying and useful for the readers if we present the contextual significance of the seven communication perspectives that we have discussed in the earlier sections; and the importance of communication planning and strategies; both as stand-alone as well presenting holistic and integrated scenario of ongoing communication decades.

Communication Scenarios and Anecdotes

A few communication scenarios through anecdotes presented in this section highlight integrated and holistic approach to communication. The salient anecdotes presented highlight the applications of ICTs, development communication, political communication, e-development and e-readiness, e-campaigns, international and intercultural communication, conflict management and resolution, opinion leadership as barriers to health care and dialogue strategies.

First communications scenario. We narrate a true story; it presents an integrated communication perspective to achieve a balance in our daily lives. This story **Let us serve ourselves** is based on some of the interviews done in 2000 for a project "Role of Information Communication Technologies (ICT) — experiments in civil society participation in development of urban colonies in Delhi, India". The project aims to include residential areas at different socio-economic levels particularly where lower income group resides.

This is the story of one of the upscale colonies surveyed. And this can be the story of many residential colonies in Delhi. People were interviewed at random to assess the problematic issues in the colony and suggestions of people about the opportunities to handle them through media power and civil society participation.

The story traced the growth of ICT accessibility in the residential area in the last four decades. The accessibility was from TV in its all phases to Cable TV, video, copying machines, computer, fax, Internet, telephone booths, cyber cafes and mobile phones.

The accessibility of different medium overtime has created increased commerce activity in this residential area market and prosperity for its people. This has changed the shape and face of the colony. The important point is that the growth of ICT overtime and its current status has created an awareness to their rights to demand for better quality of life as well necessity of civil society participation to improve quality of life. The media exposure has given understanding to the residents that they can use the power of new media to improve their quality of life.

People should not just focus on ICTs for entertainment but the awareness and knowledge gained through ICT channels should be geared to improve quality of life through cooperative participation.

They want to experiment. The action plan is to experiment with two ICT channels initially for solving problems of their living conditions in the colony. The two channels are, Cable channel and Internet.

The cable operator in the colony assigns one local request channel. They planned to use this cable channel to post their grievances, issues, solutions to the problems and actions to be taken by one and all.

They planned to harness the power of the Internet in three ways: (a) to further co-ordinate the local actions of the residents, (b) to get official attention to the problems, issues and actions taken for solutions, (c) to know how others around the world are solving similar issues. Since knowledge is the key element of tackling and scaling-up of upgrading efforts.

Further, residents suggested four pronged interpersonal communication strategies. One, Residents Association (which is defunct now) should be their strong interpersonal forum. Two, a Bulletin Board should be set up at a strategic place in the shopping complex. Grievances, issues raised, solutions, and actions to be taken should be posted on the bulletin board by all residents, businesses and visitors. Three, interpersonal dialogue strategy should be used to communicate their discontent, demands to the official agencies concerned and local political leaders involved. Four, local residents, community groups and businesses need to take a participatory approach cooperatively with local authorities, official agencies and NGOs.

This is their proposed *ICT and Interpersonal Communication Model* for consensus building in the colony to upgrade their living conditions. Their assumption is, it may even have trickle-down effects on peripheral slum colonies. Their aim was that the upgrading should have a broad development agenda with social, health, education and commerce components.

They felt it is imperative that residents must avail of opportunities for empowerment through ICT channels. They must express discontentment about the neglect of infrastructures in the colony and demand investments from appropriate authorities in infrastructure such as roads, housing, utilities, and provision of critical services such as health, education, water and sanitation.

Our surmise is that people working on similar initiatives can plan projects on similar lines. There is tremendous opportunity to use technology to solve these important problems in a cost-effective manner. The ICT channels salient to particular communities can be experimented to solve the pressing problems with the cooperation of socially aware information technology corporations and caring NGOs.

The project can be expanded to cover other income level residential colonies. It is assumed that even those at lower level income and with less education have direct or indirect access to ICT. Moreover, they are quite excited about the exposures, awareness and knowledge gained. They have more problematic issues and also less attention from the concerned agencies to their problems. They feel more helpless and dependent since they have limited resources. It will be interesting to study effectiveness of *ICT and Interpersonal Communication Model* in these areas also.

Second communications scenario from District West Godavari, Andhra Pradesh, India 2000-2004 Project e-Seva (e services) kiosks.

The District Administration visualized that the lack of empowerment to the marginal citizens was primarily due to information gap. The low capital requirement of information technology and adaptability for deploying human resources gave lead for this innovation to make women self-help groups in the villages self-reliant and economically productive.

Project e-Seva (e services) kiosks are set up for women self-help groups from poor economic strata. The unique point is that these centers are run and managed by the women self help groups and the rural women are information leaders to access government services to the citizens in user friendly and transparent manner. Kiosks empowered the women.

They were trained to handle the computer and the package. The others involved in this partnership are: district administration (government), self-employment agencies, district computer center, banks and international aid agencies.

The project e-Seva (e services) is a tool to bridge the digital divide in the rural areas and use IT to provide C2C (citizen-to-citizen) and C2G (citizen-to-government) services to the people in rural areas. Web-enabled rural kiosks at the mandal (sub district) level are set up.

The citizen centric services focused on from issuance of various certificates, to getting information on various programs, and networking citizens. Moreover, the citizens can file grievance and applications for loans, pensions, agriculture inputs, drinking water problems, land records, mutation etc. for various government programs in these centers. They do not have to go to a government office but field level action is taken on line. This way rampant corruption through government agencies is avoided in providing these services and even bogus cases of pension are weeded out. Even basic and primary health care expert advice and prescription is provided on line.

Tele-agriculture helpline, marriage bureau is operative through the portal round the clock. The centers through the portals expect to provide a virtual meeting place for the citizens to discuss issues relating to the district villages, and its problems and prospective solutions. The citizens can freely interact with each other and post their ideas. This acts as an online forum to express their grievances, air their opinions, and cause necessary social change. It also provides opportunity to conduct opinion polls on the important topical issues and improved decision-making. The digitized inputs on computer enabled education is provided to rural students in these centers to encourage analytical and thinking abilities. Even the administration uses this to pass down important social communication and advocacies to the communities.

All these centers are doing good business and are self-sustainable. The philosophy behind this intervention is that citizen does not approach the government because of discourteous treatment and corrupt practices. This improves accountability and transparency of the government operations. Kiosks have empowered the women as well the citizens. Citizens from poor economic strata are the major beneficiaries.

The above-mentioned scenario dispels the myth that IT is anti poor and unaffordable luxury. It can empower citizens in many ways for economic self-reliance, productivity, overcoming digital divide and self-initiatives in development. This also sets up the case for communication partnership with different agencies. Communication strategies planned for its success focused on public dialogue and participatory strategies; and the diffusion strategies helped in diffusing this innovative approach. The e-development strategies focused on making the self-help group of women e-ready.

Consider a third communication scenario. In 2000 decade thousands of white collar jobs, even in highly professionalized areas are being outsourced to India, China and other developing countries for mainly two reasons: the developed countries want to save costs of operation and maximize the profit margins. Secondly, these developing countries have educated, highly skilled personnel at comparatively low wages to deliver the products and services. Moreover, the advantage of being in different time zone facilitates the services. The outsourcing has meant booming economy for developing countries. But the personnel who are losing jobs in USA, and other European countries are feeling the grunt of depressed economy. They are expressing their discontentment, depression through urging the government to ban outsourcing, (based on news items in the press).

This story does highlight the advantages of advance computerization and telecommunication and economic impact of globalization. But at the same time these very factors are challenging.

This is another communication scenario in India in 80s. Once upon a time...this is an almost true story.... An official in the Ministry of Information and Broadcasting was told that private video parlors in southern state of Karnataka were showing pornographic movies, encouraging students to miss schools, and being run for the profit of undesirable elements in the community. Concerned, he asked a government research institution to do a study that addresses three questions: (a) should private video parlor be permitted to operate? (b) what materials are being shown to the public? and (c) what is the effect of viewing these materials? Some months later, the technical research report was submitted. Based on the findings of this report, the official introduced legislation designed to regulate the operation of the video parlors by censoring pornographic material and subjecting the parlors to hefty entertainment tax.

The issue arose in the context of discovery and for verification and the government had the authority to legislate a social policy for it.

Researchers asked the patrons, do you want video parlors in your community? And having been told, 'yes', the researchers interpreted as strongly endorsing private rather than public video parlors. It was the researchers' judgment that materials were porno. Neither the patrons nor the parlor operators were given the chance to explain why that is not porno and need censoring.

The report was neither disseminated to the patrons nor to the parlor operators, so they were disempowered from participation in the legislative process; the tacit coalition among the officials and researchers used this for their own interests. One of the most curious findings of the 'effects' of video parlors was that the operators were making profit. The Minister's interest was clear: is this operation significantly popular and profitable so that it can be and should be subjected to entertainment tax?

The actual scenario was that in these far-flung villages, there were no cinemas and villagers have not ever seen movies. There was video boom time. The villagers needed entertainment; private enterprise provided them on nominal charge through private video parlors. Government was committed to provide them public parlors that it did not. Villagers felt unhappy and cheated when these were banned and censored formally. They felt the hidden agenda of government was to levy entertainment tax. But if operators had to pay tax, then they would charge more from the villagers and video entertainment would have become unaffordable (Narula 1990).

On the sly, the private video parlors continued operation. The communication scenario would have been different: if officials, operators and the patrons could have been in dialogue to assess the need for video parlors and to plan for private enterprise if government had resource limitations, rather than denying them exposure to a communication technology and means of entertainment. Moreover, the villagers felt they were not being trusted to define their entertainment needs and materials.

In 2000 decades the communication scenario is entirely changed. Since the revolutionary technology of the Satellites has connected many villages with cable television reach and infrastructure. Both the government and the private cable television channels could provide adequate entertainment and infotainment to the villagers. TV sets could be operated efficiently because of advances in rural electrification. Secondly, the video and the DVD boom provide additional infotainment. Now government concerns for entertainment tax or censoring private video parlors have changed.

Think about a communication scenario from African countries in 2000 decades: where rural telecoms are being set up. Cyber-schools are set up for computer literacy, training and e-commerce in the villages and for low-income group people. Women are being trained in Internet working technology. They are using satellite technology to disseminate critical knowledge. ICTs are helping stop HIV/AIDS in Zambia. Many websites are put up for e-commerce of arts and crafts, for information, knowledge and entertainment for youths and teenagers.

Thus they are making tremendous efforts for e-readiness. In fact, they are leap-froging in ICTs applications for development and self-reliance for socially and economically deprived segments of the society with the economic aid from many international organizations. On the other hand, educated group, though comparatively much ahead in communication consumption also leap-frog by using the update communication applications, products and services and supporting and facilitating the efforts of the unexposed segment. This scenario was different a decade back, when people were exposed to mostly traditional interpersonal communication channels and a smaller percentage of the population was exposed to other conventional media such as radio and television.

Here is an update communication scenario from China that is opening up now. It has been quite conservative about letting its people use latest technology. Though it is outsourcing for computer hardware and software. But in 2000 onwards, it is getting tech savvy for its people also. Chinese engineers are developing a computer that will have a chip on which Asian languages can be etched. Therefore, it will be easy to set up language software in such computers and there would be no need of translation software. Such computers will be less expensive and accessible to people in their own languages and not necessary to use English. People can use their native languages. They can easily use such applications as e-mail etc. (based on news item in the press).

These are few illustrations. But people around the world are making demands and efforts to leap frog in communication technologies and its applications. Such efforts are resulting in changed communication scenarios, innovations and innovative applications of the old and new technologies for changing people's aspirations and demands.

The developing and developed countries are forging ahead with new ways to deal with communication issues that are arising overtime; through different communication plans, strategies, models and channels. How they deal with it makes significant differences to their lives. Smaller and poor countries are also in the race for development assisted either by developed countries or by international organizations. But the initiative to develop comes from them. Self-initiative makes difference in how communications help them in development.

Here are few instances of political communication, conflict management and communication management of positive and negative communication strategies.

Planned communication strategies are needed for conflict management between India and Pakistan. They planned official peace talks in Feb 2004 after three years (of initial talks on the issues) to resolve the conflicting issues.

Why the urgent need is felt now for the two countries to communicate about the conflicting issues? Analysts and diplomats believe that both countries have recognized the futility of their struggle over Kashmir and the damage it is doing to their domestic political situations. Neither side believes there is a military solution to the Kashmir issue nor war is an option; rather both the countries should find a peaceful resolution of the outstanding disputes between the two countries.

Pakistani analysts believe Pakistani President Musharaf is convinced militants are a threat to domestic stability. Pakistani leaders are using their entire machinery to curb Jihad and this is the worst form of state terrorism. Meanwhile, Pakistani former foreign secretary Khan observed, "the Kashmir conflict is holding back India's aspirations to be a global power. It has become sensitive to its self-image. It has many trappings of a major power...but it feels Kashmir is dragging it down". Another reason is that Musharaf and Vajpayee — the India's (then) Prime Minister are keen to be remembered as peacemakers.

The third hidden reason which observers and analysts suggest is the subtle pressure of Bush Administration on Pakistan and India to make peace in the region.

The need to communicate felt by both the country leaders urged them to set up an agenda and plan communication strategies for it.

The agenda focus on eight issues mainly border issues (includes Kashmir issue, disputed areas of Siachen, Sir Creek a border region in Gujarat state). Indian plans for a river dam in Kashmir that Pakistan says could deprive its portion of water supplies from the river. Terrorism and drug-related are other major issues; confidence–building measures in the nuclear field, economic cooperation, trade and travel (based on news items in the press).

Both countries planned for face-to-face dialogue strategy to discuss the issues. It is a positive strategy since both strive for a positive outcome. It is a five-tier strategy. They also planned conflict management strategy through understanding of reality, flexibility of rigid attitudes, to enhance their images and the need for economic cooperation and political stability for progress.

1st tier is to iron out preceding agenda for negotiations for top diplomats and eventually for two political leaders meet. This "talks about talks" would start with lower rank leaders and officials.

2nd tier strategy is to have a composite dialogue strategy to discuss simultaneously main points of disputes between the two countries in face-to-face talks.

3rd tier, two days preliminary discussions will set the agenda for final talks between the foreign secretaries of the two countries when high level officials begin thrashing out detailed agreements on emotional issues.

4th tier, beyond these weeks of talks, back-channel negotiations will continue.

5th tier is the action plan.

In political communication, the communication strategies are planned ahead with caution and sensitivity for the agenda issues and the people. Many players are involved in this —

the political leaders, international interests, bureaucracy and even the people's concerns. These are not achieved in a single brainstorm session but these are complex strategies that involved many political, administrative, social and religious systems and sub strategies. These have to be connected with myriads of attitudes, hostilities, political pressures, needs of times and timeliness and people's concerns on both sides. It sends a powerful message that conflicts can be managed if not totally resolved.

Communication management is crucial for its success. First, the management of conflict process and negotiations; and secondly political communication among the multiple actors and their concerns must be managed well to let the dialogue proceed through all five tiers.

In this very context, those who oppose this meet and dialogue disrupted it with strategies of violence — killing people, soldiers, and local political leaders in Kashmir region to express their rejection of the proposed solutions for Kashmir issue. They even blocked the streets in violent protests for two hours in Islamabad where talks were being held (based on news items in the press).

Communication strategies both interpersonal and media to channel violence must be managed so that they do not disrupt the communication and 'Meet' among the leaders as well the positive outcome expected.

Another instance of management of conflict process and negotiations between American government and Iraq. Iraqis and US officials have wrangled over how to create a new Iraqi government to keep the country from sliding into civil war after American official handover power to Iraqi on June 30, 2004. In this context, there are few options which Iraqi politicians are considering: (i) they say they are ready to drop regional caucuses, which is the key component in the plan for democracy to choose a national Iraqi government. "A government can also be established through consensus and consultations". (ii) other option considered is diverse national conference of religious and political leaders, similar to Afghanistan's loya jirga after the 2002 war. A leadership will emerge from this conference to take over. “This option is likely to enjoy the greatest support among Iraqis.”

In this context United Nations is also considering whether direct elections could be held before the handover or to recommend other options. “Americans are also worried whether Bush is managing the conflict properly and whether he has clear goals for nation-building in Iraq.”

US administrator in Iraq — Paul Bremer III said, “We are not walking away. US will remain heavily involved even after July. After June 30, coalition will no longer be sovereign but Iraqi government will be sovereign.” Iraqi people echo American optimism in Baghdad for stabilization of political situation.

Meanwhile there is ongoing civil violence, the two massive suicide bombs killing more than 100 Iraqi people who were applying for new Iraqi police and military forces and many anti-American attacks expressing resistance and undermining American and Iraqi politicians’ efforts for peace. The power struggle for the ensuing political leadership between the two religious groups — Shiite and Sunni erupts in off and on violence (based on news items in the press).

A US finance poll survey by the International republican institute between 24th Sept and Oct 4, 2004 suggests that leaders of the Iraq’s religious parties have emerged as the country’s most popular politicians and would win the largest share of votes if elections were held today, while the US backed government of interim Prime Minister Iyad Allawi is losing serious grounds.

The above instance highlights the communication strategies for managing conflict process in Iraq both by American and UN officials, and Iraqi political leaders after the Iraqi war. This called for negotiations to start the process of political handover, and avoiding political instability and threat of civil war. Many options are being considered and negotiated by officials and leaders involved from the three parties — US, UN and Iraqi. The ongoing civil violence is being managed to create sense of security, optimism, and confidence among the Iraqi people.

Another scenario when lack of cultural communication and understanding leads to political blunders and wars. Recently Robert McNamara wrote a book referring to waging war on Vietnam by Americans said that "we went into Vietnam, ignorant of its history and culture and that it had been all a mistake". Like McNamara Donald Rumsfeld went into Iraq knowing nothing of the place and its culture and would not listen to those who tell him. There are perhaps more dissimilarities than similarities between Vietnam and Iraq but once again led by the best and the brightest and bewitched by American power, this country has been swept by hubris into yet another catastrophic quagmire with no end in sight. (Boston Globe 21 Oct 04).

Here is the latest in e-campaign for national elections in India — a developing country in 2004. The parties were using for the first time modern means of communications such as mobile phones, fixed line phones, Internet, radio, cable television channels, e-mail etc. on a mass scale to supplement the traditional forms of campaigning, such as door to door campaigning and public meetings, print medium and advertisements and wall posters to get the message across. The latest technologies were expected to transmit the message to an estimated 15 crore voters, roughly a fourth of the total electorate.

BJP the then ruling party for their campaign (for Atal Behari Vajpayee Ex Prime Minister) planned to flood these channels with a one minute message to the voters from Vajpayee persuading them to give him another chance 'to build a new era'. Besides this message, governments' main accomplishments encapsulated in the 'India shining' campaign was also relayed through mobile and fixed line phones.

The party formed a database of over 2 crore e-mail addresses to which newspaper and magazine articles lauding the government achievement was forwarded at regular intervals during the election campaign (based on news items in the press).

Interpersonal communication channels and opinion leaders can pose barriers to fighting polio in Nigeria. Local Muslim clerics told villagers to reject the polio vaccine because it was part of American plot. Muslim leaders in hundreds of northern Nigerian communities limited or halted door-to-door polio immunization. They told millions of Muslims in this region that American government has tainted the vaccine with either infertility drugs or HIV, the virus that causes AIDS — the statement that proved false by independent laboratory tests.

Some leaders admitted that they did not believe it but kept silent in order to stop anything associated with USA. The US led wars in Iraq and Afghanistan had led them to believe that USA wants to control the Islamic world; and the polio vaccination effort gave them (people) an opportunity to resist a US funded initiative though it puts their own children to risk.

Another opinion leader commented expressing anti-American feelings, "population is the most important factor in US hegemony in the world. Since they cannot rapidly increase the US population, the only way for them to dominate the world is to depopulate the third world. This is their motive in the garb of polio vaccine".

The villagers acted upon the opinion leaders' advice since they were their in-group. The IECM campaigns by WHO and USA to create awareness about polio risks came not only from alien sources but has also lost its credibility with the people. They were not ready to counter the rumors with factual data. (based on news items in the press).

Think about this scenario: India does not want its people to be exposed to the political culture and ideology of its neighboring country — Pakistan by being exposed to Pakistan TV. Not only its beaming is banned in India but the Pakistan TV channels are also scrambled. This is done off and on according to political correctness. Pakistan also does the same to Indian television channels. Geographically and culturally, these countries are so close that they can have very good reception of their programs both technically and culturally.

Familiar images make false and lasting impressions. Certain images are so familiar and so deeply embedded in the consciousness of human beings that they have become cultural icons. Unfortunately many of these images — and the understanding they convey — are seriously misleading and creating false impressions of those cultures. They are remarkably difficult to correct.

In an era of satellite communications and other advance technologies, to what extent, and how long it is possible to be a close society and shut its people to intercultural influences from world media exposure? It is also not favorable and possible to minimize personal intercultural exposures in a shrinking world made possible by all the advanced technologies.

Another scenario in intercultural and international communication: A French law in Sept 2004 bans wearing conspicuous religious symbols in school including Jewish skullcaps, head scarves for the Muslim girls, large Christian crosses and turbans worn by Sikh boys. The objective is to promote assimilation of the diverse ethnic groups in the school environment. But the ethnic groups feel that their religious sentiments are being violated and their diversity must be respected.

This situation has created intercultural tensions and conflicts in Paris. Disciplinary action was taken and 10 Muslim girls were expelled from school for wearing head-scarves. Further, it has taken political twist since Islamic organization President denouncing the law said that they will no longer be 'blackmailed' into silence by concern over the two French hostages held in Iraq. The kidnappers have demanded that French abolish the law (based on news item).

Think about how Negative strategy of Violence can jeopardize human rights. There are formidable ongoing obstacles to women becoming full participants in Afghan public life. As a symbol of their liberation, officials have cited the fact that women comprised 40% of the registered Afghan voters in the 9th Oct 04 Presidential elections in Afghanistan. But women face continued threats when they exercise their basic rights. In some southern provinces women were as few as 10% of registered voters because of fear of continued Taliban attacks. Many were not able to vote without the permission of their husbands. Worse Mullahs and local male elders staffed some voting sites, which may explain why women did not cast vote at all.

Human rights watch recently documented how Afghan women working in government, in journalism, as aid workers or as human right activists have been threatened with death, harassed, and sometimes violently attacked. They were even threatened by local strongmen, "you are doing things you should not. We will kill you as an example for other women". The primary reason, women's security situation is so bad because of lack of commitment of the Afghanistan current leaders to women's rights. Many shares the same extremist views that of Taliban. Warlords wield their influence in local government to retaliate against women who promote women's rights (based on news item).

The Future

We may foresee that the above-mentioned seven perspectives from which we have analyzed communications *per se* may undergo several changes. The changes may occur when particular perspective's scope is widened. The change may occur due to changes in modalities of communications, both people oriented and technology oriented. New communication technologies may come up. Along with this, newer needs and demands may turn up. Social attitudes and values may change due to IECM strategies for newer needs and demands. People become more aware, educated and motivated in these diverse contexts and setup new modalities for both interpersonal and media communication. In order to present and explain the widened scope of these perspectives; more and advanced level Communication Models will evolve. Therefore, over the coming decades we look forward to more and more of advance level Models supporting the changing and newer perspectives from which communications may be studied, analyzed, applied, and practiced. The academicians and practitioners in communication discipline would be looking for innovative approaches.

To achieve the optimum, communication planning is a must. For achievement of targeted goals, such a planning must zero to reality with certain degree of idealism.

Our discussions have revealed that both positive and negative communication strategies have significant role in the study, analysis, applications, and practice of communications in various domains of our life and work. Media planning and interpersonal communication planning can be done on the basis of which communication strategies are being engaged.

IECM strategies have been the most powerful, both in its positive and negative roles. At the same time, participatory and dialogue strategies are assuming powerful roles whether for development, conflict and peace. E-readiness through e-development is the key for success in various domains in the 2000 decade.

With all these hopes and assumptions, we look forward to a holistic and integrated communication scenario for people, society and governance.

Post Script

Updates

The communication scenarios in all the perspectives, and outlook for planning and strategies are advancing fast. Updates would be given in this section without disturbing the text within.

Here are few updates in information technology in India:

1. Aug 2004. Railway platforms across the country will soon have multiple cybercafes and communication centers. At least 51 cybercafes will be operational before March 05. There is great demand both by Indian and foreign tourists. The maximum number of STD/ISD booths is now operational on platforms.

2. Aug 2004. The Indian government is planning a legislation to strengthen the guidelines for FDI in print media. The government is contemplating legislation to amend the Press and Registration Act for giving legal sanctity to cabinet resolution of 1955 that bars foreign newspapers and magazines in India.

3. Aug 2004. Doordarshan (Indian TV operated by government) will soon launch its DTH at a cost of 164 crores with 4 transponders envisaging 40 channels including private ones. A licensee can use bandwidth capacity of both Indian as well as foreign satellites to beam programs directly to DTH but use of Indian satellites would be extended preferential treatment.

4. 2004. QUBE digital player. This Innovation is developed by Chennai based company 'Real Image'. Digital film production is set to change the face of the Indian cinema for the better. It promises to effectively curtail piracy. The technology does away with film reels, projectors, and carbon-

arc. Digital player uses computer hardware and intelligent software to project movies. It will do away with cans of film reels. Producer makes one digital copy of the film. He can then distribute it to any number of cinema halls, either through satellite dish antenna or through a portable hard disk. Real Image plans to send movies to theatres through satellite dish antenna. Through this even remote locations are covered and transport costs are eliminated.

The movie reaches theatres in encrypted mode and requires a decryption key. Each print comes with a start and end date so only the prescribed number of shows can be screened. Any camcorder copy of the movie can easily be traced back to the exact theatre due to a specific watermark on the print.

5. Attendance check, Delhi goes hi-tech. Delhi government plans to install finger impression bio-metric machines in its offices to mark attendance. The age-old registers would go. The person would be able to log in only if the computer recognizes the persons finger impression. For that one has to be physically present. This will check absenteeism, late coming and proxy attendance.

6. Update in Cell technology world over is that it is fitted with camera, can receive your e-mail and explore websites on the screen. Soon 3rd generation cell phones coming in the market would be digital, slicker, lighter and with additional and more update features!

The latest is advertisement on the cell. This will be the third screen for advertisements after the two screens of TV and the computer Marketeers are excited about the immense potentiality but consumers are worried about their privacy and scams.

In 2004 Japan is developing different kind of cell phones, such as likely to have multiple cameras (for portraits, landscape) and 3D graphics. There will be cell speakerphones and phones for hearing impaired.

In 2004 MIT has demonstrated the latest fuel cells for Cell phones and PDAs. These micro fuel cells (mobion) will empower cell phones for longer duration.

Appendices

APPENDIX I

Telegraph

Samuel Finley Breese Morse built the first American telegraph around 1835 (the telegraph was also being developed independently in Europe).

A telegraph sends electrical signals over a long distance, through wires. In 1830, Joseph Henry (1797-1878) made the first long-distance telegraphic device — he sent an electronic current for over a mile on wire that activated an electromagnet, causing a bell to ring.

Morse patented a working telegraph machine in 1837, with help from his business partners Leonard Gale and Alfred Vail. Morse used a dots-and-spaces code for the letters of the alphabet and the numbers (Morse code was later improved to use dots, dashes and spaces: for example E is dot, T is dash, A is dot-dash, N is dash-dot, O is dash-dash-dash, I is dot-dot, S is dot-dot-dot, etc.). By 1838, Morse could send 10 words per minute. Congress provided funds for building a telegraph line between Washington D.C. and Baltimore, Maryland, in 1843. Morse sent the first telegraphic message (from Washington D.C. to Baltimore) on May 24, 1844; the message was: "What hath God wrought?" The telegraph revolutionized long-distance communications.

Telephone

The telephone (meaning "far sound") is the most widely used telecommunications device. It was invented in 1876 by (Alexander Graham Bell with Thomas Watson). Bell patented his invention on March 1876. His device transmitted speech sounds over electric wires, and his idea has remained one of the most useful inventions ever made.

Radio

Radio was invented by Nikola Tesla and promoted and popularized by Marconi in 1895. the first radio transmission across the atlantic ocean occurred on Dec. 12, 1901.

Televison

Inventors anticipated the public demand for television before the advent of radio broadcasting. So many participated in the development that it is impossible to answer the question "Who invented television?", but a few were so important as to be recognized as pioneers.

Paul Nipkow proposed the first practical mechanical scanner in Germany in 1884. The scanner was a rotating disk with holes arranged in a spiral around its edge. Light passing through the holes as the disk rotated produced a rectangular scanning pattern or raster that could be used to either generate an electrical signal from the scene for transmitting or to produce an image from the signal at the receiver. As the disk rotated, the image was scanned by the perforations in the disk, and light from different portions of it passed to a photocell. The number of scanned lines was equal to the number of perforations and each rotation of the disk produced a television frame. In the receiver, the brightness of the light source would be varied by the signal voltage. Again, the light passed through a synchronously rotating perforated disk and formed a raster on the projection screen. Mechanical viewers had the serious limitation of resolution and brightness.

John Logie Baird, a Scottish engineer-inventor, successfully promoted a television system based on the Nipkrow principle, received backing and sold transmitters and receivers. Laboratories in the United States and Great Britain worked to develop an all-electronic system. In Britain, the Electric and Musical Industries Ltd., provided a system along with Baird's, and these were experimentally used to broadcast television programs by the BBC in November 1936. The EMI system won overwhelmingly. An American inventor, Charles Francis Jenkins, followed with a rotating ring whose thickness varied and increased around its circumference, forcing a rotating prism. By using two rings overlapping at right angles, a beam could be made to scan both horizontally and vertically, which unfortunately produced small, dim and fuzzy images. Jenkins' system, like Baird's, failed on the basis of poor quality.

AT&T first demonstrated a television system developed by one of Bell Lab's scientists, Herbert Ives, again based on the Nipkow disks. GE also demonstrated a mechanical system developed by Ernst Alexanderson. David Sarnoff, however, would turn to research for a successful electronic system.

Since Marconi's invention of wireless telegraphy in 1897, the imagination of many inventors have been sparked with the notion of sending images as well as sound, wirelessly. The first documented notion of sending components of pictures over a series of multiple circuits is credited to George Carey. Another inventor, W.E. Sawyer, suggested the possibility of sending an image over a single wire by rapidly scanning parts of the picture in succession.

Up until this point, the concept behind television was established, but it wasn't until electronic scanning of imagery (the breaking up of images into tiny points of light for transmission over radio waves), was invented, that modern television received its start. But here is where the controversy really heats up.

In the 1920's, Alan A. Campbell-Swinton, a prominent electrical engineer in London, proposed a system that would use CRT's displaying the picture at the receiver, with electromagnetic scanning to form the raster. His transmitter tube, using a chamber filled with gas that could conduct electrons, was not suitable. Credit for the first practical TV signal-generator of pickup must be shared by Vladimir K. Zworykin and Philo T. Farnsworth, who invented the iconoscope and the image dissector respectively.

FCC Takes Steps to Promote Digital Television

The Federal Communications Commission (FCC) in USA has adopted a Report and Order that implements several steps necessary for the continued progress of the conversion of the nation's television broadcast system from analog technology to digital television. The Order will hasten the completion of the transition by:

Commencing an open channel election process in November 2004 that will provide certainty to the marketplace and ultimately result in a Final DTV Table of Allotments.

Establishing firm deadlines for digital stations to increase their power levels to serve additional viewers or lose interference protection to the un-served areas.

Requiring broadcasters to include PSIP information in their digital broadcast signals, thus promoting closed captioning, v-chip, channel numbering, and other functionality.

Eliminating, for now, the simulcasting requirement to permit the transmission of additional innovative programming on broadcast digital channels.

Providing clarity regarding the interference protection for broadcasters in TV channels 51-69.

Clarifying the digital closed captioning rules in order to ensure that those services are consistently and effectively delivered.

Mandating that, after an 18-month transition period, all digital television receivers contain v-chip functionality that will permit the current TV ratings system to be modified. Committing to opening a fast-track proceeding on distributed transmission technology while agreeing to consider individual deployments on a case-by-case basis in the interim.

Source: Tvhandbook.com

Appendix 2

History of Broadcasting Time Line

History has been marked by occasional dramatic jumps in technology. The majority of progress, however, has been made in incremental amounts — one development leads to a second, and so on. With the technology base available today, the future of broadcasting will be exciting.

Major Broadcasting Industry Milestones:

The Pioneers

1875 Thomson transmits wireless signals

1876 Bell invents the telephone

1884 Scanning disc for mechanical television invented by Paul Nipkow

1886 Principle of magnetic recording discovered by Oberlin Smith

1887 Hertz sends and receives radio waves

1889 Film developed by Eastman and camera developed by Edison combined to produce the first motion picture system

1895 Marconi develops radio transmitter and receiver

1896 Kodak develops first motion picture film designed for projection

1897 First cathode ray tube scanning device constructed by German Scientist, Karl Ferdinand Braun

1898 Poulson patents principles of magnetic recording

The Nineteen Hundreds

1900 Sarnoff emigrates to the U.S. from Russia at age 9

Professor Reginald A. Fessenden transmits speech without wires

1901 Marconi receives first transatlantic radio signals

1904 Vacuum tube diode developed by Fleming

1905 Nipkow disc demonstrated

Cathode-ray picture tube (CRT) demonstrated

1906 Vacuum tube triode developed by DeForest. First amplifier constructed

1907 Boris Rosing in Russia and A.A. Campbell-Swinton in England simultaneously develop image reproduction methods using electromagnetic scanning

1909 Herrold makes first successful radio broadcast at San Jose, CA

The Nineteen Tens

1910 First federal communication law, the Wireless Ship Act, enacted

1912 DeForest and Armstrong independently discover regeneration

Sarnoff intercepts first distress message from the doomed ship Titanic

1913 Edison uses first diamond stylus in Amberola phonograph

1915 First practical radio telephone communications system constructed by Bell Labs

1917 9XM-WHA begins radio transmission from the University of Wisconsin at Madison

1918 Armstrong invents the superheterodyne receiver

1919 Hoxie develops a means of recording sound on motion picture film

Radio Corporation of America founded

The Nineteen Twenties

1920 KDKA airs the world's first scheduled radio-broadcast from Pittsburgh

WWJ, Detroit, begins operation

1921 Aeriola Jr. designs the first affordable home radio

Radio Central, Rocky Point, NY, opened by RCA

1922 Armstrong invents super-regeneration system

WLW, Cincinnati, receives broadcast license

Farnsworth investigates electronic picture transmission

1923 Zworykin patents the Iconoscope pickup tube for television: complete TV system including kinescope, or picture tube, demonstrated

National Association of Broadcasters (NAB) formed

1924 Radio Manufacturers Association, predecessor of EIA, founded

1925 Rice and Kellogg develop first practical loudspeaker

Baird (Great Britain) demonstrates first TV pictures via a mechanical system

1926 National Broadcasting Company founded

Alexanderson develops scanning disc TV system

1927 Farnsworth transmits first electronic TV picture; applies for patent on electronic television

Bell Telephone Laboratories demonstrates wireless TV between Whippany, NJ and New York

Columbia Broadcasting System founded

AC bias discovered for recording machines

1928 Federal Radio Commission established

Pfleumer patents magnetic tape

Image Dissector developed

WGY-TV, Schenectady, NY, transmits 40-minute stage production using Alexanderson TV system

Sound added to motion pictures; the "talkies" are born

First experimental TV station permits issued by federal government

First successful trial of video delivery through telephone lines; motion pictures sent from Chicago to New York by AT&T

1929 Zworkin demonstrates all-electronic TV system; Zworkin joins RCA

The Nineteen Thirties

1930 Farnsworth receives patent for Image Dissector pickup device

RKO experiments with theater television in Schenectady, NY

1931 AEG engineers begin work on Magnetophone recorder

CBS conducts experimental TV broadcasts

Blattner phone steel band recorder used by the BBC

1932 Langmuir conducts research on the physics of gaseous discharges, improving the vacuum tube

NBC begins experimental telecasts

Schroeter describes method for recording pictures on magnetic tape

1933 Armstrong demonstrates FM transmission to RCA

NBC Red and Blue radio networks move into 30 Rockefeller Center studios

First TV broadcast from an educational institution (W9XK, State University of Iowa)

1934 FCC established as a permanent regulatory agency

AEG demonstrates Magneto-phone at annual German Radio Fair

WLW-AM beings super power operation at 500kW

Mutual Broadcasting System founded

Orthicon camera tube developed

1935 Armstrong begins 50kW experimental FM station at Alpine, NJ

Iconoscope camera developed using improved pickup device

RCA chief Sarnoff announces a $1 million TV research program

First TV broadcasts in Germany and England

I.G. Farben (BASF) makes tape with iron oxide powder on a plastic film

AEG-Telefunken produces the Magneto-phone tape recorder

1937 CBS announces TV development program

1938 Marzocci files patent application for rotary head audio recorder

1939 GE demonstrates FM for mobile communications

GE inaugurates FM broadcasting in Schenectady, NY

WLW-AM loses its experimental license and is ordered to return to 50kW operation

Volume Unit (VU) meter adopted as industry standard of program level measurement

The principles of ac bias recording developed

Image Iconoscope developed

TV demonstrations held at World's Fair in New York and Golden Gate International Exhibition in San Francisco

Roosevelt becomes first U.S. President to give a speech on television

DuMont company begins producing television sets for consumers

First baseball game ever televised, the Princeton/Columbia contest, covered by NBC at Baker Field, NY

First television sets offered for sale in U.S. by RCA, GE, DuMont, Philco, and two other companies

The Nineteen Forties

1940 Paramount puts first TV station on the air in Chicago

1941 Magnetophone goes into regular service on German radio stations

FCC authorizes commercial TV stations

1942 Digital computer conceived

Sarnoff awarded the rank of Brigadier General

1943 Nobel buys NBC Blue Network and forms the American Broadcasting Company

Image Orthicon developed

1945 Orr and Mullin bring German magnetic tape technology back from Europe

FM broadcast band moved to 88-108 MHz

Clarke suggests geosynchronous satellites for communications

1946 Mullin demonstrates German Magneto-phone at San Francisco IRE meeting

DuMont Network founded

Zoomar introduces first professional zoom lens

Tokyo Tushin Kogyo founded; name changed to Sony in 1955

1947 First taped US radio network program airs, featuring Bing Crosby

3M introduces Scotch 100 audio tape

Transistor effect demonstrated at Bell Labs

First Hollywood film production for TV, *The Public Prosecutor*

1948 ABC begins regular use of Ampex model 200 audio tape machine

1949 Liberty Broadcasting System founded

The Nineteen Fifties

1950 FCC approves CBS whirling disc color system

Rectangular kinescope developed

Vidicon developed

Installation of first CATV system begins

Tricolor kinescope developed

Mullin begins work on video recorder for Crosby Enterprises

Stereo tape recorder, Magnecord 1250, introduced

1952 FCC approves UHF-TV broadcasting

Ampex VTR team reproduces barely recognizable picture from tape

Crosby Enterprises demonstrates VTR with fixed heads and high tape speed

Axton (England) begins work on VERA video recorder project

Theater television reaches its peak with the broadcast of the Walcott/Marciano fight

1953 Wireless microphone demonstrated

AM transmitter remote control authorized by FCC

405-line color system developed by CBS with "crispening circuits" to improve apparent picture resolution

FCC reverses its decision to approve the CBS color system, deciding instead to authorize use of the color-compatible system developed by NTSC

Color TV broadcasting begins

RCA demonstrates its longitudinal video recorder

Toshiba begins work on helical scan video recorder

RCA develops shadow-mask color CRT

ABC merges with Paramount

1955 First FM picture off tape accomplished by Ampex VTR team

Experimental 1/2-inch videotape system is displayed in closed-circuit telecast from New York to St. Paul, MN

RCA prototype videotape machine used briefly on air at NBC

RCA demonstrates prototype single-tube color camera

Paramount Pictures develops forerunner of Sony Trinitron CRT

1956 First VTR demonstrated by Ampex at National Association of Radio and Television Broadcasters (hereafter referred to as NAB), using un-tested experimental 3M 2-inch videotape

Broadcast-quality solid-state camera (except for pickup tube) developed

Black-and-white portable TV era begins

Computer hard disk introduced

1957 Laser developed

2-inch quad VTR makes its network debut on CBS

RCA introduces the TRT-1A quad VTR

Radio-Electronics-Television Manufacturers Association changes name to Electronic Industries Association (EIA)

1958 Ampex demonstrates color VTR

1959 *Broadcast Engineering* magazine founded

National Stereophonic Radio Committee formed to decide on an FM stereo system

Audio cartridge recording system introduced at NAB by Collins Radio

Broadcast Electronics introduces Spotmaster cart machine

Ampex VTR at Moscow trade fair records the Nixon/ Khrushchev "Kitchen Debate."

The Nineteen Sixties

1960 Stereo FM tests conducted over KDKA-FM, Pittsburgh

Ampex introduces Intersync system for VTR

Toshiba proposes a videotape recorder using a helical scanning process

Echo I and II passive reflector satellites launched

First rectangular screen TV introduced

First battery-operated transistorized TV for sale

1961 FM stereo transmission system approved by FCC

Electron beam recording demonstrated

Ampex SloMo Disc developed

First live televised presidential news conference (John Kennedy)

First Western viewing of live television from USSR on the BBC (Moscow welcome for Yuri Gagarin)

1962 FCC issues FM licensing reallocation rules

Philips introduces audio-cassette tape player

Telstar communications satellite provides first international relay of TV pictures

Legislation passed in U.S. creating Comsat

Legislation passed requiring all-channel tuning (UHF and VHF) in television receivers

RCA announces first fully transistorized video recorder

1963 RCA develops metal oxide semiconductor (MOS) process

FCC releases new FM table of assignments

TV transmitter remote control authorized by FCC

ITFS service established by the FCC

Electronic line-store (625-405 and 405-625) standards converter developed by the BBC

TV used on a U.S. manned space flight, the Mercury 9

1964 RCA develops complementary MOS (CMOS) technology

Society of Broadcast Engineers holds first official meeting at NAB in Chicago

Intelsat organization formed

Character generator system introduced

RCA videotape cartridge developed

First TV program automation system installed

TV camera placed on board Ranger 7 explorer to moon

TEAC provides slow-motion color video playback system for NHK coverage of 1964 Olympics

Industry committee formed to establish videotape standards, with SMPTE as secretariat

1965 "Early Bird," first international communications satellite, launched (Intelsat I)

1966 First bipolar IC amplifier introduced

1967 PAL/SECAM standards announced

First high-band color disc recorder for playback of short program segments in normal, slow or stop action is used on ABC-TV coverage of the *World Series of Skiing*

First timecode editing system for video, called On-Time, is developed by CBS, Hollywood

Solid state imaging technology demonstrated

Intelsat II satellite launched

1968 CBS uses a portable minicam for political convention coverage

Trinitron tube developed

1-inch Plumbicon developed

First radio/TV business automation systems installed

1969 Instant random-access audio cartridge machine introduced at NAB by IGM Communications

SMPTE timecode established to end the chaos of incompatible time codes for various editing machines

Neil Armstrong walks on the moon (July 21); worldwide audience watches the event live

The Nineteen Seventies

1970 PBS network established

Color-under recording used in first 3/4-inch VTR from Matsushita, Victor Company of Japan and Sony

ACR-25 random access video-cassette recorder introduced by Ampex

1971 U Format introduced by Sony/TEAC and JVC

CMX formed after a joint experiment between CBS and Memorex

NHK (Japan) begins experiments with high line number TV systems, and discusses the feasibility of an 1125-line system

RCA joins EECO to develop and market the TCE-1000, an electronic editing system based on timecode

Cinema Products CP-16 news film camera introduced

Electronic tuning first seen in U.S. TVs

1972 Teletext experiments begin in United Kingdom

Time base corrector introduced by Consolidated Video Systems

BBC develops "sound-in-sync" digital encoding system for audio-video combining

CMX 300, the first computerized editing system, is introduced for on-line editing and auto assemble of pre-edited shows

Adapted Sony camera and 3/4-inch U-matic VTR used for roving reports at the national political conventions

MCA gives first public demonstration of laser videodisk

First prerecorded videocassette tapes offered to consumers

1973 *A* Format 1-inch VTR shown by Ampex

First ENG cameras used in electronic field production

First multi-point distribution (MDS) microwave system launched

Giant-screen projection color TVs marketed

1974 First microprocessor used in broadcast equipment

2/3-inch Plumbicon developed

Frame reducer/recorder introduced

Sony introduces Betamax home VCR

1975 *B* Format 1-inch VTR shown by Bosch

Study group begins work on a digital video world standard

HBO begins program distribution via satellite

1976 Sony shows 1-inch VTR at NAB in Chicago

Ampex shows VPR-1 helical recorder with automatic scan tracking; also introduces a portable model, the VPR-10

World's first digital PAL TV transmission via satellite (Intelsat IV)

Ampex shows first electronic still store system, the ESS

VHS home recording format introduced

1977 PBS begins operation by satellite

TEAC introduces PCM digital audio disk recorder

Type *C* format VTRs introduced

Last tower of historic Radio Central, Rocky Point, NY, is destroyed

1978 Teletext experiments begin at KSL-TV in Salt Lake City

NHK experiments with HDTV via satellite relay

NHK begins multiple audio channel television in Tokyo

Fiber-optic technology demonstrated

Digital VTR demonstrated

1979 Mutual Radio Network and National Public Radio begin operation by satellite (analog)

B format and *C* format for VTRs accepted by SMPTE and ANSI

B format and *C* format portable VTRs with battery power shown

CCD telecine introduced by Bosch (FDL-60)

The Nineteen Eighties

1980 First of second-generation type *C* machines introduced

1981 Beta Format introduced by Sony

M Format introduced (Matsushita, Panasonic, RCA and Ikegami)

First space shuttle launched

1/2-inch Plumbicon (Phillips) and Saticon (NHK) introduced

HDTV demonstrated in United States at SMPTE in Los Angeles

Digital video sampling frequency selected as 13.5 MHz for worldwide use

ZDF, Rohde & Schwarz, and Siemens introduce multiple audio channel television in Berlin

TEAC develops optical laser write/read disc system

Ampex introduces ADO digital video processor

First camera/recorder ENG systems shown at NAB

Ampex and Dynamics Control show all-digital studio cameras

1982 FCC issues the "marketplace" decision on AM stereo

Low power TV service established by the FCC

First LPTV station begins operation in Bemidji, MN

Quantel Mirage introduced at NAB

NEC DVE effects system introduced at NAB

Bosch shows first 1/4-inch camera/recorder, the KBF-1 in prototype form

CMX/Orrox shows a disc-based editing system

Two HDTV systems are shown at IBC in Brighton (Sony and Philips). Two other systems are proposed for Germany and England using a doubled 625-line PAL signal

1983 Network radio distribution by satellite (ABC, CBS, NBC and RKO) using digital format

Digital TV receiver shown by ITT-Intermetall in Germany

Multiple audio channels TV system selected by EIA for U.S.

Ku-Band satellite transmission for broadcast tested by NAB and during space shuttle launch

FCC issues 80-90 decision on FM radio

Use of FM subcarriers deregulated by FCC

First long-distance inter-city digital TV transmission sent via fiber optic cable

NEC introduces the SPC-3 CCD camera

1984 RCA introduces CCD-1 solid-state camera at NAB

Varian/EIMAC introduces Klystrode tube as a product

FCC approves use of AM subcarriers for broadcast and non-broadcast functions

FCC eliminates programming guidelines, ascertainment, commercial rules and program logging requirements for commercial TV stations

FCC replaces the 7 stations ownership rule with 12 station limits

Montage Picture Processor introduced by Montage Computer Systems

Lucasfilm/Convergence shows the Editdroid disk-based editing system designed to emulate film style editing

Multi-channel TV sound broadcast authorized by FCC; first stereo TV broadcasts begin. Sales of stereo color TV receivers and adapters begin

First color TVs with all-digital signal circuitry marketed

1985 FCC adopts RF radiation protection standards for human exposure

Panasonic introduces M-II format at NAB convention

Natuel introduces first totally solid state 50 kW AM transmitter

U.S. Court of Appeals rules the FCC's "must-carry" rules regarding cable television are unconstitutional

FCC inquiry into "fairness doctrine" concludes the policy no longer serves the public interest

SMPTE working group on digital TV tape recording votes approval of the D-1 component digital format

The National Radio Systems Committee (NRSC) begins to study proposals for a standardized AM transmission pre-emphasis curve

Data transmission on vertical blanking interval authorized by FCC

Harris signs licensing agreement with rival Motorola on AM stereo transmission standard

CCIR approves D-1 digital component recording format for worldwide program exchange

Color TVs with 35-inch picture tubes marketed

1986 Sony introduces DVR-1000 digital videotape recorder based on CCIR 601 (D-1) standard

Ampex shows ACR-225 prototype composite digital cartridge VTR

Ampex, Thomson and Bosch sign manufacturing and marketing agreements with Sony to produce Betacam products

NBC announces purchase of M-II products from Panasonic

SMPTE forms *ad hoc* group on high definition studio systems to document specifications for 1125/60 HDTV

Ampex submits its composite digital format (D-2) to SMPTE for standardization

Scrambling of satellite-fed cable TV programming starts; sale of decoders and program subscriptions to home dish owners begins

Stereo-sound in television broadcasting available in all major U.S. population centers

1987 Super-channel DBS service begins in the U.K.

Abekas introduces the A-64 digital disk CCIR 601 recorder

NEC introduces SR-10 solid state video recorder

Dolby introduces SR noise reduction system

Advanced Television Systems Committee announces plans to conduct over-the-air tests of HDTV transmission formats

FCC issues a Notice of Inquiry to determine the status of advanced TV systems

Enforcement of the “fairness doctrine” ends

SMPTE working group on HDTV approves 1125/60 standards document

NRSC announces voluntary standards to reduce AM band interference

NAB forms HDTV technology center to study future of television

Super VHS (S-VHS) introduced

1988 FCC refuses to reconsider marketplace decision on AM stereo

NRSC issues second voluntary national standard (NRSC-2) for AM radio

Ampex and Sony introduce D-2 digital composite tape machines

Harris introduces DX-25 digital solid state AM transmitter

First Klystrode-equipped 60 kW UHF transmitter goes on the air in Wrens, GA

FCC rules that advanced television systems designed to deliver improved pictures to consumers must be compatible with existing NTSC receivers

Europe’s Eureka 95 HDTV system demonstrated at IBC in Brighton, England

NBC proposes a 1050/59.94 HDTV system with the backing of ABC, Zenith, Thomson Consumer Electronics, North American Philips and others

Philips laboratories demonstrates its HDTV system designed for satellite transmission (HDS-NA)

Advanced Television Test Center announces plans to begin over-the-air tests of proposed advanced and high definition TV systems

First improved definition television (IDTV) receivers marketed

1989 American National Standards Institute (ANSI) gives final approval to 1125/60 HDTV production standard

Varian/TVT announces plans to install multi-stage depressed collector (MSDC) klystron transmitter

The Nineteen Nineties

1990 Production of giant-screen (over 27-inch) color TV picture tubes starts in U.S.

Legislation requiring close captioning decoders in all larger color TVs manufactured after July 1, 1993 signed into law

All-digital high-definition television (HDTV) system proposed; FCC sets testing schedule

1991 First TVs with built-in closed-caption display capability introduced in U.S.

U.S. testing of HDTV systems begins

1993 16:9 aspect ratio (widescreen) television sets marketed in U.S.

1995 First television program (*Computer Chronicles*) delivered via the Internet

First television station (KOLD 13) uses a networked digital video server in its daily on-air operations

Interactive cable modem trials with consumers started

Flat-screen plasma display TVs introduced

1996 First TV sets equipped with VCR Plus+ introduced in U.S.

HDTV is broadcast and received live at test station WHD-TV in Washington, D.C.

Set-top boxes plug into TV and telephone and allow viewers to surf the Internet's World Wide Web via remote control

Zenith introduces the U.S. market's first HDTV-compatible front projection TV

Agreement between broadcasters, TV manufacturers, and PC makers sets inter-industry standard for digital HDTV

1997 FCC assigns digital spectrum to broadcasters and sets schedule for digital broadcasts

Source: enchanting learning.com

NOTES

2.1. PROTEIN Program (Poverty reduction outcomes through education, innovations and networks).

3.1. New World Information and Communications Order (NWICO).

In 70s it has been suggested that an imbalance in information production and distribution might underlie uneven world economic development. Fraught with ideology, the debate about a New World Information and Communications Order (NWICO), tended to focus upon media ownership and upon the contending concepts of information as commodity and information as social good, upon the freedom of information as an individual *versus* a collective right.

The NWICO debate flourished, or perhaps one might more aptly say, raged, throughout much of the 1970s and 1980s in the halls of the United Nations, and particularly within Unesco. NWICO proponents and opponents alike accepted the premise of a link between economic progress and the availability of information. However, liberal theorists maintained that national cultures and sovereignty were not threatened by information concentration, while structuralist and socialist analysts argued that they were. In particular, the NWICO proponents, mostly drawn from the ranks of non-aligned nations, claimed that Western ownership and control of both the news media and their distribution channels constituted a form of cultural dominance whose covert goal was capitalist economic expansion.

This argument, played out in fora such as the Non-Aligned Movement and Unesco Conferences drew support from the Soviet Union, and hostility from Western administrations. It was partly due to fears of the growing "politicization" of Unesco that the United States and Great Britain withdrew from that organization in the mid 1980s.

The NWICO movement began as a protest over the concentration of print and broadcast media ownership among de facto cartel, and developed into an argument about the cultural dominance of poor nations by wealthy ones. However, even before the Soviet collapse, some NWICO proponents were beginning to suggest that the issue of news imbalance was a red herring, and that supplying developing nations with current banking and business information was more crucial.

Principles and Premises

The basic premise of the movement for a New World Information and Communications Order (NWICO), was that an imbalance existed in the direction, volume, and types of information exchanged between adequately developed countries and the Third World, which was detrimental to development and systemic in nature. Of equal importance with, and logically prior to this conception, is the ethical notion that information should be viewed as a shared resource or as a social good rather than as a commodity.

The major documents of the NWICO include the Unesco Media Declaration of 1978, Unesco's Statement on Journalistic Ethics, and the report of the International Commission for the Study of Communications Problems. The MacBride Commission was set up in late 1977, and its report was published in 1980. NWICO premises included the assertion that information is necessary to economic development, and that any attempt to establish a New International Economic Order (NIEO) must incorporate, or even depend upon, reform in the world communications system.

In the main NWICO paradigm, (the structuralist model), the current world situation is characterized by the dominance of information producing nations over those which consume cultural and information 'products'. The set of relations between these 'know' and 'know-not' nations has been described variously as a centre-periphery situation, as a North-South conflict, or as a relationship of neo-colonialism or neo-imperialism. The structuralist school included "neo-Marxian journalists, many Third World diplomats, and theorists like Johan Galtung." Galtung's major contribution to the platform is his "centre-periphery" typology, which provided a perspective on cultural dominance.

"According to this schema, nations at the Centre... dominate a 'feudal network of communication'. The Centre owns the major news agencies and 'Centre news takes up a much larger proportion of Periphery news media than vice versa'... users in the Periphery 'come to see with Centre eyes.'" (Galtung 1979, 165-166).

UNESCO terminated NWICO in 1989. But efforts are continuing for communication development in third world countries.

Currently UNDP has a Sustainable Development Media Program functioning which goes into Third World countries and works with universities, libraries, NGO's, non-profit institutions, to set up Internet capability and as many aspects of the so-called Superhighway as possible. The great merit is that this effort is much less costly than the old idea of total infrastructure development and it allows potential leap-frogging in technology to overcome the primitive starting conditions that exist.

Further advantages are that this is being done apart from government sponsorship, so it cannot be taken over as a government control vehicle and it is much closer to the grass roots than any other programs have been. So far, about 30 countries have been helped and UNDP plans further ongoing efforts.

UNESCO's international programs for development of communication (IPDC) set up in 1979 continues to function, providing seed money and start-up help along more conventional lines of communications and media facilities.

The deliberations of dependency theorists have led to the 'New world information and communication order' (NWICO). It was advocated that developing countries have the right to present information about their countries in the global context. Moreover, they must have control over their communication channels. If development has to occur then this role must change. The communication strategies should focus on educating people about the vicious nature of the stifling dependency relationships, to mobilize national and regional support for the structural support of the society. They emphasize the use of interpersonal channels, having indigenous mass-media system and having control over the content of their mass media channels.

New World Information & Communication Order (NWICO) can be best constructed by developing communication competence for the voiceless. Pluralism in voices however requires pluralism in structures of media access. No single system of media control (governmental, public or community commercial) can alone guarantee the plurality of voices. A balance among them might use the expanding channels of communication for an expanding plurality of voices more reflective of the international community.

It calls for free and balanced flow of information among the billions inhabitants of this world who are caught up between the imperatives of pre-modern, modern, and postmodern worlds to which they belong. NWICO may be conceived of as a network of NGOs, to mobilize the global civil society, to empower the urban and the rural communities, to enhance their communication competence and media capabilities, to negotiate with the State and Non-State actors to redress their conditions.

Now that we are freer of the bonds of conflicting East-West ideologies, perhaps the time has come for technocrats — librarians, computer programmers, journalists, and communications specialists to address the problem objectively, and from a holistic, information science perspective. This effort might consist of developing better ways of exporting development information from the rich nations of the North and West, to the poor ones of the South and East, and of importing knowledge of developing countries through development education activities.

For working definitions, let us say that development education is the activity of acquainting Western populations with the problems of Third Word and with its various cultures. Development information is required for economic growth and the improvement of social conditions. Most importantly, since information technology is increasingly becoming the key to economic prosperity, it behooves us to help redefine the debate as an information science issue, rather than a media studies problem.

3.2. A World of Outsourcing

Globalization goes white collar. *China*: Strengths are hardware design and embedded software; Call centers for Japan and South Korea are growing in coastal cities. *Philippines*:

Accountants, software writers, architect, tele-marketers, and graphic artists. *Mexico*: IT and engineering outsourcing for US companies boost demand for engineers. *Costa Rica:* Cheap telecom and educated workforce makes a thriving spot for Call centers targeting Spanish-speaking consumers in Europe and US. There is IT support and bookkeeping operations. *South Africa:* In Johannesburg and Mauritius, Call centers catering European countries by well-educated, French, German and English speakers. *Eastern Europe*: Indian and American service providers are opening IT services in Hungary, Poland and Czech republic. Romania and Bulgaria have set up IT workshop for German multinationals to tap German and English speaking workforce for European clients. *Russia*: 100 local software service exporters employ 10000 engineers specializing in complex projects. Boeing, Nortel, Motorola and Intel have R&D centers. *India:* IT services, Chip Design, Call centers, business back office work. Indian providers like Tata, Infoysys, Wipro are global leaders in providing IT services.

(*Source*: Data, Gartner, and Mckinsey. Business Week, Feb 3, 2003).

4.1. Quantum Computing

Classical physics is when ball is put into a box and hidden from view. It will be the same color when someone looks at it. In quantum physics a red ball could be put into box and manipulated to be in a state of super-imposition. In quantum physics objects can be different states at the same time called superimposition. For example, a ball would be — both red and green at the same time — and would be either red or green when someone looked at it.

The notions of quantum computing had their start in early 80s when Richard Feynman came across the problem of use of computer to perfectly calculate the behavior of atoms in a solid using programs. It proved impossible task. Feynman figured out, in theory, that if you could build a computer that operates on quantum logic, it might be feasible to perform these calculations.

Digital bits follow binary logic i.e. either it is one or zero whereas. Quantum computers use qbits that can be one and zero at the same time. Thus qbits are more powerful than ordinary bits. They can carry the information of 2 classical bits and so far any N number of qbits you can store 2 to the power N numbers simultaneously. The computing power grows exponentially.

Lloyd and Cory with their coworkers are experimenting with quantum computer programming. They have been able to set up simple programming by shooting radio frequency pulses at molecules in liquid alanine. The molecules act like tiny radio receivers; by tuning to the correct frequency it is possible to make contact with individual qbits.

Their other experiments are with quantum analog computer. The idea is to use radio pulses to set up a quantum computation in the atoms of the crystal that would mimic how the atoms in the solid behave. This new system would enable the researchers to carry out simulations that are too complex for any normal computers.

The essential step to real quantum computation is Photon fission experiments (Jeffery Shapiro, Franco Wong of MIT). Each photon going in generated two photons going out, equal in energy to the input. Now the two photons are entangled, the properties of one are tied in intimately with those of the other.

Even so there is limit to what molecules in liquid and calcium fluoride computers can do. A general-purpose quantum computer (like desktop PC) is decades away. As Lloyd said, for that kind of work a different kind of quantum computing might be needed. Nonetheless the interest is high in its applications like ultra secure communications, cryptography and other infotech applications.

4.2. An Internet call travels from home/business over a copper phone line until it reaches a special computer at the local phone company's switching hub. The computer converts the call into Internet data. These tiny packets of digits are sent like a roving swarm of bees through the Internet many paths, and reassembled at their final destination where they are turned back into voice. By contrast traditional phone call uses a technique called circuit switching, in which a dedicated electronic path is opened between user's each call, over which the call is sent as one uncut stream of signals.

REFERENCES

Alan Hancock. *Communication Planning for Development,* East West Communication Institute, Honolulu 1978.

Albrow M. and King E. *Globalization, Knowledge, and Society.* Sage Publications, London 1990.

Basu A. (1987) Grassroots Movements and the State, in *Theory and Society,* 16(5): 647-674.

Battison, John, "Making History," *Broadcast Engineering,* Intertec Publishing, Overland Park, KS, June 1986.

Berg Ann-Jorunn. *The Smart House,* in Heap Nick, Ray Thomas *et al* (eds). *Information Technology and Society,* Sage Publications, London 1995.

Bell Daniel. *The Coming of the Post-industrial Society,* Basic Books, New York 1973.

Beniger J.R. *The Control Revolution: Technological and Economic Origins of the Information Society,* Harvard University Press, Cambridge 1997.

Boafo, S.T. Kwame. *Communication Technology and Dependent Development in Sub-Saharan Africa,* in G. Sussman and J.A. Lent (eds) Transnational Communications, Sage, London 1991.

Cairncross Francis. *The Death of Distance: How the Communication Revolution is Changing Our Lives,* Harvard Business School Press 2001

Christensen Clayton M. *Innovator's Dilemma,* Harvard Business School Press 1997.

Cooley Charles Horton. *Social Organizations,* Charles Scribner's Sons, Boston 1909.

Curras E. Smith *et al* (eds). *Information, Communication, and Technology Transfer,* North Holland, New York 1987.

Dance Frank E.X. *The Concept of Communication,* Journal of Communication, 20: 201-10, 1970.

Daly John A. & Patricia Daly. Series of Essays on *Information Communication Technology. Applied to Millennium Goals.* World Bank 2003.

Derek H. Chen & Carl J. Dahlman. *Knowledge and Development: A Cross Section Approach,* World Bank Paper 2003.

Dunning John H. (Ed). *Regions, Globalization and the Knowledge Based Economy,* Oxford University Press 2002.

Dutton William H. (ed). *Information and Communication Technologies: Visions and Realities,* Oxford University Press, New York 1996.

Easterly Williams. *The Elusive Quest for Growth: Economists' Adventures and Misadventures in the Tropics,* MIT Press 2001.

Edge David. *The Social Shaping of Technology,* in Heap Nick, Ray Thomas *et al.* (eds). Information Technology and Society, Sage Publications, London 1995.

Ellul, J. *Preconceived Ideas about Mediated Information,* in E.M. Rogers & F. Bally (eds). The Media Revolution in America and Western Europe, Ablex Norwood, NJ, 95-107.

Enchanting learning.com

Fukuyama Francis. *Our Foreign Legions,* Wall Street journal, Jan 26, 2004.

Giddens Anthony. *Beyond Left and Right,* Polity Press, Cambridge 1994.

Gore A. *Basic Principles in Building Information Society* in Global Issues on Line Serial, Sept 1996.

Guntz Bob. *Information Counting on Digital Interview,* 15th June, 99, Wall Street Journal.

Hafkin Nancy and Nancy Taggart. *Gender, Information, Technology, and Developing Countries: An Analytic Study,* June 2001, www usaid.gov/wid.

The Southern African Gender and Media Baseline Study, 2003 www misa.org/

Harrison, Lawrence E. *et al* (editors). *Culture Matters: How Values Shape Human Progress,* Basic Books 2001.

Hall Stuart. *The Question of Cultural Identity* in S. Hall. D. Held and T. Mcgrew (eds*). Modernity and Its Futures,* Polity Press, Cambridge 1992.

Hanson J, Narula Uma. *New Communication Technologies in Developing Countries,* New Jersey, Lawrence Erlbaum Associates, 1990

Heap Nick, Ray Thomas *et al* (eds). *Information Technology and Society.* Sage Publications, London 1995.

H.D.S. Greenway Déjà vu in Baghdad Boston Globe, 21 Oct 04.

Irving I. *New technologies benefits all nations* in global issues on-line serial Sept 1996.

Human Development Report 2001: *Making New Technologies Work for Human Development.*

K4D Program, World Bank Institute 2004.

Kato H. The Information Is There but Is It Accessible, Intermedia, 13(6): 13-16, 1985.

Katz Elihu. *The Two-step Flow of Communication,* Public Opinion Quarterly, 21:161-78, 1957.

Kuo E.C.Y. *Information among Asian NIEs* in Asian Communication Handbook, AMIC, Singapore 1993.

_______ Singapore in G. Wang (ed). Treading Different Paths: Informatization in Asians, (pp 141-159) Ablex Norwood, NJ 1994, 141-59.

I*CT@ The Bank – An Overview,* World Bank 2003.

Knight P. *The Electronic Revolution and Developing Countries* in Global Issues On-line Serial, Sept 1996.

Lerner Daniel. The Passing of Traditional Society: Modernization in Middle East, Free Press, New York 1958.

Lull James, Media, Communication, Culture: A Global Approach Polity Press, Cambridge.

Lipton M. *Why People Stay Poor: A Study of Urban Bias in World Development,* Harvard University Press, Cambridge 1977.

Nagy Hanna, *Mainstreaming E-Development,* World Bank 2003.

Nick, Ray Thomas *et al* (eds). *Information Technology and Society,* Sage Publications, London 1995.

Lyon David. *The Roots of the Information Society Idea.* Nick, Ray Thomas *et al* (eds). Information Technology and Society, Sage Publications, London 1995.

Mackay Hughie. *Theorising the IT/ Society Relationship,* in Heap.

Mainwaring S. (1987) *Urban Popular Movements, Identity, and Democratization in Brazil.* Comparative Political Studies, 20: 131-59.

Mann M. *The Sources of Social Power* Vol. 1 Cambridge University Press, Cambridge 1986.

Marshal McLuhan. (1962) *The Gutenberg Galaxy: The Making of Typographical Man,* Toronto University Press, Toronto.

——— (1964) *Understanding Media: Extensions of Man,* Mentor, New York.

——— & Q Fiore. (1967) *The Medium is the Message: An Inventory of Effects,* Bantam New York.

Mcgrew T. *Global Society* in S. Hall. D.Held and T. Mcgrew (eds), *Modernity and its Futures.* Polity Press, Cambridge 1992.

Michio Kaku. *Visions,* Anchor Books, Double Day, New York 1997.

Mohammadi Ali ed. *International Communication and Globalization,* Sage Publications, London 1997.

Narula Uma. *Development Communication Theory and Practice* (revised 1994) HarAnand Publications, New Delhi revised 2000.

Narula Uma. *Communication Theory and Practice,* HarAnand Publications, New Delhi 1994.

Narula Uma. *Communication Perspectives: Cultural Diffusion, Dynamics and Challenges,* HarAnand Publications, New Delhi 2000.

Narula Uma. *Media Communication Technologies — New Perspectives,* HarAnand Publications, New Delhi 2001.

Narula Uma. *Let Us Do It Ourselves,* World Bank 2000.

Narula Uma. *Technology Revisited: India Case Study.* Mimeographed 2003.

Narula Uma. *International Communication: Discourses.* Mimeographed 2003a

Narula Uma. *Indian Women across Generations,* Atlantic Publishers, New Delhi 2005.

Narula Uma. *Perception of Pakistan in Indian Media,* Paper presented at Wisconsin University 1998.

Narula Uma. *Second thoughts on Development,* Unpublished paper CNET, New Delhi 1997.

Narula Uma. *Development Bureaucracy in India : Dilemmas Dependencies,* in Perspectives in Development Communication. Sage Publications, New Delhi, India 1993.

Narula Uma., *Grassroots Movements in India,* in I. Singh & J. Hanson (eds), *Advances in Telematics* Vol. 1, 127-134 Ablex Norwood, NJ 1990.

Narula Uma & Pearce W. ed. *Culture, Politics, and Research programs: An International Assessment of Practical Problems in Field Research,* Lawrence Erlbaum Associates, New Jersey 1990.

Narula Uma. *The Cultural Challenge of Communication Technology, American Behavioural Scientist* Vol. 32, No. 2, Nov-Dec 1988, Pg 194-207, Sage Publications, CA. 1988

Narula Uma & Pearce W. *Development as Communication,* SIU Press, Carbondale 1986.

Narula Uma. *New Communication technologies in Developing Countries: A Case of India.* Paper presented at IAMCR International Conference, New Delhi 1986.

Narula Uma. *Dynamics of Development,* Unpublished Ph.D Dissertation, University of Massachusetts, Amherst 1984.

Norderstreng Kaarle and Schiller Herbert. *National Sovereignty and International Communication,* Ablex, New, Jersey 1979.

Robertson Ronald. *Globalization: Time-space Homogeneity and Hetrogeneity* in Mike Featherstone *et al* (eds) Global Modernites, 25-44. Sage Publications CA 1995.

Rogers Everett, M. *Diffusion of Innovations,* Free Press, New York 1962, 1983, 3rd edition.

——— *Communication and Development: Critical Perspectives,* Sage Beverley Hills,1976.

Rogers Everett M. & F.F. Shoemaker. *Communication of Innovations: A Crossroad Approach,* Sage Beverley Hills, 1971.

Rubin R.B. and Rubin A.M. *Communication Research strategies and sources* Wadsworth Belmont CA 1990.

Scherer F.M. *New Perspectives on Economic Growth and Technological Innovations* 1999.

Schneider S.C. *Information Overload: Causes and Consequences*, Human Systems Management 7: 143-153.

Schramm Wilbur *The Unique Perspective of Communication: A Retrospective View,* Journal of Communication 33: 6-17.

Singhal Arvind. *Combating HIV/AID: Shout, and Shout and Shout,* Span, New Delhi, May-June 2003.

Smith M. J. *Contemporary Communication Research Methods,* Wadsworth, Belmont, CA 1988.

Soni Tara. *Computer and Kids,* Unpublished Research Study 2004.

Thomas Ray. *Access and inequality.* in Heap Nick, Ray Thomas *et al* (eds) *Information Technology and Society.* Sage Publications, London 1995.

Tvhandbook.com

Tomlinson J. *Cultural Imperialism: A Critical Introduction.* Pinter London 1991.

UNESCO Information, Communication and Knowledge: Building Contemporary Societies 2003.

UNESCO Understanding of Education in an African Village: The Impact of Information and Communication Technologies 2003.

William F. (ed). *Technology and Communication Behavior,* Wadsworth. Belmont CA. 1973.

World Summit on Information Society Dec 2003 in Geneva.

World Institute of Development Economics Research, *WIDER Study 2003.*

World Social Forum (Jan 2004).

SUBJECT INDEX